Evil Empire

John Gilligan, his Gang

and the Execution of Journalist Veronica Guerin

Paul Williams

MERLIN
PUBLISHING

Published in 2001 by
Merlin Publishing
16 Upper Pembroke Street
Dublin 2
Ireland

www.merlin-publishing.com

Text Copyright © 2001 Paul Williams
Arrangement and design Copyright © 2001 Merlin Publishing
except
Photographs courtesy of the individuals and institutions noted
beneath each picture.

ISBN 1-903582-07-5

A CIP catalogue record for this book is available from the British
Library.

Reprinted May 2001

Typeset by Gough Typesetting Services
Printed by Cox and Wyman Limited, Reading

The following is a list of officers of the Garda Síochána who formed the nucleus of the Lucan Investigation Team. Their current ranks are included.

Assistant Commissioner Tony Hickey
Superintendent Len Ahern (District Officer, now retired)
Superintendent Jerry O'Connell
Det. Inspector Padraig Kennedy
Det. Inspector Todd O'Loughlin
Det. Inspector John O'Mahony
Det. Sergeant Noel Browne
Det. Sergeant John Geraghty
Det. Sergeant Maurice Heffernan
Det. Sergeant Pat Keane
Det. Sergeant Shay Nolan
Det. Sergeant John O'Driscoll
Det. Sergeant Fergus Treanor
Sergeant Con Condon
Det. Garda Pat Bane
Det. Garda George Butler
Det. Garda Tom Fallon
Det. Garda Tom Fitzgerald
Det. Garda Michael Gaynor
Det. Garda Bernie Hanley
Det. Garda Bernard Masterson
Det. Garda Michael McElgunn
Det. Garda Michael Moran
Det. Garda Michael Murray
Det. Garda Sean O'Brien
Det. Garda Bob O'Reilly
Det. Garda Brian Woods

The following are some of the officers who, although not full-time members of the Lucan Investigation Team, participated in crucial operations during the Gilligan investigations.

Detective Inspector Gerry O'Carroll
Inspector Dominic Hayes
Inspector Jerry Healy
Det. Sgt Tony Hughes
Det. Sgt Gerry Kelly
Det. Sgt Pat Lynagh
Det. Sgt Gerry McGrath
Det. Sgt Des McTiernan (Retired)
Det. Sgt Gabriel O'Gara
Sergeant John Connors
Det. Garda Tom Byrne
Det. Garda Dick Caplice
Det. Garda John Clancy
Det. Garda Bobby Cooper
Det. Garda Marion Cusack
Det. Garda Dominic Hunt
Det. Garda John Kelly
Det. Garda Dick Reidy
Det. Garda John Stafford

Other units which provided essential back-up included:
Crime and Security Branch
Criminal Assets Bureau (CAB)
District Detective Units throughout Dublin
Garda Bureau of Fraud Investigation (GBFI)
National Bureau of Criminal Investigation (NBCI)
National Drug Unit (NDU)
National Surveillance Unit. (NSU)
Special Detective Unit (SDU)

Acknowledgments

This was a difficult book to write because it was for personal, rather than business, reasons. It is a story that has taken almost five years to tell. I didn't rush to bring this book out because to do so would have been an injustice to the memory of a murdered colleague. It would also have been an insult to the group of police men and women who risked their lives and made sacrifices so that John Gilligan's evil empire would never again threaten our society in the way it did on June 26, 1996.

I had built up a large database of information in my work for the past fourteen years as the crime correspondent with the *Sunday World* and from the research done for the books *The General* and *Gangland*. It provided a valuable base from which to work, but I couldn't have written *Evil Empire* without the generous assistance and help of many people.

I want to thank past and present members of the Garda Síochána for their assistance and help in piecing together this complex story, which effectively spans thirty years. To those of you who gave up so much personal time to give me interviews and other information, my sincerest thanks. The same goes to former members and associates of Gilligan's various gangs, his victims and others who did not want to be identified in these pages.

I would like to express my deepest thanks to *Sunday World* editor Colm MacGinty, his deputy John Shiels, and news editor John "Bram" Donlon, who gave me the time and support to complete this book, as well as Managing Director Michael Brophy for giving me so much scope over the past seven years. My thanks also go to

Diarmaid MacDermott of the Ireland International News Agency in Dublin, picture editor Gavin McClelland and former colleague Mark O'Connell BL for his excellent and comprehensive legal research. My gratitude goes also to the *Sunday World*'s investigative photographic team, Padraig O'Reilly and Liam O'Connor, who travelled all over Europe with me these last five years, tracking down various publicity-shy members of the Gilligan gang. They have come closer than most to the nastiest men in gangland and have had many close scrapes.

As always, my thanks to Gary, my book-writing mentor, and Paul for his friendship and help.

To Gerard Fanning, of Fanning Kelly Solicitors in Dublin, for his expert advise and long hours of hard work. After working for the *Sunday World* over the past several years, Gerard probably knows as much about organised crime as the D.P.P.!

I also want to take this opportunity to congratulate my old friend Kieran Corrigan, Chief Executive of Merlin Films, whose new company, Merlin Publishing, is responsible for the production of this book. My thanks to Managing Director and editor Selga Medenieks and Chenile Keogh, Sales and Marketing Manager. They make for a formidable and dynamic team and will no doubt provide a welcome and much-needed alternative in the stuffy, pedantic world of Irish publishing.

Finally, I would like to express my love and gratitude to Anne, Jake and Irena who have had a tough few months while I prepared this book. I couldn't do without them.

Contents

PART THREE – THE FALL OF THE EVIL EMPIRE

PART FOUR – JUSTICE

"Gilligan had a motive for murder: the necessity of having to protect an evil empire."

– Peter Charleton, Senior Counsel for the prosecution during the trial of John Joseph Gilligan for the murder of Veronica Guerin

Introduction

No crime in gangland's blood-soaked history has so outraged a nation as the execution of Veronica Guerin. It was an act of terrorism against society by a criminal organisation whose shady membership believed themselves untouchable and steps ahead of the law.

It was what the international law enforcement community describe as "narco-terrorism", where big drug syndicates use terror tactics against individuals and states to protect their interests. They are motivated only by greed.

The flip side of greed is fear. As far as conspiracies go, this atrocity had an uncomplicated motive. A journalist had meddled in a multi-million pound drug business. The gang boss had beaten her up and now faced an assault charge and a potential jail term of a few months.

His forced leave of absence would have worrying consequences for the gang's all-important bottom line. Each month, week and day inactive in the "business" would cost obscene amounts of money. He had the international connections and the organisational skills. Without his presence the gang was in trouble and his cocky lieutenants hatched a murderous plot. There was only one option: the meddling journalist had to be removed permanently. The murder would send an unequivocal message to anyone else intent on upsetting this evil empire: politician, judge, cop, tax man, criminal, Joe Public – don't mess with us. We have the bottle to destroy you.

When the gang's henchmen were sent out to spill blood on that sunny afternoon in June 1996 they were displaying their contempt for society. It was their version of a criminal coup.

The Guerin murder had an unprecedented effect on the Irish psyche and caused a universal outpouring of emotions: shock, fear, anger and grief. In many respects the phenomenal expression of outrage was greater than that which followed some of the worst atrocities committed during almost thirty years of violence in Northern Ireland. The crime also sent shock waves throughout the rest of the world. Organised crime had certain boundaries beyond which it would not go. Unwanted publicity was an occupational hazard which success brought. It was a cross the gangster must bear. Calling attention to oneself by shooting the messenger simply was not done.

The level of international shock at the murder was reflected in the fact that major TV networks, newspapers and magazines throughout the world covered the story. The prestigious CBS "60 Minutes" programme in the U.S. made two documentaries about the case. The murder emphasised to the leaders of the European Union the urgency of a fully integrated, pan-European effort to fight organised criminals who did not respect national borders. Narco-terrorism was no longer confined to the streets of downtown Bogota or Moscow.

Why should this have occurred in Ireland? Why not elsewhere in the civilised West, where organised crime is more prevalent? What factors contributed to the gangsters' mindsets that they thought they could get away with murder?

Before the late 1960s Ireland had no problem with organised crime. It didn't exist. In the early part of that last decade of innocence the only serious crimes were murders and they were invariably crimes of passion. The Garda Síochána (the Irish Police) numbered less than 6,500 men; in Dublin, for example, seven patrol cars were quite adequate to help keep law and order.

All that changed with the outbreak of the Troubles in Northern Ireland. The various republican groups began robbing banks and post offices throughout the country to fund their war with apparent impunity, while the police struggled to respond. During the 1970s and early 1980s the State threw much of its police and security resources into fighting terrorism and a perceived threat of a takeover by the Provos (the Irish Republican Army). In the space of five years, from 1980 to 1985, seven gardaí were shot dead by various subversive groups involved in armed robberies.

Commensurate with this situation was a dramatic upsurge in serious crime, or what gardaí classify as "crime ordinary". The street-corner pickpockets and burglars from Dublin's most deprived estates took their lead from the lawless Provos and full advantage of the distracted police. Guns were more freely available than previously and there were plenty of renegade Provos around to show novices the ropes so that they could move into armed robbery themselves. Large families with reputations for petty crime, such as the Cahills, the Dunnes, the Hutches and the Cunninghams, became the first generation of organised crime in Ireland. Between them they ushered in a new era of violence. Gangland had arrived.

The robbers of the 1970s then discovered that one good drug deal could make more cash than holding up ten banks or security vans. There was a large, ready market, particularly in the depressed inner-city ghettos and sprawling estates. The new hard drug scourge brought devastation to thousands of families. It also made the former robbers wealthier than in their wildest dreams – and very dangerous. Gang wars and contract killings became an occupational hazard for the underworld's nouveau riche.

The slow and inadequate response of both the gardaí and the legislature in dealing with organised crime gave the new godfathers good reason to believe that they were untouchable. After three decades of poor resources and a lack of strategic planning in the police, a disorganised, plodding criminal justice system, political corruption and no mechanism by which the authorities could seize drug profits, organised crime was an attractive proposition for the aspiring thug.

It was from this bleak situation that a small, vicious gangster called John Gilligan emerged to make his mark on the underworld. Through the 1970s and 1980s he had been part of the new generation of thief specialising in robbing warehouses and factories. But he, too, discovered drugs. In less than three years in the mid-1990s Gilligan built a multi-million pound drug empire through corruption, fear and violence. He controlled the most dangerous criminal organisation ever to emerge from the underworld.

Gilligan had played the system for over twenty years and, despite a few periods in jail, considered himself invincible. Like so many of his underworld cronies, he was laughing at the police. They had not succeeded in putting his old crony Martin Cahill, the General, behind bars despite an appalling litany of outrageous crimes. Cahill had blown up a forensic scientist, shot a social welfare inspector and an unarmed police man, robbed the Director of Public Prosecutions' most sensitive crime files, and kidnapped one of the country's top bankers as part of his war with the State. When the police went after him, they managed to put most of his gang out of action but not the ultimate target, Tango One. Gilligan arrogantly considered himself much more clever than Cahill. To him the General was an inferior villain, a "gobshite" in his own parlance.

As Gilligan's mob contemplated the journalist's death, they could also take encouragement from the increasing number of gangland assassinations and murder attempts taking place. None of them had been solved. Added to this was the fact that morale among the police was at an all-time low. After several years of inaction, neglect and controversy the force was suffering from a chronic lack of self esteem. By the mid-90s most detective units were understaffed and there was dire need for a reform of specialist squads. Successive management regimes had frowned upon such units and, to the detriment of serious crime investigation, a dedicated national crime squad, the Technical Bureau, had effectively been disbanded.

Experienced serious crime investigators had often complained at the lack of resources for intelligence gathering and overtime bans. At one stage in the 1980s the investigation of serious crime was on a ludicrous nine-to-five basis. If an officer wanted to work outside those hours, then he did so without being paid. On top of this, a bitter dispute was raging between the rank and file of the Garda Representative Association (GRA) and a breakaway group, the Garda Federation. By 1996 the then outgoing commissioner Pat Culligan had begun the mammoth task of revitalising and galvanising his force. He and his successor, a talented, dynamic officer called Pat Byrne, could never have realised how much John Gilligan would help their cause.

Another significant factor the young Turks probably gave thought to was the shooting of Veronica Guerin in January of 1995. A lone gunman called to her home and shot her in the leg. The crime was never solved and the investigation fizzled out within a few months. Gilligan heard the absurd rumours being spread by certain gardaí and journalists that she had organised the shooting herself to increase her profile as a crime reporter. Taking these circumstances together, the indicators were favourable to ruthless gangsters with sinister ambitions.

In the case of most major events in social history it takes a cataclysmic event to force change and focus minds. A similar situation arose in Sicily in the early 1990s when the authorities there targeted the Corleonese godfather, Toto Riina. The Mafia boss thought himself so powerful that he blew up the two prosecutors who had begun investigating his empire. The fallout from those atrocities finally galvanised the Italian government and the Sicilian people to take on the Cosa Nostra for the first time in centuries. Toto Riina, his henchmen and several of his corrupt officials were jailed. In this country the Veronica Guerin murder was a catalyst for unprecedented change in the fight against organised crime.

In one of his excellent books on organised crime English journalist Duncan Campbell wrote: "If journalism is the first rough draft of history, then crime journalism has a habit of being rougher than most."

I have been working as a crime correspondent for over thirteen years in Dublin and witnessed this rough draft of history unfold first-hand. I have written crime books about criminals and the crimes before, but this book is different. It was prompted by the murder of a colleague, a competitor in the business who did the same job and dealt with the same people. She had burst onto the scene two years earlier, producing a string of exclusive crime stories which kept me on my toes. In the year before her death she warned me to be careful in my dealings with various crime gangs, particularly members of Gilligan's gang. She wrote the same message on a Christmas card she sent to me in 1995, six months before her death. Ironically, on the day of the murder I was the first journalist on the scene.

I will never forget that day for many reasons. For almost five years I have followed every step of this extremely complex story of drugs, greed, violence and murder. This book is about the most terrifying episode in recent Irish criminal history. It is about Gilligan's rise to power and the establishment of one of the most dangerous gangs to emerge from the underworld. It pieces together the life and crimes of Gilligan and his murderous henchmen and describes how they organised the country's largest drug smuggling operation. The book tells the inside story of the gang's reign of terror in the underworld and the plot which ultimately brought them a step too far.

Out of the crisis and tragedy that marked 1996 in our history the police emerged with a new resolve to smash organised crime. This book also charts the extraordinary story of the dedicated Lucan investigation team who led the international fight against Gilligan and finally smashed his evil empire. It examines the controversial introduction of the witness protection programme, which sheltered members of Gilligan's organisation who decided to turn State's evidence against their old boss. In addition, it investigates the establishment of the Criminal Assets Bureau which has become a model for law enforcement agencies throughout Europe. The book follows how the CAB traced the gang's ill-gotten gains before turning attention on the rest of the criminal underworld.

This is a very complex story of law and order, good and bad, life and death. It has the dramatic plots, sub-plots and twists of a thriller, except that it is all brutally true. This is a story which should never be forgotten.

Paul Williams
May, 2001

Prologue

Wednesday, June 26, 1996

At dawn the clouds parted, unveiling glorious sunshine and a perfect blue sky. It was one of those rare days in recent Irish summers, a tantalising reminder of what every day of an ideal summer should be like, free of grey skies and downpours. It made one feel good to be alive.

By the time the sun had slipped below a blood-red horizon, this day would be forever etched in a nation's memory as one that witnessed a terrifying crime.

Veronica Guerin was no doubt uplifted by the sunshine as its warm rays steeped her north-County Dublin home in a golden glow. After breakfast she said goodbye to her husband Graham and six-year-old son, Cathal. Graham, a builder, was to bring Cathal to work with him in Malahide, where he was renovating a cottage. It was the last time they would see their beloved wife and mother alive.

Veronica had a busy day ahead and was probably thinking that she wouldn't get much time to enjoy the sunshine. First she had to drive twenty miles to Naas, County Kildare, to answer a speeding summons in the local district court. In the previous December she had been caught by traffic police driving at 103 miles per hour in her sporty Opel Calibra car on the Naas dual carriageway. She was also summoned for not having a tax disc displayed on her car and for failing to produce her driver's licence and insurance documents.

Veronica was concerned that she might lose her licence. She had been previously fined for speeding at 104 miles per hour. She loved driving fast. The previous day she had met with her solicitor to hand over the documents the police required. Everything, he assured her, was in order and she had no need to be worried.

On her return to Dublin the crime journalist was scheduled to meet with lawyers for her newspaper, _The Sunday Independent_. They were to draft a High Court affidavit in response to a threatened injunction being sought by an underworld contact, John Traynor: Veronica had threatened to write a story about his involvement in drugs. Traynor wanted the story stopped.

She must have been growing weary of courts and lawyers. The previous day she had been in Kilcock District Court, also in County Kildare, as the State's witness in an assault case against another gangland figure and Traynor's close "business" associate, John Gilligan. The previous September, the diminutive godfather also known as "Factory" John had beaten Veronica up when she had called to his multi-million pound home and equestrian centre near Enfield.

She was probably looking forward to spending the evening with her family watching England play Germany in the European Championship. Veronica was a fanatical Manchester United supporter and loved the sport. The following day she planned to fly to London to take part in a forum entitled "Journalists Under Fire: Media Under Siege". Veronica was to contribute to a discussion under the title: "Dying to Tell a Story: Journalists at Risk."

As she set out on her journey to Naas, chatting to contacts and acquaintances on her mobile phone, four other mobile phones began crackling with a deadly conspiracy. A motorbike was inspected and driven away from an anonymous shed in Dublin to pick up a pillion passenger. At the same time, another man was driving to Naas with a sinister mission. A cold-blooded, murderous plot had swung into action.

Veronica arrived too early for her court appearance. She parked her car and decided to fill in the time with a cup of coffee and a newspaper in a local hotel. She left the hotel at 10.40 a.m. to meet her solicitor, Brian Price. They met on the steps of the court and he told her the police were satisfied that her documents were in order.

Shortly before 12.30 p.m. Veronica's case – one of 225 listed for the day – was called before Judge Thomas Ballagh. Mr Price told the judge that his client wanted to apologise to the court for the offence. He assured the court that Veronica's driving was improving – this time she was going slower than the previous time she had been caught speeding! In future she would stay within the limit. The case was over in a few minutes. Veronica was fined £150 for the speeding offence. She walked to the door of the court, thanked her solicitor for his help and expressed her appreciation that the judge had been fair to her. Veronica got into her car and headed back towards Dublin. It was now just after 12.30 p.m. and the day was getting warmer.

The four mobile phones began crackling again as the gangsters moved in. Curt messages and orders were being relayed and received between Naas, Dublin and the Continent. Predatory eyes had spotted the red Calibra head out of town towards the motorway. A gang member was following close behind in a red van. The diabolical plot was coming to fruition.

Veronica was relieved that she hadn't lost her licence. She made a number of phone calls as she drove. She called her boss to tell him her plans for the rest of the day. As she drove past the Airmotive plant on the Naas Road, the mobile phones crackled. "She's passing Airmotive," was the message from the van.

"I see it," replied the rider of the motorbike, who had parked with his pillion passenger up a lane way. The bike swung out into the traffic and sped up behind the red Calibra.

At 12.50 she called her mother, Bernie. Her voice was cheerful. "Hi, mum. I'm on top of the world, mum. I just got a one hundred pound fine. Love you, mum."

Veronica stopped for the red lights at the junction of Boot Road and Naas Road. She dialled the mobile phone number of a Garda friend to tell him the good news about her court appearance. At that same moment the motorbike drew up beside her car. The pillion passenger pulled a magnum revolver from his jacket.

Veronica was leaving a message on the policeman's answering service. "Hi. I did very well... eh... fined a maximum of 150 quid... alt..." The cheerful voice suddenly disappeared with a sharp crack. There was the sound of a phone key being pressed and then another crack.

Silence. It was 12.54 p.m.

The motorbike's pillion passenger smashed the driver's window of the car, sending shards of glass over Veronica. He fired two shots at point blank range into her chest. The crime reporter slumped to her left across the passenger seat. The gunman reached in and fired another four shots into her body, hitting her in the back. The powerful bullets caused devastation as they tore through her body.

The driver of the bike shouted: "That's it... that's enough!" His pillion passenger casually put the weapon back in his jacket and the bike roared off into the traffic. Two other cars pulled out and drove at speed behind it.

When the lights changed to green, none of the vehicles stopped near the Opel Calibra moved. Drivers and passengers sat in shock, staring at the red car, its engine still running. They'd all seen it in the movies, but never in horrifying reality. One of the drivers, a nurse, ran to the car. She pulled Veronica back into her seat and felt for a pulse. There was none. Veronica Guerin, wife, mother and courageous journalist was dead.

Part One

The Gang

One

The Little Man

Ballyfermot, West Dublin, circa 1960

The man out enjoying his evening stroll was the first to spot the group of small kids scurrying from cover at the edge of the golden field of wheat. It didn't take much deduction to work out that the little terrors were up to something. They tittered nervously and glanced back into the huge field of crops that was ready for harvesting.

The first hint of fire was a single pillar of smoke rising up from the crops about five hundred yards into the field. Within minutes the plumes of smoke were blocking out the sun as flames devoured the crops.

"I will never forget that day. Ever since the kids had moved out to the new council houses they were always messing in that field lighting fires, but this was the worst I ever saw. It was pure devastation," recalled the elderly gentleman forty years later.

He distinctly remembered one of those kids. His cherubic face was full of excitement and his deep-set, hazel eyes twinkled with mischief. As fire engines rushed from the city to quell the raging flames, he and his chums giggled 'til tears streamed down their cheeks. This would not be the last time the eight-year-old would cause panic and mayhem in his lifetime. The child was called John Gilligan.

Forty-one years later, as Gilligan began the longest sentence ever given to a drug boss, the old man sat in his home and shook his head with disbelief. "When you look back you never think that an innocent kid like that would turn out to be such a gangster," he reflected somberly. "I always thought that he was a grand kid who just dabbled in a bit of ducking and diving... but don't use my name, I wouldn't like the trouble," he added cautiously.

It said a lot about little John Gilligan, the kid who would progress from childish vandal and petty thief to international gangster and boss of a dangerous criminal empire. Even old neighbours who had always liked and got on well with him were in fear of him. Despite being universally reviled and safely locked away in a maximum-security prison for the next twenty-eight years, a lot of people in "Ballyer" consider it safer to keep their views on little John to themselves.

John Joseph Gilligan was born on March 29, 1952. He was the fifth of eleven children, four boys and seven girls, born to Sally and John Gilligan, both of whom came from the Grangegorman area of Dublin's north inner city. The Gilligans were among the thousands of families who were moved from the squalor of inner-city slums to new, sprawling estates on the edge of the capital in the 1950s.

The governments of the day had done commendable work in clearing the appalling tenements in which impoverished Dubliners had been forced to exist for centuries. Unfortunately, the new public housing projects erected out in countryside areas such as Ballyfermot, Cabra, Crumlin, Inchicore, Donnycarney, Glasnevin and Marino would create a whole new set of social problems.

Despite having more space, privacy and decent sanitation, the new estates were lonely places for many of the new tenants. In the move to better living conditions, whole communities were uprooted and broken up. Lifelong neighbours found themselves living miles from one another. The new working class suburbs had very little to offer apart from accommodation. They would later become notorious breeding grounds for the country's first generation of organised criminals.

The Gilligans were allotted number 5, Loch Conn Road, a modest three-bedroom house with running water and toilet facilities. Although a vast improvement on the slums, the new homes were small and pokey for large families. Loch Conn Road was on the edge of the maze of concrete roads and houses that marked the new border between city and country.

Just a few hundred yards away were the wheat fields which stretched as far as the eye could see. A kid could stroll through the fields of areas called Clondalkin, Palmerstown and Ronanstown, which would later also be gobbled up by voracious urban expansion. At the back of Loch Conn were open fields nicknamed the "California Hills" by the locals who had made the exodus to new lives in the "wild west" of Dublin. Like most of their neighbours, the Gilligans arrived with all their worldly possessions in prams and carts. When most of the residents moved into Ballyfermot the infrastructure was still not complete and the bus service did not go as far as the estates, so everyone had to walk the rest of the journey.

Gilligan's mother, Sally, had a hard life. Her husband, a heavy drinker and gambler, was also a well-known petty thief. In drunken rages he regularly beat his wife in front of his children. In between short periods in jail for house-breaking, John senior worked as a seaman with B and I and was away from home a lot. In a time when crime was still not a major problem in Ireland, John Gilligan senior was the first member of the family who would attract Garda attention.

The hallmark of his break-ins to houses was a lower door panel kicked in with the heel of a boot. One older detective who had arrested him recalled how Gilligan couldn't understand why the police knew so much about him. "Gilligan senior was one of our habitual thieves and he couldn't work out why we kept catching him. He often gave us information in return for dropping charges. His son obviously picked up a lot of his characteristics. He was a nasty, evil little man," the officer recalled.

However, the Gilligans were well liked in their area. Even though the family was poor, their mother ensured that the children were turned out clean and tidy in the best clothes they had. They were considered good, helpful neighbours. The parents of kids who had heard that the Gilligans' father was in prison warned their children not to talk about it, not because they were afraid but out of respect for Mrs Gilligan. "I remember my Da saying that that woman was too good for John Gilligan. She was a very quiet, pleasant woman," one of her acquaintances explained.

Gilligan junior's sisters were hard-working girls and they helped babysit the neighbours' children. When they were older the children would not tolerate their father beating their mother and barred him from the house on Loch Conn Road until he had recalled his manners. One time when an elderly neighbour's wife died, Sally

Gilligan ensured that her kids helped out the widower. "They were decent, hard-working girls," recalled a former resident. "You couldn't ask for better neighbours than the Gilligans."

Those who knew him growing up described John junior as a pleasant young guy but otherwise quite unremarkable. Some of his contemporaries thought he was not very bright. "Years later when he was caught robbing sweets we said, 'Ah, sure, what would ya expect from that little dimwit?' Other lads were out robbin' banks and Johnny was nicking sweets," one of his contemporaries joked. Gilligan certainly wasn't a scholar. He attended the Mary Queen of Angels national school in Ballyfermot village but spent more time "mitching" (playing truant) than pursuing his education. He and his pals roamed around the wheat fields and rode the wild ponies and goats which wandered freely in the area. Gilligan left school when he was twelve years old to pursue his chosen career: crime.

In 1966, at the age of fourteen, Gilligan joined his father as a seaman with the B and I Line, the only legitimate job he would ever hold, but which he used to engage in criminal activity for the next ten years. During the 1970s the B and I Line, which had a passenger ferry and freight service, was being run into the ground. Successive governments were told that nothing could be done with the company because it was in the grip of the unions. An internal investigation was conducted and it was discovered that the Gilligans, father and son, and a small group of employees were running a major corruption racket on board.

A secret survey conducted among passengers illustrated just how much the company was being ripped off. On one sailing the manifest recorded two hundred and twenty passengers, but a head count found that there was actually more than seven hundred people on board. The little cartel had pocketed the other almost five hundred fares in just one sailing. In the early 1980s the then Minister for Transport, Jim Mitchell, reorganised the company and cleared the Gilligans and their associates out. Thirty years after getting the job Gilligan produced his seaman's record (number E 10214) to a journalist to prove that his conduct with the company had been "very good" during thirty-six voyages.

Within a year of joining his dad on the high seas, young Gilligan notched up his first criminal offence on dry land. He was convicted of larceny on July 3, 1967. His maiden crime was rather unremarkable compared to his later endeavours. Gilligan was caught stealing a farmer's chickens in Rathfarnham. On that occasion the District Court Judge decided to give the teenager the benefit of the doubt and applied the Probation of Offenders Act. The Act is intended as a slap on the wrist to a first-time offender and as an incentive to guide his return to a law-abiding life. Practically every gangster who ever made his mark in Ireland has the Probation Act typed on his record alongside his first conviction.

When John Gilligan was eighteen he met the woman who would one day be described in the courts as his able "partner in crime". Geraldine Matilda Dunne from Kylemore Road in Lower Ballyfermot was thirteen when she fell for the diminutive young thief. "Everyone wondered what Geraldine saw in him – the size of him – but she was mad about him. Everyone thought he was a bit of a gobshite and she was the real brains of the operation," recalled one of Geraldine's former female friends.

One of six children, Geraldine was born on September 29, 1956. Like her boyfriend, she dropped out of school when she was twelve. She was described by a former friend as a "real live wire". From the time she was a child she had a deep interest in horses. It wasn't unusual to see the fifteen-year-old "Dunne lassie" galloping bareback on a pied ball pony up Loch Conn Road to pick up her man. "She was a real character then, a real live wire. She used to drink Kiskadees and laugh that she had had several 'kiss me gees'," a friend recalled.

Geraldine worked in Abbots Belts, Buckles and Buttons and later as a basic line operative in a ladies underwear factory in Ballyfermot. At lunchtime she would go with friends to see Gilligan, who invariably was hanging around the house on Loch Conn Road. She would instruct her friends to tell her employer that she was sick and then would go off for the afternoon with her man. After several sick days she lost her job, so she went to sea for three months with Gilligan, working as a chef on board a merchant navy vessel.

In January 1974 Geraldine discovered that she was pregnant. She was eighteen. On March 27, just before Gilligan's twenty-second birthday, the couple were wed in the Church of Our Lady of Assumption in Ballyfermot. They moved to live in a flat at the North Strand in Dublin near John's "work". In 1977 the Gilligans moved to a local authority house in Corduff Estate, Blanchardstown, one among many such new estates built during the 1970s. In September Geraldine gave birth to a daughter, Treacy. A year later, in September 1975, the Gilligans had their second child, a son, Darren. John Gilligan was staunchly loyal to his family and twenty years later declared that he would murder anyone who upset them. It was a sentiment that would have sinister consequences.

Now that Gilligan had responsibilities to his wife and babies, he felt he had to knuckle down at his work and provide for them – by robbing. The following October he was taken away from home after he was convicted of larceny in the Dublin District Court. This time the judge was not as lenient and Gilligan was given a six-month prison sentence for his efforts. A young Garda called Tony Sourke had caught him breaking into a shop in Ballyfermot. When Sourke took Gilligan into the local station to be charged with the offence, the diminutive would-be gangster warned the cop: "I'll blow your fucking head off for this."

By now gangland was undergoing a major transformation. The burglar had been replaced by the armed robber and the level of serious crime was increasing at a dramatic rate. Gilligan and his pals were part of that new breed. Among his associates were the Cunningham brothers, Michael, John and Fran, from Le Fanu Road in Ballyfermot. John and Michael, career armed robbers, would gain notoriety when they kidnapped Jennifer Guinness, the wife of John Guinness, the millionaire chairman of the Guinness Mahon Bank. Fran, who was nicknamed the Lamb, preferred to spend his time in the fraud game, robbing banks with dud cheques and dodgy bank drafts. One of the Lamb's closest associates was another suave con man called John Traynor, who also befriended Gilligan. Traynor had also served on the B and I Line with Gilligan.

Among Gilligan's list of criminal associates was another up-and-coming underworld heavy-hitter, George Mitchell, also known as the Penguin, who would become one of the wealthiest drug traffickers in Europe. Through these contacts Gilligan was also acquainted with Martin Cahill, alias "the General", and several members of his mob, including Martin "the Viper" Foley and Michael "Jo Jo" Kavanagh, all of whom would play significant roles in the story of Gilligan's evil empire.

In the 1970s Gilligan was associated with members of the Dunne family from Crumlin, the first truly well-organised armed robbery outfit in Dublin. The Dunnes were the first major league criminals to move from heists to heroin in the early 1980s and gave the lead to other criminals. They were singularly blamed for sparking the heroin scourge in Dublin, though eventually it destroyed them too.

Gilligan and his father were useful to the new crime gangs. They helped smuggle firearms sent from Britain and other European ports when they worked on the ships. By the mid-70s Gilligan was "working" with various members of the young crime families. At weekends he and the rest of the criminal community would meet on the beach at Portmarnock for trotting races, where they also planned various jobs. Gilligan was gaining a reputation for violence and was fond of handling firearms. Like his father he developed a serious gambling problem. Sometimes he combined both. In September 1976 he was caught and charged with an attempted robbery of a bookmaker's shop on Capel Street in Dublin's north inner city. He had begun to make a name for himself.

The following year Gilligan received three prison sentences. In July he was sentenced to eighteen months for receiving stolen goods, the load of a van that he had liberated from a shop. In September he got another three months for larceny and a year for the botched bookmaker's job.

Gilligan developed a particular area of criminal expertise. From his time on the container ships he realised that they were veritable floating Aladdin's caves, with every conceivable type of domestic product rolling off the ramp into Dublin. Security was lax and he had solid, corrupt contacts in the shipping business. He saw a comfortable niche for himself in the burgeoning crime industry. He would have no problem selling a container load of goods in the working class estates across west Dublin. The punters would appreciate a bargain and he would turn a tidy profit in a short time.

He was also growing tired of prison. Like the other young turks

of organised crime, he was learning to play what the General referred
to as the "game". During Gilligan's sojourn in Mountjoy Prison in
1977 he spent time with Cahill, who was doing time for car theft.
There were many loopholes in the law which could be exploited
using a clever lawyer to play the "game". Trials could be scuppered
by scaring off potential witnesses or simply shooting them. In fact,
Gilligan's sixteen convictions over a thirty-year period of intense
criminal activity, which were recorded before the Guerin murder
and most of which carried relatively short jail terms, is evidence of
how he used both legal and criminal means to thwart the law. During
the same period he was charged over thirty times with larceny,
burglary and robbery.

When Gilligan came out of prison after serving less than a year
of his combined three sentences, he organised a team of local
criminals around him and went back to work. One night in November
1978 Gilligan hijacked a truckload of frozen bacon as it left a storage
depot at Grand Canal Harbour off James Street in Dublin. Gilligan
produced a .45 pistol and dragged the driver from his cab. He chained
the terrified man by the neck to a lamp post and left him there in
freezing temperatures.

A few days later the young policeman who had arrested him
four years earlier, Tony Sourke, heard information that Gilligan had
been behind the robbery. His informant led him to where part of the
haul had been hidden by Gilligan, behind a ditch in a field near
Ballyfermot. The rest of the haul was hidden in a shed belonging to
a certain husband and wife. Sourke discovered that Gilligan had
been paying the couple for the use of the shed for several months to
hide various truckloads of goods. He found that Gilligan was robbing
everything from frozen bacon to sheets of galvanised metal.

The husband and wife were arrested and taken in for
questioning. The wife was the first to crack. She described "John
Gilligan, a small, little man who wears a big crombie overcoat," as
the man who paid them for the use of the shed. Gilligan was arrested
and the woman identified him in a line-up in Kevin Street garda
station. On November 17, 1978 Gilligan was charged with the crime
and freed on bail.

Three months later Gilligan was again arrested by Sourke. This
time he was charged with taking part in an armed robbery at the

Allied Irish Bank branch on the Naas Road in Bluebell, West Dublin. Almost six thousand pounds had been taken in the heist by a team of three armed men. When Gilligan was being questioned he swore on his children's lives that he hadn't been involved. Geraldine arrived at the station in tears, pleading her husband's innocence. She told the detective that Gilligan had been with her at the time of the heist.

Gilligan was not convicted on either the hijacking or armed robbery charges. In the hijacking case the woman who identified him later withdrew her statement after Gilligan threatened to harm her and her husband if she went into court. In the armed robbery case forensic evidence was not strong enough to sustain the charge and the State bowed out. Before that, however, Gilligan had the audacity to offer a policeman in Ballyfermot three thousand pounds for the name of the person who informed on him and his cronies in the AIB robbery. The officer declined the offer.

The police were particularly interested in the .45 pistol that they knew Gilligan carried with him on his various jobs. Some time later they got another tip that he and his team were organising a major factory job on Bluebell Avenue in Ballyfermot. Gilligan had organised the theft of a truck and was to be the driver. As usual, a night watchman was to be tied up, the truck loaded and the cargo taken to a safe warehouse he had rented in the country.

While a team of detectives from Kevin Street station were keeping the area under surveillance, they spotted another group of men hiding some distance off. They turned out to be detectives from Ballyfermot who had received the same information. Neither team knew that the other was in the area and both were after the prize: little John Gilligan, his team, the stolen goods and his .45 pistol. On the second night of the operation the Kevin Street team, again led by Tony Sourke, was about to abort the operation when they spotted the stolen truck pull up outside a flat in Bluebell not far from the factory. Gilligan was behind the wheel with two members of his mob. They got out and went into the flat.

At this stage Sourke's backup team had moved off. He and another detective, Gary Kavanagh, decided to move in and arrest the three in the flat. When they burst in, Gilligan and his two pals were sitting on a couch. They were arrested and searched, but the woman who lived in the flat was left behind. Outside they found that the truck was empty. Unfortunately for the police, the thieves had been on their way to do the job. There was no sign of the gun. They later discovered that Gilligan had wanted to open fire when the detectives first banged on the flat door. He quickly changed his mind and handed the weapon to the woman, who shoved it down her panties.

Gilligan began organising an impressive network of fences (receivers of stolen goods) and hiding places for his loot around the country. He made a point of acquainting himself with truckers in a Ballyfermot pub frequented by drivers. They would tip him off about the various cargoes coming in and he would pay them for the privilege of hijacking their loads. He branched out and began hitting large warehouses and factories in the sprawling industrial estates across west Dublin. The Robin Hood estate at Tallaght was one of his favourite targets. By now he had earned such a reputation that other criminals would not encroach on certain industrial estates because they were known to be "Gilligan's turf".

Gilligan learned how to short-circuit alarm systems and often knocked holes in factory walls to get inside. In fact, Gilligan's robberies during the 1980s were so frequent that it caused alarm and security companies to utilise more sophisticated systems to prevent the heists. But, in the case that the security system was too elaborate for him, Gilligan often had a few security men on the payroll to ensure that things went smoothly. He was meticulous in carrying out surveillance work and knew the response times of both security staff and the police. He became known in the underworld as "Factory John".

Of that time he later bragged: "It was great fun and I got a buzz out of it. Sometimes we got stuff and other times nothing. We were chased by the cops now and again and we had plenty of near misses. There were a lot of times when we were in and out of a place and no-one knew a thing for ages afterwards. The strokes [crimes] were a win-win situation for everyone. The victims, the owners of the truck or the factory got the insurance money ... and me and the lads [got a few bob]. It was the perfect crime and doing no harm to anyone."

Gilligan's favourite time of year was winter. The long, dark nights provide excellent cover for a thief. As the evenings grew shorter each year the police in stations covering the big industrial estates braced themselves for a string of burglaries. In November 1981 members of the crime task force attached to Ballyfermot station had a lucky break when they spotted Gilligan and two of his pals driving his van near Greenhills Industrial estate in Walkinstown. When they stopped the van they found three thousand pounds worth of chocolates which had been stolen from a warehouse. Factory John was stocking up for the Christmas market.

The three were arrested, taken to Ballyfermot and charged with burglary. Gilligan's van was impounded and the three were freed on station bail. The following night an eagled-eyed officer spotted Gilligan and his two friends in the process of trying to steal the van and the chocolates from the police station yard. The audacious thieves were again arrested and charged.

The following March Gilligan was given a twelve-month prison sentence and banned from driving for fifteen years for using his van to commit a crime and then trying to rob it back from the police. Two months earlier he had been given another twelve-month sentence for burglary. But Gilligan didn't mind. The two sentences would run into each other and he would be out in a few months. He was beginning to play the system. In the course of 1981 Factory John was arrested and charged a total of nine times for larceny and burglary offences. He was convicted of only two.

It wasn't cunning or luck alone that kept Factory John in business. He utilised his favourite "get out of jail free" card – terror and intimidation. He threatened to murder anyone who crossed him or might consider giving evidence against him on behalf of the State. The members of his gang were too scared to begin touting to the police. They knew Gilligan was a potential killer. According to some of those who "worked" with Gilligan, he would conduct his own "court-martial" to see if there was an informant in the gang.

Once when a member of his gang was arrested for the offence of buggery Gilligan quickly identified a potential weak link in the gang. At the time homosexuality was still a criminal offence and the police used it to put pressure on various gangsters who were known to be closet gays. In testosterone-charged gangland, calling a hard man a "queer" was as bad as calling him a tout (an informer). The man they nicknamed "Jeremy Thorpe", after the British politician who had been at the centre of a gay scandal, was exiled from Gilligan's inner sanctum. At one stage members of the gang thought he was to be murdered.

Gilligan was never afraid of the police. When they sat outside his house monitoring his various underworld visitors Factory John would confront them, hurling abuse and threats. When he was arrested he threatened to murder officers and burn down their homes.

In the early 1980s a factory involved in making Atari computer games was burgled in Tallaght. The night before the burglary Gilligan and his crew had set a large fire there, made from wooden pallets and other debris from around the industrial estate. The fire caused the mortar in the rear wall to dry and had the effect of weakening it. The next night the gang attacked the wall with sledgehammers and even a truck to break a hole in it to get into the premises and bypass the security system. It was part of Gilligan's notorious modus operandi. The police immediately suspected him.

A few weeks later they got tipped off that Geraldine Gilligan was selling the Atari games to unsuspecting workmates in a factory in Blanchardstown, West Dublin. Detectives from Tallaght began to investigate. A woman who had bought one of the games made a statement to the detectives and Geraldine was charged with receiving stolen goods.

Geraldine sought depositions in the case. This is a form of pre-trial hearing during which the various witnesses for the prosecution relate the testimony that they intend giving in the actual trial. It was a tactic Gilligan used many times to delay trials; it gave him an opportunity to convince people that the witness box was bad for their health.

On the Friday before the depositions hearing John Gilligan arrived at the home of the woman who had made the statement against his wife. He pushed his way inside and threatened to have her fourteen-year-old son shot if she gave evidence. The woman was deeply disturbed and by Monday withdrew her statement. Similarly, a nineteen-year-old youth who had also bought one of the games pulled out of the case after Gilligan threatened him on the morning of the hearing. The police informed the court of the intimidation but no action was taken.

The case eventually foundered and Geraldine was off the hook. Gilligan openly scoffed at the detectives when his wife walked. In the meantime Geraldine was fired from her job. Thanks to her husband's efforts, she actually sued the company for unfair dismissal and received ten thousand pounds in compensation. Geraldine went on disability benefit for the stress which she claimed was caused by the regular police raids on her home. She never worked again.

By the mid-1980s John Gilligan and the Factory Gang were among the top three organised crime gangs on garda intelligence files in the country. Gilligan ranked next to Martin Cahill, the General and the north side-based gang led by the clever young villain Gerry Hutch, who was known as the "Monk". Intelligence reports describing Gilligan as the most prolific large-scale burglar in the country were being circulated to detectives in every police division in the State. Gilligan and his associates were being spotted by garda units throughout the country and at one stage it was estimated that he was responsible for one major "job" every week. At any one time Gilligan and his network were plotting up to a dozen robberies around the country.

One detective who took a particular interest in Gilligan and would remain his nemesis for over twenty years was Felix McKenna. In 1978 McKenna, who was originally from County Monaghan, was appointed a detective and sent to the Tallaght garda district. This was the area where Gilligan was committing most of his crimes; he treated the industrial estates in the area as if they were his exclusive turf. As an investigator McKenna earned a formidable reputation for his abilities and tenacity in pursuing serious crime. Throughout his career he would be on the cutting edge in the fight against organised crime and would be one of the founding officers, and later chief, of the Criminal Assets Bureau (CAB).

Shortly after he arrived in the M District in the winter of 1979, McKenna had his first encounter with Gilligan when he caught him in possession of a stolen lorry and charged him with larceny. The case was dropped when the owner of the truck refused to give evidence because Gilligan had threatened him.

On Saint Patrick's Day, 1981, McKenna and his colleagues

thought that they had at last nabbed Factory John. Gilligan and his team stole a truckload of colour televisions from an electrical engineering warehouse in the Cookstown Industrial Estate. The haul at the time was valued at one hundred and forty thousand pounds, the equivalent of around a million pounds in 2001. Gilligan broke in and disabled the alarm. He reversed a full-length transport lorry, stolen especially for the job, into the factory. After Gilligan and another criminal figure from Ballyfermot loaded it up, they drove the truck to Sligo where it had been arranged that the televisions would be sold to a local specialist in the sale of smuggled goods.

Within a few weeks of the heist McKenna and his colleagues, Det. Sgt John McLoughlin and Det. Garda Noel Whyte, received intelligence about who had carried out the crime and the name of the fence who was selling the televisions. By the time the three detectives arrived in Sligo most of the televisions had already taken pride of place in the corners of dozens of living rooms. In the early '80s colour televisions were considered an absolute luxury. The unsuspecting customers thought they were getting a smuggled bargain. McKenna and McLoughlin raided the fence's house and recovered thirty sets. The list of customers included some of the most respected people in the town. Over the following days word filtered out into the community that detectives from Dublin were tracing stolen televisions. For weeks unsuspecting customers were handing in their television sets to the local garda station or hiding them in attics. In at least one case, a television was broken up and dumped.

The Dublin detectives recovered seventy per cent of the stolen haul and charged four people with receiving stolen goods. The fence identified Gilligan as the man who had offered him the televisions and had actually delivered them. In the end, despite the opportunity of making a deal with the State, the fence opted to take the rap. Gilligan and one of his cronies had visited him in Sligo, produced a gun and threatened to blow the fence's head off. Like Gilligan's other erstwhile "clients", the fence was terrified. The risk of a stretch in prison was better than a stretch in intensive care or the grave, he told the frustrated investigators. Meanwhile, it was business as usual for the factory thieves. Demand was booming and the money was flowing in.

On the morning of January 6, 1982 the head of the State's forensic science laboratory, Dr James Donovan, was driving to his workplace in Garda Headquarters when a bomb device ripped his car apart. The country was shocked by the horrific leg injuries that the scientist suffered in the attack. It was the work of Gilligan's old pal, Martin Cahill. The forensic expert had been about to give vital technical evidence in an armed robbery case against the General and his close friend Christy Dutton. Dutton was from Ballyfermot like Gilligan, another of his associates. The General and Dutton had held up an amusement arcade and left vital forensic clues on the motorbike they had used to get away after the heist. The O'Donovan attack would have repercussions for Gilligan.

As part of the huge follow-up investigation involving the Murder Squad, Special Branch and local detective units, every piece of information received at the incident room in Tallaght station was processed in detail. One caller reported seeing a suspicious white van and a car in the Belgard area of west Dublin where Dr Donovan lived a few nights before the bomb attack. Det. Sgt John McLoughlin and Felix McKenna were given the job of tracing the van and car. The detectives discovered that the van belonged to a security man who patrolled the Cookstown Industrial Estate. He was a highly respected individual who had been appointed a peace commissioner with the power to sign garda search warrants and other sensitive police documents. The investigators then uncovered something sinister. The security man was also associated with Gilligan. On the night that the white van had been spotted, Factory John had met the security man.

Over a number of weeks the investigation team pieced together the case and found that the security man had been working for Factory John as an inside man on various robberies. It was estimated that, in the year before the attack on Dr Donovan, Gilligan had robbed goods in the estate to the value of around a million pounds at the rate of one job every month. If an alarm was raised the security man would head off the local police coming to investigate, assuring them that everything was fine. The security man confessed to his involvement and detailed his dealings with Gilligan. There was enough evidence on which to bring a criminal case against Factory John. The case, however, was a non-starter. Once again the principal witness, this time the security man, was too afraid to testify. He preferred to plead guilty to complicity in the crimes.

One of the incidents in which the security man had been of assistance to Gilligan was a burglary from the RTV Rentals warehouse on the Cookstown Estate. The gang punched a hole in the warehouse wall, even though it had a state-of-the-art alarm system. This time Gilligan headed off in a stolen truck with half a million pounds worth of video recorders. At the time these were the first of the front-loader video machines to come on the market in Ireland.

McKenna and Det. Garda Noel Whyte got information that Gilligan had this time transported the stolen goods to the midlands. He had hidden them with a farmer near Mullingar who was helping to sell them. The investigation team uncovered half of the stolen machines in a hay shed in a raid on the Mullingar farm. Most of the video recorders that had been stolen were eventually recovered, although there was one that they had some difficulty bringing back. A local priest had bought one to watch the Pope's special commemorative video. After the priest had watched his favourite tape, the detectives got the machine back. The farmer later agreed to make a statement outlining Gilligan's involvement in the crime. A file was prepared for the Director of Public Prosecutions and a decision made to charge John Joseph Gilligan with burglary and receiving stolen goods.

Gilligan used every legal device open to him to stall the criminal case. On the morning that it finally went ahead, the farmer arrived in court shaking and ashen faced. "I met John Gilligan last night and he stuck a shotgun in my ear and told me if I give evidence I am a fucking dead man," he told the police. The farmer was adamant that he would not testify. He would take the rap himself. The Director of Public Prosecutions was forced to enter a *nolle prosequi* in the case and drop the charges against Factory John. Gilligan laughed across at the detectives as he strutted confidently from the courtroom.

As his confidence grew, so did the size and frequency of the Factory Gang's "jobs". Just keeping tabs on the number of large-scale burglaries being reported throughout the country was an awesome task. Whenever Gilligan was in custody, the police, the factory owners and freight operators were given a respite. When he was released, urgent Criminal Intelligence Bulletins, including a photograph, description and list of associates, were sent to every station in the country with the warning: "Gilligan has returned to active service organising burglaries on a grand scale."

The Factory Gang was robbing everything that could be sold on the black market. The astonishing "shopping list" included cattle drench, hardware goods, double glazed windows, pharmaceuticals, clothes, lingerie, chocolates, household foodstuffs, alcohol, cigarettes, computer games, television sets, video recorders, and music systems. The gang hit warehouses, factories, large stores and hijacked freight vehicles throughout the length and breadth of the country. Gilligan's fleet of trucks was purloined from transport companies around the country. The size of truck being taken depended on what the gang intended stealing.

Gilligan began travelling independently of the loot while in transit, scouting ahead of the stolen goods and watching for police checkpoints. He used walkie-talkie radios to co-ordinate the various burglaries. If the truck carrying the loot ran into the police, Gilligan would move to distract them. He and his gang were always armed. The gun was a helpful persuader if a security man became stupid. Officers were warned to approach the Factory Gang with caution and with armed backup. In Dublin the experienced officers involved in the investigation of serious crime were finding it impossible to get the resources to place around-the-clock surveillance on the Factory Gang.

Garda management had switched resources away from such specialist areas of investigation with the result that the organised crime gangs had virtually free reign. An internal report, colloquially known as the "Three Wise Men's Report", directed a move away from specialist squads. The theory was that every man and woman in the force should be able to do any job required. Gilligan was taking full advantage of the inadequacies in the system. Inaction was creating a monster. Ironically, Factory John would single-handedly be responsible for a dramatic change in the standard and style of policing in Ireland.

In the meantime, while the police continued to play catch-up,

Gilligan began doing business with Tommy Coyle, the country's biggest fence on either side of the border. Coyle also had extensive underworld contacts in Britain and Europe. The fence, who lived and operated from Drogheda, County Louth, was an extraordinary character in gangland terms. He was the middleman for every illegal group, both paramilitary and criminal, on both sides of the border and the Irish sea. Both loyalist and republican terrorists were among his clients. A policeman once commented that to be handed a list of Coyle's contacts would be every investigator's dream. He was the essential cog that kept the wheels of organised crime and terrorism turning.

A lot of gangland observers still wonder why Coyle was never murdered by one of the many disparate groups he played footsie with (he died from cancer in October 2000). The truth was that, in addition to his complicated working arrangements, Coyle developed a relationship with the police and acted for several years as a double agent. It was also suspected in garda and criminal circles that Coyle worked as an agent for Britain's MI 5. His death from natural causes was testament to the fact that his usefulness outweighed the damage done by his wagging tongue.

In 1985 Coyle took delivery of a consignment of half a million pounds worth of televisions from Gilligan and Michael "Jo Jo" Kavanagh, which had been liberated from Sony's main warehouse in the Cookstown Industrial Estate. Kavanagh, from Crumlin in Dublin, was a key player in the General's gang but frequently took part in jobs with Gilligan. He also organised his own armed robberies.

This was part of a now-regular arrangement between the Factory Gang and Coyle, who had an impressive network of safe warehouses and distributors for practically any merchandise. Gilligan stole the goods and dropped them off to Coyle. In turn Coyle had them stored and distributed within days. On this occasion the police were on to the scam and arrested Coyle. After a long interview the fence agreed to show Det. Inspector Mick Cannavan, an experienced serious crime squad officer, where most of the televisions were hidden in a shed near Slane, County Meath. In the following weeks the police "recovered" a number of other hauls of stolen merchandise around Counties Meath and Louth. Coyle gave no evidence or statement to link Gilligan or Kavanagh to the crime. He was subsequently charged but was let off on a legal technicality.

Gilligan and Coyle were rumoured to have fallen out over the busts but nevertheless continued to deal with each other. In November 1985, for example, Coyle helped dispose of one hundred and fifty thousand pounds of cigarettes stolen in a hold-up from a warehouse in Clondalkin. The truck stolen for the heist was later found in Newry.

In some respects, despite being greedy and volatile, Gilligan could be pragmatic. Part of a stolen consignment could be recovered by the police as long as it did no long-term damage to the operation. It was an acceptable occupational hazard. On his part Gilligan was suspected of informing on some of his partners in crime. However, investigators who tried to break him during the heady days of the Factory Gang recalled how he would steadfastly refuse to give the names of any of his fences. They were his bread and butter and therefore non-negotiable.

In January 1986 Gilligan had one New Year's resolution: to keep on robbing 'til he was gangland's wealthiest hood. Two days into the new year he was doing just that. At 6 p.m. a gang of armed and masked men burst into the Nilfisk warehouse in Tallaght. Gilligan used a stolen van to get into the complex belonging to Initial Services, an office sanitation company which serviced many of the factories across Dublin. The foreman was tied up at gunpoint. Gilligan's men used a stolen tractor unit to reverse a stolen forty-foot container truck inside and began loading it with hundreds of brand new vacuum cleaners. The gang made off with over a hundred thousand pounds worth of Nilfisks. If there had been prizes given out for the country's most efficient cargo loaders, Gilligan would have had difficulty finding space for the trophies his gang would have won. With so much experience, they were incredibly efficient.

Felix McKenna, who by now had been promoted to sergeant and moved out of Tallaght, was brought back for the investigation because of his experience in dealing with Gilligan. He was under the command of Det. Superintendent Ned Ryan, known as "Buffalo", the tenacious serious crime squad chief and the General's sworn enemy. McKenna had an impressive network of informants throughout the underworld. Within three days he got the tip he had been looking for. Gilligan had stashed the vacuum cleaners in a safe warehouse in the Weatherfield Industrial Estate in Clondalkin, only three miles away.

This time Ryan ensured that McKenna got the manpower he needed. He was given the go-ahead to mount a long-term surveillance operation, if necessary. Detectives from Clondalkin, Tallaght and the Central Detective Unit were involved. During a discreet search of the warehouse McKenna and his men discovered most of the stolen vacuum cleaners. In addition to the Nilfisk loot they found the stolen tractor unit and forty-foot trailer which had been used in the robbery, a stolen Leyland truck and a Ford Sierra car. The team pulled back and waited for their target to appear.

Eight days later the squad's diligence paid off. A van drove into the estate and stopped outside the warehouse. John Gilligan got out of the passenger seat. He carefully scanned the area for anything unusual and then opened the warehouse doors. He directed a van inside that was being driven by a young member of his gang, 22-year-old David Weafer from Finglas. Gilligan looked around again before closing the doors. McKenna waited for ten minutes to allow Factory John to feel comfortable inside his Aladdin's cave before the team pounced.

Eight armed detectives burst through the doors with weapons drawn, screaming at the two men to get down on the floor. Gilligan, who was in the process of loading the Nilfisks into the van, soiled himself with the shock of the bust. Det. Sgt Tony Hughes almost threw up as he arrested Gilligan and brought him in for questioning under section 30 of the Offences Against the State Act. On January 11 Gilligan was charged with the aggravated burglary in Tallaght and placed in custody.

Two days later another of Gilligan's jobs went ahead as planned without him. This time an armed gang struck at Connolly Haulage in the Bluebell Industrial Estate in Inchicore and drove off with a truck full of £107,000 worth of cattle drench. During the robbery the truck driver was locked into the back of a refrigerated lorry and almost died of hypothermia. Two old friends of Gilligan's, George Mitchell and Gerard Hopkins, were caught with the drench and subsequently sentenced to five years each in prison.

When he was released on bail a few weeks later, despite his

friends' misfortune, Factory John was back at work. On April 6 he took a truckload of video recorders from the Kersten Hunik warehouse in the same Bluebell Industrial Estate. They were never recovered.

As a result of the ongoing Sony television investigation the police discovered that the gang was also using a lockup shed in Finglas, north-west Dublin. A team placed the lockup under surveillance for a number of days when a locally-based criminal associate of Gilligan's turned up. Just before the detectives moved in, Gilligan turned up in his car with the wife and sister-in-law of another major criminal. The officers moved in and everyone was arrested. Inside the shed the detectives found clothes which had been part of a truckload stolen from a factory in County Kildare, crates of cooking oil taken from a warehouse at the Dublin docks, and pharmaceuticals purloined in a £138,000 burglary from the Glaxo factory in Rathfarnham, Dublin.

Gilligan was charged with the Glaxo burglary on July 9, 1986. He was also charged with receiving the other stolen goods in the shed. Gilligan opted for trial by judge and jury, but his associate made a statement and pleaded guilty. The man was then subpoenaed as a witness against Gilligan, but when it came to the case being heard, the State's only witness disappeared and Gilligan walked free yet again.

A month after he was charged with the Glaxo burglary Gilligan was in Limerick, this time with two associates, robbing mail bags from the city's train station. On September 14 the three were arrested, charged, and then freed on bail. The growing number of outstanding charges was not putting Factory John off his stride. Two weeks later he took part in an armed robbery in Portlaoise with members of the General's gang. On the job was Martin Cahill's brother, John, Martin Foley and Eamon Daly, one of the General's closest lieutenants. The four got away with a total of one hundred thousand pounds in cash, cheques and registered letters.

In December the Limerick case was dropped in the District Court, much to Gilligan's amusement, on a legal technicality. On the same day he was arrested and taken to Portlaoise for questioning about the armed robbery. He was released after two days. No charges were laid.

For every seizure being made by the police there were several they never managed to recover. In one case Gilligan and his team robbed two forty-foot container loads of the latest Adidas sportswear. The robbery took place in Cork on a Saturday night. By Wednesday the residents of Crumlin and Ballyfermot were wearing the very latest Adidas sports gear, including some designs which hadn't made it into the shops yet.

In another job Gilligan, with the help of Martin "the Viper" Foley, robbed a truckload of Aran sweaters from a factory in Falcarra, north Donegal. Somehow Gilligan headed back to Dublin with the load of sweaters and forgot to take Foley with him. The truck was later recovered in Dublin and taken to Crumlin garda station for examination. Gilligan stole it back from the station yard and it was never seen again.

In April 17, 1987 the police pressure on Gilligan was mounting. For the second time they nabbed him red-handed. This time he and two associates were in the process of loading a truck with eighty thousand pounds worth of sweets at Rose Confectionery in the Robin Hood Industrial Estate in Tallaght. A security man had spotted them and called the police. When a member of the gang spotted the squad cars Gilligan remained calm. He joked that one of the gang should put him into a sweet jar and close the lid. But the fun wore off when he was charged again. Prison was now inevitable for Factory John.

Meanwhile, Geraldine Gilligan was enjoying being the wife of one of the country's most notorious criminals. Police on the Gilligan case always suspected that she was his loyal partner in crime. Geraldine drove her husband to meetings with other gang members, as he was now banned from driving for a total of forty years as a result of various convictions. Geraldine was also privy to the planning of various jobs.

But she had plans of her own. Geraldine harboured pretensions of respectability which she felt she could buy with the proceeds of her husband's crimes. She still had a deep interest in horses and had eight stabled in Kilcock. Treacy was also taking riding lessons. Geraldine was ingratiating herself into the horsey set on the proceeds of crime. She was attending riding schools around the country. In order to pursue her ambitions, she decided to buy a farm in the country which she intended developing into an equestrian centre.

In September 1987 the Gilligans bought a derelict farmhouse on five acres of land in a secluded area called Mucklon, near Enfield, County Kildare. Geraldine spotted the place for sale one day as she was driving through the village. She paid seven thousand pounds in cash for the property. The couple immediately began reconstructing the house and building stables for horses at the back. Like his wife, Gilligan had a wish to appear respectable and they both joined the Meath Hunt. Gilligan also began describing himself as a horse breeder and trainer. In the country very few people knew anything of their new neighbour's real profession.

In December 1987 and the first six months of 1988 garda management finally launched a major offensive against organised crime in Dublin. It was long overdue. In 1987 alone there were almost six hundred armed robberies throughout the country, with five hundred of them in Dublin alone. Only one hundred had been solved. The number one target of the campaign was the General and his gang. Cahill had cajoled and embarrassed the authorities so much that they were finally forced into all-out action. He had robbed the Beit paintings, blown up the car of the State's forensic scientist, robbed millions of pounds in cash and jewels and, out of spite, actually burgled the offices of the Director of Public Prosecutions and stole several sensitive crime files.

The Tango Squad was a novel approach to taking on the criminals. Young, enthusiastic officers from around the city were recruited for an overt surveillance operation which forced the gang to make mistakes. Most of them were arrested and jailed, except Cahill. Among those targeted were Christy Dutton, Seamus "Shavo" Hogan, Martin Foley, Eamon Daly, Michael "Jo Jo" Kavanagh and Cahill's brother-in-law, John Foy.

The intense pressure on gangland was unearthing intelligence about other criminal gangs. Det. Sgt Felix McKenna was now one of the Tango Squad's team leaders. He received a tip-off that Gilligan was planning to hit a hardware store in Enniscorthy, County Wexford, and stash the stolen goods in a yard at Ballymount, in west Dublin. Gilligan had begun concentrating on robbing hardware stores around the country in order to equip his new ranch in Kildare.

On January 26, 1988, Gilligan and gang members Christy Delaney, from Finglas, Robert O'Connell and James "Fast 40" Kelly, both from Tallaght, hit Bolger's hardware in the town and took off with fifteen thousand pounds worth of materials. In the previous weeks another large hardware store had been hit in Athlone. The next evening McKenna and his Tango team moved into the yard they had been told about and found a lorry with half of the stolen hardware goods inside. The rest had already been moved.

The owner of the yard, Maurice Griffin, admitted to McKenna that Gilligan had left the loot there for safekeeping and would be returning later to pick up the rest. Nine officers concealed themselves in and around the yard and the stolen goods and waited for Factory John. At 11 a.m. two men drove up to the container in the yard and began transferring the stolen gear to their van. As the two villains, Delaney and Kelly, chatted away, detectives were listening to them from under the truck.

McKenna decided not to arrest the two thieves in the yard. He ordered his men to allow the pair to leave the yard and arranged for them to be intercepted a mile away on the motorway. With a good result, McKenna bosses back at Harcourt Square wanted them to pull out and go back to watching Cahill. But his immediate superior, Det. Superintendent Noel Conroy, agreed to leave the Tango squad in situ for the rest of the day in the hope that Gilligan would walk into the trap.

Luckily for the police, mobile phones were not yet widely in use. When Kelly was taken in, he tried to make a phone call to Gilligan to warn him off, but couldn't make contact. At 5 p.m. another van drove into the yard. This time it was being driven by Robert O'Connell and Gilligan was in the passenger seat. The pair loaded up the rest of the stolen material in canvas bags and threw them into the back of the van. Again McKenna waited until they had driven down the road before he had them arrested. Gilligan, already on bail for the sweets burglary, was given bail again. He told the arresting officers that he had only been "getting a lift" from Delaney. Gilligan would use every delaying tactic possible and the case would not come to court for two years.

Three nights later Gilligan, Kelly and O'Connell were again arrested. This time uniformed officers caught them stealing wood from Chadwick's builders suppliers in Sandymount, south Dublin. They were released on bail. Gilligan assessed the various cases facing him and opted to plead guilty to both in the hope of getting shorter sentences. On May 13, 1988 he was given eighteen months for the burglary at the Rose Confectionary warehouse. At Gilligan's hearing in the Circuit Criminal Court Det. Inspector John McLoughlin, who had been stationed in Tallaght as a detective sergeant, took the opportunity of publicly exposing Gilligan for what he was.

He told Mr Justice Frank Roe that Gilligan was "one of Ireland's biggest criminals in organised crime". McLoughlin said he had known Factory John for fifteen years and he was the leader of gangs which robbed warehouses all over the country. His only source of income was crime. On the other hand, a woman with whom Gilligan stabled three horses said that he was a "kind, generous and considerate person who placed his ponies at the disposal of disadvantaged children". Two months later Gilligan pleaded guilty to the Sandymount job and was jailed for four months.

When he was released from prison in July 1989 Gilligan was still facing charges for the Nilfisk case, which he had decided to fight. Because of his previous convictions and the size of the haul of stolen goods recovered, he was facing a much longer stretch. David Weafer had pleaded guilty to the charge and had been jailed for two years. Gilligan believed that Weafer had secretly done a deal with the police and was informing on the gang. He decided to send Weafer a message in prison. One day while he was showering Weafer's face was slashed with a knife by one of Gilligan's associates. He was rushed to hospital for stitches. The attack was also intended as a message for any other would-be snouts in the gang.

Before the trial anonymous calls were made to Nilfisk's headquarters in Dublin threatening that the place would be burned down if employees gave evidence. The matter was reported to the police and Gilligan was placed in custody for almost two months. After pre-trial hearings Gilligan had been returned to the Dublin Circuit Criminal Court on a charge of receiving the Nilfisk cleaners. The trial lasted for two weeks. In the witness box Gilligan directly addressed the jury and claimed that he had been offered a lift in the van by Weafer. He protested that he had been helping a mate move a few things when the police burst in.

Gilligan's lawyers made an application to the court on a point of law. They pressed the case that there was substantive evidence that Gilligan had in fact actually robbed the vacuum cleaners. Quoting English legal precedent, they pointed out that you cannot receive that which you stole in the first place. Gilligan had only been charged with receiving. Factory John's major gamble paid off. He was acquitted and walked free. The case caused consternation in the offices of the Director of Public Prosecutions, who sent an edict to all District Court judges informing them that when a defendant was returned for trial, he should be returned on all the charges outlined by the police. Gilligan had played the system again and won.

Factory John was still facing the Enniscorthy case. Every time he appeared in court Gilligan and his pals instilled a sense of fear and intimidation. He would stare out policemen, witnesses and jurors. McKenna and his colleagues were determined that Gilligan would not disrupt the system for his own advantage this time. In the meantime, Gilligan used Geraldine in a bid to compromise an individual on the prosecution side by blackmailing him.

McKenna furnished an extensive report on John Gilligan's history for the Director of Public Prosecutions. He itemised the number of times Factory John had used intimidation and fear to get off various charges and that he was suspected of threatening jurors. He urged the D.P.P. to issue a certificate returning Gilligan for trial to the non-jury Special Criminal Court.

At a pre-trial hearing for Gilligan, James Kelly, Robbie O'Connell and Christy Delaney, Gilligan's lawyers argued that he should not be returned for trial because of insufficient evidence. The judge, having read the book of evidence, said there was a case to answer. He was about to return Gilligan for trial by jury at the Circuit Criminal Court when the prosecution's barrister stood up. She handed the judge the D.P.P.'s certificate directing that Gilligan be sent forward to the Special Criminal court. Gilligan was stunned and he turned pale with shock. His three co-accused were sent to the Circuit Criminal Court. O'Connell got three years while Kelly and Delaney's sentences were suspended.

During the day-long trial Maurice Griffin, the owner of the yard, was called to give evidence for the prosecution. He contradicted his earlier statements to the police and claimed that stolen goods had been brought to his yard before the Enniscorthy robbery. He said he had been visited by a Mr Gilligan but that he wasn't the man in the dock. Felix McKenna told the court that Gilligan was the leader of the gang and heavily involved in serious crime. On November 7, 1990 the court cleared Gilligan of a burglary charge but convicted him for receiving and jailed him for four years. Mr Justice Robert Barr, in handing down the sentence, said that he accepted Gilligan was the gang leader.

"He has been involved in serious crime for many years and it appears probable that he has never had lawful employment," the judge said. Leave to appeal was denied and Gilligan was sent to serve his sentence in Portlaoise maximum security prison in E Wing, where other members of organised crime gangs were incarcerated. As he left the court, Gilligan was white with rage. It was a significant victory for McKenna, the Tango Squad and the Serious Crime Squad. The Factory Gang had finally been smashed

A number of subsequent appeals by Gilligan were turned down, but he wasn't finished with the courts. While serving his sentence he was also charged with a vicious assault on a prison officer in November 1992. An additional six months were added to his sentence and he was moved to Cork prison. In September 1993 he was granted temporary release and in November was given his full freedom.

John Gilligan left prison a changed man. He swore he would never serve another jail sentence in his life. With a new ambition and new associates, he was determined to be a big-time drug smuggler. He was about to build an evil empire.

Two

The Coach

Gangland is a parallel world which exists with its own subculture alongside legitimate, law-abiding society. Like ordinary society, organised crime has its different "professions" and pecking order. Armed robbers, drug dealers, fraudsters, hit men and fences are the professionals. In each case there are gang bosses, the underworld equivalent of "businessmen", and their subordinates, the "workers".

There are also a handful of individuals who do not necessarily fall into any particular category but who are nevertheless vital to the workings of the underworld. Shady and very clever criminals act as fixers and advisers for the big gangs, organising money for drug deals and inventing scams to launder the profits. Some make contacts and set up supply routes, or obtain information about potential crimes and then assist in their organisation. Still others act as the front men in dealings with the legitimate world. They are invariably suave and articulate, which the average hoodlum is not. They walk the perilous fine line between the law and the outlaws, gathering intelligence for the godfathers while at the same time passing on information to the police. They work hard to keep everyone happy while at the same time lining their own, very deep, pockets. For thirty years the undisputed king of the fixers in Ireland was a colourful and cunning character called John Traynor.

Experienced police officers described Traynor as an "extremely clever, manipulative and duplicitous" gangster, who played games with everyone he ever did business with. In 1996 Traynor earned infamy as Veronica Guerin's underworld informant who, at the time of her murder, was seeking a High Court injunction to stop her publishing a story about his involvement in drug trafficking. Traynor is the man gardaí suspect was responsible for the first gun attack on the journalist in 1995, when she was shot in the leg. He is also suspected of passing on the information about her Naas court appearance to the Gilligan gang, which ultimately led to her murder on June 26, 1996.

Once dubbed "the Coach" by Guerin in an anonymous, boastful interview he gave her for the *Sunday Independent*, he was a charming, articulate and very convincing informant. Traynor was an accomplished fraudster by profession but his many talents made him invaluable to organised crime. He worked hard at portraying himself as the former villain who had opted to go straight. A big, strong man over six feet tall, Traynor did not have the appearance of the quintessential criminal. Ironically, he was often mistaken for a policeman and, being an inveterate opportunist, often posed as one. He craved respectability and social status away from the company of criminals, but the reality of his life was much more sinister.

Traynor was a vital cog in the Martin Cahill's criminal organisation. He initiated and helped mastermind several of the General's most spectacular crimes. He was to Cahill what in Mafia terms is called a "consigliori", a counsellor and right-hand man to the boss. Like most aspects of Martin Cahill's bizarre personality, his relationship with Traynor was paradoxical. He had a deep-rooted suspicion of con men like Traynor, considering them too flashy and smart for their own good. After Cahill's murder, the Coach would also be John Gilligan's full partner in crime when he began building his evil empire, organising drug contacts and an elaborate money laundering operation.

Together with his other infamous associates in the fraud business, Sean "the Fixer" Fitzgerald and Fran "the Lamb" Cunningham, the notorious trio hatched some extraordinary scams which are still talked about by both cops and criminals. Fitzgerald, who was originally from Drimnagh, south Dublin, was Traynor's closest friend and associate for over thirty years. Like his best pal, Fitzgerald portrayed himself as the well-spoken businessman. He has a string of convictions for various fraud and forgery offences.

In criminal circles Traynor was somewhat of a snob. He considered himself a cut above the rest of the underworld riff raff. In interviews he often gave the impression that he felt he was actually lowering himself by dealing with most of the criminals in Dublin. Whenever he spoke about some of the bigger gangsters, he invariably curled his upper lip and described them in a sneering tone as "dirty, filthy cunts".

Unlike most of his criminal associates and friends, Traynor came from a comfortable, respectable background. He was born on February 2, 1948 in Charlemont Gardens, off Charlemont Street between Kelly's Corner and Ranelagh Bridge on the edge of Dublin's south inner city. He was one of eight children. The Traynors were somewhat better off than many of their neighbours. His father, who was never involved in criminal activity, was an electrician by trade. When John was ten years old the Traynors moved to live at Clogher Road in Crumlin, Dublin 12, one of the many new local authority estates which were sprouting up across west Dublin. Traynor attended Synge Street national school, where he was described as a very bright pupil, but did not go on to second level education. Instead, he began dabbling in crime.

Traynor received his first criminal conviction at the age of thirteen, on January 13, 1961, for housebreaking. He was given the benefit of the Probation of Offenders Act. The following month he notched up another two convictions for larceny and housebreaking and spent a month in detention on the orders of the metropolitan Children's Court. Over the next five years he received a total of nineteen months in custody for larceny, housebreaking and robbery.

In between his scrapes with the law, and to avoid them, Traynor became a seaman at the age of fifteen with Irish Shipping and the B and I Line, where he befriended and worked with John Gilligan. While working on the high seas, Traynor's natural talent for smooth talk and leadership paid off. He was elected to the executive of the Seaman's Union, which effectively ran the then deeply troubled State-owned shipping companies.

In the meantime, Traynor's family moved to live in County Kildare, where his father bought pubs in Kill and later in Rathcoole. He also owned a greyhound track at Hazelhatch in Kildare. In 1973 John married 26-year-old Michelle Sexton, an attractive country girl from County Sligo. Michelle Sexton had never been involved in crime. She would have to endure her husband's constant infidelities and long absences from home, either while doing time or on the run. Just before his wedding Traynor had been convicted on a charge of car theft but the sentence was suspended because of the impending big day. The couple lived in Rathcoole and later moved to Glenvara Park in Templeogue, Dublin. Between 1974 and 1985 the Traynors had four children: two boys and two girls.

In 1977 Traynor received his most serious conviction when he was jailed for possession of a firearm with intent to endanger life. Years later he recalled the incident with typical bravado: "Most of my convictions were for stupid things I did when I was drunk. I was in a pub in Newcastle, outside Dublin, and had a .22 pistol which I had bought for a hundred pounds. I got in a row with a cop who was there. I hit him with the gun and swung it around, threatening the people in the bar. It was more of a joke than anything else." On December 14, 1977 Traynor was sentenced to five years of imprisonment for his "joke", as well as for firearms, assault, burglary and larceny charges. A few days later he was given another five-year stretch, to run concurrently with the others, for assault causing harm.

In between crimes the Coach drove heavy goods vehicles and subsequently managed the a greyhound track for his father at Hazelhatch. But Traynor was addicted to money, and spending it. He loved the high life. A womanising heavy drinker and gambler could not live on legitimate wages alone and still feed a family. Traynor discovered that fraud was a lucrative source of badly needed funds.

The first time Traynor came to the attention of the Garda Fraud Squad was in 1976 when he set up a bogus insurance company. He managed to rip off a number of punters before the police moved in to investigate. Traynor shut up shop and moved on before he was caught. It gave him an appetite for more. During the 1970s and '80s the stock and trade of the fraudster was stolen and counterfeit cheques and bank drafts. Typically fraud had not been treated very seriously by the Irish legislature and this was reflected in the relatively short sentences given at the time to convicted fraudsters. This situation only made fraud more appealing to jail-shy chancers like Traynor. He and his cronies were an invaluable source of cash for robbery gangs; during heists they often got more cheques and drafts than actual cash and needed someone to launder them.

In 1981 Traynor bought a large batch of bank drafts from the renegade republican group the Irish National Liberation Army

(INLA), who had robbed them from banks in Old Castle, County Meath, and Shercock, County Cavan. Like the organised crime gangs, the paramilitary thugs found that they, too, needed Traynor. He had a precious skill for moving stolen goods and knowledge of the financial world. In turn, Traynor had no problem getting into bed with the INLA. A born opportunist, he recognised how such a relationship could be useful for the future. Traynor would maintain his links with the terrorists-turned-organised criminals for twenty years.

Garda intelligence reports classified Traynor as an associate of the INLA and the Provos. In the 1970s he was also listed as a member of Saor Eire, a quasi-republican group that emerged for a short time after the outbreak of the Troubles in Northern Ireland. The group's main interest, however, was not political. They robbed banks for their own benefit. It was the kind of activity which attracted a lot of Dublin criminals who found it advantageous to act under the guise of "patriotism". Stealing was a revolutionary action and crime an economic necessity against the dominance of the capitalists! Traynor, like the many other criminals identified as having "political" leanings at the time, was using the "cause" as a flag of convenience for criminal activity. In any event, Saor Eire faded away after the murder of Garda Dick Fallon, an unarmed uniformed officer who was shot dead in a bank robbery in 1970.

For three years the gardaí made several efforts to catch Traynor and his cronies with the stolen Shercock and Oldcastle drafts, but without success. Traynor, Fran Cunningham and Sean Fitzgerald altered the drafts by simply gluing different company on them, using letter transfers commonly used at the time by school children. Then they used a network of expendable down-on-their-luck drunks and gamblers to cash them around the country. They were called "kite men". If the runners were caught, then that was tough luck. There would be no evidence linking the drafts to the big-time con men. Traynor and his pals recruited their lackeys in pubs around Dublin. Their favourite watering hole at the time was Bartley Dunnes, the famous city centre gay bar, colloquially known as "Bartley Bums", where most of the criminal fraternity hung out.

When other criminals or the paramilitaries ran out of stolen bank drafts Traynor and his chums decided to go out and rob their own. However, they weren't prepared to take the risks involved in obtaining the valuable pieces of paper with sawn-off shotguns. Traynor often bragged about his favourite scam. Using an inside man he and his cronies worked out a way of stealing mail bags from the Collector General's Office. The bags contained cheques from companies and individuals which were made payable to the Collector General. Traynor and his pals altered the words "Collector General" so that they appeared as "Collette Gerhardt". The cheques were endorsed with the signature of the fictitious woman and her "address", care of the Germany Embassy. The cheques were cashed throughout the country and Traynor later gloated that they had defrauded the tax man to the tune of £2.75 million, although it is more likely that they got only a fraction of that amount. In any case, the Coach could afford to blow a fortune within weeks on women and booze.

Traynor had a talent for spotting a way of turning a fraudulent penny. One day he walked into a bank on College Green in Dublin to cash a cheque – a legitimate cheque. The system in the bank required the customer to go to one hatch for authorisation by a designated official. The official checked the bank balance on which the cheque was drawn, then initialled and stamped it with the branch's official stamp. The customer then returned to the cashier's hatch where the cheque was cashed. Traynor noticed that there was no communication between the two bank officials. It was a wonderful opportunity to make money.

Traynor went to work. He discovered that an employee of the branch with a fondness for drink was a regular in Bartley Dunnes. Within a week the fraudster had convinced the employee to take the bank stamp. He sent in a number of runners to have cheques for small amounts cashed. When the cheque had been passed and stamped, Traynor's pals slipped out around the corner to a pub where he was waiting. The signature was forged onto a cheque for a much larger sum. It was stamped and the runner was sent back to collect the cash. Traynor reckoned he pulled over £47,500 in three days. He later described it as "great craic".

John Traynor first met Martin Cahill when they were children hanging around the same area. Traynor used to visit his odd little friend with a taste for sweet cakes in Hollyfield Buildings, the run-

down tenement block in Rathmines where the General's family lived
with other troublesome Corporation tenants. After Traynor moved
to Kildare he stayed in contact with Cahill. When he was jailed on
the firearms charges in 1977, he served his time in Mountjoy with
Cahill. John Gilligan, who was inside on an eighteen-month stretch,
was also with them for part of the time.

Shortly after they came out of prison, the three cronies came
together for a warehouse burglary. Cahill, Traynor, Gilligan, George
"the Penguin" Mitchell and Paddy Shanahan took part in the theft
of a hundred thousand pounds worth of cigarettes from the ADC
wholesalers in Johnstown, County Kildare. Paddy Shanahan, a friend
of Traynor's who came from Kill, carried out the surveillance for
the "job". Like Traynor, Shanahan was a most unlikely criminal. A
member of a respectable family, he grew up in the heart of County
Kildare's stud farm belt, a world away from the newly emerging
gangland in the big city. Another thing that made him different to
the rest of the underworld was the fact that he was university
educated, having studied history and English at University College
Dublin. Shanahan made a conscious decision to become a villain.
He was hooked on the adrenalin rush of serious crime and became
a prolific robber with a reputation for violence.

Traynor and Cahill had a close but strange relationship. They
were gangland's odd couple. Traynor was everything that the
General despised, namely a flashy, womanising hard drinker.
Traynor described Cahill as "totally odd and very paranoid". But
the two crooks needed each other. Traynor was Cahill's adviser and
organiser. Cahill did the robberies and shared out the cash.

In May 1981 the two bought a grotty little bar at the North Wall
near Dublin docks called the Jetfoil, which became a notorious haunt
for drug dealing and barroom brawls. Traynor was the front man
and the money for the purchase came from one of Cahill's heists.
The bar's stock of alcohol and cigarettes was either stolen by the
General's men or bought at a competitive "wholesale" price from
John Gilligan. Gilligan, in turn, had sourced the goods from one of
the many west-side warehouses he considered his own. Most of the
equipment in the bar was bought by Traynor using counterfeit or
stolen bank drafts and false addresses. Gardaí from all over the city
were regular visitors to the Jetfoil in their search for stolen goods.

Cahill and Traynor also bought a dry-cleaning business on Aungier Street on the south side of the city. Again Traynor was the beneficial owner on the registered deeds. Upstairs a brother-in-law of one of Traynor's criminal associates had a massage parlour, which the Coach regularly visited. For his kicks, the General used to shin up a drain pipe and peep through the window at the action inside!

There was no written, legal agreement between the two unlikely partners. There was no need. Cahill knew that if there was a "legal" problem he could sort it out in his own inimitable fashion. On his part, Traynor knew that Martin Cahill was the one man in the world he could never rip off. It was the classic underworld version of a gentleman's agreement.

In January 1983 Traynor brought Cahill information on a robbery which would earn his colleague the nickname "the General" and confirm his position as the country's most notorious criminal mastermind. Traynor had for months been nurturing an employee who worked for O'Connor's jewellers in Harold's Cross, Dublin. The corrupt employee had been selling Traynor small quantities of uncut jewels and gold dust. Traynor showed Cahill a matchbox full of gold dust which the employee had given him, worth a thousand pounds. If this was what you could pick up off the floor in a tiny box, Traynor reasoned to his pal, then imagine what you would get if you robbed the place.

Over the next six months Traynor and Cahill planned every aspect of the O'Connor's heist. Traynor did most of the surveillance and worked with the inside man. He obtained photographs and detailed plans of the security system and the layout of the building. Traynor would meet his source in Ashton's pub in Clonskeagh. The inside man was never allowed to meet Cahill face-to-face, although the General made it his business to know everything about him. Years later, when Traynor related the O'Connor's story, he explained that even though they were planning the job together, Cahill still did not fully trust him.

On the Sunday prior to the robbery Traynor called to Michael Egan, an aluminium fitter from County Offaly who lived on Sundrive Road, Crumlin. Egan was a Walter Mitty character who had been involved in several failed business enterprises. He was drawn to the company of flashy criminals and Traynor exploited that interest.

Egan was told that Cahill needed to hide a van in the workshop at the rear of his house that was accessed by an alleyway. There was "a small stroke going down", he told Egan, and members of the gang would be hiding there the night before. The following morning at exactly 9 a.m. Egan was to open the workshop door and a van would return with the loot.

Eventually the robbery went ahead during the evening of Tuesday, July 26, 1983 and the following morning. That date was chosen because most of the staff were on their summer holidays. A few members of the gang broke into the O'Connor's complex through a boiler house which had not been alarmed and lay in wait for the staff to arrive the next morning. The job was pulled off with military precision. The gang rounded up all of the staff members as they arrived for work. In thirty-five minutes they removed the contents of the strong room, including gold bars, gems, diamonds and thousands of gold rings. The haul weighed over half a ton and was valued at £1.5 million. It was the largest robbery in the history of the State at the time and eventually closed O'Connor's down. Just after the robbery Cahill led his gang back to Egan's workshop in Crumlin on his Harley-Davidson motorbike in rush hour traffic.

With the rest of the gang dispersed, Traynor, Cahill and Ballyfermot criminal John Cunningham spent the following day and night counting and sorting the huge haul of mesmerising gold and jewels. At one stage two detectives conducting a follow-up search stopped outside the workshop door. When they tried to open it, the three armed criminals pulled their guns; if the cops came in, they were prepared to shoot their way out. Traynor later claimed it was the nearest he ever came to killing a policeman.

When the three hoods had the O'Connor's haul sorted, they drove in two cars to a garden off Ballymount, west Dublin, and buried the guns and jewels. They returned to the workshop and took away the van. Traynor drove behind in his BMW car. They took the van to Poddle Park in Crumlin to burn it using petrol bombs. As John Cunningham was throwing one of the devices into the van, it prematurely ignited, causing serious burns to his right hand. Cahill and Traynor drove Cunningham back to his home in Tallaght where they dressed the wound. Two days later Cunningham went to hospital for treatment to his burns. He told doctors that he had been injured when a chip pan caught fire in his home. When the gardaí subsequently searched Cunningham's house as part of the O'Connor's investigation, they found no evidence of a fire.

Traynor and Cahill negotiated the sale of the O'Connor's haul. Despite its legitimate value they could only realise a fraction of it on the black market. Eventually they agreed to sell the sapphires, rubies, emeralds and diamonds to a London fence called Les Beavis for a hundred thousand pounds. In addition, each gang member had a bag of gold which he could offload as he wished. Each bag was equal in size and Beavis agreed to buy each one for forty thousand pounds.

Traynor oversaw the movement of the gold and jewels to London. He made around fifty thousand pounds in cash from the heist. While the gold was being smuggled out of the country, one consignment went missing. The incident led to the infamous "crucifixion" incident, in which the General literally nailed the suspected thief to the floor of a derelict house. Traynor in later years could describe the scene in graphic detail as Cahill "nailed down" his problem. Traynor admitted helping to abduct the errant gang member and taking him to the derelict house, but denied that he actually took part in the appalling torture. He claimed that he was horrified by what he saw but felt powerless to do anything about it. He knew that he couldn't talk down the General. John Traynor had an innate sense of self-preservation. The crucified courier, who still denied that he robbed the robbers, was cleared by the General's court. Cahill said no guilty man could tolerate such pain without spilling the beans. The stolen gold was subsequently dug up by a dog in the garden of a house in Terenure, Dublin.

In the weeks that followed the O'Connor's job, the General and his gang ran into conflict with the Provos over the proceeds of the heist. Coincidentally, that group had also examined the prospect of hitting O'Connor's, but had decided to abandon the idea on the grounds that it was too risky. A week after the robbery the IRA asked for a meeting with Cahill. The General and Traynor attended the meeting, which took place in a coffee shop in Crumlin Shopping Centre, next door to the local police station where officers were still investigating the robbery. Two senior IRA figures sat across the table from them.

The Provos said they wanted half of the O'Connor's haul. Cahill was having none of it and told them: "If you want gold, then go out and rob yer own gold like we did." When he was warned that there would be very serious consequences if he failed to comply with the demand, the General stood up and moved his face closer to the IRA men. "You do your strokes and we'll do ours. Ye're not gettin' a fuckin' penny." He marched out of the coffee shop with Traynor in tow. It was not the approach the Coach would have taken in the situation. He argued that Cahill should give the IRA something to get them off their backs but the General refused. Traynor knew that to push the issue any further would show that he was scared of the Provos. Cahill did not like fear in an associate.

The tension continued to mount for several months and eventually came to a head in February 1984, when the Concerned Parents Against Drugs (CPAD) marched on the homes of Cahill's gang members. At the time it was believed that the organisation had been infiltrated by the Provos. In response, Cahill organised his own group, the Concerned Criminals Action Committee (CCAC) to march on the CPAD. Traynor and Sean Fitzgerald were among those who led the march. They did so not out of a deep-rooted belief in their cause but because Cahill ordered them to take part. The crucifixion was still foremost in their minds. The following month all hell broke loose.

A close friend of Cahill's, Tommy Gaffney, was kidnapped by an IRA active service unit. Martin Foley, who was a leading member of the General's gang at the time, worked as Cahill's front man in what was building up to an all-out bloodbath between the two groups. Three weeks after the abduction, another IRA unit tried to kidnap Foley. Luckily for him, the police were quickly on the scene. The Viper was rescued after a high-speed chase and shootout between the Provos and the police. The four-man Provo unit was arrested and subsequently jailed for the incident. The day after the Foley abduction fiasco, the IRA released Gaffney with a chilling message: "Tell Cahill that we won't kidnap him... we'll stiff him on the street."

Both sides pulled back from the brink of an all-out bloodbath. Traynor had managed to stay out of the firing line but, just to make sure he had covered his own back and kept his options open, Traynor secretly met with the Provos and assured them that he would do everything to convince Cahill to pay up. In the end it never came to anything.

After the dust settled on the O'Connor's episode, there were other difficulties to be dealt with. The Jetfoil had succeeded in becoming one of the worst pubs in Dublin. Its regular patrons were the dregs of the city, punters who wouldn't even have been allowed into an off-licence to buy a can of beer. There was constant heat from the police, so Cahill and Traynor decided that the Jetfoil should go on fire. They estimated that they could claim fifty thousand pounds from Dublin Corporation for the "malicious" damage to the property. They would turn a tidy profit on their original investment and still be in a position to sell the pub. In the build-up to the "accident", they orchestrated a number of "threats" against the premises. In the early hours of May 25, 1984 they moved out most of the bar's stock. Chairs and tables were piled up in the middle of the lounge, paper was placed on top and forty gallons of petrol poured throughout the building. When the fire brigade arrived, the door to the pub was open with the key in the lock. The place was gutted.

In October 1988 the High Court heard a compensation claim brought by Traynor for £47,700 worth of malicious damages against Dublin Corporation. The judge hearing the case said it was clear that the "worst type of disorderly persons" frequented the Jetfoil. It was a place also well known to the Garda Drug Squad. Traynor, who by then was out of the country, had claimed in a written submission that he had taken all necessary precautions to avoid such damage and was, rather ironically, relying on the police to protect him and his fine establishment. The Judge cut Traynor's claim by a quarter but was forced to award him and his shadowy partner £35,675.

In the period following the O'Connor's job, Traynor went back to what he did best, namely stolen cheque and bank draft scams. By the mid-1980s all government departments were fair game. Cheques from the Departments of Agriculture, Social Welfare, Defence and Justice all ended up in the hands of Traynor and his associates. In particular, he took immense pleasure from stealing and cashing scores of stolen garda cheques.

He, Cunningham and Fitzgerald had learned a lot about the workings of the police through their many encounters and regularly passed themselves off as policemen. On one occasion, when a member of the Cahill gang was being held in Rathfarnham garda station, Fitzgerald phoned up pretending to be a senior officer from the Serious Crime Squad. He demanded that the Cahill gang member be released because he was vital to an ongoing investigation. The criminal was let go. Whenever the con men were organising to hit certain city centre banks with a string of cheques to be cashed, Traynor would call the local detective units pretending to be from Garda Headquarters and inquire if an operation was going on in the area to catch fraud men. If the answer was no, then he and his cronies went to work. On other occasions, again posing as garda brass, he actually directed garda units to other areas to ensure that he had a police-free run at the banks he had targeted.

Traynor's most sinister scam involved blackmail. Throughout his career the fraudster had a string of girlfriends, most of whom were high-class prostitutes. Traynor would organise for them to pick up wealthy businessmen and other individuals he considered useful for inside information or assistance in various frauds or thefts. Traynor had purchased video surveillance equipment for use when organising robberies with Martin Cahill. The girlfriend would take the unsuspecting target back to an apartment for sex, which event Traynor would tape. Intelligence available to the Serious Crime Squad in the mid-1980s suggested that Traynor was demanding up to twenty-five thousand pounds from each victim in return for a copy of the tape, although it was never clear how much money he actually made from the scam or what other "assistance" he obtained from the victims. None of the victims ever reported a crime.

Together with another well-known member of the fraud community, James "Danger" Byrne, Traynor got involved in an international scam which became known as the Great Norwegian Fish Scandal. Byrne, from Elphin, County Roscommon, had been associated with Traynor for several years. The former Roscommon county footballer dreamed up the idea of purchasing dried fish in Norway and shipping them to Nigeria. The complex scam involved a promissory note for £3.6 million which was drawn by Byrne from the Norwegian Tromso Spare Bank after being endorsed by a friendly bank official at the Northern Bank in Carrick-on-Shannon. A further two promissory notes valued at over twelve million pounds were stopped before Byrne and Traynor could cash them. The scam made international headlines and the Norwegian bank took legal action in Ireland, but never recovered the money. Although the bank official was fired for the offence, there was insufficient evidence to merit a criminal investigation against the pair and the case was eventually forgotten.

Traynor was also to play a role in another world headline-grabbing criminal event when he was involved in the organisation of the Beit art robbery with Martin Cahill in 1986. In 1985 Paddy Shanahan had returned to Ireland after being released from a sentence for armed robbery in England. He had begun to specialise in the theft of expensive antiques and paintings from stately homes and was working with a criminal gang from London's East End when he was caught by police. When he came home, Shanahan began planning the robbery of Russborough House, the stately home of Sir Alfred Beit, a retired member of the House of Commons and a member of a wealthy South African diamond-mining family. The Beit collection of Dutch Masters alone was considered one of the most valuable private collections in the world.

Shanahan's mistake was to discuss the idea with Martin Cahill, who decided that he would do the robbery behind Shanahan's back. He began planning his own job after Easter 1986. Traynor and Cahill spent several weeks visiting Russborough House doing surveillance on the security system and the layout of the place. In the early hours of May 21 Cahill and a team of twelve gang members made international criminal history when they walked off with some of the world's most valuable paintings. Traynor did not take part in the robbery itself but would later play a major role in attempting to sell off the paintings for his boss, as would John Gilligan.

Traynor was targeted during the follow-up investigation into the Beit robbery. In August 1986 the Serious Crime Squad raided a shop off George's Street in the south city centre that was owned by a relative of Traynor's. Instead of Dutch Masters, the cops recovered thirty-three thousand pounds worth of stolen cigarettes. The consignment was believed to have been part of a haul stolen earlier by Gilligan and the Factory Gang. Traynor was arrested in connection with the haul and accepted responsibility for it. He was charged with receiving stolen goods and released on bail. He had also been arrested and charged with receiving over fifteen thousand pounds worth of video game machines.

Traynor had run into more trouble than he felt he could handle. One of his stolen cheque scams came back to haunt him when the Fraud Squad traced Revenue cheques which had been lodged by one of his runners. The runner, a 25-year-old car salesman from Tallaght, was arrested after cashing four of the forged cheques for nearly five thousand pounds between July and August 1986. The man told detectives that he had been given the cheques by Traynor. The runner was convicted and given nine months in prison. The Fraud Squad went looking for their old adversary.

To add to his growing number of problems, the wife of Michael Egan, the owner of the workshop used after the O'Connor's robbery, walked into Sundrive garda station in January 1987 looking for Det. Sgt Gerry O'Carroll, who was an old adversary of the General and his gang. Eileen Egan was involved in a bitter dispute with her husband and decided to spill the beans about his involvement in the robbery. The unexpected breakthrough shocked the gang. When Egan was taken into custody he made a full statement of admission. He also told the police that he had been paid only five thousand pounds from the robbery and had suffered "trouble and threats" from Traynor.

When the General got word of Egan's arrest and learned that he had been ripped off by Traynor of a share of the proceeds, he was furious. One disgruntled member of the gang, no matter how peripheral he was to the job, was a threat to the others. Traynor's greed was exposing Cahill to danger.

Cahill also suspected Traynor of ripping him off in their various property deals. In addition to the shop on Aungier Street, they now had a small shop in Arbour Hill. The pub was closed and the subject of an impending compulsory purchase order by the Dublin Port and Docks Board. In his paranoia Cahill believed that Traynor had secretly sold the pub behind his back, pocketing Cahill's share. One night in March 1987 Cahill stormed into the dry cleaner's in a fit of rage when he couldn't find Traynor. In one of his blood-curdling fits of anger he actually ripped every garment in the shop and smashed up the dry-cleaning machines. Armed with a gun, he went in search of his erstwhile partner with his brother-in-law, John Foy, and Martin Foley. Later that night they questioned Sean Fitzgerald about his missing friend and the whereabouts of Cahill's cash. But John Traynor, con man and survivor, had left town in the nick of time and gone to England. He would not return for almost five years. Traynor knew when to keep his head down to avoid trouble.

It didn't take Traynor long to organise work for himself. He began operating with a number of English and Irish fraudsters, dealing mostly in stolen and counterfeit drafts and cheques. One extraordinary Irish character he began associating with was John Francis Conlon from County Mayo. Conlon was the quintessential international man of mystery who dabbled in the high stakes world of spying and gun running. He had documented links with the Israeli secret service, Mossad, the American CIA, and the British MI5. Conlon did international arms deals in the Middle East and with Eastern Block countries. He was also mixed up in international fraud. James "Danger" Byrne, an old associate of Conlon's from their west of Ireland days, also appeared on the English scene.

In 1990 Traynor and his cronies came into possession of a batch of stolen treasury bonds worth several millions of pounds which were registered with the Bank of England. Traynor planned to obtain the millions by placing the bonds with a bank as collateral for a mortgage on a huge international "development". In London the group befriended a Swiss bank official who had a weakness for the high life and frequently needed cash. They went to work.

The friendly bank official with the cash flow problems was approached with a "business" proposition worth several millions of pounds. Plans had been drawn up for a huge, luxurious holiday complex on an island in the Caribbean. The project required a hundred million pound mortgage. The stolen bearer bonds, with their numbers altered, were produced as collateral and a deal was agreed.

The gang managed to draw down an initial payment of around two hundred thousand pounds and sent a runner to collect it from the bank's headquarters in Geneva. In the meantime, the City of London Police and the Serious Fraud Office had been tipped off about the stroke and an investigation begun. The fraud syndicate made another application to draw down mortgage funds from the Geneva bank. This time the figure was one million pounds.

In July 1990 Traynor dispatched his courier to collect the new tranche of funds for the "Caribbean project". The conspirators kept in touch by mobile phone. When the courier went into the Geneva bank he was told that there would be a slight delay with paper work and was asked to wait. The courier rang Traynor, who was sitting on a park bench near Bayswater Road in London. As they talked, Swiss police arrested the courier for fraud. At that same moment the City of London police arrested Traynor. He was charged with handling stolen bearer bonds and remanded in custody to Wormwood Scrubs. On October 18, 1991 Traynor was sentenced to seven years of imprisonment for his part in the international operation. He was devastated and blamed Conlon for informing on him.

While he was on remand and later serving his sentence in England, Traynor made frantic efforts to sort out the sale of the Jetfoil pub and lease out the shop which he owned with Cahill in Dublin's Arbour Hill. He knew that he had to convince the General that he was not being ripped off. In letters to an associate at the time he stressed that Cahill had to be convinced that Traynor was not trying to cheat him. He even instructed his friend to burn all of his letters in case the wily General burgled his office and found the correspondence. Eventually Traynor sorted things out to Cahill's satisfaction. The Jetfoil pub sale to the Port and Docks Board eventually went through in 1992 for a hundred and eighty thousand pounds, half of which Cahill received. The General forgave his old pal for past grievances and assured him that when he came back to Dublin he would not find himself nailed to anything. In the meantime, Cahill organised money for Traynor's wife and children.

In Dublin, Traynor's wife and children had befriended a neighbour who had moved into the area since his departure. Ironically, the young man was a detective attached to the Serious Crime Squad. At another time Traynor would have considered him a neighbour from hell. The policeman became very fond of his neighbour's children and felt sympathy for Michelle Traynor, who was rearing four children on very little money. He knew that the children dearly wanted to visit their father in prison and he helped them collect Ryanair flight discount coupons, which came with loads of Bord na Mona peat briquettes. After a few months enough coupons had been collected for Traynor's wife and one of the children to fly to London. Traynor was greatly impressed by the cop's kindness and unexpectedly wrote to the Garda Commissioner requesting a visit from the detective.

The unusual twist of events was warmly welcomed by the Serious Crime Squad. They were now in the process of trying to track down and recover the Beit paintings and the highly sensitive crime files stolen from the Director of Public Prosecution's office. Traynor was probably the only person in Cahill's organisation who could, if he was fully on side, lead them to the General's hidden loot. The request could not have been more opportune. Traynor was extremely vulnerable. He hated prison, particularly English prison, and was homesick. Added to that was the prospect of still facing at least one serious charge for the stolen cigarettes haul when he was released.

The detective and one of his superiors talked with Traynor over a two-day period in Wandsworth Prison. Traynor, who looked drawn and had lost a lot of weight, was anxious to know where he stood in relation to the charge awaiting him in Ireland and suggested that he was prepared to do a deal of some kind. The two detectives bluntly informed him that the State wanted the D.P.P.'s files back and, in particular, the file relating to the suspicious death of Father Niall Molloy, which had caused a national scandal.

The Roscommon priest's battered body was found in the bedroom of the home of Richard and Therese Flynn, called Kilcoursey House, in County Offaly in 1985. The Flynns were wealthy landowners and horse breeders. Fr Molloy, a close friend of theirs, had been involved in a number of horse and land deals with Therese Flynn. There were subsequent allegations of a major cover-up of the whole affair and of both political and religious interference in the case. In 1986 Richard Flynn was acquitted of the manslaughter of Fr Molloy.

The file that the authorities were most anxious about having returned, which was now in the General's possession, contained highly sensitive notes and statements that would cause great embarrassment if aired in the public domain. Traynor was told that if the file was returned, then his outstanding warrants in Ireland could be "looked at". The receiving charge was already a weak case, something that Traynor did not know, and it was highly probable that he would not be convicted for it. Traynor told the two cops that Cahill had absolute control over the files and all he could do was talk to the man whenever he got home. However, he did offer information on a number of Irish criminals, including John Francis Conlon. As the two cops were leaving the prison interview room, Traynor called the young detective back and thanked him for the help and compassion he had shown to Traynor's family. He promised that he would never forget it and would return the favour.

Traynor was a model prisoner and qualified for temporary home leave from Highpoint Prison, to which he had been transferred, in November 1992. He had been in custody since his arrest in July 1990. Traynor was due to return to Highpoint on November 23, but he never returned. He had had enough of prison life.

The escapee was welcomed home with open arms by the General. By 1992 gangland was a completely changed place. Most of Cahill's gang were now serving long sentences for serious crimes and he had tried to organise a new gang around him. According to Traynor, Cahill confessed to him that "everyone has let me down except the fraud man I didn't trust".

When Traynor cautiously explained his meeting with the two officers from the Serious Crime Squad, Cahill agreed to dig up the file. Within a few weeks of his return to Ireland the young detective was in his office in Harcourt Square. It was late in the evening when the phone rang. It was Traynor. "I think that we can do that bit of business tonight. Meet me outside the Garda Club."

Within a few minutes the detective found Traynor sitting in a car outside the Garda Social Club on Harrington Street. The fraudster explained that he had consulted a solicitor who told him that he could not be extradited back to England and he had decided to stay put. He told the detective to get out and walk around the corner to Stammer Street. The detective felt for his revolver as he walked slowly around the corner. There was no one in sight. About a hundred yards down the street a figure suddenly stepped out of a bush. It was Martin Cahill.

Under Cahill's arm was a Dunnes Stores plastic bag. He handed it over to the cop. There was a strong, damp smell from the bulky file inside the bag. It had obviously been buried somewhere for a long time. Then Cahill spoke. "I'm doin' this for John. I appreciate what you did for his family. This is where you and me start and finish." The General turned and walked off into the night.

Less than a year later the cigarettes case against John Traynor was dropped by the State in view of the amount of time that had elapsed since the initial charges had been laid. John Traynor decided to make a fresh start in life.

Three

Dutchie Holland

The hit man is the most feared individual in the underworld. He is a cold-blooded assassin who can kill without emotion simply because it is his "job". It's never personal, it's always business. Once a contract is accepted, it must be executed. No-one messes with the hit man, making him an invaluable asset to a gang boss. The enforcer's very existence ensures debts are paid and guarantees loyalty. Probably no other gangland character has been portrayed as often in television and movie crime dramas as the assassin. In the real world, the man whom gardaí openly admit they have suspected of being Ireland's top hit man would defy the imaginations of Hollywood's best crime writers. Patrick Eugene Holland, or "Dutchie", certainly wouldn't fit the Hollywood bill.

In criminal and police circles Holland's name was well known and associated with serious crime for several years. He is the criminal the Lucan Investigation Team identified as the man they suspect actually murdered Veronica Guerin on the orders of John Gilligan. But, if he was the actual killer, he was a most unlikely choice of gangland hit man. On the day of the assassination "Dutchie" Holland was fifty-seven years old. He was a bald, unattractive man with a boxer's deformed nose and a medium build. To the ordinary observer there was nothing threatening about Holland. He was a gentle, soft-spoken man heading for retirement.

Criminals who served time with him in prison and gardaí who investigated him share the same description of Dutchie. He was a very strange and complex character with a dark, dangerous side. A non-drinker and non-smoker, Holland projected himself as a deeply religious man, self-righteous, with a keen belief in an afterlife. He rarely used bad language and was courteous and friendly with everyone.

Born on March 12, 1939, just before the Second World War,

Patrick Eugene Holland grew up with his family in St Lawrence's Road, Chapelizod, west Dublin, which at the time was still the countryside. He once told how he had an idyllic, privileged childhood and was very close to his parents and siblings. The family was middle class and well off. Holland's parents presented him with his own car when he was seventeen. In his younger years he was a dedicated athlete and played professional soccer for a time.

When he was in his late teens Holland went to America with a local boy he grew up with and joined the United States Marine Corps. He spent a few years with the Army before returning home to Ireland in the early 1960s. Shortly after that he had his first problems with the law. Unlike most other criminals, it is hard to find a reason why someone like Patrick Holland became a professional criminal in the first place. He grew up at a time when there was effectively no serious crime in Ireland. He came from a respectable background without criminal influences. He had never been in trouble with the law throughout his teenage years or in his early twenties. His first recorded conviction was in 1965 at the age of twenty-six.

Once, while he was being questioned about a gangland murder, Holland confided to a detective that it was the 1965 conviction which had turned him to a life of crime. After returning from the Marine Corps Holland got a job as an assistant manager in the Donnelly's sausages plant in the Coombe area of inner-city Dublin. He was highly regarded at work and seen as a good staff motivator. Holland claimed that one day at work a man he knew came to see him in the factory and gave him two theatrical fur coats to hang onto for him. Holland said he placed them in his car for safekeeping. Some time later the police arrived looking for stolen furs. After finding the furs in his car, Holland was arrested and charged with two counts of receiving stolen goods. Holland claimed that he had been set up. In March 1965 he was jailed for six months on the two charges. He appealed the sentence and it was subsequently reduced to two months. Holland claimed that after that incident he developed a hatred for the authorities.

In the early 1970s he married Angela Swords, the only woman with whom he would ever have a relationship. Acquaintances said that, apart from his mother, she was the only person he ever really cared about in his life. At the same time as he was beginning his married life, he was becoming a serious criminal. In the 1974–1975 period a mysterious "lone raider" began hitting banks throughout Dublin. Holland was a loner in practically everything he did. At a time of Provo and organised crime gangs, this novel new character attracted the attentions of the police.

The Central Detective Unit (CDU), based at Dublin Castle, put a team on the case of the lone raider. Before each incident a mini car was stolen and after each robbery a plump, male figure was described as the only assailant. The targets had been well chosen and the raider knew what he was after. In a period of less than a year he had got away with at least a dozen robberies. In one incident a member of the public tried to grapple with Holland as he made his exit from a bank. This have-a-go individual clung on to the robber's jumper. Holland squirmed out of the clothes to make his escape and the bystander was left holding three jumpers in his hand. That gave the police a vital clue about their target. He was a master of disguise. In fact, it was not unusual for Holland, despite his flattened nose, to dress up as a woman for a "job".

Eventually, in 1975, Dutchie was caught and charged with two robberies, one at the Mater Hospital and the other at the Bank of Ireland on Merrion Road. With two cases pending against him, Holland broke with his own rule of working alone and teamed up with Michael and John Cunningham from Ballyfermot. At 9.40 p.m. on December 29, 1976, Holland, Michael Cunningham and two other criminals burst into the manager's office at the Carlton Cinema on O'Connell Street, while the main feature of the evening was being shown.

Two were armed with handguns. An accomplice covered the staff and Dutchie demanded the keys to the safe. He began filling a white shopping bag with the contents of the safe, but it wasn't big enough to hold all the cash, so Holland demanded a box. As the raiders left, they pulled the telephone wires from the wall and warned the staff not to alert the police. They got away with £13,500 in cash.

The gang wasn't to have a happy new year with the loot. Detectives arrested Michael and John Cunningham at a New Year's party two days later. In a search of Cunningham's house at

Scholarstown Estate in Rathfarnham, the police recovered the guns and the cash stolen in the job. On January 3, 1977 Holland, Cunningham and two other men were charged with armed robbery.

Now facing three armed robbery charges, Holland decided to leave the country. On February 7 a warrant was issued for his arrest when he failed to appear for a remand hearing in the Dublin District Court. Dutchie had fled to America with Angela. The couple spent two years in Chicago, Illinois.

In March 1981 they came back to Ireland for a family wedding and decided to stay for a number of months. It wasn't long before the lone raider was back in action. On May 2, 1981 Holland walked into the Commercial Banking Company at College Green in Dublin, wearing a hat and glasses. He politely inquired of one of the bank assistants if there had been a phone call for a "Mr Kavanagh". He was told that there had been no call. Holland thanked the assistant but remained standing beside the counter.

A few minutes later the bank assistant inquired if he was "Mr Kavanagh" because a phone call had just come through on the bank's phone for him. Holland remained talking on the phone until there was just one customer left in the bank. He put down the receiver, pulled out a revolver and threw a hold-all bag to the manager, ordering him to "fill it up". Holland walked out with £4,200 in cash. Within a few hours the police at Pearse Street station had identified Holland as the culprit and an alert was issued to all units throughout the city. While the search continued, Dutchie was planning other robberies.

The lone raider robbed staff at the Berkeley Court Hotel and robbed thirteen thousand pounds in cash. Then, on May 13, he stepped into a lift in Hawkins House, at Hawkins Street, where the Department of Posts and Telegraphs had offices. A courier was carrying a payroll which Dutchie duly demanded at gunpoint. When the elevator arrived at the ground floor, he casually strolled out of the building with twenty-two thousand pounds in cash. Holland had plans to return with his wife to America the next day.

The plan was to leave the country the same way he had returned in March, by taking the ferry from Rosslare to France. From there he intended to board a flight to Boston. Unfortunately, the police had been tipped off about Holland's plan and were waiting for him at the harbour. He arrived for his journey with Angela, her mother and her nephew. All four were arrested and brought back to Dublin for questioning. Dutchie was found to be in possession of a false passport in the name of Patrick Kearns and to be carrying twelve thousand pounds in cash.

The following day detectives searched a temporary address which Holland had been using in Sandymount, Dublin. During the search they discovered a large cache of firearms, including an Ingram machine gun, a .357 Magnum revolver, smoke grenades and ammunition. Holland was held in custody until his trial. On July 17, 1981 Dutchie was convicted of all three robberies and sentenced to a total of seven years.

He was released from prison in the summer of 1986 after serving five years of his stretch. Within two months a garda intelligence report was circulated to all Dublin detective units alerting them to the formation of yet another armed robbery gang. This time it was headed by John Cahill, the older brother of Martin, the General. John had recently been released after a ten-year stretch for armed robbery. Martin had given him a "coming out" present of six handguns, and Thomson and Uzi machine guns. The weapons had been stolen by the General from the Garda Technical Bureau. There were four other names in the new gang. The third was that of Patrick Eugene Holland. The new Cahill gang became very active but were eventually arrested after a shootout following an armed robbery a year later. Dutchie was not among those caught.

While the gang was active, Holland set up a little printing business at a premises in Gardiner Street in the north inner-city. Holland produced television guides to sell to shops around Dublin. It was a modest operation and Dutchie knew that it wouldn't make him a millionaire. But he had other plans.

In late 1988 Holland began making contact with members of the IRA. He and his wife moved to live in a Dublin Corporation house on Sherrard Street that was registered in her mother's name. By November, after a senior IRA figure was observed visiting, the house was under surveillance by undercover officers from the anti-terrorist Special Detective Unit. It was then that the police discovered the connection to Holland.

At the beginning of March 1989 Michael Anthony Maughan

arrived in Dublin from London and stayed with Holland. Maughan, who was originally from County Mayo, had met Holland in prison. A rapist, Maughan had been jailed in 1982 for seven years. The two pals began planning robberies around the country. They identified two targets: a bank at Maryfield in Cork city and a post office in Bray, County Wicklow.

Holland told Maughan that he had been in discussions with the Provos with a view to obtaining guns but he needed something to trade with. Maughan suggested that another prison friend, Patrick Waters, could probably help. Waters was from Arigna, a few miles from Drumshanbo in County Leitrim. He had worked in the Arigna coal mines from the age of thirteen until he was jailed for robbery ten years later. After coming out of prison he worked with Maughan in London and bragged that he could still get explosives. On Friday, March 31 Waters arrived in Dublin for the purpose of a health check. He was planning to be married at the time. Maughan had asked Waters to bring him to Arigna to pick up explosives and return them to Holland's place at Sherrard Street.

In the meantime, Holland contacted IRA figure Michael O'Reilly, whom he knew through a family connection, and proposed swapping the guns for explosives. O'Reilly, who was involved with procuring explosives and munitions for the Provos, said he was interested. In the evening of Wednesday, April 5, Maughan and Waters stole seven-and-a-half pounds of gelignite, six detonators, a roll of cortex and fuse wire from the mines in Arigna. They brought the haul back to Sherrard Street at 3 a.m. on the following morning, where Dutchie was waiting for them.

At the same time, unknown to Holland and his friends, they were being secretly monitored by a combined squad of detectives from the Special Detective Unit and the Serious Crime Squad. The operation was under the overall command of Det. Superintendent Noel Conroy and his second-in-command, Det. Inspector Tony Hickey of the Serious Crime Squad, both of whom had impressive reputations as top-class investigators. Conroy, who was originally from County Mayo, had been involved in the investigation of serious crime in the city for twenty years and would be promoted to the ranks of assistant and then deputy commissioner. (He is currently the Deputy Commissioner in charge of Operations in the Garda Síochána.)

Tony Hickey, a native of County Kerry, had also been involved in serious crime investigation for two decades. A recipient of the prestigious Scott Medal for bravery in the line of duty, Hickey had played a major role in the investigation of scores of high-profile crimes. He was the man who would eventually lead the Lucan Investigation Team against Gilligan and his gang.

Hickey had a major interest in Dutchie Holland. He had been one of the officers who had spent several months investigating the lone raider cases ten years earlier and had actually charged Holland with an armed robbery at the Mater Hospital.

At this stage the police teams were in place and were aware the explosives were in Sherrard Street. But there was one person missing, the Provo. He did not arrive until 2.25 p.m. Michael O'Reilly was visiting Holland's house to view the explosives he had been promised. Ten minutes later Hickey and Det. Sgt Denis Donegan moved in with their team. Armed officers covered the rear and the front of the building. As Hickey rang the doorbell, Donegan looked through the letterbox and saw Holland and O'Reilly inspecting the bag of explosives. Donegan kicked in the door and the officers rushed inside. O'Reilly made a dash for the back garden. Donegan raced after him. At the same time Hickey and other officers charged upstairs, where Maughan and Waters were immediately arrested. O'Reilly was stopped at gunpoint trying to get across a wall and Donegan arrested him.

When the detectives came crashing into his world again, Dutchie simply put his hands up and sat down into an armchair. Holland had recovered enough by the time Tony Hickey came back into the room to be able to shake hands with his old adversary and say hello. Holland told Hickey that he was taking full responsibility for whatever was found in the house. In addition to the haul of explosives and detonators from Arigna, a search uncovered a replica pistol, wigs, theatrical make-up, balaclavas, maps, garda radio code books, and books on combat and explosives. On one map the Premier Dairy plant in Finglas, west Dublin, had been clearly marked and what appeared to be an escape route plotted. The officers also found computer data which suggested that Holland was planning to hack into the computer mainframes of major companies in order to defraud them of large amounts of money.

All four were arrested under the Offences Against the State Act and were later charged with unlawful possession of the explosives. While Holland was being interviewed by detectives he began an informal chat about his life and what he had been up to while in America. The officers were astonished when he suddenly revealed that he had worked as a contract killer for the Mafia in Boston and Chicago prior to his 1981 arrest. Dutchie claimed that he was wanted by the FBI. He had also boasted to other criminal associates about "two or three" murders he had allegedly carried out for the mob, a claim that was considered strange for a man who normally kept everything to himself. The Irish police investigated Dutchie's extraordinary story through the FBI, but found no evidence to substantiate it.

On June 26, 1989 Holland, Waters and Maughan all pleaded guilty to the explosives charge in the Special Criminal Court in Dublin. Michael O'Reilly, who denied the charge, was also found guilty. Jailing the four men, Mr Justice Robert Barr said the court was satisfied that O'Reilly was a member of or associated with the Provisional IRA. His intention was to receive the explosives and put them to a criminal use. The Judge said that the court was also satisfied that the other three men had played a significant role in the crime. They must have been aware that bombs could have been made from the explosives they provided and that such bombs could possibly cause death or serious injury.

"The court must impose exemplary sentences to deter those who might be tempted to supply explosive substances to the IRA," the Judge said. Holland, Maughan, and Waters were each jailed for ten years. O'Reilly was given twelve years. In May 1990 the Court of Criminal Appeal reduced each of the four sentences by three years. At fifty-one years of age Dutchie had to endure another four years behind bars. He was not released from Portlaoise Prison until September 1994.

Four

The Brat Pack

In the early 1980s a member of the notorious Dunne drug family was led away in handcuffs to begin a long jail sentence for heroin distribution. The drugs scourge was only a few years old and had brought unbelievable devastation and hardship to large sections of working class Dublin. There was a palpable sense of joy and victory at another of the Dunnes being sent down, as though the problem would now somehow go away.

Just before he got into the prison van, Dunne turned to the pack of reporters and members of the public who were swarming excitedly around the steps of the Circuit Criminal Court. "If you thought we were bad, just wait 'til you see what's coming next," he warned, before disappearing inside.

No member of the Dunne family, or any other criminal for that matter, had ever spoken such chillingly prophetic words. The new breed of young professional criminal would be more callous, calculating and ruthless than the older gangsters who paved the way for them. The young hoods who emerged during the mid-80s were entering an underworld which was almost twenty years in existence. Organised crime was an established way of life in Ireland. The shock from the sudden upsurge in serious crime had long worn off. The public was cynical and desensitised to violence and murder. The gangland Brat Pack didn't need blooding or encouragement in the hands of an experienced godfather. They were enthusiastic students. On June 26, 1996 the lethal combination of the new, young criminal breed and the older, ruthless gangsters, resulted in the murder of Veronica Guerin.

The investigation which followed exposed a clique of young thugs who had been John Gilligan's loyal lieutenants. They were flash and brash, and prepared to wipe out anyone who got in their way. The most loyal and ruthless of them was a brutal, young hoodlum called Brian Meehan.

Born in Crumlin on April 7, 1964 Meehan was the very epitome of the new swaggering gangster. In underworld terms he displayed a natural talent for serious crime and had earned a formidable reputation as a hardened criminal by the time he was twenty years of age. Meehan, or Meenor as he was known to his friends, was the second of four children, two boys and two girls. For a time he lived with his parents, Kevin and Frances, at the Stanaway Road family home in Crumlin. Brian was reared for most of his childhood with his grandmother in Fatima Mansions, a huge Dublin Corporation flats complex in south Dublin that had been devastated by heroin abuse.

Meehan did not become a hard drug abuser like so many of his peers. Instead, he became a dedicated "joyrider" from his early teens, robbing high performance cars and racing them through Dublin, playing cat and mouse with the pursuing police. Around the same time that the Dunne family member was making his chilling prediction, Meehan recorded his first criminal conviction for larceny in 1981 at the age of sixteen. He received the Probation Act. Over the following years the majority of his convictions were for car theft and driving without insurance. Before he even qualified for a full driver's licence, Meehan had been banned from driving for five years. He was eventually banned for over fifteen years.

As a young, talented "wheels man" with plenty of "bottle" (nerve), it wasn't long before Meehan was noticed by the major players involved in organised crime. He showed little fear and was also extremely violent. He could put a squad car out of action by ramming it in a certain way, while keeping his own car fit to drive away. Meehan particularly enjoyed jousting with police squad cars. He was also fascinated by guns and armed robbery. Michael "Jo Jo" Kavanagh, a close associate of the General's, was the first to see the potential in the young tearaway. He started robbing high performance vehicles for Kavanagh to use in robberies.

Meehan was used as a driver on a number of jobs by both Kavanagh and Cahill, which gave him immense credibility on the street as an up-and-coming hood. In 1986 and 1987 Kavanagh began organising armed robberies with Meehan and a loose grouping of young criminals from south Dublin. They were soon making their mark.

On the afternoon of February 19, 1987 a security van was delivering wages to Buckleys Builders Providers at Robinhood Road in Clondalkin. As they drove into the yard at the premises, three armed and masked men jumped out and forced one of the security men to open the rear of the security van. The robbers took over twenty thousand pounds in cash and left the yard. As the van made its getaway up Greenhills Road, it was intercepted by a police car with three officers on board who were responding to a 999 call from Buckleys.

The getaway van drove into a nearby housing estate and stopped in the driveway to a garden. The three officers got out and ran to the van. Garda John Leonard opened the driver's door and attempted to grab the driver's leg as he made for the passenger door. One of the raiders aimed a gun with both hands at the officer's head and squeezed the trigger. The weapon misfired. As the other raiders scrambled out of the van, Leonard caught another one of them, who turned around and shot him in the forearm.

Leonard's colleague, Pat McNicholas, ran after the driver of the van, Brian Meehan, as he climbed up onto a boundary wall. As the cop dashed towards him, the raider pulled a pistol from his belt, aimed, and squeezed the trigger. This shot, too, misfired. He squeezed the trigger a second time. This time the weapon fired. "Stay back, you bastard, or I will kill you!" the 21-year-old hood warned the unarmed officer. Meehan was joined by the other raiders who fired warning shots in the air before making their escape through gardens. Despite a major investigation, no-one was ever charged with the robbery.

The gang were undeterred by their close shave and the furore caused by shooting a cop. The police hit the underworld hard in their search for the raiders. Two weeks later, however, on March 5, "Jo Jo" Kavanagh, Meehan and company were back at work. This time the target was the Ringsend Bus Depot in east Dublin. Shortly after wages were delivered to the garage, a car drove up to the administrative offices. Four armed and masked men ran inside, while a fifth remained behind the wheel of the car. The raiders snatched forty-nine thousand pounds and were heading back to the getaway car when they were confronted by an armed detective who was protecting the premises. The officer ordered them to put down their guns, but instead they pointed them at him. The cop fired several shots at the gang, who scrambled into their car and drove off at speed. Later two men, one of whom had been injured, were arrested and charged with the robbery.

During the shoot-out Kavanagh was wounded by one of the policeman's bullets. Meehan and another gang member brought him back to his house in Crumlin and tried to dress his wound. Kavanagh was later brought to County Wexford, where he was cared for by a person with a medical background. By the time the police caught up with Kavanagh he had made a full recovery and his injuries had healed. He was questioned, but released. Kavanagh refused to speak. There was insufficient evidence to sustain a charge and the two captured raiders would not identify him.

By now Meehan's name was beginning to feature in reports circulated by the Serious Crime Squad. Information from units on the ground and underworld informants was that he was becoming a very serious player. Apart from Kavanagh and Cahill, he was being observed in the company of several hardened criminals around the city. In 1987 he had been spotted on a number of occasions driving Gilligan and Kavanagh around town in the company of another criminal figure. Gardaí had also spotted Gilligan calling to see Meehan at his home.

One incident particularly irritated the then head of the Serious Crime Squad, Det. Superintendent Noel Conroy, and put Meehan on the wanted list. One night in 1987 Meehan had been stopped at a checkpoint in Clontarf while driving a high-powered, stolen jeep. In the passenger seat was armed robber P.J. Loughran, a former IRA member from Northern Ireland. In 1990 Loughran was shot and paralysed when he and his gang were surrounded during an armed robbery in Athy, County Kildare. Another raider was shot dead. At the Clontarf checkpoint the unarmed garda asked Meehan his name and address. Instead of bluffing an answer, Meehan pulled a pistol and pointed it at the cop, telling him to "fuck off". Then he drove away.

Kavanagh and Meehan had teamed up with some other very serious players. Paddy Shanahan from Kildare, the former university student turned robber, was part of the team. So, too, was Norman McCaud, a self-styled Canadian godfather in his late forties. McCaud was reportedly a Mafia hit man who had been hiding in Ireland for several years. The Canadian authorities had tried unsuccessfully to extradite him to face a murder charge.

It gave the impressionable "Meenor" quite a buzz to think that he was working with men of such eminent gangster pedigree. McCaud was eventually taken back to Canada in the mid-90s when the Irish government signed an extradition agreement. He was cleared of the murder charge, but didn't enjoy his freedom for very long. He was soon found dead behind the wheel of his car with his trousers around his ankles. The big-time Mafia hit man had died of a heart attack while having sex with a prostitute.

On December 21, 1987 the gang planned to hit the Allied Irish Bank branch on Grafton Street. McCaud and Shanahan provided backup while Kavanagh and Meehan hit the bank. It was a daring daylight robbery. Posing as a pair of window cleaners, they gained access to the bank using a ladder and then crossing a number of roofs. When they were over a cash-counting room at the bank, they broke through a skylight and lowered themselves down inside. They held up the staff at gunpoint and took fifty-five thousand pounds in cash before climbing back up the ropes to the roof. Meehan and Kavanagh took a bus from nearby Suffolk Street and McCaud and Shanahan took the money away for safekeeping. As far as the Serious Crime Squad was concerned, Meehan had made the big time.

Intelligence indicated that Kavanagh and Meehan were the two raiders who had hit the bank. The two were placed under surveillance and, on December 28, were both brought in for questioning about the case. Both men were released but, based on the strength of evidence gathered by the squad, the Director of Public Prosecutions decided to charge only Meenor with the heist. Ironically, the man in charge of the team investigating Meehan was Det. Inspector Tony Hickey, the man who had also caught Dutchie Holland and who would have a significant effect on the criminals' future careers.

Meehan did not want to go to prison. Before this he had served relatively short stretches for car theft and other road traffic offences. Armed robbery carried a much longer sentence. While he was being questioned, he suggested helping the detectives "recover" other criminals' firearms. Criminals regularly hand over firearms in the hope of doing a deal with the police and beating the rap. Taking weapons off the streets has traditionally been given a high priority by city detective units. Meehan eventually organised for the officers to find the .45 he used against the uniformed cop in Clontarf. The weapon was found near the Royal Canal in Phibsboro. He also arranged for an officer to find two sawn-off shotguns in Crumlin.

On bank holiday Monday, while out on bail, Brian Meehan and John Bolger, a friend Gilligan's, took part in an armed robbery at Powerscourt Estate near Enniskerry, County Wicklow. During the heist Meehan had taken the manager of the premises hostage and made off with the safe. The gang drove a stolen van to Crone Forest car park, off the Glencree Road in the Dublin mountains, and got into a car. Unfortunately for Meehan, Det. Garda Pat Keane was lying in the bushes watching for another criminal gang as part of a separate undercover operation. Keane decided to investigate and went to the driver's door of the car, where he saw Meehan. The robbers drove off at speed, as the officer opened fire on them. They escaped, but Meehan was subsequently charged with driving without a licence.

On bail for the Grafton Street "job", Meehan took part in the robbery of almost a million pounds worth of pharmaceutical drugs from the Dublin Drug Company in Glasnevin Industrial Estate. The crime had been organised by Martin Cahill and involved several members of his gang. Meehan was again brought in by the Serious Crime Squad. This time they threatened to charge him with firearms offences in relation to the weapons he had given up to them. Meehan offered to help them recover the drugs haul and also to set up for capture a number of other armed robbers operating in the city.

Meehan was placed back in custody while awaiting his trial. One afternoon he walked out of prison. He simply pretended to be another prisoner who was due for release. Meehan went to live with a girlfriend in Ballybough in the north inner-city, with whom he later had a son.

Meehan's garda handler kept a close, but discreet, watch over him. Meehan passed on information about a planned robbery that was to go down at the Irish Permanent branch in Phibsboro. The robbers had already cut through bars on the window at the rear of the building. A large team of detectives kept the place under surveillance for weeks but nothing happened. It later transpired that a member of the gang, an acquaintance of Meehan's, had recognised one of the detectives watching the branch and the job was aborted. The gardaí decided that Meehan was only playing for time. He was "found" and brought back to Mountjoy.

Later in the year Meehan went on trial for the Grafton Street robbery in the Circuit Criminal Court. Each day the trial was attended by Kavanagh and Meehan's associates. On the fifth day of the trial the Judge was informed that members of the jury were being intimidated. Two female jurors told the police that they had been followed home from the very precincts of the court. The Judge immediately ordered an investigation and the jury was discharged. Later one of the jurors positively identified a close associate of both Meehan and Kavanagh as the man who had tried to intimidate her. But the criminals had done their job. The jurors were too frightened to give statements and refused to co-operate with the investigating police. No-one was ever charged with the incident. A second trial was set for April 1989. This time Meehan pleaded guilty to the robbery and was jailed for six years.

Rumours had leaked out about Meehan's attempts to do a deal with the police over the Grafton Street job and about his involvement in handing back guns. As a result he lost face in the eyes of his fellow criminals, although he was still feared. To rebuild his reputation with the other prison inmates, Meehan began a campaign of protest over conditions in Mountjoy. In the summer of 1990 the simmering tension spilled over into a full-scale riot, led by Meehan, that caused millions of pounds worth of damage to the prison over several days. Meehan and dozens of other prisoners staged a protest on the prison roof.

Following the riot, Meehan was moved to serve the remainder of his sentence in Portlaoise maximum security prison. He served his sentence in E1, the wing reserved for men considered to be the hardest criminals in the country. Meehan, although considered a big-mouthed thug, was accepted by the rest of the criminal fraternity. During these years he developed a strong friendship with the man who would become his underworld godfather and make him wealthy beyond his dreams, John Gilligan. Here he also met Patrick "Dutchie" Holland.

Another prison troublemaker who would become close to Gilligan was Paul Ward, a former neighbour and close friend of Meehan's from Windmill Park in Crumlin. Ward, who was known as "Hippo", had earned a reputation as a violent thug from the time he was a teenager. He had taken part in several robberies with Meehan and later lived with Meehan's younger sister, Vanessa.

Also born in 1964, one of the youngest in a large family of mostly boys, Ward followed a predictable route. He dropped out of school in his early teens and was first convicted at the age of fifteen of causing malicious damage. He began dabbling in drugs and developed a heroin problem. Ward carried out several violent robberies while strung out and terrorised his old neighbourhood. Police who dealt with Ward and locals who knew him describe him as a "two-bit violent robber" who was not afraid to inflict pain or shoot anyone. In November 1989 Ward joined Meehan in Mountjoy prison after he received a four-year sentence for the armed robbery of a bookmaker's shop in Crumlin village. He narrowly missed killing a detective as he and another accomplice made their escape and were eventually cornered near Crumlin Shopping Centre. Like Meehan, Ward also took part in the Mountjoy riot and was moved to Portlaoise around the same time.

The third member of what become gangland's most notorious brat pack was Peter Mitchell, from Summerhill in Dublin's north inner-city. Physically big and known as a loudmouth, he was nicknamed "Fat Head" or "Fatso" by associates and police. Mitchell also met Meehan in Mountjoy prison around the time of the infamous riots. The pair became best friends and later even lived with two sisters. Mitchell's history was remarkably similar to that of his pals. Born in the inner-city in 1969, his mother was a street trader and his father a coal delivery man. He had no interest in school and dropped out. His only job was helping his mother sell wrapping paper, sweets, cigarettes and fruit on Henry and Moore Streets. From an early age he was known as a "hard man" and not afraid to use violence, including against the police. Apart from minor offences for casual trading, he also incurred convictions for larceny, burglary, receiving stolen goods, assault and robbery.

While his pals were in prison, it was Mitchell who became the first member of the brat pack to be seriously involved in drug dealing in the north inner-city. He specialised in cannabis, ecstasy and, later, cocaine. During visits to see Meehan in Portlaoise, Mitchell would brag about all the money he was making from his new business. There were enormous opportunities for a new gang that wasn't afraid of the opposition. The formation of John Gilligan's evil empire had begun. Gangland would never be the same.

Five

Inside

In the late 1980s and early 1990s Portlaoise Prison became organised crime's premier training academy. The huge prison complex in County Laois was the underworld's Alma Mater. It was here that contacts were made, plans laid and gangs formed. Friendships made behind the high prison walls were long lasting, like the bonds between old college chums. Portlaoise Prison was the birthplace of John Gilligan's evil empire.

Until the late '80s Portlaoise was almost exclusively used to house "subversives", mostly members of the Provisional IRA, the INLA and other political paramilitary groupings. Through the years there had been various high-profile attempts to spring the terrorists from inside its walls. In one case a helicopter was used and in another a truck was converted into a crude "tank" used in an attempt to smash through the prison gates. The result was that Portlaoise Prison became one of the most secure places of detention in Europe.

The ratio of prison officer to prisoner is the highest in the country at two to one. A detachment of a hundred and twenty troops, armed with rifles and anti-aircraft machine guns, patrol the perimeter, the rooftops and man the watch towers. An air exclusion zone operates over the entire complex. Getting in and out, even for prison staff, is difficult. Access between the outside and inside is a time-consuming journey through several layers of security screens and gates. The perimeter consists of high walls, cameras and sensors. There are even acres of tank traps. There is no escape.

In the annual prison report of 1988 the average daily population in the prison was one hundred and ninety-six, forty of whom were so-called "non-subversive" prisoners. These were mostly Dublin petty criminals who, in return for working as glorified servants on the subversive wings, earned up to fifty per cent remission. But that was to change.

From 1988 onwards there was a dramatic increase in the number of hardened criminals being jailed. Limerick Prison, which was also high security with military protection, had been used traditionally for holding members of organised crime gangs, but the prison was small. Portlaoise became the obvious choice for accommodating the growing numbers and E1 became the wing designated as home for the country's most notorious hoodlums.

In the two years between 1988 and 1990 when John Gilligan, Brian Meehan and Paul Ward were sent there, most of the General's gang were already in residence. Cahill's brothers, John and Eddie, his brother-in-laws, Eugene Scanlan, Albert Crowley and John Foy, and his lieutenants, Eamon Daly and Harry Melia, were all serving long stretches for armed robbery and drugs offences. Another gang member, Seamus "Shavo" Hogan, who had been sent to Portlaoise to serve a seven-year stretch for possession of firearms, had been segregated after three other inmates tried to slice off his ears. He had been accused of informing to the Tango Squad and the injuries were intended to make his ears resemble those of a rat, a term which in gangland parlance is used to describe an informer.

Eugene "Dutchie" Holland was also serving his sentence for the explosives find at Sherrard Street. E1's other "respected" residents included three members of the notorious Athy Gang and two members of the infamous Dunne crime family, Larry and Christy "Bronco". Larry was doing fourteen years for running the family's heroin operation and Bronco had been given ten years for kidnapping and robbery. Former INLA members Fergal Toal and Dessie O'Hare, "the Border Fox", also shared the wing. They were doing forty years for the brutal kidnapping of Dublin dentist John O'Grady. O'Hare was also suspected of carrying out several cold-blooded, sectarian murders in Northern Ireland. Dublin pimp John Cullen was doing life for burning to death one of his prostitutes, Dolores Lynch, her mother and aunt. There were another twenty, lesser-known crime figures on the wing, all of whom were equally hard cases. It was a fearsome collection of Ireland's ugliest and most dangerous drug dealers, robbers and killers.

When "Factory" John Gilligan finally cooled down about his four-year sentence for the theft of three thousand pounds worth of hardware goods, he settled into life in E1. He might even have been well pleased with himself. The State was acknowledging his status as a major-league villain by giving him an address in the penal system's "des res" for gangland's hardest men. Portlaoise was a well-run prison and not overcrowded. There were plenty of educational and training programmes to chose from. Several of the inmates during the early 1990s took art classes and even put together an impressive exhibition that went on tour around the country. It included works by Eddie Cahill, Larry Dunne and John Cullen. Gilligan, however, had no interest in messing about with paint brushes. His art was networking, making contacts and winning the respect of his fellow inmates, a lot of whom he had associated with in the past.

Gilligan already had a formidable reputation making up for his small physical stature. He was known as a criminal not to be messed with. As one former inmate recalled: "For a small fellow Gilligan had a tougher reputation than some of the biggest fellas in E1. He was known for having mad bottle (daring) and he was a violent bastard who wasn't afraid to 'do' anyone who fucked around with him. Gilligan was a big mouth and always demanding to be the centre of attention, but he was still well liked. He was always slagging the other lads and having the craic and trying to help out. But he was making connections, nurturing fellas who could help him on the outside. Gilligan was a great grafter [worker]."

Gilligan developed close relationships with Brian Meehan and Paul Ward. He had already known Meehan for some years, admired his "bottle" and treated him like a son. It seemed to him that the two kids had a lot of potential. In Gilligan's warped criminal mind, they were a credit to the new generation of violent thugs whom they represented. Meehan and Ward reciprocated the affections of their new godfather. They would have no reservations about working for him in the future. They would be the backbone of his criminal organisation.

It was in Portlaoise that Gilligan became interested in the drugs business. While lounging around Gilligan's cell, Meehan and Ward would talk about how well Peter Mitchell was doing on the outside running a small operation selling hashish and ecstasy. Another fearsome and violent brute, Mitchell controlled an area that stretched from his own neighbourhood of the north inner-city out as far as

the working-class suburb of Coolock. There were huge profits to
be made. One good deal could yield more hard cash than a whole
fleet of trucks full of sportswear or chocolates, and it didn't appear
to involve the same level of risk or aggravation.

Armed robberies and the large-scale holdups of the Factory
Gang were becoming a lot less attractive. In three armed robberies
in 1990, three raiders had been shot dead by the police, one had
been crippled and four others were shot and injured. A total of ten
individuals had been jailed with long sentences. The police were
becoming better organised and armed to deal with the gangs. In
Dublin a new squad called the Cobra Unit had been set up to target
armed robberies. Teams of heavily armed officers wearing bulletproof vests and driving high performance cars cruised every division
in the city. Their response times shocked the serious blaggers
(robbers).

Drugs had brought a lot of hassle to organised crime. The trade
brought turf wars and gangland murders. To stay on top a godfather
had to be prepared to fight fire with fire. Gilligan knew that with
such violent characters as Meehan, Ward and, of course, a lot of his
other old contacts, he had the ability to become a serious player
with the ability to protect his turf. But Gilligan wasn't the only
criminal re-evaluating the future of crime. By the 1990s gangland
was already undergoing change. Demand for so-called soft drugs
had increased dramatically. But, in order to get a foothold in the
business, hard cash would be required to set up deals.

An underworld "businessman" cannot stroll into a high street
bank for a loan when starting up an illegal venture. Fortunately for
Gilligan, he still had some "business" interests on the outside with
the potential of raising the investment money. Some time before
Gilligan was jailed in late 1990, Drogheda fence Tommy Coyle
contacted him with an interesting proposition. Coyle was
experiencing difficulty selling off the General's priceless haul of
Beit paintings. Each attempt to offload them had failed because of
worldwide sting operations and traps set by police forces. This time
Coyle had been approached by a representative of the Portadown-
based UVF, a group that was responsible for some of the worst
sectarian atrocities against Catholics in Northern Ireland. The
loyalists were interested in buying the paintings to raise cash for a

number of arms deals with a South African gunrunner.

Coyle had also arranged a number of meetings between the UVF representative and the General. For Cahill, now desperate for cash, politics meant nothing. The loyalists' blood money was as good to him as the Provos'. Gilligan, through Coyle, became a go-between in the complex negotiations which took place over the period of a year. Cahill, who was suspicious to the point of sheer paranoia, trusted Gilligan. He knew, at least, that Factory John would not have a cop on his shoulder. When Gilligan was jailed, his wife Geraldine continued to participate in the complicated negotiations, on his instructions.

In late 1990 Detective Superintendent Noel Conroy and Detective Inspector Tony Hickey of the Serious Crime Squad received intelligence about the proposed deal. It was decided that the units' surveillance team would target Geraldine Gilligan and her home at Blanchardstown. In January 1991 the undercover team watched a representative of the Portadown terrorists visit Geraldine at Corduff Estate, Blanchardstown. The UVF man actually asked one of the undercover surveillance men for directions to Gilligan's house. The cop had been posing as an ordinary pedestrian.

According to reliable sources, there were several meetings between Geraldine and two loyalist representatives that were monitored by the surveillance team. The meetings took place in pubs on the outskirts of Dublin, including a bar in Blanchardstown and another near Dublin airport. At one stage, while in the company of the two loyalists, Geraldine tried unsuccessfully to cash a thirty thousand pound bank draft in the Ulster Bank at Walkinstown Cross in west Dublin. She tried a number of other institutions, but these also refused her. In February 1991 two loyalists from Portadown and Scotland were arrested in Turkey after trying to sell a Metsu, one of the least valuable paintings of the Beit collection, which Cahill gave them. The Turkish businessman they were dealing with turned out to be a police officer. It was later discovered that, unknown to the gardaí, Scotland Yard also had planted an undercover man in the complex sting. There was no more contact between the Gilligans and the Portadown men.

John Traynor also tried to sell the paintings for Cahill. This time, at Cahill's request, he offered to sell them back to the police.

The opening demand was £1.6 million. Traynor approached the same detective to whom he had handed over the controversial D.P.P.'s file on the Fr Molloy case. At one stage Traynor gave the officer a Polaroid photograph of one of the paintings, a Reubens called "Portrait of a Man". The deal fell through when another business contact of Traynor's was arrested with most of the art haul in Belgium. Other works were recovered by police in London.

In the meantime, "Factory" John served his time and began planning for the future. He was homesick and greatly missed Geraldine. He worried that she might not be there for him when he got out of prison. He wrote romantic letters expressing his love for her and how much he wanted to be home.

On Saturday, May 23, 1992, the prisoners in E1 organised a soccer match with a team from the Republican wing of the prison. Because they considered themselves political prisoners, the terrorists refused to associate with the criminals or allow them in their wings. In the scheme of things, the idealistic "politicals" considered the gangsters to be nothing more than undisciplined riff raff. But, there was enough room to compromise on soccer tournaments in each other's exercise yards. The games were classed home and away.

Gilligan had organised to have a video camera brought in to record the event and he provided the commentary for the seven-a side match. The "home" game was played in the exercise yard beside E1 in beautiful sunshine. The video is a most remarkable piece of gangland memorabilia, as criminals and paramilitaries jostle, dribble and shoot at goal in a good-humoured atmosphere. It also provides rare insight into how Gilligan had ingratiated himself with the rest of the prison population.

Gilligan's commentary, in his flat Ballyfermot brogue, was monotonous. He showered praise on his team, which included Brian Meehan, Paul Ward, Harry Melia, Eugene Scanlan, Martin Farrell, Fergal Toal and Warren Dumbrell. He was particularly glowing in his remarks about Toal, Ward and Meehan. He slagged off the referee John Cullen, who was obviously a close friend, and he gave nicknames to the Provos because he didn't know their proper names. The video recorded one, almost comical, irony. Three years earlier the Provos had tried to murder the criminal team's star striker, Harry Melia, because of his drug dealing activities in Tallaght. Now Melia was exacting some revenge by scoring most of the goals to beat the paramilitaries sixteen goals to five.

Gilligan cracked jokes on camera about the players. At one stage a Republican supporter reminded the criminal side that there were at least ten minutes more to play in the match. The criminals disagreed and said that the match had only a few minutes to run to the full-time whistle. Gilligan jokingly reminded the Provo: "When we're winning, there isn't another ten minutes to go. We're criminals for fuck sake... we have to rob, yes!" It was all in good humour.

After the match Gilligan pointed out other major criminals who had come out into the sunshine to watch the two most unlikely soccer teams in Ireland. Like a celebrity-spotting television reporter, he pointed to Larry and Christy Dunne and described what they were wearing. Gilligan ordered the E1 team to line up to be filmed and praised each individual as they stood in front of the camera. He then prompted the cameraman to pan across to the Republican team. Smiling, he walked over and congratulated each of them on a good game.

In the film Gilligan looks like a caricature of himself, dressed in blue shorts and a stripped sweatshirt with white socks and runners. He literally had to look up to most of the prisoners. Dessie O'Hare, who had missed the match, appeared in the yard. Gilligan's commentary became excited. "The Border Fox has come into the yard. He missed the match because he was on a visit. It's himself, the Border Fox! Would you come over here, Dessie, and say a few words to us, or I'll blow the whistle on ya," Factory John quipped at the baby-faced psychopath. O'Hare smiled but didn't reply. The fun continued as the criminal team and their supporters gathered for a group photograph. Gilligan snuggled up next to Dessie O'Hare. John Cullen held his hands over Gilligan's eyes (a still shot from the video can be seen in the picture section). On video it all looks like a jolly day out for the lads.

The film continued in a recreation room where the criminals and terrorists celebrated the match with soft drinks, tea and cakes. The paramilitaries have distinctive, strong country and Northern Ireland accents. The criminals have heavy, loud Dublin accents. Gilligan continued chattering into the camera's microphone and calling out to the two sets of teams and their supporters. After almost two hours of video footage and little John's droning on, the players seemed to grow tired of his insistence on being the centre of attention. It is obvious that he was working hard at being popular. Four years later the tape would provide the Lucan Investigation Team with further corroboration of the close relationship between Gilligan, Meehan, Ward and the renegade terrorists, Toal and O'Hare.

In November 1992, Gilligan's happy days in E1 came to an abrupt end when he lashed out violently and assaulted a chief officer. Gilligan claimed that he "lost the rag" because he had been left waiting for prison paper work. He was forced to bid farewell to his chums when he was transferred to serve the rest of his sentence in Cork prison. He was later convicted of the assault and given an additional six months.

On September 9, 1993 John Gilligan was granted temporary release and went home to his family. Until his final release date two months later, he was required to sign on each week at Portlaoise Prison. Three days after Gilligan's release, Brian Meehan was also granted temporary release. His full release date was set for April 1994. Paul Ward had been released six months earlier.

As John Gilligan walked out of the prison gates for the last time, he swore that he would never again serve another jail sentence. He was instilled with one ambition in life: to make the criminal big time and become so big that no cop or judge could touch him.

Part Two

Building an Evil Empire

Six

The Firm

While Gilligan was in prison John Traynor had also evaluated the drug scene and come to the conclusion that it was the only way of becoming rich quick. Traynor was a very intelligent man who carefully worked out his strategy before making a move. He closely examined the trade in heroin and cannabis and did his own market research. Both drugs were in huge demand with the guarantee of prodigious profits. He began drinking and socialising with known drug dealers to analyse the workings of the business.

Traynor was reluctant to dabble in heroin, but his reluctance was only partially born out of a deep-rooted revulsion at the devastation heroin was causing on the streets. It was in many ways a very attractive business. Heroin was a lot easier to transport than hashish and, depending how the supply was "cut" or diluted for distribution, the profits could be enormous. Traynor hesitated because heroin dealers were hated in the community and thought of as the scum of the earth. Heroin dealing, while lucrative, brought the kind of bad luck and unnecessary aggravation that he had spent all of his life skillfully avoiding.

Added to this was the difficulty that the Provos were prepared to murder heroin dealers, supposedly for the good of the community. Dealers low down on the heroin distribution chain tended to be addicts themselves and therefore untrustworthy, adding to the main supplier's risk of being informed on to either the vigilantes or the police. The courts also tended to be harder on heroin dealers than hash dealers. In any event, Traynor detested heroin pushers. He thought himself higher up the evolutionary scale. It was John Traynor's remarkable sense of self-preservation which dictated that cannabis would make him the millions he had always craved.

During his time in English prisons, Traynor had used his conniving charms to make invaluable international underworld contacts. In Wormwood Scrubs and Wandsworth he had befriended major players from England, Holland, Belgium, Turkey, Spain, and Morocco. Most of them were involved in drug-related criminal activity, either supplying large consignments of every kind of drug, from heroin to cocaine, or laundering the profits. Traynor listened and learned a lot from his fellow inmates. The profits they discussed had the greedy Coach drooling. But Traynor needed a partner, someone with clout in the underworld who could be trusted, and who could take most of the heat.

Always the cunning chancer, Traynor did not want to be the front man himself. He was happy staying out of the limelight so long as he could live the high life on the proceeds. Gilligan was the obvious choice as his partner in crime. Big John had been a friend of Little John since their days on the high seas. They'd also done a lot of business in the years of the Factory Gang. In 1995 Traynor described Gilligan in glowing terms: "He is the best grafter I have ever met. In criminal terms he is a great businessman. He can turn money into more money, no problem, and is prepared to be hands-on, if necessary. But he is very dangerous if you fuck with him."

By the time Gilligan came out of prison he was already thinking the same way and needed no convincing. The crooked pair made the perfect team. Each had something the other needed in order for the scam to work. They were totally dependent on one another. Gangland's equivalent of "little and large" began plotting for the future. Buying drugs was an expensive business; the two hoods needed cash.

Two months before Gilligan's release, Traynor and Cahill had begun planning one of their most ambitious strokes yet. If it worked out, Tarynor's part of the haul would provide the capital to set him and Gilligan up in business. Thanks to a source on the inside, Traynor was able to compile information on the main cash-holding centre of the National Irish Bank ("NIB") in central Dublin. He gathered intimate details of the lives and routines of the bank's top officials. He established that, at certain times of the week, the vaults held over ten million pounds in cash. The difficulty was how to get his hands on it. A traditional armed hold-up would be pointless because of the centre's location and the level of security around it. In order to get away with the crime, the thieves would have to be able to enter the building unchallenged and ensure that the police weren't called.

Traynor and Cahill devised a plan. The gang would abduct the bank's chief executive, Jim Lacey, his wife and four children late at night. The wife and children would be taken to a hiding place and Lacey left under no doubt that the lives of his family were in his hands. Meanwhile, a member of the gang, posing as another kidnap victim, would convince the banker that his family had also been abducted. Lacey would have to arrange for the gang member to collect the cash in order to secure the safe return of both families.

Traynor confided to Gilligan that this job would set them up for life. Gilligan did not play a major role in the Lacey kidnap plot but Cahill recruited Brian Meehan as part of the gang. Micheal "Jo Jo" Kavanagh, who was already facing major trouble with the law at the time, volunteered to act as the other "victim". Kavanagh, Meehan, Cahill, Traynor and another criminal conducted surveillance of the movements of Jim Lacey and his family. They secretly followed Lacey as he drove to and from work each day. They even tested the security system at the Lacey's home in up-market Blackrock. One night they deliberately activated the alarm system to test the response times of the police.

On the night of November 1, 1993 Cahill and six members of his gang, including Meehan, went about their brutal work. Traynor had organised most of the logistical support for the operation. A born coward, he preferred to be a safe distance from the action. The gang lay in wait outside the Lacey home until 1.25 a.m. when Jim Lacey and his wife, Joan, returned from a bank function. The armed and masked gang rushed the couple as they walked through their front door. There was a violent struggle as the Laceys fought with their attackers. Jim Lacey was struck across the head with a pistol, causing a large gash in his forehead. The Lacey children were awakened and ordered out of bed. The whole family was terrorised by Cahill and his gang.

One of the most aggressive members of the kidnap gang was Meehan. He cocked a gun over the heads of the Lacey children for added emphasis as Cahill was telling Jim Lacey that he would never see his family again if he did not do as he was instructed. Around 6 a.m. Joan Lacey, her children and their babysitter were hooded and taken away in a van driven by Meehan to a disused stable at Blackhorse Avenue in north Dublin.

Kavanagh was presented before the dazed and terrified banker. Before leaving the two men alone, Cahill convinced Lacey that his son had been shot. Later that morning Kavanagh drove with Jim Lacey to NIB headquarters, where he informed his senior staff of the unfolding drama and the instructions he had been given by the gang for the safe return of his family. Despite being enormously shaken by his ordeal, Jim Lacey outwitted the General's "victim" when he told his staff to take the quarter million or so pounds in the vault and put it in bags. Kavanagh was handed two large cash bags stuffed with money and told that was all the money there was in the vaults. The "victim" grew impatient and dropped his guard. He said that there were supposed to be millions in the vaults but in order to maintain his story he couldn't push the issue any further in front of the staff. He left with the money. That afternoon the Lacey family were found safe and well after their ordeal.

At the same time that Kavanagh was driving through the city with the NIB money, John Traynor and John Gilligan were seen by plenty of eyewitnesses. They strolled down O'Connell Street together and visited a bookmaker's shop to place a bet. There was no way that the police could even put them at the scene of the crime, never mind in the dock of the Special Criminal Court.

One astonishing aspect of the Lacey kidnap is that before the crime Traynor had actually tipped off the detective he was dealing with in the Serious Crime Squad that there was "a big stroke" being planned involving a bank. He was no more specific than that. The police at the time did not have the resources to mount a major surveillance on such vague information. It was part of the Coach's duplicitous way of playing all sides to cover his own end. He was making it clear that he had only heard a "whisper" and was simply doing his duty as an informant. If he was involved, then why should he tip off a cop that something big was going down? It was another example of Traynor's rat-like cunning. On the day of the crime he made sure he was at a safe, highly visible distance.

It had been a bad day for Cahill and his mob. They got away with £233,000 in cash, but the next day the newspapers reported that there had been in excess of seven million pounds in the bank vaults. Cahill and Traynor were furious that they had been duped. Over the following two months the gang members were identified, arrested and questioned about the kidnapping, including Cahill, Meehan and Traynor, but with no success. The same officers who had dealt with Meehan during his stint as an informant in 1988 and 1989 interviewed their old friend. This time he wasn't opening his mouth. He was confident that they had nothing to put him away with this time. The men were released without charge. Jo Jo Kavanagh was the only gang member to be charged with the crime and in October 1997 he was jailed for twelve years. He is serving his time in Portlaoise's E1 wing.

The Lacey fiasco convinced Traynor and Gilligan that large-scale crimes were a thing of the past and drugs the way of the future. Traynor had become Martin Cahill's most trusted adviser on all things shady. He knew that the General was not interested in drugs and would refuse to get involved, but he could convince Cahill to loan him and Gilligan the start-up money. Cahill was promised a major return on his investment within a certain time. The loan of over a hundred thousand pounds was part of the estimated half a million Cahill had received for the Beit collection. In addition, Gilligan had been dealing in large quantities of smuggled cigarettes and tobacco. Traynor also had his share, twenty-five thousand pounds from the Lacey kidnap. The hoods were ready for business.

Gilligan and Traynor's first priority was to find a reliable drug dealer with whom they could do business. Through Traynor, Gilligan had been meeting two English drug dealers with a view to setting up a supply route into Ireland. The little man had even been secretly videotaped by undercover Scotland Yard detectives in a hotel in Brighton. The two drug dealers were subsequently caught and charged; Gilligan had to find a new source.

He recruited an old friend from Ballyfermot, Denis "Dinny" Meredith, to assist in the new venture. Dinny, who had grown up with Gilligan, had been a member of the Factory Gang and had driven the container trucks used in their many robberies. Dinny had worked for a number of transport companies which had fallen victim to Gilligan. Through his job as a long distance trucker he still had serious criminal connections and a network of dodgy contacts in the transport industry. He had already been successfully involved in smuggling tobacco and alcohol from the Continent, as well as small quantities of drugs. Gilligan trusted Dinny and appointed him the gang's first bagman.

Dinny was also closely associated with John Traynor. Between the trucker and Traynor's contacts in Amsterdam, they were introduced to one of the country's major international drug traffickers. Both the trucker and Traynor had contacts in Amsterdam, from where Europe's drug trade is organised and supplied. That city is to drug traffickers what Wall Street is to stock market dealers.

Simon Ata Hussain Khan Rahman was a major league criminal who made gangsters like Gilligan, Traynor and Cahill look like schoolboy pranksters. Rahman had criminal connections throughout Europe, former Soviet block countries, the Middle East and North Africa. Born in January 1942 in Suriname, Rahman had moved to live in The Hague. From there he ran a criminal empire which, apart from narcotics, dealt in smuggling, fraud and firearms. His convictions included burglary, road traffic offences and "vandalism". In 1989 he had been arrested by Dutch police under "opium laws". He had also been charged with drug trafficking in Britain, but was acquitted in court and promptly returned to Holland. He was estimated by the Dutch authorities to be worth between twenty and fifty million pounds. A practising Muslim, he nurtured a veneer of respectability and was the chairman of a Muslim socio-cultural association.

His front was that of a legitimate millionaire businessman who specialised in the import and export of goods from foodstuffs to furniture. He had a superior, aloof presence about him and he privately sneered at Gilligan and his mob as uncouth ruffians. Rahman sourced his cannabis in Nigeria and Morocco. He exported container loads of rice and nuts, for example, to the Gambia. When the containers returned to Holland they would carry various "imports" of foodstuffs and furniture to conceal shipments of thousands of kilos of hashish. Rahman had well-established supply routes organised throughout Europe for the import and export of his illegal wares. He supplied gangs in England, France, Belgium, Germany and former Eastern Block countries. Rahman was the quintessential businessman. If you were willing to pay the cash, he would supply whatever you required. Rahman had a large network of people working for him and he stayed a safe distance from the physical operation of the business. He would live to regret the day that he sat down to deal with a vulgar Irish gangster called Gilligan.

Two weeks after the Lacey kidnap, Gilligan and Denis Meredith flew to Amsterdam to meet with Rahman. They also met with one of Rahman's closest associates, Johnny Wildhagen, a Dutch national from The Hague. Forty-year-old Wildhagen, a tall man with a ponytail, was a violent cocaine addict who worked as an enforcer for Rahman. He organised consignments of drugs and guns for export. He also oversaw the movement of cash. Rahman was not impressed by Gilligan during their first meeting. He told Gilligan that each deal would have to be paid for in cash, upfront. The prices of the first shipments were in the region of £1,300 per kilo. This, explained Rahman, would be cheaper depending on the quantities being ordered. The price would later average £1,200 per kilo. Rahman also explained that, as trust and goodwill developed between the two sides, the payment for shipments could be broken into three parts: part would be paid in advance, upon delivery and shortly after the drugs were sold, but before a new shipment was sent to Ireland.

Gilligan and Dinny stayed overnight, returning to Dublin the following day. The negotiations and talks continued. On November 22 Meehan was sent to Holland and returned the same day. A week later Traynor and Gilligan travelled to Amsterdam where Traynor, who controlled the money which had been loaned by Cahill, finalised a deal 170 kilos. Rahman and Wildhagen were impressed by Traynor, who they would later describe as "Big John, the real boss of Gilligan". Traynor, it is understood, convinced Rahman that if he reduced the price of the initial shipment from £1,300 to around £1,000 per kilo, it would mean more cash for Rahman in the long run. It was a sort of introductory offer.

Acting on Traynor's advice, Gilligan had prepared himself well for his new profession as a drug trafficker. He joined the Aer Lingus Gold Circle Club before his first flights to Holland. Using the business class frequent flier card, Gilligan could get a seat on an aircraft minutes before it was scheduled to take off. This is a facility used by airlines to accommodate business class customers in need of a last-minute flight. Catching a plane without warning enabled

Gilligan to shed unwanted police surveillance. The morning after their meeting with Rahman, Gilligan and Traynor arrived back in Dublin on one-way tickets they had purchased in Schipol airport. The previous day in Dublin they had paid for two pre-booked open return tickets on Gilligan's Aer Lingus card. The return tickets could be used at any time over the following twelve months. When the flight arrived in Dublin, Gilligan was the first passenger to go through Customs, while Traynor ensured he was last off. Gardaí attached to the immigration unit were not so easily fooled. The pair had also been spotted flying out the previous day. The purchase of tickets that were never used was a scam intended to mislead the police about their movements. A report about the trips was immediately circulated to all Garda units with an interest in them. Little did the police know just how significant this event would be.

Traynor had worked out the gang's strategy. He advised Gilligan that they should vary the size of the drug shipments. Each large consignment should be followed by a smaller one, in case the route was discovered and the drugs seized. It also gave them breathing space to collect their money. Traynor also suggested the concept of operating what is known in bookie circles as a "tank". Simply put, the gang would use the initial investment money as the "tank" and split up the profits. This was an operational cash base and a kind of insurance to lessen the financial blow if the drugs were intercepted.

On December 5 the first consignment of drugs arrived in Dublin port on a transport truck organised with Dinny's assistance. The hash was packed into six boxes, each of which were specially sealed and labelled as leather jackets and addressed to an industrial premises in Chapelizod, west Dublin. The truck delivered the boxes to the unsuspecting company's warehouse. The following morning the boxes were picked up by a courier, who also happened to be a friend of Dinny's and a criminal associate. The following day the driver went to the warehouse. Gilligan and Traynor had the truck followed to ensure that it was not under surveillance. When the truck stopped at traffic lights Brian Meehan turned up and knocked on the window and said he had been sent to collect the boxes. He signed for them using the fictitious name "Frank O'Brady". The deal went off without a hitch.

Later that same day Gilligan and Dinny again flew to

Amsterdam and returned the following afternoon. On December 12 the second part of the deal, twenty kilos, arrived on a transport truck from the same company. This time it was packed in one box labelled "compressor parts".

In the early days of the operation Gilligan and Traynor distributed the hash through Peter Mitchell, Brian Meehan and Paul Ward. They had set up a network of dealers who bought the drugs from them. Over the following months the operation gradually got bigger with dealers throughout Dublin buying their wares from them in turn. The money was collected for Gilligan and Traynor and then shipped out to buy another shipment.

Following the first successful arrivals to Dublin, each subsequent shipment was preceded by one or more trips to Amsterdam, most of them by Gilligan. On January 4, 1994 another fifty kilos arrived in two boxes of "oil coolers". Gilligan had gone to Amsterdam on December 14. On January 7 Gilligan flew again to meet Rahman and his representatives. Rahman did not want to be paid in Irish currency and suggested that the most efficient method of changing the cash was to use a Bureau de Change. Later Gilligan changed £31,950 into Dutch guilders, which were then handed to Rahman. That visit was followed four days later by another fifty kilos packed as "oil coolers". The following day Gilligan was back in the Bureau de Change in Amsterdam and changed £65,860 into Dutch guilders. Two days later fifty-five kilos arrived in Dublin. On January 20 busy "Little John" handed Rahman £63,460 in guilders and three days later seventy-five kilos of hash arrived in Dublin. On January 28 Gilligan flew to Amsterdam and changed £117,865 into guilders which was followed, on January 30 by a hundred-kilo shipment. On most of these earlier occasions Dinny also arranged for money to be brought to the Continent by one or more of his truck driver friends to make up the balance of each transaction.

Gilligan's plans to fly to Amsterdam were rudely interrupted on January 31 when a team of armed detectives from Blanchardstown arrived at his home in Corduff estate. He and his son Darren were arrested under the Offences Against the State Act and taken to Cabra and Blanchardstown stations, respectively, for questioning about a shooting incident in December. A doorman at

French's nightclub in Mulhuddart was shot and injured shortly after 3 a.m. in the morning. Investigating officers felt that the Gilligans could help with their enquiries. Darren Gilligan had been accused of selling drugs and thrown out of the club some time before the shooting. He had been barred by the doorman who had been wounded in the subsequent attack. A file was sent to the Director of Public Prosecutions on the case but the injured man withdrew his complaint. Neither of the Gilligans were ever charged.

Gilligan did not have time to be annoyed about the arrest. He was too busy building a drugs empire. On February 4 Traynor flew to Amsterdam instead of Gilligan. This time a forty-five kilo shipment was arranged and it arrived on six days later. On February 11 Gilligan flew to what he now referred to rather affectionately as "the Dam". That visit was followed up with a twenty-five kilo shipment. On February 14 Traynor also returned to the Dam and changed thirty thousand Irish pounds.

The following morning Gilligan checked onto the 7.25 a.m. flight to Amsterdam. By now he was enjoying the hustle and bustle of being a high-flying drug baron. Dressed in an expensive overcoat and carrying a briefcase, he snuggled up in the comfort of the business class cabin rubbing shoulders with people whose companies and homes he would probably have robbed four years earlier. This was an infinitely more civilised and lucrative way of making a dishonest living than breaking into factories in the middle of a frosty winter night. Later that day Gilligan visited a Bureau de Change in central Amsterdam and changed £44,845 sterling into Dutch guilders. The money was paid over as part-payment for a hundred kilos of hash. Gilligan took the next flight home.

The previous day a forty-foot container truck from a legitimate and unsuspecting company arrived in Hoofdorp, near Schipol Airport in Amsterdam. The innocent driver had been instructed to pick up several pallets of computer parts for a computer company in Ireland. The truck was then dispatched to pick up five pallets of truck parts in Mechelen, near Antwerp, across the border in Belgium. The trucker then had to make a further pickup from a warehouse near the port in Antwerp. At the warehouse a pallet containing two boxes of "oil coolers" was loaded. The driver was asked to hang on – there were other boxes for Chapelizod to be delivered to the warehouse. As far as the driver was concerned, this was a perfectly legitimate transaction and he had no reason to suspect that there was anything untoward occurring. About an hour and a half later these extra boxes were brought to the warehouse by Johnny Wildhagen in a Mercedes car. The truck headed for Antwerp's Euro Port and crossed on the ferry to Dover. It drove to Liverpool to catch the róll on–roll off ferry to the North Wall in Dublin.

As the truck arrived off the ferry on the morning of Thursday, February 17, members of the Customs National Drug Team decided to conduct a routine search. They discovered that the "oil coolers" were not what they purported to be and seized the truck and the hundred kilos of hashish. The driver was questioned but the officers were quickly satisfied that the he was totally innocent and had just been doing his job. The customs officers called in the North Central Divisional Drug Squad based at Store Street Garda Station. The squad and the customs officers removed most of the hashish and released the truck the next day, which returned to a warehouse at Bluebell Industrial Estate. Officers from the customs and the drug squad placed the warehouse under surveillance in the hope of nabbing the drugs gang when they came to collect the "oil coolers".

On the following Monday morning at 10 a.m. Dinny arrived in a red van to pick up the "machine parts" from the warehouse. The police and customs later learned that the van was also under surveillance by Gilligan's mob. The van drove to Chapelizod but failed to make the delivery while the cops watched. The courier made another legitimate delivery and then returned the machine parts to the warehouse in Bluebell. Dinny and Gilligan's gang had smelled a rat and decided to pull back. Dinny was later interviewed about the incident and claimed that he had tried to make a delivery but there had been no-one to meet him. He admitted to having made seven other such deliveries but denied that he had any knowledge of what was really in the boxes. When the courier reported back, Gilligan and Traynor decided that they needed a new, safer route. At the same time business was picking up for the fledgling gang and there were dealers to be supplied. If they weren't able to keep the goods coming, then their customers would find another source.

Dinny, the courier, had known John Dunne for over four years. Dunne, who was 38 years old, was originally from Finglas, west

Dublin, but had moved to live in Cork in November 1991 with his wife and three children. Dunne worked as the operations manager with the Sea Bridge shipping company at Little Island in Cork. This legitimate company was about to be used by an unscrupulous employee for the benefit of a ruthless criminal gang. No-one in the company knew that Dunne was using his pivotal position breach his employer's trust.

Dinny had befriended Dunne through a relative living in Neilstown. Dunne often arranged driving jobs for the courier. Dinny informed Traynor and Gilligan that Dunne was the type of guy who wouldn't turn down the opportunity of earning some extra money with no questions asked. In his position he would be perfectly placed to ensure that shipments from Holland were collected and transported safely to Dublin. If Customs swooped, then Dunne could warn the gang off and no one would be caught.

Shortly after the seizure in Dublin port, Dunne was spending the weekend with relatives in Dublin. Dinny arranged to meet him in the Silver Granite pub in Palmerstown for a drink. Gilligan was with Dinny when Dunne arrived. Dinny introduced Gilligan by his first name only and the three had a few drinks together. Factory John was charming and chatty with his new-found friend.

In late March Gilligan called Dunne at work and introduced himself as "John, Dinny's mate". Gilligan asked to meet Dunne, as he was down in Cork on business. Dunne agreed. An hour later Gilligan rang him again. He told Dunne he was outside Sea Bridge and asked if he would come out for a chat. When Dunne went out to the car, Gilligan was in the passenger seat and Traynor was behind the wheel. Dunne sat into the back seat.

Gilligan and Traynor were friendly and made small talk before they got down to business. They wanted to know what services Sea Bridge had from the U.K. and the Continent, particularly Holland. Gilligan asked Dunne for the names and telephone numbers of reliable shipping agents in Holland he could use and asked Dunne if he would handle the Irish end. Dunne agreed and explained the system to Factory John. Gilligan would arrange to have his shipments taken to the unsuspecting agent's depot in Holland from where they would be shipped to Sea Bridge in Cork. Dunne would be expecting the arrival and take care of it from there.

Gilligan then discussed money and told Dunne that he would be paid a thousand pounds for every shipment he handled. Out of that Dunne would have to pay the shipping fee and the rest was profit. Dunne immediately suspected that the whole business was "shady" but, as Dinny predicted, decided not to ask any questions. He would later claim that he thought the boxes he handled for Gilligan were full of smuggled tobacco and admitted that he was motivated by greed. Gilligan and Traynor were delighted with the new arrangement. It was back to business.

In the meantime, the Gilligan Brat Pack were anxious to get a piece of the action. Ward, Mitchell and Meehan, along with two other associates, got their investment money the way they knew best, at the point of a gun. On morning of April 28, 1994 the young gangsters hit the Jacobs biscuit factory on the Belgard Road in Tallaght. They held up security staff delivering wages and got away with seventy-eight thousand pounds. They drove their getaway car through a hole in the perimeter fence which they had cut the previous night. Ward was subsequently arrested along with another criminal but released without charge. The Jacobs money was now buying a lot more than biscuits.

In March Gilligan had arranged the largest deal yet with Rahman which was to be shipped to Ireland the same month. The first shipment was to contain sixty kilos and the second 175 kilos. Gilligan made three trips to Amsterdam to organise the deal and collect money sent by truckers to the Continent. On March 2 and March 16 he took the 7.25 a.m. flight to Schipol airport to meet his Dutch contacts. He returned on the same day on both occasions. On March 25 he was again recorded taking the early morning flight. Later that day Gilligan changed almost ninety thousand pounds worth of Belgian francs, sterling, punts and dollars into Dutch guilders at the Bureau de Change near Centraal Station in Amsterdam. The following day he returned to Dublin. On April 4 he called John Dunne in Cork and told him that the first shipment would be left with a Dutch shipping company the following day. Three boxes, one large and two small, would be addressed to a bogus engineering works in County Cork. The cargo was described as being a type of chair. The boxes had been packed and the false invoices prepared by Wildhagen and his associates.

But things did not run as smoothly as planned. The sixty-kilo shipment was mistakenly unloaded at Dublin port on April 11 and then transported by road to Sea Bridge in Cork. Gilligan was furious. He rang Dunne several times to find out what time his precious cargo was due to arrive in Cork. An hour after the three cartons were offloaded at Sea Bridge, Brian Meehan and Paul Ward arrived to pick them up. Meehan introduced himself to Dunne as "Joe". The drugs were on their way back to Dublin for the second time that day.

A week or so later Gilligan rang Dunne again. Another load was coming through Holland and would be due in Cork on April 25. Gilligan said he had changed shipping agents. This time the shipment contained 175 kilos of hashish disguised as machine parts from a bogus Dutch company. Dunne called Gilligan when the cargo arrived and was instructed to drive it to the car park of the Ambassador Hotel on the Naas Road just outside Dublin. Dunne did as he was ordered. At the Ambassador Brian Meehan was there to meet him and transferred the large boxes to another car. Half an hour later Gilligan arrived. He smiled and handed Dunne £1,000 in cash. It was to become one of the most secure and lucrative illegal drug smuggling routes in gangland history. Between April 1994 and October 1996 over twenty thousand kilos of hashish would arrive by the same route for the Gilligan gang, in ninety-six individual shipments, none of which were detected. They had worked out the perfect system. The Gilligan gang was open for business.

Seven

The Soldier and
The General

Charles Joseph Bowden was a perfect candidate for a "job" in John Gilligan's burgeoning drug "business". He was a hard man with military training and discipline, flash, arrogant, with a natural talent for organisation. Most importantly, unlike the rest of the gang, he was not a convicted criminal and therefore unknown to the police. When he first got involved in the drug business, anonymous Charlie Bowden could never have foreseen just how infamous he would become.

Bowden was born into a large Finglas, west Dublin, family on October 15, 1964. It was a family of eight boys and four girls. Charlie was the second youngest in the house, after twins who were four years younger than he. As a child he was considered high-spirited and intelligent. Unlike many of his peers, he did not get involved in criminal activities. Instead, he expended his energies enjoying sport. He was particularly interested in martial arts. Bowden dropped out of school after his Intermediate Certificate exams and went to work in a factory at Store Street in the inner-city as a chemical sprayer. He had other ambitions however, and was attracted to a career as a soldier. Bowden wanted action and adventure in his life.

On August 9, 1983 Bowden enlisted in the Defence Forces and underwent sixteen weeks basic recruit training before passing out as a two-star private. Bowden was posted to the 5th Infantry Battalion based at Collins Barracks in Dublin, where he completed another six weeks training to become a three-star private. Throughout his training and his subsequent career, Private Bowden, Army number 849069, was considered a born soldier who loved military life and had the potential to rise up through the ranks. Tall and athletic, he was one of the fittest soldiers in his entire brigade of over 2,500 troops. Bowden won a gruelling Army Pentathlon and was the All-Army Karate champion three times. He was also an expert marksman and won the Eastern Brigade rifle championships once. At nineteen years of age it seemed that nothing could go wrong for Charlie Bowden. He was on top of the world. The same year he joined the Army, he married pretty Anna Thompson, who was from the same neighbourhood in Finglas. The couple had three sons together.

In October 1984 Bowden volunteered for the United Nations peacekeeping service and did a six-month tour of duty in South Lebanon with a Company of the 56th Infantry Battalion. In the early 1980s several Irish troops were killed in confrontations in the war zone between Lebanon and Israel. During his tour Bowden was injured when his post was shelled. He was hospitalised for a short while but then returned to active service and completed his tour. Like the rest of his Army record up to that time, Bowden's overseas record of his conduct and performance was "excellent". Back home, Bowden's superior officers selected him for promotion. In late 1986 he passed a punishing four-month, non-commissioned officers (NCO) course with distinction. He was promoted to the rank of corporal in April 1987. He was twenty-two years old.

The upper ranks felt that Bowden had a bright future in the Defence Forces. At one stage he was considered an ideal candidate for selection to the elite special forces unit, the Army Ranger Wing. If he agreed to study part-time and completed his Leaving Certificate exams, he could qualify to apply for a full commission as an officer. But it all went terribly wrong.

Early in 1988 Bowden was selected as one of the instructors to train a recruit platoon. On the night of February 2, 1988 he and another Corporal stormed into the recruits' billet. They had both been drinking. The two Corporals challenged the recruits to a fight and then attacked them. Bowden and his colleague beat up eight of the recruits using their martial arts training. One recruit put on a helmet to protect his head in the bloody melee, but Bowden put his fist through the front visor, damaging the man's eye. Two of the recruits had to be hospitalised after the incident. The following day Bowden approached a recruit and warned him to tell the two injured soldiers to keep their mouths shut. "Tell [soldier A] that he hit his head off a locker, if anyone asks, and tell [soldier B] that he just fell or something, and if anything gets out about this tell them they are going to be here for the next three years and I have a lot of friends in the battalion. Tell them that is not a threat."

It was no use. The incident and Bowden's threat were reported and the Military Police were called in to investigate. On March 31 an Army court-martial convicted Bowden of seven charges of assault against the recruits. He was busted back to the rank of private and given twenty-four days of detention at the Army's detention barracks in the Curragh Camp. When he returned to his unit Bowden had lost his taste for soldiering. Any chance of ever joining the Ranger Wing or becoming an officer were gone. One of the essential attributes of a Special Forces soldier is his ability to control his aggression. He would also have to spend years proving to his battalion commander that he was fit enough to regain his corporal stripes.

Bowden decided to leave the Defence Forces and was discharged on August 8, 1989. His conduct assessment on discharge rated him "unsatisfactory". By the time he left the Army Bowden's marriage was also on the rocks and in the same year he split from Anna and moved out of the family's Corporation house in Finglas. His marriage and army career had died together. The two great loves of his life had lasted just six years.

The ex-soldier was at rock bottom. Behind the facade of a womanising tough guy, he was shattered inside. Bowden found himself in dire financial straits. He had to support three small children and pay for a flat, his new home. Bowden went back to work in the factory that he had left six years earlier full of enthusiasm and hope for the future. He also began working as a bouncer in a number of city-centre nightclubs.

In early 1992 Bowden joined a kick-boxing club in Buckingham Street in the north inner-city. It was here that he met Peter Mitchell, who was running a cannabis and ecstasy racket in the north city. At the time Mitchell was also involved in running a protection racket that forced club and pub owners to "hire" his doormen. Bowden was finding it hard to pay maintenance money to his family and approached Mitchell looking for "work". The work involved selling drugs for Fatso. Mitchell liked Bowden because he was tough and he was unknown to the police. Bowden didn't care how he earned his cash.

A short time later Mitchell called to see Bowden at a pub where he was working as a bouncer. Mitchell told him that a guy would deliver a parcel to him and he was to hold onto it until he got further instructions. The following evening Bowden took possession of a parcel containing three thousand Ecstasy tablets – with a street value of almost fifty thousand pounds – which he hid away. The same evening Mitchell called Bowden and told him to divide the tablets into batches of a hundred tablets each. Dealers would call to Bowden to pick up batches of the tablets. Mitchell would call in advance and tell him how much to give each pusher.

As he got more involved in the racket, Mitchell paid Bowden five hundred pounds each week in cash. Bowden also began distributing cannabis for his new boss, about five or ten kilos per week, for which Mitchell paid him fifty pounds per kilo. The arrangement continued until around September 1993 when Bowden decided to go back to school to study bookkeeping and domestic science for his Leaving Certificate exams.

This return to the straight-and-narrow was short-lived. In 1994 Bowden again found himself in financial trouble and was drawn by the lure of easy money. He had been in a new relationship and living with a friend's sister in a flat in Ballymun. The relationship broke up and Bowden fell behind in his rent. The former soldier was fond of nice clothes, drink, drugs and women. He contacted Mitchell again. By now the gang's drug trade was booming and Bowden was welcomed back with open arms. The Cork route had been established and was working well.

Mitchell met Brian Meehan and Paul Ward for the first time. Meehan approved of Bowden because of his tough image and military knowledge. Gilligan, who would not meet him for several months, also approved. Gilligan was enthralled by Simon Rahman's organisation and, like an impressionable kid, was trying hard to emulate the slick Dutch operation. Bowden was the kind of unknown muscle who gave the gang an edge. Like Rahman, Gilligan had decided to stay out of the physical end of handling the drugs. Bowden and the other young gangsters could do that.

By the time Bowden rejoined the "business" in the summer of

1994, more than a thousand kilos of hashish had already been brought through Sea Bridge and shipped to Dublin by John Dunne. Gilligan was now buying the hashish at an average of £1,200 per kilo. Meehan was Gilligan's managing director and confidant. Gilligan sold the hash to Meehan for an average of £2,000 per kilo. Meehan then co-ordinated the wholesale activities with Paul Ward and Peter Mitchell, who each had his own customers. The cannabis was sold on to these clients for an average of £2,300 per kilo. Until July, Gilligan and Traynor's profits were in the region of eight hundred thousand pounds. Meehan, Ward and Mitchell's take was around three hundred thousand.

Bowden began by delivering eighty kilos each week, for which they paid him fifty pounds per kilo. Meehan and Mitchell would tell him how much and to whom to deliver each consignment. Their customers were all regulars. The demand for Gilligan's hash was growing so rapidly that the gang could barely stay on top of the operation. Very soon Bowden became a vital cog in the workings of the gang's business. By late summer huge amounts of cash were being collected, counted and then shipped out to Holland and Belgium to buy further shipments. Each month the quantities grew larger.

In August, for example, Rahman shipped almost nine hundred kilos to the Gilligan gang, whose collective profit was in the region of nine hundred thousand pounds. Within a few months Meehan and Mitchell bought Bowden a car to deliver the drugs around the city. The fact that he had been banned for drunken driving was not viewed as an obstacle for the greedy courier. He registered the car in his brother's name and used his brother's licence. As the quantities began to increase, so too did the problem of where to store the consignments securely.

At first Bowden kept the stuff in his Ballymun flat, but that was proving too much of a risk. In October 1994 Bowden rented a lockup garage at Emmet Road in Inchicore, again in his unsuspecting brother's name. In the middle of 1995 he moved to a more secure lockup in the Kylemore Industrial Estate, but left that in a hurry after the police raided another factory unit nearby. In November 1995 he rented a small industrial unit at Greenmount Industrial Estate, in Harold's Cross, south Dublin. Bowden would take in the boxes of hashish that came from Cork and organise a list of customers and delivery times. Within six months his weekly wages increased from five hundred to three thousand pounds per week. Bowden had become the gang's line manager.

Meanwhile, as the gang began to prosper, Gilligan and Traynor had a problem. Martin Cahill had begun hearing rumours that his two pals were doing well in the drug trade. He began putting pressure on Traynor for a return on his investment. Cahill reckoned that over half a million pounds was a fair amount. Traynor called to see Cahill every day and put him off with excuses that the gang was not yet in profit. Both Traynor and Gilligan had decided that they weren't yet going to pay Cahill his money, but they knew that there were only two ways of getting the obsessive, paranoid General off their backs: either pay him what he was demanding or kill him.

    At this time, Cahill was a major mobster in decline. Chronic diabetes, for which he was not receiving medication, had made him irrational and unpredictable. But then an event occurred which would eventually get Gilligan and Traynor off the hook.

    On the night of Saturday, May 21, 1994 a team of killers from the dreaded Ulster Volunteer Force (UVF), based in Portadown, travelled to Dublin. On the same night Sinn Féin were holding a fundraising function in the Widow Scallan's Pub on Pearse Street in the south inner-city. It was a regular venue for Republican functions and the event had been advertised in the Provo newspaper, *An Phoblacht*. At the time the UVF had dramatically escalated sectarian violence in the North and, as the negotiations towards an IRA ceasefire continued, they had carried out some of the worst atrocities in the history of the Troubles.

    At 10.50 p.m. two members of the UVF hit team arrived at the door of the upstairs function room, which was packed with over three hundred people. One of them carried a handgun, the other a hold-all with an 18 lb bomb inside. IRA man Martin Doherty, a thirty-five-year-old father of two from Ballymun, who was stationed at the door, stopped the two men getting in. In an ensuing scuffle Doherty was shot several times and died instantly. A second man was seriously injured when he was shot through a locked door leading to the function room. Having failed to throw the bomb into the packed function room, the UVF men abandoned it and made their escape. Their getaway car was later found on the North Strand. Miraculously, the bomb failed to explode. If it had, the blast would have been powerful enough to kill everyone inside and knock the actual building down.

In the aftermath of the incident gangland was in a state of fear. The Provos conducted an extensive investigation throughout the underworld to discover if gangsters had given the loyalist killers logistical assistance for the attack. Cahill became their main source of interest because he had dealt with the UVF in his attempts to offload the Beit paintings two years previously. Police and underworld sources believe that neither Cahill nor any other criminal had been involved in helping to organise the Widow Scallan's bomb. Intelligence sources later revealed that the UVF gang had actually got lost in the inner-city as they tried to find the pub where the meeting was to occur on the night of the attack. A number of Republican figures even approached this writer seeking information which pointed the finger at Martin Cahill. I hadn't any.

Cahill had nothing to do with the incident, but the suspicion was enough to seal Cahill's fate. During the research for this book a likely motive for the General's murder emerged which underworld, police and Republican sources seem to agree on. In the follow-up to the Widow Scallan's attack, several underworld figures were "invited" to Dublin interviews by the IRA. Martin Cahill told the Provos to "fuck off" when his presence was requested, but two individuals who were helpful were John Gilligan and John Traynor. Ever the smooth-talking, convincing con man, Traynor is understood to have given the IRA the clear impression that Cahill had been involved [in the attempted bombing]. Gilligan, who was not as subtle, clearly pointed the finger at the General. The two had also spread rumours that the drug shipment seized at Dublin port was Cahill's.

At the same time, Traynor and Gilligan had been developing a strong relationship with a Republican breakaway group, the Irish National Liberation Army (INLA). Traynor had known members of the quasi-criminal gang for several years. Gilligan, too, had become close to a number of INLA members, including Fergal Toal, while in prison in Portlaoise. Gilligan often visited Toal and other

INLA prisoners in Portlaoise and regularly lodged sums of money to the prison account for them to buy snacks, cigarettes and clothes. INLA member John Bolger, a brother-in-law of "Jo Jo" Kavanagh, was also a close friend of Gilligan's. Bolger was shot dead in an internal INLA feud in the summer of 1994.

Traynor, Gilligan and Paul Ward were also supplying drugs to the INLA for their own rackets. Over four kilos of high-quality cocaine had been smuggled through Sea Bridge for a member of the INLA based in Tallaght. The INLA had already had a number of confrontations with Cahill during which he burned an INLA member's flat. They, too, could now assist the Provos with their enquiries.

In the aftermath of the Widow Scallan's incident, Gilligan and Traynor had several meetings with Cahill. Following one of those meetings, Cahill told a close friend and confidant that he had thrown Gilligan out of his home. "He is a dirty bastard," Cahill told the friend, although he did not divulge the nature of the row. Most significantly, Gilligan had two meetings with the General at the house of the General's sister-in-law at Swan Grove in Rathmines in the days before his murder. On both occasions the Garda surveillance team who were keeping tabs on the Cahill spotted Gilligan, who went to great lengths to try and avoid being seen arriving. On each visit Gilligan parked his car several streets away and went to the meeting on foot, through side streets and alleyways.

On the afternoon of August 18, 1994 a gunman stepped from the kerb at the corner of Oxford Road and Charleston Road and pumped five rounds into the General as he sat behind the wheel of his car. The modus operandi of the crime was chillingly similar to that later employed in the murder of Veronica Guerin, and the weapon used was the same type, a .357 Magnum revolver. On the day of the assassination, John Traynor was on holidays with his old friend Sean Fitzgerald.

Gilligan and Traynor's pals, the INLA, were the first to claim responsibility for the murder, but within minutes the IRA announced that they had done it. Incredibly, a short time later radio newsrooms around Dublin were again contacted by the INLA saying that they had nothing to do with the crime and they would murder anyone who claimed they had! The Provos then came back with a statement giving details about the location of the getaway bike and other details of the assassination in their bid to claim the credit.

In the following edition of *An Phoblacht* the Provos issued a statement which read: "It was Cahill's involvement with, and assistance to, pro-British death squads which forced us to act. Cahill's gang was involved closely with the Portadown UVF gang which, apart from countless sectarian murders in the twenty-six counties, was responsible for the gun and bomb attack on the Widow Scallan's pub. The IRA reserve the right to execute those who finance or otherwise assist Loyalist killer gangs. We have compiled a detailed file on the involvement of other Dublin criminals with Loyalist death squads. We call on those people to desist immediately from such activity and to come forward to us within fourteen days to clear their names."

Seven years after the murder of Martin Cahill there is still intense debate about who really killed him. It is a question which has divided everyone involved in the whole bloody business that is crime. Since Veronica Guerin was killed, there has been speculation that it was the INLA and the Gilligan gang who actually murdered the General and then gave the credit to the publicity-hungry IRA. Some underworld sources have claimed that Dutchie Holland and Brian Meehan were seen in the area at the time. In 1997 a woman came forward and told the police that she remembered seeing Meehan in the vicinity of Oxford Road around the time of the murder. She recognised Meehan from his picture in the *Sunday World* newspaper. The two claims have never been substantiated.

The IRA later "questioned" practically every gangster in Dublin, except Gilligan or Traynor. They used the Cahill scare to extract large sums of money from various drug dealers for their "cause". Some observers believe that certain members of the IRA were making plans for how they would make a living after the ceasefire. The relationship between the Gilligan gang and the INLA grew even stronger. In early 1995 the INLA provided "protection" to John Traynor on the orders of John Gilligan when members of the Cahill family and gang began putting pressure on him for the General's money. The INLA threatened to shoot one of Cahill's sons and a message was sent to other members of the gang in Portlaoise that they had better back off. Traynor later gave Martin's widow, Frances, the money to buy a chip shop in south Dublin. Whether this was "conscience" money or a gesture of loyalty, only Traynor knows. The General's murder will remain one of the most perplexing episodes in gangland history.

One truth is that, following the murder, the Gilligan gang went from strength to strength. On the day of the killing, Gilligan's loyal courier, Dinny, was in Amsterdam to meet with Simon Rahman's bagmen. Around the time that Cahill's assassin was producing his gleaming silver magnum revolver, Gilligan's man was changing £142,000 into Dutch guilders. Ironically, it was almost the same amount that Cahill had given the gang to do their first deal nine months earlier. On the day after the murder, August 19, two consignments of 180 kilos and 205 kilos of hash were booked in for shipping to Cork. The boxes, addressed to one of the gang's bogus companies, were being sent as "motor parts" from one of Rahman's companies. Astonishingly, despite all the IRA's guff about taking on organised crime, the country's most dangerous gang had been given a free hand to operate. Perhaps the Provos were afraid of little John, or he was paying them off. In any event, Gilligan's evil empire was about to thrive.

Two months later another of Gilligan's former associates, Paddy Shanahan, was gunned down as he walked into his gym in Crumlin. A north-side criminal was initially suspected of ordering the killing and Dutchie Holland was arrested on suspicion of being the hit man. He was later released without charge. One of the theories about the killing was that certain members of the Gilligan gang suspected that Shanahan was an informant. It was also suspected that the gang were afraid that Shanahan was going to re-form the General's old gang, some of whom were due out of prison. Shanahan's murder remains a mystery. In 1995 two former members of Gilligan's old Factory Gang, David Weafer and Christy Delaney, were shot dead in separate incidents in June and December. Both deaths were officially classified by gardaí as "drug related".

Gilligan was losing a lot of old friends and his mob was also experiencing problems with the police. In his extraordinary arrogance, Gilligan did not consider the authorities as much as a threat as a nuisance. He had begun to believe himself untouchable and was indignant at the interference of the boys in blue.

The week after the Cahill murder, on the evening of Wednesday, August 24, 1994, the crew of a garda patrol car spotted Brian Meehan and Peter Mitchell driving on Dorset Street. The two underworld pals had just collected over forty-six thousand pounds in cash and were in the process of bringing it to Gilligan. When the squad car pulled the two over to be searched one of the officers, David Cherry, spotted a plastic bag full of money behind the front seat. Meehan told him that the cash belonged to him. Meehan and Mitchell were arrested under the Misuse of Drugs Act and taken to Fitzgibbon Street for a drug search.

In the station Meehan had a change of heart and told the officers that the money belonged to a friend, but he refused to name the friend. The police held on to the money, gave Meehan a receipt and released him around 10 p.m. John Gilligan arrived at the station and told Garda Cherry that the money was his and that Meehan was a "good friend who has been minding it for me". He said he could prove ownership of the cash and arranged an appointment at the station the following day.

In a rare display of willingness to co-operate with the police, Meehan made a statement in which he named Gilligan as the true owner of the cash. Gilligan also made a statement. These were the only statements the two hard men ever made to the cops. Gilligan claimed the money and produced photocopied cheques that he claimed had been received from winning bets on horses over the previous few weeks. "I am a gambler, a successful one," he claimed in his statement. He also produced documents stating that he was a horse breeder registered with "Wetherbys Ireland Ltd". The gardaí decided to seize the money under the Police Property Act.

Gilligan applied to the courts to have the money returned. He was furious that his precious cash flow had been interrupted. In the following days Traynor approached the detective in the Serious Crime Squad and asked if there was a chance that some kind of deal could be made to get the cash back. Traynor said that Gilligan was prepared to give the police a few "good arrests" by tipping him off about a number of drug dealers. In fact, the dealers on offer were Gilligan's customers. The proposed "deal" fell down when the cop told Traynor that he would be happy to do a deal, but the drug dealer he wanted was called Gilligan!

The gang's main logistical problem was organising and shipping hard cash from Ireland to Holland to pay for the drug shipments. The smuggling route into Ireland appeared secure but moving large sums of cash was a constant headache. In the first months of the business Gilligan brought the cash with him in briefcases. Apart from a few trips, Traynor had cleverly stepped back from that side of the operation. Dinny, who was acting as the gang's bagman, also brought large amounts of cash. In 1994 alone he personally changed £1.6 million into Dutch guilders at the GWK Bureau de Change in the hall of Centraal Station in Amsterdam. He handed it to Rahman, while Gilligan changed over two hundred thousand pounds. In addition, Dinny had organised a network of truckers travelling to the Continent to bring parcels stuffed with cash to be changed in Belgium and Holland. The drivers were paid fifty pounds for each delivery and were told that the parcels contained cash for cigarettes and tobacco.

The truckers were instructed to hand over the parcels of money to Thomas Gorst, another key member of the Rahman organisation. Thomas Gorst was born in the Kirby area of Liverpool in 1940 and moved to live in Antwerp in Belgium in 1970. He had been involved in international drug trafficking for several years and organised Rahman's smuggling routes through Belgium. He also organised warehouse storage and transport. His brother, Eric Gorst, was a major drug dealer in England and bought his supplies, through his brother, from Simon Rahman.

Gorst, who was also known as "scouser", was well known to Interpol and several European police forces. In 1992 a Tangiers court gave him a year in prison after he was caught with twenty-five kilos of powdered hashish that he was preparing to smuggle to Spain. His second wife, Mariette, who had been arrested with him, was acquitted. In April 1983 Gorst was convicted and jailed for four years by a court in Plymouth, England, for drug trafficking. Gorst and his wife were also identified on Interpol files as running a brothel in Antwerp and were also regularly observed in the company of known South American drug traffickers.

Johnny Wildhagen introduced Gilligan to Gorst and his wife early in 1994 during one of his visits to Holland. Gorst also met and socialised with Traynor. He would later tell police that he liked

Traynor but detested Gilligan, whom he considered a loudmouth. Gorst had agreed, on behalf at the behest of Rahman, to help with the delivery and conversion of the drug money coming from Ireland. Mariette Gorst was working in a sleazy lap-dancing bar near Antwerp. Gilligan loved the place. In fact, when he discovered how cheap sex could be bought in such clubs in Holland and Belgium, he was known as an enthusiastic regular customer on the overnight visits when his wife or mistress weren't with him.

Gorst knew Gilligan as "Gillon". He began collecting the parcels of cash from the truckers coming from Ireland and then organising the transport of the money for the short journey by road across the border into Holland. Gorst took delivery of scores of parcels of money, each containing sums ranging between five and eighty thousand pounds at a time. The money would be delivered by different drivers on different days. Dinny instructed the drivers to call Gorst's Belgian telephone number when they arrived at Zeebrugge Ferry Port. The meetings with Gorst normally took place at a BP filling station on the main motorway on the outskirts of Antwerp.

Between November 1994 and January 1995 Mariette Gorst changed over one hundred thousand Irish and English pounds into Belgian francs at the KB Securities Bureau de Change in Antwerp; Belgian nationals obtained a better rate of exchange than foreigners. Her husband and Gilligan would watch while the transactions took place – but not all the cash being sent to Gorst actually made the journey to Belgium.

On December 11, 1994 Dinny approached Dennis Larrissey, who was preparing to board the ferry at Dun Laoghaire. Dinny appeared beside the truck and tapped on the window. He threw in a parcel wrapped in Christmas paper and asked him to drop it off when he got to Belgium. The forty-year-old trucker from County Meath had done a number of such deliveries for Dinny and two other associates. He was led to believe that he was delivering wages and that there wasn't anything illegal about it. Following Veronica Guerin's murder, Larrissey also told the Lucan team about the incident and said that he had been doing a favour for Denis Meredith.

When Larrissey arrived in Holyhead port he was stopped by a Customs officer for a routine search. She spotted the package sitting on the passenger seat of the cab and asked what was in it. Larrissey said that he didn't know, but that he had been asked to deliver it to the Continent. When the officer opened the package and saw the money, the driver was brought to the Customs hall where the cash was counted. It took the Customs staff five hours to complete the count, which amounted to seventy-six thousand pounds in used notes. Larrissey was released later that day and was contacted again by Dinny. When he told the bagman what had happened, Larrissey was informed that the money belonged to Gilligan and that he should call him immediately. When Larrissey rang Gilligan in Dublin, Gilligan said that the trucker had nothing to worry about and claimed that it was all a mistake. The money was being sent out to build a golf course on the Continent and there should have been "documents" in the parcel explaining this.

Gilligan then rang Her Majesty's Customs at Holyhead and spoke to a senior officer there named Dave Winkle. In an aggressive tone Gilligan demanded the return of his money and claimed that he could produce documentation proving that it was for "investment in property in Ireland". He was clearly getting fed up with police and Customs interfering in his "business". The case concerning Gilligan's drug money had been passed for the attention of Roger Wilson of the Customs National Investigation Service based in Manchester. An experienced investigator, Wilson believed that the money was suspect and decided that it should be confiscated under drug trafficking legislation. When Gilligan was informed about Wilson's decision he flew into a rage.

"He's [Wilson has] backed me into a corner... it's not a problem for me to get someone to shoot him... I'm not goin' down that road, I just want me money back. But if someone messes with my family I'll have them fucking shot," Gilligan snarled down the phone at the Customs officer. The threat against Roger Wilson was taken seriously and he was subsequently placed in a special protection programme by his superiors.

While Larrissey was driving on the Continent the following day, he received another call from Gilligan. He instructed the trucker to call to the Customs people in Holyhead on his return journey and sign forms confirming that he had no claim to the money.

In the meantime, Gilligan instructed his legal team to fight the case at Holyhead Magistrates Court. A week after the Holyhead incident, on December 22, Gilligan was fighting another legal battle for the return of his cash. This time he was in the Dublin District Court seeking the money which had been taken from Brian Meehan in August. The case was heard before Judge Thelma King. During the hearing Gilligan gave evidence of how the money was the proceeds of his activities as a professional gambler. Counsel for the State wanted to know why he had entrusted such a large amount of money to a convicted armed robber. Meehan, Gilligan replied, was a trusted friend and he had no reservations about leaving the cash in his possession. The court ordered that the money be returned to Gilligan. On December 23 Gilligan strutted into Fitzgibbon Street and was handed back his drugs money. He grinned at the officers across the front desk.

Gilligan was not going to give up on the money now in the possession of HM Customs, either. He visited Holyhead on four occasions seeking the return of the cash. On three occasions he attended the Magistrates Court where Customs sought various adjournments. Gilligan's solicitor insisted on each occasion that he and his client were prepared to go ahead with the case and accused Customs of delaying the proceedings unnecessarily.

On July 21, 1995 the Magistrates heard the case and ordered that the money be returned to Gilligan. He left court a happy man. Everything, both legal and otherwise, seemed to be in his favour. Ironically, on the same day, Simon Rahman's couriers booked a shipment of one hundred kilos of hashish for Gilligan. It was business as usual and no-one was touching his money.

Eight

Dirty Money

Peter "Fatso" Mitchell was sitting across a table from two Serious Crime Squad detectives in an interview room at Coolock garda station. He was complaining and mouthing off in a loud, hoarse tone, but Mitchell's diatribe was not about police harassment or the fact that they could hold him for two days. The cocky underworld mouthpiece was giving out about drug dealers – the ones who worked for him!

"Youse think that drugs is an easy business? Well, it's fuckin' not. I'm payin' fellas £1,000 a week to sell hash and a few Es for me and do you think I can get the bastards to work? You can't get the fuckers out of the pubs or their beds. It's just not fuckin' easy," Mitchell whined to the two bemused cops.

Fatso then complained about an RTÉ programme which he claimed had referred to his drug-dealing activities. "They claimed that I was makin' £50,000 a week from drugs. Well, that's a fuckin' lie. I don't know where they got that figure," Mitchell frowned, as he leaned across the table to impart a confidence to his two new friends. "I'll tell ye I don't earn anything like that... I'd say that I'm only makin' about £30,000 a week and nothing more and that's the fuckin' truth, lads."

It was an extraordinary outburst, but illustrated how Gilligan's henchmen thought the police were powerless to touch them.

Mitchell had been arrested on Monday, May 8, 1995 with Brian Meehan and three other north side thugs for questioning about a gun attack on the home of Garda Inspector Willy Stratford in Raheny. Around 4 a.m. the previous morning a gunman had fired two shotgun blasts through Stratford's downstairs and upstairs windows. A brick with a note wrapped around it was thrown through the window of the policeman's car. It read: "Concerned criminals against intimidation. Move it or lose it." Miraculously, no-one was injured in the attack. It was another reminder, as though any were needed, that the crime gangs were getting out of control.

Inspector Stratford's two sons, John and Kevin, were young, enthusiastic cops based in two north-central police stations. They were dedicated policemen who believed in giving criminals a hard time and were well known to Meehan, Mitchell and their associates. A week before the shooting incident John Stratford and his colleagues stopped a car with Mitchell and Meehan inside. When they searched the car, the officers found a sword, baseball bat and other weapons. The two drug dealers were on their way to dispense summary justice to a dealer who hadn't paid for Gilligan's merchandise. The pair were arrested and Mitchell was charged with possession of an offensive weapon (the sword). As he and Meehan were being brought to the station, they threatened Stratford, told him the address of his family home and the registration number and type of cars his brother and father drove.

When the shooting took place, Mitchell and Meehan were the obvious suspects. They and Paul Ward were true protégés of Gilligan's. Like him, they were arrogant and threatening. They were afraid of neither ordinary, law-abiding "civilians" nor other criminals. They were not intimidated by the police and were openly antagonistic towards them on the street. An incident in the previous February illustrated this contempt of authority. When Meehan, Mitchell and Gilligan were stopped while driving through the north city, they immediately became aggressive and abusive, even though the officers had simply asked them their names. The three had been going about their drugs business and did not appreciate the intrusion. Gilligan gave the impression that he simply didn't have time for this messing about. The cops responded by arresting Meehan on an outstanding warrant for dangerous driving.

Mitchell's astonishing outburst at the Coolock Garda Station was prompted when the Serious Crime Squad officers told him that they meant business over the Stratford shooting. "If you had anything to do with this, Peter, we'll hound you until you and your friends are charged. You'll get big time for this, we'll see to it. The good life will be over," Fatso was told.

Mitchell gave them some information about a number of other known drug dealers who were, of course, his competitors.

Subsequently, Gilligan's boys were cleared of the attack and a cocaine-addicted drug dealer, known as "Psycho" Doherty, was eventually caught and given four years for the incident.

To the officers involved in taking on the new-look gangland in the wake of the General's demise, Mitchell's boasting was an ominous development. Mitchell and the other gang members were swaggering and supremely confident that the police couldn't get them. The lack of legislative support and resources to mount major operations against them seemed to validate the gangsters' attitudes. Mitchell's words were interpreted as a vulgar boast designed to annoy them.

When Mitchell told the detectives about his income, it was probably the first time in his criminal career that he had even approached the truth. In any case, the police at that time did not know or believe the amounts of real cash being made by organised crime. That dramatic discovery would only be made in the wake of Veronica Guerin's murder. By 1995 the Gilligan gang were making more money than they knew what to do with. Four days before the arrests in May, for example, a consignment of two hundred and fifty kilos of hash had arrived at Sea Bridge in Cork, delivered by John Dunne. As the consignments got larger, the gang got more greedy.

Garda investigations, which were partly based on shipping records obtained in Holland and Ireland, would later show that during 1995 Gilligan and Traynor imported an estimated 8,700 kilos of hash into Ireland. Based on an average profit of eight hundred pounds per kilo, Gilligan's take was almost seven million pounds, out of which Traynor got his cut. The rest of the gang, collectively, made another one and three-quarter million pounds (based on an estimate that their wholesale profit margin on each kilo varied between one hundred and three hundred pounds). These figures, based on detailed, painstaking analysis by the Lucan Investigation Team, are still considered conservative. From investigations in Holland, Belgium and Ireland it was understood that there had been many other shipments.

In 1995 Bowden was "appointed" an equal partner in the business. Shay Ward, a brother of Paul Ward, who had a long criminal record and a heroin habit, had also joined the gang. Bowden and Shay Ward would collect the consignments from John Dunne at the Ambassador Hotel. Dunne, who had gotten lazy, began paying a Cork van driver to do the Dublin deliveries. Each week Bowden drew up a list of customers from information compiled by the members of the gang, including Gilligan and Traynor.

Each man had his own set of customers. The list gave a fascinating insight into the mind-boggling extent of the distribution operation. As each consignment came in, Ward and Bowden would break it up into the different quantities to be delivered. Bowden eventually had to buy a van from Traynor in order to make the deliveries. At the peak of the operation the gang were delivering an average of two hundred kilos per week. Deliveries were made to customers at pre-arranged locations and at the same time each week. Without Bowden the system would not have worked as well as it did. He recalled how the other members of the gang could disappear for days on a drinking binge.

Each Friday the five gang members met in Meehan's flat and counted the week's turnover. The money for Gilligan was counted and packed for delivery to him. The rest they divided amongst themselves. Each man earned an average of seven thousand pounds per week. A slow week earned them a paltry three thousand. Money was invested in large consignments of ecstasy and cocaine as a sideline. The good times were rolling and it wasn't long before they began displaying the signs of their ill-gotten gains: expensive clothes, cars, holidays, gifts, drugs, drink, women. Whatever they wanted, gangland's Brat Pack could buy it.

Bowden had a major problem about where to put his cash. He would store the money in a washing basket in the bathroom of his Ballymun flat, but it wasn't a bottomless pit, so to speak. The basket could hold more than forty thousand pounds. In the meantime, he started a hairdressing business called Klips on Moore Street in Dublin, run by his girlfriend Juliet Bacon, and also bought a comfortable new home at the Paddocks near the Phoenix Park which he paid for with a sixty-nine thousand pound mortgage. Ironically, his next-door neighbour was Senan Moloney, the crime reporter with the *Star* newspaper. The mortgage repayments and the hairdressing salon, which never turned a profit, soaked up some of the mountain of cash. He spent as much as a thousand pounds a week just socialising. His cocaine habit cost another four hundred. He bought BMWs for himself and Juliet. He paid his brother to have a special safe sunk in a shed at his house to store more of the cash and he hid a large carrier bag stuffed with more than a hundred thousand pounds in a friend's flat. Bowden was intoxicated by his criminal life.

Peter Mitchell also lived the high life. He bought two houses at Summerhill Parade which he converted into flats. He had top-of-range cars and a string of bank accounts which he opened in the names of relatives. Paul Ward, who had begun living with Brian Meehan's sister, Vanessa, bought a detached house in Walkinstown in Dublin which he had lavishly refurbished and decorated. He even had a jacuzzi fitted and bought Vanessa a car for ten thousand pounds in cash. The couple, like the rest of the mob, splashed out on expensive holidays and designer clothes. Ward also developed an expensive drug habit after he began using heroin. He had a number of investment bonds in the names of various relatives, including one for twenty thousand pounds which he bought for a daughter from a previous relationship.

Meehan, as Gilligan's managing director, was the wealthiest of the gang. In July 1994 he bought a luxury apartment at Clifden Court on Ellis Quay that overlooked the Liffey river in central Dublin. Like the other members of the gang, he obtained a mortgage using false papers to suggest he was a "roofer". His father, Kevin, and his uncle, Thomas, had a roofing business. Meehan grew impatient for the apartment and paid almost fifty thousand pounds in cash two months before the bank had finished arranging the mortgage. In May 1995 Meehan's girlfriend, Fiona Walshe a sister of Peter Mitchell's girlfriend, Sonya, was sent out to buy a jeep. Walshe inquired about the price of a Pajero Jeep at a north-side garage which Meehan had inspected earlier. She paid for the vehicle with twenty-four thousand pounds in cash, even though she had never worked and was receiving social security payments. The following November Meehan bought a two-storey terraced house at Annesley Bridge Road for one hundred and twenty thousand pounds. The house had been divided into flats that garnered an annual rental income at the time of twenty-four thousand pounds. Over a two-year period Meehan also accumulated over a quarter of a million pounds in cash, which was deposited to bank and building accounts around Dublin with the help of his father and uncle. They would later claim that they thought the cash from jobless Brian was the proceeds from selling smuggled tobacco and cigarettes.

Times were also good for John Traynor. After the initial contacts and meetings with Rahman in Holland, Traynor stood back from the day-to-day running of the drug business. Unlike the rest of the mob, he did not go out of his way to antagonise the police. He preferred talking to them. Whenever Traynor was stopped he was courteous and friendly. In fact, between 1994 and 1996 when the empire was exposed and smashed, Traynor only visited Holland seven times. Gilligan, on the other hand, made more than forty trips recorded on his Gold Card TAB account and several others which he paid for in cash. In Dublin, Traynor and Gilligan met regularly to discuss business and to sort out money, but Gilligan had made himself the overall boss and controlled the purse strings. He drip-fed Traynor a few hundred thousand pounds at a time. Traynor once complained to an associate that "the little bastard owes me £1.75 million". Gilligan knew that the only way to ensure Traynor's loyalty was to owe him money. He needed the Coach to help launder the drug money.

As the money from the first drug shipments began to come through, Traynor began dabbling in the used car business to launder his cash. While Martin Cahill was alive he could not be seen to prosper; if he showed it, then it was likely that Cahill would have turned up one day to inform him that he now owned the business. In the months following the General's death, Traynor had a dramatic change in fortunes. He set up a number of used car garages in Rathmines in Dublin, Naas, County Kildare and County Laois. The companies were one of the Coach's clever money laundering fronts. He imported hundreds of used cars from England and sold them on at a loss. In one case he bought a fleet of used rental cars and sold them at a loss of two hundred pounds each. Traynor claimed to have two hundred thousand pounds worth of cars on his various lots at any one time. He also laundered cash through a cocaine dealer from Crumlin who owned a building firm. He bought a number of properties in Waterford and had them converted into apartment blocks.

Traynor loved the image of the well-to-do business man and liked flashing money around. He regularly splashed out on booze and drugs parties for his many girlfriends, three of whom were also high-class prostitutes. Traynor got involved in car racing at the Mondello racing track and bought three racing cars to enjoy his hobby. He drove a top-of-the-range, seventy thousand-pound car and even bought himself a small yacht. On one occasion Traynor even managed to inveigle his way into the Dun Laoghaire yacht club. Traynor staggered out of the club, drunk, and decided to take his little yacht for a spin around the harbour. As he drunkenly zig-zagged across the water, he caused a major emergency for the outgoing Holyhead ferry, which was forced to retreat back into the harbour.

But the fortunes of Traynor and the rest of the mob were modest compared to the wealth being enjoyed by John Gilligan. When the millions began rolling in, Gilligan got greedy and wanted more. As the HM Customs could confirm, little John wasn't prepared to let anyone take a penny from him. On the ground, Meehan, Mitchell and the rest of the Brat Pack ensured that the "little man", as they called him, got his money on the button. If a dealer didn't pay, then they either threatened him, broke his legs or shot him. No-one was to be allowed off the hook; if someone was let away and Gilligan found out, he would be furious and order that the dealer get an even more severe beating. The drug money had turned Gilligan into an avaricious thug. Owing him a hundred pounds was as intolerable as robbing a million.

Geraldine Gilligan had also become intoxicated with the mountains of cash her beloved husband's success had brought. At last they could be "somebodies". After all, she had stood by her little man since she was a teenager. She had supported him in his criminal activities and had suffered hard times when he was in prison. Geraldine convinced herself that she deserved all of the comforts and clout that the drug money could bring. Geraldine convinced John that they should use the money to build a world-class equestrian centre and own and breed their own race horses. The kind of rich people who John once robbed for a living could be their clients.

Within weeks of being released from prison in September 1993 Gilligan set about expanding and developing what would become known as the splendid Jessbrook Equestrian Centre, which Geraldine named after one of her horses, Jess. In 1987 they had bought the seven acres at Mucklon near Enfield. It included a derelict house which they had started renovating when John was jailed for the Wexford hardware robbery. It would also be an efficient method of laundering his drug money. The Gilligans had arrived. They had made the transformation from criminal class to landed gentry.

Gilligan was an unknown in the quiet country backwater on the Kildare–Meath border. Mucklon is on a quiet countryside road, miles from the nearest town, Enfield. At first it was thought that Gilligan was a Dublin businessman who had decided to move from the hustle and bustle of the big city for some peace and quiet. But that soon changed. Gilligan's inimitable method of conducting legitimate business soon had tongues wagging. In negotiating land deals and building work, Gilligan's preferred methods of communication were threats and intimidation. Like the rest of his gang, he didn't have an ounce of decorum. He was nothing more than a nasty little bully.

On November 14, 1994 John Gilligan purchased thirty acres of land near to his existing holding for fifty thousand pounds. Another man had a piece of land that Factory John was determined to buy but, when the man repeatedly refused to sell, Gilligan beat him up on a village street and reportedly urinated on his face. No charges were ever preferred. The people of the area were terrified of the little man from Dublin. Gilligan paid twenty-eight thousand pounds for a further fifteen acres in September 1994 and then sixteen thousand for eight acres in August 1995. In January 1996 he paid another twenty-eight thousand pounds for five acres. Shortly before Veronica Guerin's murder, Geraldine finalised a forty thousand-pound deal for twenty-one acres of land. In two years the Gilligans paid £162,000 for seventy-seven acres of land. Even though none of the Gilligans were involved in gainful employment, no mortgage or loan of any kind was sought. The land was paid for in cash.

In September 1994 Gilligan bought a new detached house as a present for his daughter Treacy's twentieth birthday. He paid seventy-three thousand pounds for the house at Willsbrook in Lucan, County Dublin. Treacy was her father's favourite and he always wanted the best for his little girl. She had been sent to an exclusive private school of a kind which only wealthy businessmen and big-time criminals can afford, but she left before completing her education and fell pregnant. On paper, Treacy's only income was a Lone Parent's Allowance of £79.70 per week; a deciding officer at the Department of Social Welfare assessed her as having no means. But in May 1994 Treacy was called in for an interview by the department to discuss her claim.

Police on the ground were watching the Gilligan family's sudden display of wealth and were powerless to do anything about it in the absence of legislation to seize the proceeds of crime. At that time their only way of getting something done was to report the financial dealings of criminals to the Department of Social Welfare or the Revenue Commissioners. Treacy denied that she had any means. When the social welfare inspectors asked about a car Treacy owned, she stated that it was a present from her father. They pressed her for evidence of this and threatened to cut off her payments.

When Treacy told her father about the inspectors' questions, he was furious and dealt with the problem in his usual way. On May 16 and 18 Gilligan telephoned and made several threats against the social welfare officer. The investigator passed the file on to the head office without recommendation. A note in Treacy's social welfare file recorded how "unspecified threats" had been made by Gilligan, who was described as a "very dangerous man". A memo by department officials stated that they had "decided to drop the subject about the car and continued paying her Lone Parent's Allowance".

It would be wrong to criticise the department officials for anything in relation to this matter. In 1989 Martin Cahill had social welfare inspector Brian Purcell abducted from his home and shot in the legs. Purcell's "crime" was that he had been unfortunate enough to be given the task of investigating Cahill's unemployment assistance payments. Neither Cahill nor any member of his gang were ever charged with the appalling crime. Civil servants were terrified by the incident, and they were reasonable in taking the action they did with Treacy Gilligan. They weren't being paid to risk life and limb over a few measly pounds. This was an anomaly in the system which allowed organised crime to intimidate and terrorise ordinary, innocent people. As Veronica Guerin herself once observed, "law favours the criminal more than anyone". This incredible situation did not change until the establishment of the multi-disciplinary Criminal Assets Bureau under the control of An Garda Síochána. In 1994 the Revenue Commissioners sent a tax demand to Gilligan at Jessbrook. Gilligan took the letter and wrote the words "fuck off" on it before sending it back. He never heard from them again either.

In 1995 Gilligan bought a house for his son Darren's twentieth birthday. This time the generous father paid seventy-eight thousand pounds for the semi-detached house at Weston Green in Lucan. At the same time, Darren was receiving £64.50 per week in unemployment assistance, even though a Bank of Ireland account in his name in Blanchardstown contained sums of up to eighty thousand pounds. In March of the following year, John Gilligan also bought his and Geraldine's rented Corporation house at Corduff in Blanchardstown for eleven and a half thousand pounds. Gilligan's spending spree continued unabated.

In the year between 1995 and 1996 Gilligan spent £78,135 in cash buying new vehicles, including two jeeps for the equestrian centre. On January 9, 1996 he walked into a car show room in west Dublin with his two children. One picked out a new car and the other a jeep, which John agreed to buy, in much the same way children pick up toys in a store. When the delighted car salesman asked his customers how they wanted to pay for the vehicles, Gilligan replied, "Cash," and produced a plastic Dunnes Stores bag full of used notes. He also produced a few thousand pounds which he was carrying as loose change in his pockets. The Gilligans left with their new toys, for which Daddy had handed over a total of over thirty-five thousand pounds.

It was particularly good day for the Gilligan offspring. On the same day as he bought them new cars, Daddy lodged twenty thousand pounds in cash to each of his children's bank accounts. Perhaps it was their pocket money! But Gilligan could well afford it. During the following two weeks, two shipments of 387 kilos of hashish arrived in Cork. Gilligan's estimated profit from the two consignments, over three hundred thousand pounds, more than made up for the losses from his generosity to his family.

In 1995 the Gilligans bought a race horse called Rifawan.

Gilligan paid for it with sixty thousand pounds in cash, which he carried in a shoe box. Rifawan was put in training at the stables of Arthur Moore at a cost of twenty-four thousand pounds between February 1995 and May 1996. Moore did not know the name of the real owner of the horse and, as far as he was concerned, he was training it for a perfectly legitimate client. Rifawan came second in two races. Following the murder of Veronica Guerin, Moore discovered the horse's true owner and returned it. Rifawan was subsequently sent to an English trainer but broke his leg in the Burns Cottage novice chase at Ayr in Scotland. Rifawan had brought the Gilligans a measure of the respectability which they craved. They had found themselves in the prestigious owners' enclosure at races in Ireland and England and swilling champagne with the hoi polloi. Gilligan once bragged how he had gotten within winking distance of the Queen Mother herself.

Meanwhile, Geraldine and John were actively pursuing their plans for Jessbrook. Geraldine wanted to build an indoor show jumping arena to world-class standards. Again, there was no difficulty with money. Over a two-year period, Geraldine, using her maiden name, Matilda Dunne, put over one million pounds through various bank accounts, although there was no "visible" source of income. In April 1994 she hired the services of an architect to draw up plans for the complete renovation of the derelict house at Mucklon and the construction of fourteen stables. The house was rebuilt with six bedrooms, a large lounge complete with private bar, a long driveway with electronic gates and a security camera system.

Gilligan used the threat of violence and large wads of cash to get things done. The builder who began working on the house was terrorised by Gilligan. One morning, when a bricklayer didn't turn up for work, Gilligan went looking for the builder with an iron bar to beat him with. When Gilligan couldn't find the builder, he rang the man's wife and told her that he would put her husband in the hospital by nightfall. He later spoke to the builder and threatened to put him in a wheelchair if the workmen didn't turn up. On another occasion Gilligan called the builder, the architect and another contractor to a meeting in his house and berated them that work wasn't progressing fast enough. During the conversation, Gilligan's mobile phone rang and he passed it to the builder. A rough Dublin accent on the other end told him that if he didn't do what Gilligan wanted, he (the caller) would be waiting for him up the road and would "get" his wife and family. The voice then asked for the phone to be passed to the architect and he was given the same message. The two men, who were honest, hard-working people, had never experienced a situation like it. They were terrified for their own safety and the safety of their families.

On another occasion Gilligan rang and asked the builder: "How many times have I said that I will kill you?" The builder answered: "Loads," and Gilligan began shouting down the phone about a piece of work which he said had not been properly finished. In the end the builder completed the house and stables and left. It had been a nightmare for the man. Gilligan refused to pay him the thirty-six thousand pounds he was owed, leaving him practically bankrupt and living in fear that the new squire of Jessbrook would kill him.

In May 1995 the Gilligans decided to proceed with a full-size show jumping arena. It would be one of the largest in the country and modelled on one at Millstreet, County Cork. Again Gilligan did business his way. The plan was to have seating for four hundred spectators, a main arena of eighty by forty metres, and a warm-up area of forty by twenty metres. Gilligan is understood to have targeted a planning official and threatened him and his family if planning permission was not granted. He had compiled information on members of the official's family and home. When building work began on the huge enclosure, Gilligan ordered that the seating capacity be increased to nine hundred.

Gilligan spent over £1.5 million on the Jessbrook development in less than a year. Most of the money was paid in cash from shoe boxes and plastic bags. The rest of payments were from cheques drawn on Geraldine's bank account. The Gilligans were proud of their masterpiece, but decided that, because of John's criminal activities, it would be safer to hide his involvement from a legal point of view. To cover their tracks, the Gilligans drew up a legal separation agreement in July 1995 in which he assigned ownership of Jessbrook to Geraldine. They reckoned they had covered every angle.

Gilligan made no effort to hide the extraordinary amounts of cash he had. He arrogantly reckoned that he had worked the perfect system for laundering his dirty money. Gilligan was a life-long gambler. He was addicted to it. In the early days he thought nothing of wagering his entire earnings from a warehouse robbery. Once he bet ten thousand pounds on a greyhound. The dog broke its toe leaving the trap and never even started the race.

But now he was in the big league. Gilligan and a network of couriers laid bets in bookmakers' shops throughout greater Dublin on short odds. He would often bet money on all the horses running in a race at up to ten thousand pounds a time. When he won money Gilligan was paid with bookmakers' cheques, which he then used as evidence that he was a professional gambler and that gambling was his source of income. He did this successfully on a number of occasions. The following is an example of how Gilligan turned drug money into bookies' money.

On March 18, 1995 Gilligan made twelve bets. The first was £5,000, to which was added £500 tax. The horse lost. He also lost the next two races, bringing his losses so far that day to £16,390. On the fourth race he bet £4,000, plus £400 tax. The horse won, paying £8,400 and leaving Gilligan down £12,000. He also won the following bet of £3,800, plus £380 tax, which paid £10,450. His losses were down to £6,120. The sixth bet, for £3,300 and £330 tax, was lost, leaving Gilligan down £9,750. In the next three races Gilligan wagered a total of £12,000. All three horses won, lowering his cumulative losses for the day to £1,220. On the next race, the tenth of the day, he lost another £2,000 and £200 tax. He called the last two races right, leaving him £2,000 up on the day's betting. With taxes, he had bet a total of £53,900 in cash. The money had effectively been laundered. It was now in his possession the form of bookmakers' cheques.

Some bookies began to limit the amounts that Gilligan could wager. It was not unusual for him to step up to the counter and empty a plastic bag full of bundles of cash for his bets. One bookmaker conducted detailed analysis of Gilligan's betting patterns, the type of races he backed, the horses and jockeys, but could not find a pattern or method to his wagers. Between March of 1994 and June 1996 Gilligan bet a total of £4,982,590. Betting tax of ten per cent put that total at £5,480,849. Gilligan's return

was £4,860,713, showing a loss of £620,135 (or 11.3 per cent).
Even by today's standards of taxation, the cost of the laundering
operation was, from a business point of view, a steal in comparison.

Gilligan also spent a small fortune on flights, mostly between
Dublin and Amsterdam, when he went to order drugs from Simon
Rahman. His Gold Circle TAB account recorded that he spent over
twenty-seven thousand pounds on business class flights in thirty
months. It is estimated that he spent several thousands of pounds
more on flights which had not been logged in his name. He also
spent large sums of cash on his mistress.

Carol Rooney, from Palmerstown, was an impressionable 18-
year-old assistant in a local bookmaker's shop when she met little
John Gilligan. She was in awe of the man who was old enough to
be her father. He piled bundles of money on the counter to bet on
horses and she found him charming and interesting. He invited her
out and they began a relationship. The teenager was overwhelmed
by Gilligan, who splashed out on lavish presents. Behind Geraldine's
back he took Carol on holidays and on trips to Holland, where she
was also helped to change drug money into guilders to pay Rahman.
He rented a luxury apartment for her in County Kildare and also
bought her a car with cash.

Simon Rahman thought Gilligan's method of laundering cash
was a reflection of the rest of his organisation and his personality –
vulgar and unsophisticated. He was aware that Gilligan was a
gambling addict and capable of throwing away a fortune in the
casinos. Rahman made sure that the drug money Gilligan delivered
to Holland was exchanged as soon as possible.

Simon Rahman had decided to get one of his own men to keep
an eye on Gilligan and to take care of the financial transactions. He
and his associates referred to Gilligan as "De Klein" (the little one).
The term was disparaging. Rahman did not trust Gilligan and
described the gang, with the exception of Traynor, as a bunch of
"Neanderthals". He refused to have any dealings with Meehan and
Mitchell whenever they travelled to Amsterdam. He referred to them
with condescension as "the others". From the beginning of their
relationship Gilligan had tried hard to project himself as a major
league international drug trafficker, a godfather with considerable
clout. Rahman was amused at "De Klein's" efforts to ingratiate

himself with the Dutch hoods. The incident at the casino had illustrated how stupid Gilligan and his mob were by attracting so much unwelcome attention. He always reckoned that their loud, indiscreet manner would someday lead to them being caught. In the meantime, they were spending a lot of money and Rahman wanted to protect his investment, but at the same time he maintained a safe distance from Gilligan so that he would not get caught himself.

Martinus Maria Cornelius Baltus became Rahman's liaison man with the Gilligan gang. Born in September 1946 in The Hague, Baltus was described as being Rahman's equivalent of John Traynor. He specialised in fraud and was a general underworld "wheeler-dealer" and money launderer. He set up dozens of bogus shelf companies through which Rahman organised various smuggling scams. In December 1994 Rahman introduced him to Gilligan as a potential investor in a holiday home development which Baltus was supposedly organising. The meeting took place in the Movepick Hotel in Voorburg. However, no investment was ever made and Baltus, on Rahman's instructions, began handling Gilligan's drug money. On January 3, 1995 Baltus was sent to Schipol airport to collect Gilligan and drove him to a meeting with Rahman in the Victoria Hotel in Amsterdam. Gilligan handed Rahman a sports carrier bag which he handed to Baltus to exchange. Rahman's new bagman changed the money at the Bureau de Change in the hall of Centraal station. The bag contained £138,000 in cash. Baltus used his Dutch driver's licence as evidence of identity. Baltus returned to the hotel and handed the bag of guilders to Rahman.

Between January 1995 and April 1996 Martin Baltus exchanged over £2.8 million pounds received from Gilligan and Denis Meredith into guilders. The conscientious bagman even used to iron out crumpled notes before he took them to the Bureau. On each of the twenty-nine recorded occasions that he made an exchange at Centraal Station, Rahman was always a short distance away to monitor the transactions. When Gilligan was in Ireland during the handover, Rahman would ring him to confirm the rate of exchange he had received on the day.

Baltus also attended meetings between Thomas Gorst, his wife Mariette, Rahman, and John and Geraldine Gilligan. On one occasion the Gilligans brought their little grandchild with them.

John Gilligan's Mug Shots

Some of the many police mug shots of "Factory" John Gilligan taken during the 1980s. The pictures were regularly circulated to police units throughout the country.
Sunday World

The Gilligan Gang

Eugene Patrick "Dutchie" Holland

Brian "Tosser" Meehan

John "The Coach" Traynor

The Gilligan Gang

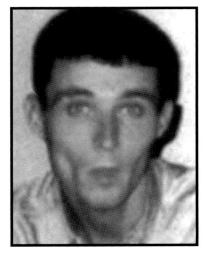

Paul "Hippo" Ward

Peter "Fatso" Mitchell

Seamus "Shay" Ward

John Gilligan (bottom right) pictured in Portlaoise Prison in 1992 with triple murderer and pimp John Cullen (top) and INLA member and kidnapper Dessie O'Hare, "The Border Fox" (bottom left).
Sunday World

Dummies on Parade

John Gilligan poses for a photo with a wax dummie of Benny Hill at Madame Tussaud's in London
Sunday World

Fun in the Sun

John Gilligan (bottom left), Brian Meehan (standing) and Peter Mitchell with Frances Meehan (Brian Meehan's mother), having fun at the Sandals Resort in St Lucia, 1996.
Sunday World

John and Geraldine Gilligan ordering a meal in St Lucia with Peter Mitchell.
Sunday World

Fun in the Sun

John and Geraldine Gilligan with World Champion Super Featherweight boxer Prince Naseem Hamed during their visit to St Lucia in 1996.
Sunday World

From left: Frances Meehan, Kevin Meehan, Brian Meehan, Brad Meehan and Peter Mitchell at the wedding of "The Tosser's" sister in St Lucia, 1996.
Sunday World

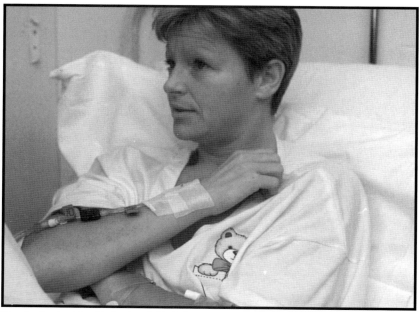

Veronica Guerin pictured in her hospital bed after the January 1995 attack at her home in which she was shot in the leg.
Sunday Independent

Graham Turly and Veronica with their son Cathal before she was attacked by John Gilligan in Jessbrook near Enfield, County Meath.
Sunday World

Veronica Guerin, murdered by the Gilligan Gang on June 26, 1996.

Veronica Guerin and John Traynor shortly before her murder.
Sunday Independent

The murder scene.
Sunday World

The author interviewing John Traynor in Portugal, July 1996.
Sunday World

Dutchie Holland being interviewed by Pat Kenny in Kensington, London, March 1997.
Colin Keegan, Collins Photos

Gilligan arriving for a remand hearing in relation to his assault on Veronica Guerin the day before her murder.
Irish Independent

Corrupt cop John O'Neill, who was on the gang's payroll, shortly after being charged with taking bribes. **Collins, Dublin**

An aerial view of Gilligan's Jessbrook Equestrian Centre, near Enfield, County Meath.
Liam O'Connor, Sunday World

Brendan "Speedy" Fegan, the Newry, County Down drug dealer who helped run the gang's drugs business following the murder of Veronica Guerin.
Sunday World

Mug shot of John Gilligan, 1993.
Sunday World

The Gorsts regularly brought parcels of money similar to the one seized at Holyhead port and gave them to Baltus for changing. Baltus also helped Rahman and Johnny Wildhagen pack shipments of hashish into wooden and cardboard boxes at Rahman's offices in The Hague. The boxes were lined with polystyrene, the drugs placed inside and expanding foam pumped in around them. Baltus then drew up shipping documents using one of his bogus companies and delivered the goods to Rotterdam port for transportation to Cork.

On June 16, 1995 Baltus attended a meeting with Rahman, Wildhagen, Gilligan, Dinny and a major Moroccan drug trafficker called Havid. Havid had smuggled a shipment of hash into Holland and the purpose of the meeting was to make a deal. The deal didn't go down in a darkened alleyway, like in the movies. This was altogether more dignified. The gangsters met in an up-market restaurant in Kiykduin for lunch. To the innocent observer it was a group of well-dressed businessmen discussing the markets over a bottle of Chablis. Rahman, acting as a broker for his client (Gilligan), agreed to purchase 208 kilos of hash at £1,200 per kilo.

Rahman bought drugs from other, bigger traffickers whenever his own stocks were low. Another trafficker he regularly dealt with on Gilligan's behalf was a man referred to as the "hash farmer". This happened whenever demand was unusually high. Following the meeting with Havid, Baltus packed the drugs in boxes and shipped them to Cork.

The most sinister development in the relationship between the Gilligan gang and their Dutch friends was the purchase of guns. From their first dealings Gilligan and his mob demanded that Rahman supply them with firepower. The gang wanted to defend its turf and also use the guns to supply their pals in the INLA and the IRA. A powerful arsenal was a must for those intent on being the most powerful in gangland. Through Johnny Wildhagen, Rahman bought Agram 2000 machine pistols, Sten sub-machine guns fitted with silencers, automatic pistols, revolvers and ammunition which were shipped to Ireland with consignments of drugs between March 1995 and January 1996.

Rahman would hide the weapons in the ceiling of one of his offices. In March 1995 Baltus helped Wildhagen and Rahman pack the weapons in Rahman's warehouse. It was a departure that would have chilling consequences. On March 9 Rahman sent Baltus to meet a criminal referred to as "Koos" in a fish market on the corner of Dierenselaan-Zuiderparkalaan. Koos handed Baltus a carrier bag, which Baltus put in the boot of a Mercedes car belonging to Rahman. As he drove around the corner, armed police were waiting for him. Martin Baltus was arrested and an Agram 2000 recovered from the bag. The gun was intended for the Gilligan gang.

Despite the arrest, Rahman continued to send guns to Dublin. One shipment in January 1996 included a gleaming new .357 Magnum revolver, the most powerful handgun in the world. Charlie Bowden, who had now become the gang's armourer, cleaned, oiled and wrapped the weapons in cloth before they were hidden away. He carefully cleaned the brand-new magnum that had never been used. He wrapped it carefully in cloth and put it in a plastic Tupperware box before hiding it with the gang's other weapons in a grave in the Jewish cemetery at Oldcourt Road in Tallaght. The next time that weapon was taken from its resting place, a brave journalist would die. Gilligan's high-rolling days as a godfather were numbered.

Nine

The Crime Reporter

When John Gilligan was released from prison and started his new career as a drug baron, a little-known journalist named Veronica Guerin was also making her mark in a new profession. Although from totally different worlds and backgrounds, their lives were destined to collide with tragic consequences. Their names would be forever synonymous in history.

In November 1993 Veronica arrived on the front page of *The Sunday Tribune* with a scoop that any journalist would have given his or her eyeteeth for. It was an exclusive series of interviews with Bishop Eamon Casey. The one-time celebrity bishop went into hiding in 1992 when it was revealed that he had fathered a child from an affair with an American woman called Annie Murphy. The Catholic Church was seriously embarrassed by the controversy and, in order to cover its tracks, Casey was spirited as far out of view as possible. He was sent to work as a Parish Priest in a secluded community in Ecuador. There, they thought, no-one would find the randy bishop and the whole embarrassing situation could be forgotten. Out of sight, out of mind.

Not so, when Veronica Guerin got on the case. For almost a year she had doggedly pursued the story and eventually found out where Casey was hiding. She flew to Quito in Ecuador at her own expense and literally doorstopped Casey. She spent several hours discussing the story with him and eventually persuaded him to give his first interview about the affair. He grew very fond of the reporter and trusted her. The Casey story put Veronica on the map of Dublin journalism and her newspaper, *The Sunday Tribune*, experienced a huge surge in sales. Veronica's tenacity and dogged determination were the characteristics which got her some of the best stories. I, like a lot of my colleagues, was envious of her. She was a natural investigative reporter and loved the sheer buzz that comes from breaking the big story.

Guerin was born in Dublin in 1958, the second youngest of three girls and two boys. The family lived in the Dublin suburb of Artane. Her father, Christopher, an ardent Fianna Fáil supporter, was an accountant. The Guerin children had a happy childhood. Her siblings would later recall how Veronica was strong-willed and full of life. She was a passionate sportswoman and a life-long, fanatical Manchester United fan. As a pupil in the Holy Faith Convent in Killester she played football and represented Ireland internationally. She played several times for the Irish national basketball team.

Like the rest of her family, she was a staunch Fianna Fáil supporter and Charles Haughey was her hero. Together with her brother Jimmy, she joined Ogra Fianna Fáil, an organisation for young party supporters, and canvassed for Haughey at elections. Even then she showed a type of courage that marked her out from the rest. She had no fear of electioneering in the roughest areas of the north side. In 1982 Haughey appointed Veronica to the board of National Institute for Higher Education, now the Dublin City University (DCU). He also appointed her to the Fianna Fáil group in the New Ireland Forum. When she married builder Graham Turley in September 1985, Haughey and several members of his family were guests at the wedding. Graham and Veronica spent part of their honeymoon on Inishvickillaun, Haughey's island retreat off the Kerry coast. The couple had one child, a son, Cathal.

Before settling on journalism Guerin had worked at various jobs and businesses. She studied to be an accountant and worked in public relations. She had also tried her hand at a number of business ventures before deciding that she wanted to be an investigative reporter. Her first major story was an investigation into the Aer Lingus holidays company which she wrote for the *Sunday Business Post*. She left the *Post* in 1993 to work freelance for the *Sunday Tribune*. Early in 1994 she moved to work at the *Sunday Independent*, where her career took off.

Veronica was fascinated by crime and began writing about the complex world that is gangland. During the summer of 1994 she approached John Traynor and nurtured him as a source. The smooth-talking con man, who was now making a fortune as part of Gilligan's organisation, was intrigued by the gutsy female reporter. True to form, Traynor saw an advantage in having a reporter on his side. He could dish the dirt on his enemies and keep himself out of print. Shortly after that, I also met with Traynor while researching the book *The General*. I had been working on the story about how he had returned the stolen Father Molloy file to the gardaí. He offered to help me if I didn't actually name him. Some time later Veronica complained to her editor at the *Sunday Independent* that I had been hassling one of her sources. Traynor had been playing us against each other. The row never developed and we both continued to talk with the Coach.

That September Veronica again came to public attention when she ran a number of speculative stories about who had actually shot Martin Cahill. In one story she wrote that she had been threatened by a north-side gang. In the same month she also ran the sensational story about Martin Cahill's tangled love life with his wife and her sister. Traynor had been the main source for the story, which had always been known in criminal and police circles but never written. The following month she ran a detailed story about the Father Molloy case. Traynor had shown Veronica a copy of the file that Cahill had given back to the police over a year earlier. In October a shot was fired through the front room window of her home in North County Dublin, presumably as a warning to stop writing about them. The shot had been fired from a handgun. The shooter was never identified.

The warning did not dampen Veronica's enthusiasm for the job. In January 1995 a north-city criminal mastermind called Gerry Hutch, or "the Monk", pulled off a spectacular £2.8 million robbery from the Brinks Allied cash holding centre in north Dublin. The heist had been meticulously planned and was executed with military precision. Ironically, the robbery took place less than a mile from Veronica's home. The Government and the gardaí were publicly embarrassed when the *Irish Independent* ran a story revealing that the police had been watching the Monk's gang in anticipation that a major robbery was being planned but had failed to stop it. On the following Sunday, January 29, Veronica added to the outcry when she exposed the fact that Hutch had availed of a tax amnesty for his robbed cash a few years earlier. Veronica was upsetting the organised crime bosses.

Shortly before 7 p.m. on the following evening Veronica heard
a knock on the front door of her home. Graham and Cathal were
out visiting and she was getting ready to go to a *Sunday Independent*
staff party. When she answered the door, a man wearing a motorcycle
helmet and brandishing a gun pushed her inside the house, knocking
her to the floor. He pointed the gun at her head and then lowered
the weapon. He shot her in the thigh, narrowly missing a major
artery. Veronica was hospitalised and underwent surgery. She made
a full recovery and courageously vowed to continue her work despite
the attack. The incident was a chilling warning from the criminal
underworld, which effectively went unnoticed. At first the Monk
was suspected of carrying out the attack, but within a week gardaí
had eliminated him from their enquiries.

After weeks of investigation, the police nominated the man
who they still believe ordered the attack, John Traynor. The Coach
had organised the shooting to show that he had the "bottle" to hit a
reporter who, he claimed, had annoyed him. He later bragged that
the incident boosted his reputation in the eyes of other gangsters,
especially to Gilligan. It was also intended to prove to the Cahill
family that he was not friendly with Guerin and had nothing to do
with the story about the General's complicated love life. The timing
of the attack was also well planned. He could have the Monk blamed
for his dirty work.

Traynor was arrested and questioned about the incident but there
was no evidence linking him with the crime. Two months after the
shooting Veronica interviewed the Monk in the kitchen of her home.
He had agreed to do the story because he had been wrongly accused
of drug dealing and of being involved in her shooting. Hutch was
also impressed by Veronica's courage. After she had been released
from hospital she personally delivered letters to Hutch's home
demanding to know if he was responsible for the attack. Despite
being on crutches, she was still determined to get to the bottom of
her own story.

Traynor and Veronica continued to talk on a regular basis after
the incident. It still remains unclear if she ever found out that he
had been behind the attack that could have cost her life. In May
1995 she warned me about Traynor. "He is a dangerous, two-faced

bastard. He would have no problem setting you up," she told me. It was clear that in the months before her death that she had begun to suspect Traynor of being involved in her shooting.

During the summer of 1995, as his drug business continued to boom, Gilligan began being mentioned in underworld and police circles as the new, big-league godfather. Veronica became interested in exposing the life and crimes of John Joseph Gilligan. A police contact had told her about Gilligan's inexplicable new-found wealth. On his part, the cop was typically frustrated by the lack of resources and legislation to enable him to take on Gilligan.

In August 1995, Traynor told me that Veronica was "chasing" a story about Gilligan. She had asked him to introduce her to the little man. Traynor said he had advised her against it. At the same time, the *Sunday World* ran a story about the new bosses of gangland alongside a picture of Gilligan. The article revealed that Gilligan was now heavily involved in the hashish and ecstasy trade and gave specific details of how he had illegally imported a number of machine guns with the drug shipments and how one of the weapons was fitted with a silencer. Traynor had given me the information. For legal reasons the *Sunday World* hadn't actually named Gilligan in the story and his eyes were blacked out of the photograph. Traynor told me that Gilligan had "gone ballistic" over the story and warned me not to write about him in the future. "He is a very dangerous man. He will come after you and your family," he warned.

Traynor said he didn't want to give me any more information on Gilligan but he was happy to share secrets about the activities of criminals he did not like. George Mitchell ("the Penguin") and Martin Foley ("the Viper") were his two pet hates. It was clear that the purpose of leaking such stories was intended to divert interest from him and fellow gangsters, but Veronica was not giving up on Gilligan. On September 7 she addressed a letter to him at Jessbrook, asking if he would consent to let her interview him. In the letter Guerin wrote that she wanted to talk to him about his sudden success and the source of his wealth. Gilligan hadn't responded.

On Thursday, September 14 Guerin decided to call on Gilligan in person and put her questions to him directly. She left Dublin around 8 a.m. and drove thirty miles to Enfield, County Kildare. Around the same time, Dinny was catching the early morning flight to Amsterdam with £156,100 of Gilligan's cash, which was then exchanged routinely by Baltus in Centraal Station. Guerin followed the signs for Jessbrook Equestrian Centre on the narrow country road three miles from Enfield. She arrived at 8.50 a.m. and drove up to the Centre, which was already open. She was stunned by the size of the place. Guerin asked a woman in reception if could she see "Mr Gilligan". The woman told Veronica that he wasn't there, but that she could get him at his private residence. She was directed to go back out onto the main road and call to a different gate.

At the main gate Veronica pressed the intercom button and looked up at the security camera overhead, so that whoever was answering could see her. The electronic gates opened. She waited to see if someone would come to meet her. When nothing happened she drove up the tree-lined avenue to the house. The little man's jeep was parked outside. Veronica was impressed with the splendour of Gilligan's country mansion. Inside, he had been watching her on the security monitors. A short-tempered bully at the best of times, this morning he had a hangover. The previous night he and Geraldine had been celebrating Darren's twentieth birthday. His blood was boiling at the nerve of the nosy reporter. Veronica got out of her car and gently knocked on the front door. Gilligan watched her on a camera which followed her every move.

Still wearing his silk dressing gown, he stormed out to the door to see off this latest irritant in his life. He opened the door. "Yeah?" he snarled at Veronica. "Mr Gilligan?" she asked. "That's right," he snapped back. Veronica explained who she was and said she wanted to ask him some questions about his wealth and the equestrian centre. Gilligan could no longer hold his temper and lunged at her. He grabbed her about the upper body, punching her about the head and face with his fists. He began screaming at her. "If you write anything about me I'll fucking kill you, your husband, your fucking son, your family, everybody belonging to you, even your fucking neighbours!" Gilligan shouted.

Later Veronica told gardaí that Gilligan seemed to be physically carrying her towards her car. He pushed her onto the bonnet, while continuing to punch her in the head and body. She was terrified and later said that she thought Gilligan was going to kill her. When he let go, she slid, battered and dazed, onto the ground beside her car.

Crying and trembling with fear, she struggled to get to her feet. "Get the fuck out of here! Get off my fucking property!" Gilligan continued to shout. As she opened the door of her car, Gilligan grabbed her again and shoved her violently into the driver's seat. He continued spitting his threats that he would murder her and everyone belonging to her if she wrote anything about him. Veronica was fumbling with her car keys in her panic to get away from the demonic madman screaming obscenities at her when Gilligan reached into the car and grabbed her again by the neck. "Have you a fucking mike? Where's the fucking wire?" Gilligan tore open Veronica's cotton shirt and ripped her jacket. "I'll kill you and your whole fucking family if you write anything about me," Gilligan continued as he slammed the car door shut. "Now get the fuck out of here!"

Veronica drove away at speed leaving Gilligan standing fuming in front of his mansion. She could barely focus on the road through tears of terror and pain and got lost on her way back to Enfield. Her upper body and head were aching from the brutal attack. When she gathered her thoughts, she phoned a number of Garda friends. One of them was Deputy Commissioner Pat Byrne. When Byrne answered his mobile phone he could only hear sobbing. Eventually Veronica composed herself enough to speak. "He's... he's after beating me up... he threatened to kill me... he beat me black and blue," she told the man who less than twelve months later would be waging war against John Gilligan.

Later she went to her doctor who diagnosed shock and extensive bruising. She was advised to rest. Veronica called to see her mother Bernie. In the hallway of her mother's home, she sat on the stairs and sobbed. Pat Byrne had already mobilised the police and ordered that Guerin be given full-time protection while the assault was being investigated. After the incident, Gilligan got dressed and went to see Traynor. He was in a rage and said that he was going to have "that interfering bitch done once and for all". Traynor tried to placate his foul-tempered partner.

The following morning solicitors for the *Sunday Independent* contacted barrister Felix McEnroy requesting that he meet with Veronica to discuss the assault. The senior counsel had represented Gilligan in a matter some ten years preciously and knew of his dangerously explosive temper tantrums. It was just before 1 a.m. when Veronica called to McEnroy's office. She was still shaken and had bruises and swelling around her left eye. As they were talking, Traynor called Veronica and spoke to her about the assault. He was being conciliatory, but Gilligan, who was standing beside him, snatched the phone and repeated his previous threats. Veronica hung up.

About five minutes later Gilligan rang Veronica's mobile phone again. This time McEnroy listened to the call. He instantly recognised Gilligan's voice. Gilligan identified himself and, in an aggressive tone, told her that he and Geraldine were separated and that "all the property is in her name". Then his voice changed. It was clear, controlled and menacing. "If you do one thing on me, or write about me I am going to kidnap your son and ride him. I am going to shoot you. Do you understand what I am sayin'? I am going to kidnap your fucking son and ride him, and I am going to fucking shoot you. I will kill you." McEnroy was shocked at Gilligan's tone. He immediately told Veronica to cut off the conversation and advised her to make a statement about the assault and the threats to the police.

Later that evening Geraldine Gilligan called Veronica. She asked her if she was "Miss Guerin". "This is Geraldine Gilligan. I was told that you are doing an article about my place. Me and my husband are separated and I am glad that we are separated. Everything is in my name. I just want you to know that," said Geraldine in a relaxed tone. Veronica told her that she could not discuss the matter any further and hung up. Later Traynor called Veronica to advise her not to have anything more to do with Gilligan. "I have told you before that he is a very dangerous man. He means what he says. Let it sit and I'll calm him down if you leave him alone," Traynor advised.

Veronica, however, ignored Gilligan's henchman and that evening gave a statement about the incident to Detective Inspector Tom Gallagher from Coolock Garda station. Her statement concluded: "I am fearful for my life and for the safety of my family. I believe that the threats made to me by John Gilligan were meant to put me in fear in relation to my personal safety and that of the members of my family. I am bruised around my upper body and head. I have serious bruising and swelling in the area of my left eye and my injuries are painful."

The *Sunday Independent* decided to run a story about the assault. On Saturday, September 16, the journalist who was writing the story phoned Gilligan to obtain a quote about the incident. The nasty little godfather was only too happy to oblige. "If anyone interferes with me or my fucking family, I'll fucking kill you. I'll find out who you are and I'll kill you, me old flower," Gilligan again snarled down the phone. The newspaper coverage of the assault infuriated Gilligan. The investigating detectives decided to question Gilligan about the incident but when they went looking for him he had gone to ground. He stayed around Dublin until September 25 when he flew to Amsterdam with Carol Rooney. Dinny, who was booked on the early morning flight, offloaded himself at the last minute and Gilligan took his seat.

He stayed in Holland for a number of weeks in the hope that the police at home would forget about the assault. He instructed Traynor to convince Guerin to drop her assault charges against him. Within a week of the incident I met with Traynor to discuss what had happened. "I told her [Veronica] not to fuck around with that man and do you see what happened? The man is mad. He feels like he is defending his family and if anyone crosses that line they will end up dead," Traynor warned me solemnly. "When Veronica arrived on his doorstep at Jessbrook it drove him ballistic. She was intruding on his part of the world. No-one ever goes near the place except he is invited and I mean that." He said he had conveyed this to Veronica but gave the impression that they had fallen out over Gilligan. I later spoke to Veronica herself about the incident. She said it had been more terrifying than when she was shot. She was happy about the way the police were handling the case but she again warned me to be careful with Traynor.

A few months later Traynor claimed that the assault had been "sorted". He said that he had offered Veronica over a hundred thousand pounds in cash on Gilligan's behalf to drop the charges. But the truth was that the courageous journalist had rejected the offer and was determined that Factory John would pay for the brutal attack. Gilligan blamed Traynor for the problem because he was still talking to Veronica. In the weeks that followed, Traynor contacted his garda handler to see was there anything Gilligan could "offer" to get himself out of the "Guerin hassle". The detective advised Traynor to urge Gilligan to give himself up and face the music, but Traynor replied that the little man was determined not to go back to prison.

On November 10 Gilligan arranged to meet with Superintendent Tom Gallagher and Chief Superintendent Jim McHugh. He was brought to Santry for questioning under section 4 of the Criminal Justice Act. Gilligan denied that he assaulted Veronica and told the detectives that he thought he must have frightened her because of the way she "flew down the driveway". "I never assaulted a woman and never will," Gilligan told the officers. He also denied that he had torn her clothes. "On the advice of my solicitor," he told them, "I have already been tried and convicted by the *Sunday Independent*. I have nothing to say." Gilligan was anxious, however, to point out that he and Geraldine were "separated". "It was a happy separation... she got everything," he smiled. A file on the case was prepared for the Director of Public Prosecutions.

Gilligan was summonsed for assault and causing criminal damage to Veronica's clothing. If convicted in the District Court, Gilligan was facing at least six months in jail. Such an enforced absence at this critical time would cause untold disruption to his burgeoning evil empire. He was determined not to go back behind bars. He had grown too big and powerful to be brought down by a woman.

On the morning Veronica drove to Gilligan's house, she also put herself in the sights of a dangerous gang. His forced leave of absence would have worrying consequences for the gang's all-important bottom line. Each month, week and day inactive in the "business" would cost obscene amounts of money. He had the international connections and the organisational skills. Without his presence the gang was in trouble and his cocky lieutenants hatched a murderous plot. There was only one option: the meddling journalist had to be destroyed.

Ten

The Untouchables

The video camera panned across paradise. Palm trees and exotic plants swayed in a mild breeze. In the background the Caribbean glistened under a blue sky. The camera zoomed back from the breathtaking scenery, past magnificent flora and manicured lawns, to be replaced on the screen with John Gilligan's grinning, sunburned face. He lifted a glass of champagne to the camera in a toast. "This is a lovely bleedin' place for a weddin', wha'? It's fuckin' beautiful it is," he declared in his thick Dublin brogue. It was March 1996 and the gang were living the high life on the island of St Lucia.

John and Geraldine Gilligan had travelled to the exotic island four thousand miles from rain-sodden Ireland, for the wedding of Brian Meehan's sister, Leslie, to an electrical engineer with no connection to gangland. Meehan's parents, Kevin and Frances, and his siblings, Brad and Vanessa, were there. Peter Mitchell, Paul Ward and three of the Walshe sisters, including Fiona and Sonia who were the girlfriends of Peter Mitchell and Brian Meehan, made up the party of fourteen. The group stayed at the Sandal's luxury resort for a week, swilling champagne, snorting cocaine, eating fine food and lounging about the pool. The Gilligans had paid seven thousand pounds in cash for the week and Brian Meehan had paid for his family's holiday. It cost him almost thirty thousand pounds.

The cherished home movie recorded the idyllic wedding. Leslie was married in a gazebo overlooking the shimmering Caribbean. Brian Meehan was the best man. He and his father Kevin looked awkward, like nightclub bouncers, in their black tuxedos. "He [Meehan] looks great. I dressed him meself. Doesn't he look great? I got him out of all those rave clothes," Gilligan commented on his lieutenant's attire. Peter Mitchell's unmistakable voice causes the staff handling the wedding ceremony to raise their eyebrows. "I have to zoom in on the bouncer [Meehan]. You'll get a job at home as a bouncer. Ya dirty fuck, ya."

The wedding party's vulgar, raucous behaviour seemed out of place on such a beautiful peaceful island. Behind the din and rude jokes, the gentle rustling of the palm trees and waves lapping on the beach nearby provided the background music for an idyllic scene bought and paid for on the proceeds of crime. Meehan was filmed signing the wedding register. "I hope that's not a fuckin' statement for the fuckin' police," Mitchell shouts. Later the camera recorded the fun around the swimming pool. Meehan and Peter Mitchell jumped into the pool with Paul Ward and began laughing and shouting for the camera. "This one's for Veronica Guerin," Meehan scoffed loudly amid cackles of laughter from everyone. "Crime doesn't pay," followed by more cackles of laughter. The crime reporter was never far from their drink and drug-soaked minds. Gilligan's Brat Pack joked with him about the impending assault charge. He was enjoying the jibes and laughed that he would win his case and never go back to prison again. Throughout the tapes Gilligan was constantly by Geraldine's side. They seemed to be the perfect loving couple and certainly did not behave as if they had been separated.

In another camera shot the wedding group sat around a hotel lounge drinking and singing songs. Gilligan sang part of the song "The Wild Rover" before forgetting the lines. Then Brad Meehan, Brian's drug-addicted criminal brother, began to sing an old country song. The lyrics could have been written with Gilligan and his henchmen in mind. "I've got everything a man could ever need. I've got dreams to dream, songs to sing in the morning, I've got a bed to hold my head and I've got eyes to watch my woman. I've got everything a man could ever need." Gilligan clapped his approval at the song. He looked smug and confident in the bosom of his mob and family, like a miniature Don Corleone. He was untouchable.

But the "Guerin problem" was never far from his thoughts or those of his gang. She had rejected an offer of compensation and was determined to pursue the assault charge. Following the incident, Gilligan had hatched an incredible plan to finally sort out the mess. He planned to kidnap Gavin O'Reilly, the son of Tony O'Reilly, the multi-millionaire proprietor of the Independent group which owned the *Sunday Independent*. Gilligan discussed the plan with

Traynor who, along with Meehan, had helped organise the Lacey kidnapping. Their lackeys in the INLA, whom they had supplied with guns, drugs and money and who had become their private little army, could be prevailed upon to help in the diabolical operation. Gavin O'Reilly, who was one of the company's directors, was to be abducted and taken to a safe house. Gilligan reckoned that it would show the newspaper executive that he meant business. The executive was to be threatened and terrorised, but not harmed. Before his release he would be instructed to convince Veronica to drop the charges; if he did not, then the O'Reilly family would be "hit" again. He would be warned not to report the matter to the police.

Traynor eventually convinced Gilligan that it wasn't a very wise course of action. He was influenced by his own sense of self preservation. Wearing his double agent hat, he even informed the detective in the Serious Crime Squad of the plot. In October 1995 an intelligence report on the information was sent to the Crime and Security Branch at Garda Headquarters. An armed surveillance squad was placed at a discreet distance around Gavin O'Reilly until the authorities were satisfied that the executive was not being watched by criminals and that the kidnapping plans were not going ahead. Gilligan's henchmen would have been more than willing to take part in what would be a very high-profile crime against one of the country's most influential families. They had no fear of the fallout from such an incident.

The gang had become the most powerful in the Dublin underworld. Their drugs empire was thriving. The distribution system organised by Charlie Bowden was working like a dream. Their Dutch suppliers were efficient and giving value for money. They had a formidable arsenal of firearms. No criminal or cop could cross them. They had all become dangerous men. They were supremely confident and cocky and even sent postcards to the police, signed "The Firm", from exotic holiday locations.

St Lucia was a welcome break from the hassle of the drugs world for Brian Meehan, Mitchell and Ward. In the month before their well-deserved break, they had been involved in two incidents with underworld rivals in Dublin. The most dramatic was the attempted murder of Martin "the Viper" Foley. The Viper had become one of the gang's smallest customers, buying a kilo of hash most weeks from Charlie Bowden. He had been given the nickname "the Viper" by Martin Cahill in the early 1990s because the General suspected him of being a police informant. Foley had been a member of the General's gang until the time of the Tango Squad investigation in 1988. His best friend, Seamus "Shavo" Hogan, had also been accused of giving the police information which led to the arrest of Cahill's brother-in-law, John Foy, when he went to collect guns for a robbery. Foley had also been a member of Gilligan's Factory Gang. But Traynor and Gilligan now hated him. Foley and Shavo Hogan had been putting pressure on Traynor for money they reckoned they were owed from the sale of the Beit art collection. Traynor, a born coward, began to fear a hit from Foley and Hogan. Something had to be done about the Viper.

Forty-six-year-old Foley had a formidable reputation as an underworld hard man. He had 37 convictions ranging from crimes of violence to road traffic offences. Foley was infamous as the criminal with nine lives. In 1984, in the wake of the O'Connor's jewellery robbery, he had been abducted by a four-man IRA active service unit. Foley was rescued and the Provos arrested when armed detectives surrounded the gang as they tried to make their getaway. In December 1995 the Viper was shot and injured in Rialto, Dublin, by a south side drug dealer in a row over a mutual girlfriend. Foley, a fitness fanatic, made a full recovery even though he still had a bullet in his chest.

Foley had an incredible propensity for irritating people. As part of his campaign against Traynor and his gang, he began spreading rumours that they were involved in heroin dealing. Criminals are notorious gossips. In January Brian Meehan was called to a meeting with the IRA and questioned about the rumours. The Provos, who had taken money from the Gilligan gang before, said they could not turn a blind eye if the gang were selling smack. They told Meehan the information had come from Foley, who wasn't one of their favourite people. Meehan convinced the Provos that the gang was not involved in heroin. Later, at a meeting in the lockup at Greenmount Industrial Estate, he told the other gang members what had happened. He suggested they kill Foley. Everyone agreed.

On January 29 Charlie Bowden got a call from Meehan telling him to meet him at the car park of Bridget Burke's pub in Tallaght.

Meehan and Ward were waiting for him. The three went to the Jewish cemetery on the Oldcourt Road. Bowden and Meehan took out an Agram 2000 machine pistol and a .45 automatic pistol, part of the arsenal of weapons carefully packed with the drugs shipments by the gang's Dutch associates. It had arrived on January 15. The Agram is a deadly, close-quarter street-fighting weapon manufactured in Croatia. Agram is the old name of the city now known as Zagreb. Its design was based on the mechanism of the German Heckler and Koch machine pistol, the MP 5, which is the favourite weapon of specialist police and army units throughout the world. The Agram is intended for use within twenty metres and has been the weapon of choice of assassins working for the Russian Mafia.

Meehan asked Bowden to show him how to use the weapon. Bowden fitted the silencer to the Agram and put a plastic bag on a bush in a field at the back of the graveyard. Meehan fired the full magazine at the bag, hitting it only a few times. He also tried the .45. Happy that they were in working order, Bowden put the weapons in a black bag and brought them to the Greenmount lockup. On Thursday, February 1, Meehan called Bowden and arranged to meet him at Paul Ward's house in Walkinstown. Meehan was to meet Foley around 7 p.m. on the pretext of collecting drug money from him. He and Ward intended ambushing the Viper.

At 6.55 p.m. Foley left his home on Cashel Avenue in Crumlin and began reversing his car away from the house to turn onto Captain's Road. Meehan and Ward were waiting for him on the corner of Cashel Avenue in a stolen car. Foley spotted them and paused for a moment. Ward, who was driving, pulled out on the road. Ward and Meehan got out and ran towards Foley's car. The two gangsters opened fire with the Agram and the pistol, peppering the car with bullets. Foley reversed up the road with the two shooters after him on foot. One of the bullets hit him in a finger. Foley abandoned the car and jumped across the side wall of a garden. Meehan, still firing his machine pistol, ran after Foley. Ward had thrown the automatic pistol to Meehan as a back-up weapon while he went back to the getaway car.

Foley burst through the back door of a house and turned the lights off. "Call the police! They're after me," Foley yelled at the stunned occupants of the house. The family, a husband, wife and their teenage daughter, were terrified. They ran to get out of their home. When they opened the front door, Meehan came racing towards them, wearing a balaclava and holding the automatic in both hands. "Where's the fucker? Get out of the way!" he shouted. The family ran out into the street. Ward by now was reversing the getaway car up and down the avenue. The woman was screaming that someone was being murdered in her home. Ward shouted over to her to keep quiet: "Shut the fuck up! There's no-one fuckin' goin' near youse!"

At the same time Foley had spotted Meehan in the doorway and raced upstairs. Meehan opened fire again, this time hitting his target once in the back. Other bullets went through a bathroom door. Foley jumped through a glass window in a back bedroom, landing on an extension roof. He got off the roof and jumped into the garden of the house next door. Meehan climbed on to the roof and fired more shots at Foley as he ran through several gardens in a desperate bid to escape. He burst through the back door of another house and bolted it. He ran through the house, locked the front door and phoned for the police and an ambulance.

Fortunately for the Viper, Meehan was a poor shot and had fired off the full magazine on the machine pistol. The .45 automatic pistol had jammed. Meehan abandoned his murder bid and calmly walked out onto the street and into the car. Ward drove off and headed back to his house on Walkinstown Avenue. Charlie Bowden, Mitchell and Shay Ward were waiting for them in Ward's house. They were listening to the police radio communications on a scanner. As soon as they heard reports of the gun attack, Shay Ward opened the garage at the back of the house. Meehan and Paul Ward arrived within seconds. They were high on adrenaline. Meehan was cursing about the weapon that had jammed. He said that he had hit Foley in the back and was wondering if he was dead.

But the Viper had survived yet again. It was his third scrape with death. Four years later he would be the victim of a fourth attack in September 2000. Although shot and injured a number of times, he also survived that attempt on his life. In the months after the incident, the Viper discovered why he had been shot. Amazingly, he and Meehan effectively kissed and made up. After that it was business as usual and Meehan continued supplying Foley.

A week before the trip to St Lucia, Meehan and Mitchell were questioned about another shooting incident, this time involving a drug dealer who worked for a notorious criminal called Peter Joseph Judge, alias "the Psycho". Judge, from Finglas, was one of the underworld's most feared killers who had more than earned his chilling nickname. He had two former associates abducted, tortured and murdered in rows over drug shipments. One of his victims, William Jock Corbally, had been murdered and buried in an unmarked grave by Judge. Everyone in gangland feared "the Psycho", that is, everyone except Gilligan's untouchables.

On the night of February 28, 1996 Brian Meehan fired two shots outside a north-side pub as a warning to Judge's dealer. He had begun selling drugs in the north inner-city area which Mitchell considered to be his turf. The encroachment on Fatso's territory rekindled an old dispute. Two years earlier the dealer had shot Fatso in the same pub, causing him minor injuries. Peace was restored on that first occasion when the dealer agreed to pay Mitchell substantial compensation. The incident was never reported to the police. Following the second shooting, officers at Store Street station were tipped off that P.J. Judge and the dealer were planning to murder Meehan. The two criminals had obtained a high-powered motorbike and were carrying sawn-off shotguns. Judge had been cruising the area looking for Meehan. To avert a bloodbath, detectives raided the homes of the dealer, Judge, Meehan and Mitchell, searching for weapons. Nothing was found. The hoods were left under no illusion that the police had found out about their feud. They decided to postpone "straightening out" the situation. St Lucia was for them a well-deserved break. When they returned to Ireland, the violence was to continue.

On April 1 Johnny Reddin, a drug dealer and underworld heavy, was sitting in the Blue Lion pub on Parnell Street in the city centre. The 42-year-old was then facing a charge of causing grievous bodily harm leading to the death of a teenager, Sean McNeill, in a north-city nightclub. Reddin was also an associate of Paul Ward's and sold drugs for the Gilligan gang. As he sipped a pint at the counter, a man wearing a peaked cap walked up to Reddin and produced a pistol. "Here, Johnny, take it out of that," he said, and then shot him once into the head. The gunman ordered the other customers to shut up and lie on the floor. He ran out the door and got away on a motorbike.

Following the murder of Veronica Guerin, the Lucan Investigation Team obtained intelligence which led them to believe that a member of the Gilligan gang was responsible for the Reddin hit. Underworld sources told officers that Paul Ward, in particular, was "very annoyed" with other gang members about it. Senior and reliable police sources have confirmed to this writer their suspicions that Reddin's killer was a member of the Gilligan gang. It is unclear, however, whether the hit man was working freelance at the time or if he was working on the orders of the gang. Although investigating officers recommended that a known criminal be taken in, no-one was ever charged with the offence.

As a result of intelligence gleaned during the Guerin investigation, the same sources believe that two members of the gang also gunned down Cork criminal Michael Crinnion in the spring of 1995. It has been claimed that Paul Ward and Brian Meehan did the hit as a favour to a Cork gang who were feuding with Crinnion's gang. They pointed out that in the cases of the Crinnion and Shanahan murders and the Foley shooting, the involvement of Gilligan's gang was not known until the Guerin investigation, the most wide-ranging nation-wide trawl ever carried out into gangland.

The gang members were growing ever more arrogant. Instead of keeping their heads down, they were openly flouting their criminal success. On one occasion Gilligan and his Brat Pack were out on the town in an up-market hotel on the south side. The hoods regularly hired a large room for "parties" in the hotel. These were basically orgies of sex, drink and drugs with prostitutes hired for the event. Gilligan and his pals were downstairs drinking at the bar. As usual, they were boisterous, aggressive and flashing money about. A detective walked into the bar for a drink. He had a bulge under his jacket and Meehan began abusing him for carrying his gun. The policeman ignored the jibes and ordered a beer. As his glass stood on the counter, Gilligan took off his expensive gold Rolex watch and slid it in the direction of the cop. It clanged as it collided with the glass. The detective looked down and the watch and said nothing. Gilligan shouted at him: "Here, take the fuckin' thing, that's worth more than you'll earn in a year." His Brat Pack cackled with laughter.

The detective shoved the watch back up the counter and left.

Two days after the Reddin murder Brian Meehan was arrested in the early hours of the morning by uniformed officers from the Bridewell garda station. He had been at the hood's funeral that day and had been drinking. He was in a belligerent mood when the cops stopped to talk to him on the street. Gardaí are entitled to stop and search known criminals under the Misuse of Drugs Act. It was and is a statute regularly used for the purposes of gleaning intelligence. The officers took Meehan to the station to be searched for drugs.

On the way Meehan taunted a female officer, calling her a lesbian and telling her: "You fancy my arse." When Garda Joe O'Connor told him to behave himself, Meehan threatened him. "I will get you, your wife and family. You think you're a big man now, but you will not be so big the next time I meet you with a bally [balaclava]." Once at the station Meehan was taken to a custody room for strip search. In front of Garda O'Connor Meehan began handling his penis and asked the astonished officer: "Do you like men with big cocks?" Meehan then began masturbating and turned around, grabbing his buttocks and exposing his anus. "Maybe you fancy me arse instead." Meehan turned around and resumed masturbating. "Do you want a repeat performance?" he asked before being told to put back on his clothes.

Gardaí found over six hundred pounds in cash in Meehan's pockets, which they seized for forensic examination. Meehan told the officers to keep it. "Youse fuckers need it more than I do. Give it to the police benevolent fund. Youse are a bunch of fucking idiots working and paying tax. I earn more in a week than you earn in a month," he sneered at them. Then he turned his attention on the desk sergeant and called him a "shite bucket". He was charged with causing a breach of the peace and indecent behaviour. Meehan couldn't have cared less.

Sometime in March Gilligan and Meehan were contacted by an underworld associate to help organise the springing of Thomas "Bomber" Clarke from a prison van. Bomber Clarke was a ruthless, violent criminal who had been involved in serious crime from an early age. He specialised in armed robbery and was an old friend of Meehan and Ward's. He had also served time in prison with Gilligan.

At twenty-seven years of age he had notched up twenty-two convictions in Ireland. In 1987 he had been given five and seven-year sentences for two armed robberies. When in January 1993 he was due to appear in the Dublin Circuit Court on another robbery charge, Clarke fled to England. He lived in Leeds and continued to rob banks.

On May 20, 1994 Clarke was convicted at Leeds Crown Court on three counts of armed robbery and sentenced to nine years. In October 1995 he escaped from prison and returned to Ireland. In December he was tracked down and arrested in County Kerry. He was initially questioned about the murder of Christy Delaney, a former member of Gilligan's Factory Gang, but was convicted on the outstanding robbery charge and sentenced to five years of imprisonment. While in custody he was charged with another building society heist and had to make a number of appearances at remand hearings in the District Court.

Gilligan and his gang had no problem doing Bomber a favour. After all, they were untouchable and a daring act would raise respect for them in criminal quarters. The police had received intelligence that Bomber Clarke was planning an escape with the help of unknown criminal associates. On a number of occasions the Emergency Response Unit (ERU) had shadowed the prison van ferrying Clarke between Portlaoise Prison and the District Court in Dublin. As a result, the break-out operation was called off.

On April 25 Clarke was being transported for another remand hearing. Brian Meehan, Paul Ward and another criminal from Clondalkin planned to spring him on the way to court. Peter Mitchell was to provide a back-up car for Clarke's getaway. A garda driver and four prison officers accompanied Clarke in the prison van from Portlaoise. As it drove past the village of Rathcoole on its way to Dublin, the three hoods followed the van in a stolen 5 series BMW. As the van approached the junction of the Naas Road and Boot Road at Clondalkin, the gang struck. This was the same location where Veronica Guerin would be shot two months later. The BMW suddenly drove into the van's path, blocking a possible escape. Two men jumped out of the car and ran to the van. One had bolt cutters and the other a handgun. While his partner broke the van window, the gunman ordered the prison officers to open Clarke's cuffs.

Bomber Clarke climbed out through the broken window and jumped into the car. The escapees sped off.

As a major manhunt began, Clarke was brought to the apartment owned by Gilligan's mistress, Carol Rooney, near Celbridge in County Kildare. Within days Gilligan had Clarke smuggled out of the country on a container truck to Holland. There he was given a safe house by Johnny Wildhagen, Rahman's henchman. Gilligan and Meehan sprang Clarke to prove to the rest of the underworld that they could do whatever they liked. It was also speculated that, in return for their "kindness", Clarke was to murder George "The Penguin" Mitchell. Mitchell was also an important player in the international drugs market, although a lot more discreet than Gilligan and his "Neanderthals". If the Penguin was out of the way, the Gilligan gang could take over his substantial slice of the action, dramatically increasing the size of their own operation. Gilligan was still trying to impress his Dutch counterparts and he offered Clarke's services as a hit man.

In any event, Bomber Clarke was arrested by Dutch police on suspicion of staking out houses for the purpose of carrying out "burglaries". He was caught loitering near the home of one of Rahman's underworld rivals. In April 1997 Clarke pleaded guilty to the additional armed robbery charge which they had proffered while he was in custody and was sentenced. When he is released in 2007, Clarke will be extradited back to Britain to serve the rest of the prison sentence he escaped in 1995.

In the meantime, business was brisk for Gilligan and the money was flowing in so fast that the gangsters could barely cope. In the first four months of 1996, up to the time of the springing of Clarke, the gang imported 3,247 kilos of hash. The figure is based on detailed analysis of shipping records conducted by the Lucan Investigation Team. Gilligan and Traynor's cut was estimated at two and a half million pounds, while the five gang members each "earned" one hundred and thirty thousand. Records from the Bureau de Change in Amsterdam showed that over one million Irish pounds had been exchanged.

In fact, the gang had become such an important client to Simon Rahman's operation that they even began returning sub-standard hash. Between August 11, 1995 and September 5, 1996, the gang returned over eight hundred kilos, which was described as "diesel". The drugs were repacked in wooden crates by Charlie Bowden and Shay Ward and shipped out with the help of John Dunne in Cork. The gang also became the single biggest supplier of drugs to Northern Ireland. A young, Newry-based drug dealer called Brendan "Speedy" Fegan began buying up to one hundred kilos per week from Meehan and the gang. Fegan was introduced to the mob by Paddy Farrell, another notorious drug baron, who had brought Fegan into the business. Fegan supplied loyalist and republican paramilitary gangs with ecstacy, cocaine and hash.

As the operation grew more powerful, the gang needed to cover its tracks. They had so much money that they could buy anything: guns, drugs, women, cars, houses and holidays. By the middle of 1996 they had also bought a cop. John "Buffalo" O'Neill was thirty-one years old when he met Paul "Hippo" Ward and was recruited as an agent for the Gilligan gang. Having a man on the inside would be of immense use in developing the evil empire.

O'Neill, from Ballyfermot in Dublin, had known Paul Ward and Meehan growing up. Unlike them he had opted for a life on the other side of the thin blue line and joined the Garda Síochána in November 1985. The married father-of-three had spent his career as a uniformed officer based in Tallaght and Crumlin. A keen GAA football player, non-drinker and non-smoker, he was considered by some to be an enthusiastic policeman with an impressive arrest record. To others in the force and in the criminal community, his enthusiasm was rather excessive. Sadly, John O'Neill, hero cop, had a weakness which would destroy all of the respect he had earned.

Friends and former colleagues recalled how O'Neill had always wanted to give his family everything that he hadn't had growing up in deprived circumstances. O'Neill bought a nice home for his family and lavishly furnished it. He extravagantly splashed out money, buying a four-wheel-drive jeep for himself and a brand new car for his wife's birthday. He bought his children the most expensive toys that money could buy, including small motorbikes for his sons. But it was all done on a garda's basic wages.

O'Neill soon found himself in debt to the tune of a hundred thousand pounds. Apart from a mortgage, he also had four Credit Union loans. Buffalo had worked as a bouncer for a criminal associate of Ward's, who used the cover of a nightclub manager. The manager was also close to Mitchell and Meehan. O'Neill was desperate for cash and approached the manager to ask if he knew anyone who could loan him money. The manager was delighted to oblige and contacted Hippo Ward.

In December 1995 O'Neill took a thousand five hundred pounds in cash from Ward in the car park of the Red Cow public house on the western edge of Dublin. Ward told his new "friend" that he might be wanted to help sort out the odd summons or warrant. Shortly before Christmas, Ward gave O'Neill another thousand pounds in the car park of another pub. Rather than pay off some of his debts, O'Neill spent the cash on presents for Christmas. In January 1996 Ward asked O'Neill to "pull" (quash) two summonses for a criminal friend of his from Drimnagh, by taking them out of the list for hearing in court. O'Neill had the documents taken from the list.

In May O'Neill was in need of more cash. This time Ward paid him two thousand pounds for pulling two arrest warrants for an associate of the gang. O'Neill took the warrants from his station and showed them to Hippo, who paid him another five hundred pounds. A short time later he pulled two arrest warrants for another gang associate from Ronanstown. This time O'Neill tore up the warrants in front of Ward and received two thousand pounds for the effort. Ward also arranged for the Buffalo to "find" three kilos of cannabis to make him look good with his bosses. He later had summonses for motoring offences pulled for Paul Ward, Vanessa Meehan and Brian Meehan. O'Neill was getting in above his head and out of control.

Ward and the other members of the gang liked to brag that they had now bought their very own policeman. Gilligan liked the idea. A bent cop was a valuable asset for a drugs gang. Early in 1996 Gilligan and Traynor discussed his Traynor's relationship with the detective in the Serious Crime Squad. Traynor claimed that the cop was working for him, although the policeman had never asked nor taken any money from Traynor. Traynor neglected to tell his boss that he had been giving the cop information about the underworld. The two hoodlums agreed that they should try to put the detective on the payroll. Traynor reckoned that the officer was vulnerable at the time because he had been experiencing personal difficulties.

During one of their frequent meetings, the Coach put his dodgy proposition to the detective. He and Gilligan were prepared to give him a quarter of a million pounds in cash if he would leave the gardaí and begin working as the gang's "security adviser". Although such an offer was tempting, the detective turned it down. Traynor had miscalculated the situation. What he did not know was that the mild-mannered and easygoing policeman had been passing on every piece of information he had picked up from the con man to his own intelligence section. He had also compiled the first major dossier outlining the activities of the Gilligan gang and recommended that action be taken. It would be too little, too late.

Eleven

The Bagman

Russell John Patrick Warren was an ideal bag man for Gilligan's gang. He was not a career criminal, was clean-cut and did what he was told. Warren was a wimpish, cowardly character and easily manipulated. He had no qualms about making money dishonestly, as long as he didn't have to dirty his hands with a serious crime and there was no aggravation involved. Russell Warren was a "quick buck" merchant. He was no match for a bully like Gilligan and he soon found himself under the little man's control. Once inside Gilligan's organisation, he was too terrified to contemplate leaving. The only way out was in a body bag. Russell Warren became John Gilligan's glorified slave.

Warren was introduced to Gilligan's criminal organisation through a friend, "the Bookie". He had an industrial cleaning company which cleaned out newly built houses and apartment blocks for construction firms in preparation for sale. One of Warren's customers recalled his work: "He was the most useless man I ever had on a site. He was a nice bloke but you always had to go over his work a second time."

Warren had been dabbling and making money from the smuggled cigarettes racket which was one of Gilligan's peripheral activities. By now Dinny had opted out of delivering and laundering cash for Gilligan and the boss needed a new, reliable bag man. Dinny later claimed that he had received a visit from the IRA warning him about his relationship with Factory John. He also claimed that he had fallen out with him. The Bookie, too, was beginning to take a back seat and concentrate on a new bookie business. He was worried at how "heavy" Gilligan had become in the drug business. He could see how the money and power had turned the little man into a dangerous monster.

At first the Bookie asked Warren to count bags of cash which he claimed were the proceeds of Gilligan's betting and cigarette-smuggling activities. After some time counting and sorting the cash, the Bookie asked Warren to fly to Holland to deliver the money to Gilligan. He would be paid five hundred pounds for each trip. Warren's first flight to Holland was on January 11, 1996. In Schipol airport he handed over a package to Gilligan and Martin Baltus and took the return flight to Dublin. Eventually Warren also took part in exchanging bags of cash at the Bureau de Change in Centraal Station, which by then had been used to exchange at least seven million pounds for the gang. Records showed that he exchanged seventy thousand pounds on February 7. In twenty-two trips over the next seven months Warren personally exchanged another £2.2 million. Records also showed that the Firm's new "accountant" exchanged a further £1.7 million while in the company of two other bagmen. He had become an essential cog in the gang's operation.

In the meantime Gilligan had brought bad luck to Simon Rahman's organisation. Early in 1995 the Judicial Police in Antwerp, Belgium, received an investigation report from their money-laundering unit concerning Thomas and Mariette Gorst. The report outlined five suspect money-laundering transactions at the KB Securities bank in Antwerp which had been carried out by Mariette Gorst between November 1994 and January 1995 on behalf of Gilligan. Large amounts of Irish currency had been exchanged for Belgian francs. The police began to investigate. On October 5, 1995 Thomas Gorst and his wife Mariette were arrested at their home in Berchem by officers from the Judicial Police under Belgian money-laundering laws.

During questioning about the transactions, Mariette Gorst said that she had changed the money for a professional Irish gambler called "John Gillon". During her detention she described what she did for "Gillon".

"Gillon tells me that on a given day the money would be here and that I should go to the bureau de change. I select the bureau de change. I wait outside the door and somebody approaches me to give me money to change. Sometimes it's a woman, other times it's a man. I presume that Gillon gave that person a description of me. The money is in a bag. Without knowing how much I am taking inside, I go into the bureau de change and change the money into

Belgian francs. The first time I don't know what kind of currency I was changing. After changing it, I gave the money back to the person who gave it to me. After receiving the money that person vanished. I don't know where. I can't put a name to that person. When you [the police] ask me why Gillon was unable to do it himself, my answer was that he was short of time. Gillon needed money here for gambling, as a professional gambler. I also heard he wanted to buy a golf course. The money originated in casinos and from Gillon's dealing in horses."

Thomas Gorst endorsed his wife's lies and described "Gillon" as a stud-farm owner in Ireland. "I have nothing to do with drug trafficking or money laundering. Gillon said he would have exchanged the money himself but it was a better rate for a Belgian national to do it. I am sure the money was for a legitimate purpose. I have never seen Gillon since January of 1995," the international drug trafficker told his interrogators two years later. In the same interview he implied that his wife and Gilligan had been having an affair. "I first met Gillon in a bar in Antwerp with Mariette. I know that John and Mariette saw each other four or five times after that. To what extent this was a friendly relationship or something more I can't tell you."

In early December the Judicial Police, through Interpol, sent a text message to the gardaí in Dublin requesting assistance in identifying a "John Gillon or McGillon". On December 7 Garda Headquarters replied: "Based on details supplied by you there is no such person known to our records. There is a person named Gilligan who has numerous convictions for larceny and burglary offences. He is considered dangerous. In order to confirm identity can you supply a set of fingerprints of the subject."

In the absence of proper identification, "De Kleine" John had narrowly avoided serious attention. There was no more follow-up by the Irish police. The Judicial Police, however, charged the Gorsts with money laundering. On January 17, 1997 they were both given six-month prison sentences for the offences. But Gilligan's days of remaining anonymous on the Continent were slowly coming to an end.

In Holland, Baltus had been cleared of the firearms charge from his arrest in March 1995. The State could not prove he had prior knowledge that the bag he had been given on that date contained the Agram machine pistol. In the meantime, he continued to work for Rahman. In April 1996 Baltus took delivery of a bag containing thirty thousand pounds from Russell Warren and exchanged it in the bureau de change. It was the last recorded occasion that Baltus exchanged money for the Gilligan gang.

Around the same time, Gilligan began supplying Rahman with forged Irish driving licences and passports. Forged documents are the stock and trade of international drug trafficking and an Irish passport tends to arouse less suspicion at the point of entry in most countries, especially the drug-producing countries. Rahman was involved in widespread fraud rackets and appreciated the quality of the Irish documents and dollars. These were being churned out by Dutchie Holland through his printing business in Dublin. The counterfeit documents were the only saleable goods that Holland had produced since setting up his company. Attempts to print legitimate publications had failed, but the business was useful for hiding his drug money. Holland was also printing hundreds of counterfeit dollar bills. Other documents were being sourced through the gang's Northern Ireland and English underworld links.

The forged documents could be sold or bartered for guns or drugs. A typical international drug trafficker could have as many as fifty passports. Rahman's violent sidekick, Johnny Wildhagen, used a number of Gilligan's fake Irish passports and licences to travel between Europe and Africa. On one of the passports he was identified as Peter McMann. The forgeries were a means for Gilligan of developing his reputation with the other major players. Forgery, he said, was just another dimension to his huge criminal empire. Gilligan had tried to model himself on Rahman, the sophisticated international criminal. By now he was on first-name terms with some of the heaviest criminals in Europe. In his own mind, Gilligan was the Mr Big they all respected. The psychotic little godfather harboured ambitions to become the big Don no one could touch. He and his mob talked incessantly about killing people. In Holland and Belgium he acted like his hero, the Italian-American godfather John Gotti, but he was loathed and mistrusted by Rahman and his cronies. They kept a safe distance from "De Kliene". When he was eventually brought down, his departure from the scene was hardly felt by organised crime in Europe.

Rahman and Baltus had been particularly impressed with the forged dollars and began passing them off through various international contacts. Rahman used them as part payment to African and Eastern European gangs for drugs and other contraband shipments. Gilligan posted samples of the dollars to the Bilderberg Europa Hotel in The Hague's coastal resort of Scheveningen. The envelopes containing the fake bills were addressed for the attention of Simon Rahman and were collected by the addressee without a hitch. On April 10 another sample consignment of thirty $20 bills was posted to the hotel. The phony cash was concealed in a white envelope within an outer brown envelope. When Rahman didn't turn up, Carol Rooney made several phone calls to the hotel inquiring if the envelope had been collected yet. The hotel management became suspicious and called the police. On April 18 Rahman received a call from Gilligan reminding him about the envelope. Rahman asked Baltus to collect it for him. When Baltus arrived in the hotel he was arrested. It was discovered that similar notes had also been found in the home of Baltus' son several months earlier.

As part of the follow-up investigation, Simon Rahman's home was searched and more of the counterfeit notes were found in a press. Rahman calmly informed the police that Baltus had given him the notes. In a statement the drug trafficker claimed: "Martin Baltus gave me those notes. I knew they were counterfeit and I threw them in the direction of the waste paper basket. When I threw them they must have missed the basket and ended up in the press." Two other criminal associates from Suriname were also arrested. In one of the calls which led to the arrests, Carol Rooney had left an Irish telephone number for the hotel staff to call in the event that the envelope remained uncollected. On May 30 an official request was sent to Dublin to trace the telephone number. It led back to Rooney and Gilligan. The Irish connection was about to be exposed.

The investigation into Rahman now also touched on Johnny Wildhagen. Rahman and his organisation considered Wildhagen a major danger. His cocaine habit combined with his violent nature made him a loose cannon. He was mad enough to spill the beans not only on Rahman but on several other arms and drug traffickers, including the "hash farmer" and Havid. One day a deliveryman called to Wildhagen's apartment at Diemanstraat in The Hague. Wildhagen appeared at the door and pointed a .357 magnum at the deliveryman, who almost had a heart attack. Wildhagen was in the throes of a coke-induced paranoia spell and looked like a creature out of a horror movie. He was wearing only pants, his long, greasy hair was draped across his face and shoulders, and his eyes seemed to be popping out of his head.

John Wildhagen, alias Peter McMann, was an accident waiting to happen. When the Dutch police went looking for him, Wildhagen had disappeared. Europal and Interpol were also alerted. Several months later, when the police discovered that he was using Gilligan's false passports, searches for a Peter McMann or Peter De Mann led nowhere. The whereabouts of Johnny Wildhagen are still unknown. He is believed to have disappeared because he was a threat to his own and possibly even been murdered. It was a course of action that Gilligan would wholeheartedly approve.

Exactly a month before the arrest of Baltus, the attentions of the Dutch authorities had also been drawn to Gilligan by his ham-fisted methods of laundering cash. On March 18 Gilligan, Meehan and the Bookie visited the Scheveningen Casino. Meehan and Gilligan exchanged 250,000 guilders, the equivalent of eighty thousand pounds, in 1,000 guilder notes into tokens at various gambling tables. None of the three played and after an hour Meehan went to the cashier's desk. He asked to have the tokens cashed and the money transferred by the casino to a Dutch bank account.

Security staff in the casino had been watching the trio on security cameras and saw that they had not played at any of the tables. The money was not profits of gambling. The cashier informed Meehan that the money could not be transferred and had to explain the legal situation on a number of times. It was hard getting through to Meehan. Detecting a problem, Meehan then asked that the money be lodged in the casino account. The request was also refused. Only money won while gambling in the casino can be lodged under Dutch law, Meehan was told again.

By transferring or lodging the money, Meehan was hoping to have documentary proof that the cash had come from gambling and was therefore legitimate. Gilligan had done the same thing on a number of occasions in the past. He also had his cherished batch of bookies cheques that he kept for whenever the police or customs stopped him. His lieutenant had been indiscreet. Gilligan and Meehan became agitated and aggressive at the refusal. They had no respect for the laws in any country. Had the casino been in Dublin or Cork, the pair would have adopted their normal approach and threatened to murder the staff and burn the place to the ground. To them there was only one law, gang law. But this was Holland and they were not on home turf.

In the company of several burly security officers Meehan's tokens were cashed and the money given back to him. Unlike most other customers, they left angry that they still had their money. The Neanderthals, as Rahman described them, through their sheer arrogance and stupidity, had attracted avoidable attention to themselves. The casino later reported the incident to the Dutch Office for the Disclosure of Unusual Transactions (MOT). The money-laundering agency began investigating the backgrounds of Meehan and Gilligan and scrutinising their Dutch links and financial affairs in Holland.

The Dutch authorities had been given the video footage of the three Irish men in the casino. Before the end of April they had contacted the police in Dublin informing them of the casino incident and the information was passed to the fledgling Money Laundering Unit at Harcourt Square. The unit, which was then part of the Garda Bureau of Fraud Investigation (GBFI), was a forerunner of the Money Laundering Unit and the Criminal Assets Bureau. The MLU were told that if they required the tape for evidential purposes, they should request it through official channels within a certain number of days. When the Dutch did not hear from the Irish, the tape was erased in compliance with the law. When the gardaí eventually went looking for the tape, they were informed that the film had been deleted. The Irish were beginning to learn the international game the hard way. In future they would have to be quicker off the mark.

Nevertheless, the events in Holland in March and April and the arrests of the Gorsts in Belgium the previous year would eventually provide vital evidence to help smash the Gilligan empire following the murder of Veronica Guerin. Also in April, Thomas Gorst's brother, Eric, was arrested by British police when they swooped on his drug distribution network. He was caught taking delivery of hundreds of kilos of hash. It had been shipped from Holland in large cardboard boxes purporting to contain machine parts. This arrest again led back to Holland and Simon Rahman. He was already known to the British authorities. The pieces of the international crime jigsaw were gradually coming together.

Back in Dublin, serious crime had spiraled, especially gangland murders, and morale in the force was at its lowest. The drug trade was flourishing everywhere. The outgoing Commissioner, Paddy Culligan, had worked hard during his tenure to stop the rot within the force. He decided that it was time to reassess the organisation's response to the sophisticated and pernicious underworld which had begun to emerge. The gardaí had, like their European colleagues, realised that crime was no longer confined by national borders. In order to catch the bad guys, the authorities would have to begin working with agencies throughout the world and use the latest technology available. John Gilligan, Georgie Mitchell and the rest of the big Irish mobs had already gone international. The gardaí were playing catch-up with the criminals, but at least it was a start. Circumstances were slowly beginning to change for the worse for Gilligan and his ilk.

Culligan had little time for the media and preferred to remain low key. Much of the work he did went unnoticed outside the police and, indeed, to many of those inside it. He is credited by his former colleagues for laying the foundations on which the force could be restructured by his successors. One of the key strategies was to promote the best people and appoint them in areas where their talents could be fully utilised. In order to achieve this, he had to loosen the link between the force and politics. For too long the gardaí had been used as a political football by government Ministers who insisted on influencing promotions. Certain Ministers had ensured that potentially embarrassing investigations were ignored by having a safe pair of hands in the right place. Good officers through the years had been forced to sit on their hands while crime thrived because those in power were not interested in changing the laws. This was most likely the result of fears among some decision-makers that wide-ranging laws on corruption could one day catch them out as well. The old, true story of the garda officer finding a politician in the pub drinking after hours summed up the relationship: "Do you want a pint, Guard, or a transfer?" Culligan was adamant that politicians would no longer decide who was promoted to the upper echelons of the force. Two officers of the new breed were Tony Hickey and Kevin Carty.

On his promotion Chief Superintendent, Kevin Carty had been in charge of the Central Detective Unit (CDU) before being tasked with organising the new Garda National Drug Unit (GNDU). A secretive Special Branch intelligence officer for most of his career, Carty had swapped chasing terrorists for drug traffickers. It was a whole new ball game. A bravery award winner, Carty had a major interest in drug crime. He had been chairman of the Drugs and Organised Crime Group during Ireland's earlier stint as European President. The body initiated far-reaching cross-border, anti-crime measures.

The GNDU would be a national and international unit. When he moved to the CDU in late 1994 Carty and his second-in-command, Det. Supt Austin McNally, set up a number of operations to target major criminals. One important area that had been largely overlooked for several years was the gathering of intelligence on organised crime, or what is termed "crime ordinary". The lack of intelligence was one of the main reasons why a thug like John Gilligan was able to become such a dangerous gangland threat.

In their first months McNally and Carty notched up a number of notable successes. One of those complex operations was the targeting of George "the Penguin" Mitchell's organisation. Thanks to sources like Traynor and the front page of the newspapers, the public had become familiar with his face and work. Although the Penguin himself escaped the net, a huge ecstasy factory capable of turning out millions of pounds worth of drugs was broken, along with the people Mitchell hired to make and distribute the stuff. Mickey Boyle, a convicted kidnapper who worked as Mitchell's hit man, was shot and arrested in London while trying to murder East London villain Tony Brindle in 1995. The Dublin team played a pivotal role in the operation. There was also the Urlingford drug sting operation. Carty's undercover people unloaded over a hundred tonnes of hashish off a trawler on the south coast, drove it to Urlingford and then "seized" it. Mitchell, a Dublin sidekick called John "The Manager" Noonan and a major U.S. drug trafficker with

Mafia links had organised the huge deal. Carty's people made up for their failure to catch the m,ain players when Noonan was later caught with ecstasy and jailed.

When Carty moved to GNDU, Tony Hickey (who was now also a Chief Superintendent), was given command of CDU. Hickey's brief was to restructure the existing unit into an FBI-style, crime-fighting organisation called the National Bureau of Criminal Investigation. The NBCI would provide a large team of experienced detectives to work on serious crime cases throughout the country. The Bureau would also provide expertise and extra manpower to local detective units. It was a revamped modern version of the old Technical Bureau. NBCI would also collate valuable intelligence on organised crime. Hickey was an expert on organised crime and all its dazzling personalities.

At the same time, Traynor and Gilligan were coming to notice. Traynor's sudden success in the second-hand car business and his newfound wealth was an intense source of interest to the police on the ground. Gilligan's attack on Veronica Guerin, the subsequent death threats he made against her and the publicity afterwards were putting the little man in the limelight. Then there was a flood of reports coming into headquarters from exasperated officers wondering, like Guerin, how Gilligan could afford such a mansion and equestrian centre, not to mention the racehorse. The intelligence gathered by the detective dealing with Traynor also outlined suspicions that the pair were involved in drugs and guns.

In April Traynor had beaten up and threatened a nightclub owner. In a bizarre twist following the incident, Veronica acted as a go-between to encourage the owner to drop the charges against her source, the very same source who would be responsible for her attempted murder. Across town Meehan and Mitchell were arrogantly making fun of the police and bragging about the money they were making. It was impossible to ignore them any longer. Action had to be taken.

In late April Carty put together Operation Pineapple. The GNDU, with some assistance from Hickey's people at the CDU, were the main players in the investigation which was designed to compile information on the gang's membership, their wealth and criminal activities. A trawl through garda reports put Gilligan in the company of Traynor, Meehan and Mitchell on several occasions. Then there was the English police investigation which caught Gilligan on tape organising a deal with other drug dealers in Brighton and the cash seizures in Dublin and Holyhead. The investigation was to include other police units and representatives of the Customs and the Revenue. Nora Owen, the then Justice Minister, had been drafting legislation to organise a united, multi-disciplinary offensive against organised crime. She was anxious that old rivalries be forgotten.

Intelligence reports and requests for assistance were arriving on Carty's desk about Irish links to organised crime syndicates in Europe. The information was being relayed through Europol, the relatively new official law-enforcement organisation for the European Union. Consisting of officers from forces throughout the E.U., including Ireland, it had been set up after the Maastricht Treaty in 1992 with the objective of pooling police resources and intelligence. Carty had built up good contacts with European forces through his involvement in anti-terrorism and his stint in E.U. policing. The main bulk of the intelligence came from Holland where the MOT had been compiling information on the financial transactions at the bureau de change in Centraal Station. In Holland the police set up a special Paddy Team to operate in tandem with the Irish investigation. Officers from the Money Laundering Unit and GNDU flew to Holland for meetings with their colleagues. There were seven targets in Operation Pineapple, based mainly on the intelligence obtained in Europe: Traynor, Gilligan, Meehan, the Bookie, Denis Meredith, Carol Rooney and another person. Operation Pineapple did not properly get off the ground until May, one month before Veronica Guerin's murder.

It is important to make a critical comment at this point in relation to Operation Pineapple because of claims made in the month before this book was published. It has been claimed that Operation Pineapple had compiled a "full picture" of Gilligan's operation and gang structure in the month before the murder of Veronica Guerin. It has also been claimed that the entire gang had been identified, including Charlie Bowden, and that they had been placed under surveillance and had their phones bugged. It has been claimed that Operation Pineapple had at that time already uncovered the links between Gilligan and the INLA. It was also alleged that an order was given to arrest the key members of the gang three days before Veronica Guerin's murder, on Monday, June 23, for the purpose of adding to the volumes of intelligence. In the light of the events which took place on June 26, these claims appear incredible and pose several questions. One, especially, is particularly poignant. Why was Veronica Guerin murdered?

In light of all the intelligence and surveillance work which it is claimed was carried out by Operation Pineapple before the murder, why would it take one hundred detectives over two months to process two hundred suspects before members of the Gilligan gang were positively identified as the prime suspects? It is altogether incredible to think that such surveillance would not have uncovered the gang's Cork drug route or their Greenmount warehouse. This route was operating with such frequency that it would have been virtually impossible *not* to have discovered the operation or at least some part of it by watching the gang members, especially in light of the claim that Charlie Bowden, the gang's most active "worker", was under watch.

In reality the Lucan Investigation Team did not discover the Cork route and the gang's warehouse at Greenmount until the arrest of Charlie Bowden on October 6. Charlie Bowden himself was *not* identified by the police until September, five months after he was allegedly identified as a member of the gang. It is only reasonable to speculate that if the gang members had been watched, bugged, tailed or arrested before June 26, Veronica Guerin's assassination would have been called off immediately. Some information would have been gleaned to suggest that they were up to something big. After all, the murder physically involved seven members of the gang. If there was a hint of police activity near them, then they would have walked away to fight another day like all cunning hoods.

Without what can only be described as tragic hype, Operation Pineapple still played a fundamental role in the investigation. It provided an excellent database from which the Lucan Investigation Team and the soon-to-be-established Criminal Assets Bureau could work. Through the contacts with law enforcement agencies in Europe it had built up a significant picture of Gilligan's contacts in Holland, principally Rahman and Baltus. It had begun to unravel the financial transactions of some of the gang and how Jessbrook had evolved. At one stage in the early days of the Guerin investigation, it was known in Garda circles that there had been a dispute between the Pineapple and Lucan teams. This was subsequently sorted out and resources were pooled for the largest anti-crime offensive in the history of the State.

Part Three

The Fall of the Evil Empire

Twelve

Murder

Gilligan and his mob had no idea that the gardaí were limbering up for a major showdown with them. At that stage they probably couldn't have cared less. They were untouchable in their own minds. Gilligan reckoned that he had all the corners covered. He never touched the drugs and the money was disguised as proceeds of his charmed life as a "professional gambler". If he did know about Operation Pineapple, he hadn't time to think about it. Gilligan's mind was dominated by Veronica Guerin. He was obsessed by her and the impending trial.

"Who does that fucking bitch think she is?" a gang member recalled Gilligan scream in a blind fury when he learned that he was to be charged with assault and causing criminal damage to the journalist's clothes. In March he received a summons ordering him to appear at Kilcock District Court on May 14. Despite the bravado that he had practically "won his case", Gilligan still wasn't prepared to risk being jailed. He had changed, but it wasn't just the Guerin case which brought about the new man. The money and the power had turned him into a depraved, greedy monster. Associates described him as being like a man possessed. He ranted on about killing and maiming people who annoyed him. The little bully took the pressure of his life out on the women in his life. He beat his wife Geraldine. He also attacked his young mistress, Carol, as a reminder that she could never cross him.

The gang's "market share" was going through the roof. The shipments were getting larger and more frequent. The average consignment was over four hundred kilos every few weeks, which netted him a profit of around three million pounds per shipment. Apart from potentially losing all that dirty money if he were to go to prison, he had grown soft with the high life. Swapping a plush, five-star hotel for a pokey prison cell was inconceivable. His cronies wholeheartedly agreed. "Who the fuck does Guerin think she is?" they said. Murder was on everyone's mind. Veronica Guerin was sentenced to death for crossing their evil godfather and putting their lucrative business at risk.

In April Traynor approached his garda handler. He was in a panic. Gilligan was "going out of control". Traynor implied that he might be prepared to set up the whole operation to put an end to it but wanted to know how he "stood" with the police if he did. The double-dealing agent said he wanted to get the money Gilligan owed him from the drug operation. Then he wanted out. Gilligan had long since bullied his way to being the overall boss. Traynor had been relegated to the position of a weekly customer shifting an average of fifty kilos. He didn't mind being out of the limelight and his ego was assuaged by the steady profit of over ten thousand pounds, which was coming in every week despite his protestations to the contrary. Like Gilligan, he was greedy.

Traynor offered to give the cops the gang's drug distribution "system". If they had that, then Gilligan was theirs for the taking. If the Garda operation was well planned, they could catch Gilligan and Meehan red handed. He did not give them the names of anyone else in the gang. Traynor had no idea that plans were being put in place to set up Operation Pineapple. In hindsight it appears that Traynor's instincts were alerting him to impending aggravation, or that he knew or suspected that Guerin was going to be murdered. In any event, Traynor knew when the time was right to quit and get out. The officer reported back to his superiors that the Coach might be in a position to do a deal. It could be a useful break for Operation Pineapple.

On May 14 Veronica Guerin travelled to Kilcock Court with her husband, Graham, and a colleague, Michael Sheridan. Sheridan, who went on to script a movie and write a book in Veronica's honour, recalled how she was frightened at the prospect of facing the man who had assaulted and threatened to kill her with chilling malice. As she stood outside the health centre which doubled as the local seat of summary justice, she tried to suppress her nerves.

Gilligan arrived in a convoy of jeeps and cars with a bunch of henchmen and Geraldine, his "estranged" wife, on his arm. The scene epitomised Gilligan and what he had become. He was actually living the life of an Irish John Gotti. He wanted everyone to know that he was a swaggering godfather no-one should dare cross. His goons crowded around him, talking on their mobile phones and eyeballing the crowd. The John Gilligan Goon Show had arrived in town. The goons could have been talking to one of his bagmen, the Bookie, who was on his way to the bureau de change in Amsterdam with a bag stuffed with money. Records later obtained by the Lucan Investigation Team, through their Dutch counterparts, showed that the Bookie changed Irish punts and sterling pounds worth £128,390 into guilders at 11.52 a.m. An hour later he played the tables at the casino in Schipol airport before catching the return flight to Dublin. The following day the same records showed that Gilligan's brother Thomas, exchanged another £122,050.

As soon as he got out of his jeep, Gilligan caught sight of his nemesis, the person he hated more than anyone else in the world at that moment. He probably had to restrain himself from running over and throttling her again. There were too many witnesses. Gilligan knew that the case would be adjourned for at least a month because of a legal technicality. He spoke briefly with his solicitor, Michael Hanahoe, outside the health centre. Gilligan continued to stare at Veronica as he walked up the steps, but Geraldine couldn't keep her distance. She sauntered across to where Veronica's group were standing with a sarcastic grin on her face. She did a twirl in front of Veronica. "You won't forget me in a hurry," she said, her voice full of contempt. Then she pranced off back to her husband's side.

Judge John Brophy adjourned the court hearing until Tuesday, June 25. The Lucan Investigation Team suspected that certain members of Gilligan's gang went to the court to see what the reporter looked like, what kind of car she was driving and whether she had police protection. The murder plot was being pieced together.

Another incident that occurred around this time also pointed to the fact that a murder conspiracy was being put in place. A member of Brendan "Speedy" Fegan's gang recently described "preparations" which were made between the beginning of May and the time of the murder. The source didn't know what the preparations were for until the afternoon of June 26. In the beginning of May, Fegan and Paddy Farrell arranged a meeting with Gilligan, Meehan and the rest of the Dublin mob. The source was left in a north side pub while Gilligan picked up Farrell and Fegan and brought them to a meeting. "I knew something heavy was going down but I knew better than to ask any questions. A few hours later Gilligan dropped Speedy back to the pub. All he said was that he would have to be in Dublin more often over the next few months," the source recalled.

A week later Meehan rang Fegan and asked him to travel to London with him for a meeting with the little man. If Fegan couldn't go, then the source was to go in his place. In the event, Fegan and the source flew to Heathrow where they were met by Meehan in a stretch limousine. They were driven to a plush hotel in central London where Gilligan was waiting. Carol Rooney was there, too.

Gilligan had a strange request for the Newry drug dealer. The source recalled that meeting: "He asked Speedy to pose for a number of pictures of him with Carol Rooney, to make it look like they were boyfriend and girlfriend. Gilligan told Fegan that the picture would be hung up in Rooney's apartment to give the impression that Speedy was her boyfriend. He said that something was going to happen which would have the cops crawling all over everyone in Dublin and he didn't want Rooney getting caught up in it. Fegan was amazed that such an ugly, old guy like Gilligan could have such a young, attractive girlfriend. She was no more than twenty. I think Brendan fancied his chances with her, anyway. Gilligan told Fegan that he was in control of the underworld in Dublin and implied he had an arrangement with the Provos.

"He said, 'No one messes with us. You have nothing to worry about from the Provos.' For about two weeks before the murder of the journalist there was no action coming from Dublin. On the day of the murder I was with Fegan in a car driving between Newry and Belfast when a news flash came on the radio reporting the murder. The minute it came on, Fegan said in a matter-of-fact way: 'That was the Dublin lads. They got her. I didn't think they would. There'll be a lot of shite flying now'."

The source's account of the events were confirmed by Fegan himself a year later when he was arrested by the Lucan Investigation Team.

Russell Warren and his friend, Paul Cradden, had been out drinking all day on Friday, June 7. They fell out of the Speaker Connolly pub around closing time. Cradden had talked about a powerful Kawasaki 500cc motorbike his employer, Ian Keith, kept in a lockup garage in Dun Laoghaire. Cradden was bitching about his employer. They decided to upset him by stealing the bike. Warren drove his van to the coastal suburb. They parked in a lane beside the lockup. Warren jumped over a wall and broke into the garage. The pair of drunken chums struggled and staggered as they heaved the large motorbike into the back of the van. They giggled as they drove away.

But the pair had a problem. They hadn't a clue what to do with the bike. Warren drove back towards Terenure and called another pal, Stephen McGrath from Saint Enda's road, who had a garage. Not knowing what the gang were planning, McGrath agreed to let them stash the bike there. They told McGrath that they had repossessed the bike, though in reality neither of them had reclaimed anything other than their change from the pub counter. The following morning, when Warren had sobered up, he told McGrath the truth. Warren tried to sell the bike and put the word around. A few potential buyers, unconcerned about the bike's previous owner, viewed it, but no-one bought.

Less than a week later Warren picked up Gilligan at Jessbrook to drive him around on business. Warren was at Gilligan's beck and call. Whenever the little man told him to jump, Warren asked how high. Gilligan treated him with utter contempt. To him Warren was just another piece of property bought and paid for with his growing mountain of dirty money. During the trip Warren made conversation and told Gilligan about the motorbike that he was considering dumping. He wondered if the nasty godfather sitting beside him in the car might have some use for it. Gilligan was interested. He asked what size it was and where it was being kept. "Don't dump it; just keep it. Don't do anything with it. I may need it," he grunted at his servant. Warren phoned McGrath and told him to hang on to the bike.

On or about Thursday, June 20, Gilligan telephoned Warren and asked if he still had "that bike". Gilligan wanted to see it. He arranged to meet his hapless bagman-come-thief at the Terenure House car park later that day. He told Warren he didn't want anyone in the vicinity of the bike; Brian Meehan was coming with him and he didn't want to be seen. They met as arranged and Warren brought them to McGrath's garage. The godfather and his sidekick examined the bike. Gilligan consulted with Meehan. Gilligan gruffly ordered Warren to fit it with indicators, fill it with petrol and do whatever else was needed to make it roadworthy. Meehan said he would be back to test drive the motorbike after the work was done. The three left the garage and got into Gilligan's car. Gilligan was doing the driving despite being disqualified from for over forty years. Before he started the engine to drive back to the pub car park where Warren had left his van, he turned around and looked at the bike thief. It was the kind of bloodcurdling look that sent a chill down Warren's spine.

"I was told not to trust you, but I will. If you ever make a statement or say anything to anyone about me, I will kill you. Your mother and father, brothers and sisters, you and your wife, and the rest of your family will be shot. I am just tellin' you to keep it in your mind. Don't think I want to do this but, no matter where you are, I'll get you."

Gilligan turned around and drove the car to the Terenure House pub. He reminded Warren about the work that had to be done to the bike. He told him to call Meehan when the bike was roadworthy. Gilligan never mentioned paying his servant for the bike or the work, but Warren knew better not to ask. Over the next two days he bought all the parts needed. He and Stephen McGrath did the repairs.

Veronica Guerin wasn't just upsetting Gilligan. In the first week of May, she declared to her friend and news editor Willie Kealy that she was going to "name them all". By that she meant that she intended to name and shame all the bosses in the criminal underworld. The competition between Veronica and this writer had intensified during the first four months of the year. It was friendly rivalry. Since her murder it has been claimed that the escalation of our attempts to get the scoop over one another in some way led to her death.

Guerin began putting pressure on Traynor to come up with more information about the Mr Bigs. She informed him of her intention to write a major story exposing his involvement in the drug trade. She was now aware of Traynor's involvement with Gilligan but, like the police, did not know the sheer scale of the operation. Relations between the reporter and the lying, cheating hoodlum deteriorated dramatically. He threatened to seek a High Court injunction against her. Veronica responded by threatening to expose him. It was a dangerous game of jousting, but not unprecedented between journalist and source. However, the argument between Traynor and Guerin was more personal than most and, indeed, confusing when one tries to analyse the events leading up to her murder.

It seems clear that Veronica knew at that stage that the Coach had been behind the attempt on her life in 1995. She told him that his name had featured in a police investigation of a Liverpool-based heroin gang, that she had heard he was a heroin dealer and a contract had been placed on his head. She was putting one last squeeze on him before finally exposing him. She met him on a number of occasions to discuss the allegations and had adopted a less aggressive approach in the hope that she could record Traynor admitting that he was in fact involved in narcotics. She still did not have the proof. On one of those tapes she can be heard discussing her assault case against the little man: "Even last week when you were saying about Gilligan and what he's capable of, and trying to stop me going to court, it makes me more determined. It's the way I am."

Traynor replied: "If he never done anything, at the back of your mind, you know what he's capable of."

It was during one of these meetings between the reporter and her source-turned-subject that Veronica's fate is believed to have been sealed. She let slip the fact that she was due to appear in Naas District Court on a speeding fine the day after the assault case was to come up again. The Naas case had been on her mind a lot. She genuinely worried that she might lose her driving licence and the mobility necessary for her work. In any event, she must have considered it small talk as she tried to pry more from the Coach. In a lot of ways Veronica was naive. She was not long enough in the dirty business of crime reporting to be a match for John Traynor in his dangerous game of wits. The cunning crook had gleaned more from the conversation than she had.

On the morning of June 7, 1996 an IRA gang murdered Detective Garda Jerry McCabe during a botched armed robbery in

Adare, County Limerick. That morning this writer was leaving Dublin to cover the story with a photographer when Traynor called on the mobile phone. He inquired if I had heard anything about a threat on his life that he said Veronica had told him about. I said I hadn't because I had only returned from a three-week holiday abroad. Traynor, who was always friendly and talkative, told me about his problems with Veronica. He referred to Veronica as "her". He had complained on several occasions in the past about "her" but I had always interpreted those criticisms as his way of playing one of us off against the other. Traynor was a consummate manipulator.

This time, though, he seemed very concerned that she was going to expose him as a drug dealer. He said that he was going to seek legal advice later that day about a possible injunction. I dismissed the whole thing as nothing more than Veronica winding up the Coach. I was aware that they had fallen out before and wasn't prepared to get involved. I told Traynor that there was nothing I could do. I was certainly not prepared to ask her to drop any story. Sean Fitzgerald, Traynor's criminal best friend, later recalled of that time: "Veronica had Traynor in the horrors. He was terrified that she was going to write about him being a drug dealer." Later that morning Veronica phoned Traynor and told him that she wasn't satisfied he was a heroin dealer and was postponing the story. He cancelled his appointment with his barrister.

Later that day I attended a press conference in Henry Street Garda Station in Limerick about Detective McCabe's murder. Veronica was also there. We greeted each other across the room but didn't get a chance to speak. It was Friday afternoon and both of us were after a front-page story. Saturday morning is the final deadline for a Sunday newspaper reporter. It was the last time I ever met Veronica. She stayed in Limerick to cover the funeral of Jerry McCabe. The incident upset her. Later she told her husband Graham that she would like the hymn "Be Not Afraid" played at her funeral. The hymn had been sung during the detective's funeral Mass.

On Monday, June 10, Veronica met Traynor again in Dublin on her way back from covering the McCabe murder. This time, the Coach claimed, she told him she now knew he was selling hash and ecstasy but not heroin. On Thursday, June 13, Traynor swore an affidavit about his dealings with Veronica in order to obtain an injunction against the *Sunday Independent*'s story alleging his involvement in drug trafficking. It was a masterpiece of the Coach's lies and half-truths. The drug dealer and user of prostitutes expressed fear for the family he was dedicated to. An article would put them all in danger from vigilantes. He would have to move home over the shame of it.

He effectively described himself as a struggling used car salesman. "I have never dealt in, touched, seen or been involved in anything to do with drugs. I have never invested any money with anybody involved in drugs and do not know or have not been in company with any of the people mentioned by Veronica Guerin at the time of writing this," Traynor's affidavit read. On Friday, June 14, Traynor's counsel, Adrian Hardiman, obtained an interim injunction against any story. Lawyers for the newspaper informed the court on June 14 and 19 that the story was not imminent. On Monday, June 24 the lawyers gave a further undertaking that the story would not be published in the following edition. The case was adjourned to July 1. Veronica was due to swear a responding affidavit. She had an appointment with the *Sunday Independent*'s legal advisers for the afternoon of June 26. Traynor had some breathing space.

Veronica Guerin's murder was now the main source of debate among Gilligan's Brat Pack. Meehan and Mitchell discussed the subject with Charlie Bowden at the end of May. Meehan said there was "hassle" between Gilligan and the reporter. He said Gilligan was "upset" over this and had told him that he wasn't going to prison for anyone and he wasn't going "to let her away with it". Meehan said that Gilligan had all the contacts for the hash in Holland. If he was inside, then the supply would dry up. A few days later Bowden, Mitchell, Meehan and Paul Ward were driving through the Strawberry Beds area on the banks of the River Liffey. Meehan brought up the subject again. Meehan asked Bowden about the .357 Magnum Rahman had sent them in January. Meehan and Ward said they would go to the cemetery to check for the weapon. Bowden knew that Veronica Guerin was to be shot, but later claimed that he thought Meehan was going to use the gun to threaten her again.

Bowden was asked about the gun again the following week at

a gang meeting in Meehan's apartment to divide up the week's earnings. Meehan said he couldn't find it in the grave where the gang's arsenal was mainly stored. Bowden had been using more than one grave and Meehan said he would go and check again. Meehan then told the former soldier that he and the gang were planning to shoot the reporter. Meehan offered to do it himself but was turned down because of his performance in the Foley hit.

He claimed that Eugene "Dutchie" Holland had been chosen for the horrific task, although Holland has always strenuously denied carrying out Veronica Guerin's murder.

The hit man had "a proven track record". He was the odd man out in the gang and Meehan disliked him, mainly out of fear. Everyone in the gang was afraid of the hit man. There was something cold and callous about him, even when he was being friendly. On Monday, June 17, Bowden met Meehan and Mitchell and brought them to the Greenmount lockup. A few hours earlier Bowden had collected another consignment of 423 kilos from John Dunne at the Ambassador Hotel. As they checked the shipment, Meehan talked about the plan to shoot Veronica. Traynor had told Meehan about her court appearance in Naas on Wednesday of the following week. Bowden wondered if she would have a police escort because of the earlier attacks on her. Meehan had it all worked out. They would know if she had an escort because they planned to have the reporter followed. Later it was discussed again by Meehan, the two Wards, Mitchell and Bowden.

On June 25 Veronica made a second trip to Kilcock District Court. Again she would have to face Gilligan. This time he behaved less ostentatiously and arrived without his goons in his solicitor Michael Hanahoe's car. The hearing lasted a few minutes and was adjourned to July 9, when the case was scheduled to go finally ahead. Before he left, Gilligan spotted two detectives who were attached to the Investigation Branch at Garda Headquarters. One of them was Detective Garda Pat Keane, who a few days earlier had been asked to assist with Operation Pineapple. Keane would also become a member of the Lucan Investigation Team within the week. Gilligan walked over to the two cops, thinking that they were watching him. "She's a fucking stupid bitch. This case will never get off the ground," he snarled before walking to his solicitor's car.

Hanahoe drove Gilligan back to Jessbrook in order to familiarise himself with the layout of the place for the forthcoming case. Gilligan asked him for a lift to Dublin airport, as he was catching the afternoon flight to Amsterdam. In Holland Gilligan met his girlfriend Carol Rooney. They met Thomas Gorst and travelled to a house which Gorst had rented for the two lovers near Aalst in Belgium. Gilligan had called him some weeks earlier and told him he wanted to stay in Belgium for at least a month and wanted a house. He would move between the house and a hotel suite in Amsterdam. The same afternoon Thomas Gilligan, John's brother, changed one hundred and fifty thousand pounds at the bureau de change.

That afternoon, as Veronica Guerin drove back to Dublin and Gilligan made his way to the airport, Brian Meehan rang Russell Warren. He wanted to meet at the garage. He told Warren to make sure no-one was around. Some time later Meehan met Warren in the car park of the Terenure House. He was being driven by Peter Mitchell. They went to the garage and Meehan took the bike for a test drive. Ten minutes later he returned, satisfied that it was working well. As he was leaving, Meehan turned to Warren and asked him if he knew who Veronica Guerin was. Warren didn't read newspapers and didn't know who she was. Meehan described the doomed crime reporter, her hair, build and age. Gilligan's sidekick didn't mention that she was a journalist. Meehan said he would show Warren a picture of her later that evening. The meeting didn't take place. Meehan rang Warren and told him that he wanted to pick the bike up the next morning at 9 a.m. and he would talk to him then. The same evening Gilligan also rang his bagman. Warren inquired if he was to pick up money for Amsterdam. Gilligan ordered him to stay put because he was needed in Dublin.

After Meehan and Mitchell checked the bike they met Bowden at a pub in Harold's Cross. He drove them to Greenmount. Shay Ward had retrieved the Magnum and twelve rounds of ammunition from the graveyard. As Meehan, Mitchell and Ward discussed the ambush that was to take place on the following day, Bowden cleaned the weapon and loaded it. He left six spare rounds alongside the gun on a bench. There was tension in the air and this time Bowden knew that the attack wasn't just talk. He could have picked up a phone and made a call to the police to anonymously inform them that Veronica was to be shot, but he did nothing. Instead, Bowden began to set up his alibi. To cover himself with his girlfriend, Bowden had told her a few weeks beforehand that he heard the gang was going to have something done about the crime reporter. He said he reckoned the IRA were going to do the dirty work. Bowden didn't want Julie Bacon knowing that he was involved. If she did know, she would certainly leave him. It was Charlie's only concern and he gave no thought to Veronica's last night with her family.

The following morning Meehan phoned Paul Ward, who was at his home in Walkinstown. It was 9.30 a.m. Meehan told him that he had to "bring the kids to school". It was the code to notify Ward and his brother Shay that the destruction of Veronica Guerin had begun. The Wards were to wait at the house and listen to the police frequencies on a scanner. Meehan and the gunman planned to return there immediately after the hit. When they heard the first reports of the shooting, they would expect the killers. Ward's job was to dispose of the murder weapon and the motorbike.

Earlier Meehan had phoned Warren and said he was delayed. Around 9.45 a.m. Meehan arrived at the garage and examined the motorbike. He said he would be back later for it. Meehan asked Warren to drive to Naas to look for a red Opel sports car with a KE (Kildare) registration. It would be parked somewhere in the vicinity of the courthouse. When he spotted the car he was to call Meehan. Again, he didn't mention Guerin's name. Once in Naas, Warren parked outside the local Social Welfare office, which he mistakenly took to be the courthouse. When he discovered his mistake, he drove down the town and asked a uniformed garda for directions. He parked the van and walked to the courthouse. Warren would later claim in court that he was in contact with both Meehan and Gilligan throughout this time. Gilligan, he claimed, was anxious to know whether he had located the red car. Gilligan told Warren that a second man was also in Naas, watching for the car from a rooftop.

It must be noted that Russell Warren's evidence in relation to the events on the day of Veronica Guerin's murder, although accepted during the trial of Brian Meehan, was rejected as unreliable by the judges of the Special Criminal Court during Gilligan's murder trial.

As Warren walked towards the courthouse, Veronica Guerin

drove out from beside the building and headed towards Dublin. Warren phoned Meehan, who by now was sitting on the motorbike parked down a side road off the Naas dual carriageway. The hit man was his pillion passenger. Meehan told the bagman to follow the red car. Warren tailed Guerin, staying about four cars behind her on the road. As he passed the Air Motive factory he phoned Meehan again. "OK, I see it," Meehan shouted into his hands-free mobile phone attachment.

Meehan weaved through the traffic, stalking the red car. The bike sped past Warren's van and behind Veronica's car. The hit man had already pulled the .357 Magnum from his jacket. The pair made their move when Veronica stopped at traffic lights. The motorbike pulled alongside her car. The hit man put a foot down on the road to balance himself. He reached over to the roof of the car and fired a shot. He fired another shot. He leaned over and fired another four shots. The pair drove off. Veronica Guerin, archenemy of John Gilligan, John Traynor and their evil empire, had been executed. A mother, wife, daughter and sister was dead.

John Gilligan probably thought his problems were over. In reality, they were only beginning.

Warren had never seen anything like this before. He froze and everything, he recalled, seemed to be in slow motion. Warren pulled out of the traffic, which was now at a standstill as shocked motorists got out of their cars and ran to Veronica's car. Warren was in shock. He got out of the van and threw up. When he composed himself, he rang Gilligan, who was in Holland in a room at the Hilton Hotel with Carol Rooney. Warren would later claim that Gilligan asked him about the hit team: "Are they gone? Did they get away?" Warren replied that the pair on the bike had just shot somebody.

"Are they dead?" Gilligan is alleged to have asked. Warren was still in shock. He said that the person in the car had been shot five times. "The same thing will happen to you and your mate if you do anything about it," Gilligan warned Warren before hanging up. Carol Rooney witnessed Gilligan's conversation with Warren and later gave the Lucan Investigation Team a statement about it. She was later, however, too terrified of her lover to ever give evidence.

Despite the drama unfolding back in Ireland, it was business as usual for Factory John. At 2.30 p.m., one hour and thirty-six minutes after the murder, Carol Rooney exchanged forty thousand pounds at the usual bureau de change in Centraal Station in Amsterdam.

John Traynor had carefully organised his alibi for the day of Veronica Guerin's murder. Between 12.10 and 12.15 p.m. Traynor was training in one of his racing cars at Mondello Park, a few miles from Naas. He had brought his two sons with him that morning. Before he had finished his first lap, he overturned the Opel Astra car on a hairpin bend known as the "Coca Cola" corner by racers. When people rushed to the car, they saw that he was shocked but uninjured. It was suggested that he should go for a check-up to the Naas courthouse. He was in the accident and emergency ward when he received the call that Veronica had been murdered. He appeared shocked at the news. Traynor knew that his life would never be the same again. That afternoon he went on a booze binge with his old friend Sean Fitzgerald and a number of associates of his from London. They all later recalled that he appeared "very upset".

After the murder Meehan and the hit man sped up the Belgard Road, across through Ballymount and down into Walkinstown using back roads. They arrived at Ward's garage within minutes of the murder. At the same time, Peter Mitchell was spotted by an off-duty garda making his way to Walkinstown from the general direction of the murder scene. Paul and Shay Ward were waiting in the house. Meehan and the hit man walked through to the house. Meehan was pumped up with adrenalin. The hit man was totally calm. He washed his hands and complimented Ward on the great job he was doing renovating his home. There was no mention of the horror they had just perpetrated. The hit man left the gun for Paul Ward to dispose of and the bike was left in the garage. He left the house. A short time later the hit man was said to be in Crumlin village to pick up his unemployment assistance payment.

Shay Ward, meanwhile, brought Meehan to the Greenmount lockup, where he quickly changed his clothes to get rid of any forensic evidence. Ward later took the clothes away in a bag and burned them. He dropped Meehan to Aungier Street at 1.30 p.m., where Meehan met Mitchell. The pair walked across town to Bowden's hairdressing salon on Moore Street. On the way Meehan called Paul Ward to check if he had disposed of the gun. Ward was already on his way to do so, on a bus. He was petrified that he might get caught with the weapon. The .357 Magnum has never been recovered.

Bowden had been in the shop all that morning and through lunchtime. It was to be his alibi. Sometime before 2 p.m. Bowden met Meehan and Mitchell outside Hallins Restaurant near the salon. Meehan told him what had happened. He said it was a "good job this morning".

"I thought the [hit man] was only going to fire one or two rounds at her [Veronica Guerin]. I was surprised at how cool he was. He emptied it into her. Fair play to him," said Meehan in admiration. About an hour later the gang members put the murder behind them and began a marathon drinking session in the Hole in the Wall pub on Blackhorse Avenue, not far from Bowden's new home at the Paddocks. The European Championships were on television. The group included Bowden, Mitchell, Meehan, Meehan's girlfriend Fiona Walsh, Julie Bacon and other friends of Bowden. Later that night Meehan got in a row with another drinker in the pub toilet. He was still keyed up after the murder. At closing time they all went back to Bowden's house. Bowden's neighbour, the *Star* newspaper crime reporter Senan Moloney, had spent the afternoon and night covering one of the most distressing stories of his career. He came home to find that his neighbours were having a party.

The following morning the gang went back to work, distributing hash, collecting cash and organising a shipment to Gilligan in Holland. Meehan later bragged about the murder to a friend of Bowden's, shop assistant Julian Clohessy. On the night of July 11 Clohessy was out with Bowden, Meehan and the rest of the gang in the POD nightclub. Clohessy was stunned when Meehan gloated that he had been involved in the murder. Meehan claimed that before she was shot, Veronica had pleaded with him. "She said, 'Please don't shoot me in the face'," said Meehan, as if he was recalling something as mundane as crossing the road. "I said, 'Fuck you, you bitch'," Meehan continued, until the pair were interrupted by another drinker.

It was shortly after 1 p.m. when this author's mobile phone rang in the *Sunday World* newsroom. It was a detective friend who had been providing protection to my family and myself on and off for the previous two years. His voice was trembling. He told me that Veronica had been shot. I laughed and told him that he had heard a sick joke. But his voice was deadly earnest. "I'm sorry... Veronica Guerin has just been shot... She's dead... I'm standing beside the car now on the Naas Road. It happened about five minutes ago," he said. "Look, for your own sake, just stay in the office or go home... Don't come up here," my friend advised.

Within a few minutes I had made my way to the scene of the outrage. As news began to filter out, the phone kept ringing. Some colleagues were asking in disbelief if the news was true. Other garda contacts were calling to tell me what had just happened. I was the first journalist at the scene of Veronica's murder. There, a few feet away, was the person I considered to be my closest rival. She was lying in the driver's seat of her car, dead, her body full of bullets and her clothes drenched in blood. It was a dreadful sight.

The police had cordoned off the road where the car had stopped. Squad cars hemmed it in and the area was cordoned off with blue and white crime scene tape. Detectives and uniformed officers looked on in utter bewilderment. Det. Sgt Gerry O'Carroll began organising officers to take down statements from eyewitnesses.

Then the horrific reality struck home. I had been threatened and received police protection. I had been lectured by senior officers about my safety and the potential dangers from organised crime – but no-one actually thought that the Irish gangs would actually step across the line and fire fatal shots. I was convulsed with fear and shock. It was fear of the selfish, self-preservation kind. This could happen to me. What effect would something like this have on my family? My mouth went dry, my legs felt like jelly. I was throwing up. Tears streamed down my cheeks. The whole world had gone completely fucking mad. I lost it for a while, until a colleague and a detective friend brought me away. Life would never be the same.

A lot of lives changed forever that afternoon. Crime reporting was no longer a "game" in the way that I had understood it to be. The fine line of journalism that we understood insulated us from criminal reprisals no longer existed. Everyone remembers where he or she was on that fateful afternoon. The entire country felt a sense of numbness and sheer terror. The murder was perceived as a type of criminal coup, a barbaric attack on the foundations of our society. In the halls of power and justice there were a lot of ashen faces. If organised crime could callously take out such a high-profile reporter, then anyone was fair game.

The Deputy Commissioner whom Veronica had called when Gilligan beat her up was in his office when the news came through. Pat Byrne was minding his younger son that otherwise quiet afternoon. Byrne had to immediately go to the scene of the crime. He was one of the top cops in the country and he, too, later recalled how scared he was that afternoon.

Nora Owen, the Minister for Justice, was out of the country on Government business in New York when she was told the news. She was a good friend of the dead journalist and was heartbroken. She also knew that the Irish public would want answers to what was going on. A price would have to be paid to avenge this savage deed. In the days and weeks that followed, Nora Owen, who was an effective minister, suffered a ferocious hammering from the media, this author included. In hindsight I felt bad about that. Nora Owen didn't deserve it. She hadn't pulled the trigger, nor was she responsible for the rot of longstanding complacency which had been allowed to set in by several Governments and all the political parties. She was the first Justice Minister to make a serious effort at grappling with reorganising the mess that was Ireland's criminal justice system at the time. In grief and anger, the media had to blame someone. Nora Owen was the scapegoat.

Veronica's colleagues and friends at the *Sunday Independent* were understandably in a state of shock. Willie Kealy, one of the last people to speak with Veronica, could barely verbalise his sense of grief. He and Veronica had a close working relationship. She reported directly to Willie, who was her news editor. A book of condolences was opened in the public office of the Middle Abbey Street headquarters of Independent Newspapers and was signed by thousands of people, including church, political and business leaders. Among them, The Monk, Gerry Hutch, took his place in the queue of signatories to record his own revulsion at the crime. It was an extraordinary sight to behold, one of the country's most notorious crime bosses registering his sympathy at the murder of a journalist who had originally exposed him and his gang. It was a microscopic image of those surreal days in the summer of 1996. Nothing would be the same again.

Never before had the Irish nation seen such an outpouring of anger and emotion. A veritable wall of flowers at the railings of the Irish parliament building, Leinster House, symbolised the feeling of the people. There were hundreds of notes and prayers pinned to the flowers calling for action to be taken. Across the world the murder made the news headlines. The morning after the murder, the *Irish Independent*'s main headline summed up the feelings of frustration: "We know who killed her – and he's untouchable".

While all this was happening, John Gilligan spent most of his waking hours on the mobile phone to Dublin. His gang remained calm. The outrage would pass and the investigation would fizzle out in no time. On Friday afternoon this author decided to contact Gilligan to see what he had to say for himself. I called Geraldine at Jessbrook to inquire about her husband's whereabouts. She sounded angry and put out. Within less than two days Jessbrook's once thriving business literally died. Work on the huge show-jumping arena was almost completed and several major events were already booked to take place there. Work stopped and the events were cancelled overnight. The people whose patronage Geraldine had longed for would not set foot on the place. Her dreams were shattered by her husband's gang. On the phone Geraldine was anxious to point out that she was separated from Gilligan and that he didn't live at Jessbrook: "Do you want his phone number? Because he doesn't live here, so I don't know why everybody keeps ringing me. Thank you, goodbye."

Gilligan answered his mobile phone almost immediately. I introduced myself and announced that I wanted to discuss Veronica Guerin's murder with him. He needed little encouragement to talk about the case. "I was terrible sorry to hear about that and I had nothing to do with it," was his opening remark. The following is an edited extract from the transcript of that 45-minute telephone conversation. It served to illustrate Gilligan's reaction to the horror. This was the first interview given by Gilligan after the murder, in which he admitted he was the prime suspect in the murder. Later he also spoke with a reporter from the *Sunday Tribune* and made the same admission.

P.W.: Do you know that they are putting your name around a lot, John, for doing it?

J.G.: The only ones putting my name around is the newspapers. Terrible, terrible sorry to hear it. I had nothing to do with it. I had nothing to worry about the [assault] case. I'd have had the case over and done and won. It's only a Mickey Mouse case.

P.W.: Yeah?

J.G.: Six months is all it'll take at the very worst [in prison] and I've no problem. I had it won, it's home and dried and I certainly wouldn't have got time.

P.W.: Well, who do you think would have it done, John?

J.G.: I don't know, Paul, and that's telling you one thing. I don't know, I don't know, I didn't do it, I didn't get it done. Not in a million years did I get it done. I'm very sorry for her. I don't deal in drugs.

P.W.: But you are not in the country at the moment. It seems a bit suspicious that you left the country on Tuesday night, the day before the murder?

J.G.: I wasn't in the country when anything happened [to] that lady.

P.W.: Well, we know that you left beforehand. It all looks very suspicious, John. This stuff isn't being made up by the papers. Even your old cronies in the underworld, they're saying that it is you who organised the murder of Veronica Guerin.

J.G.: I'm telling you one hundred per cent I don't believe the police are doing this, saying I did it, it's the fucking newspapers.

P.W.: So you are saying, John, that the newspapers just want to set up John Gilligan?

J.G.: I am, yeah, I think that's what they are trying to do. They're trying to get me in trouble.

P.W.: I work in the same business as Veronica and was friendly with her. We are all absolutely gutted over what has happened. Do you understand that?

J.G.: Well, so am I. I like Veronica.

P.W.: Why did you fucking beat her, then, if you liked her?

J.G.: I didn't beat the shit out of her.

P.W.: You gave her a fair few digs. I saw her afterwards. We talked about it. Jesus, John, beating up a woman?

J.G.: No, I don't beat up women. Before I go any further, I don't beat up women. I had no problems with the case. She lied and she went home and changed her clothes. I don't know who beat her up. All her statement was lies. It's a terrible thing to say about the lady, she's dead. Lord have mercy on her soul.

P.W.: But what about the statement you made after the assault when another *Sunday Independent* reporter phoned you? 'I'll fucking kill you and your family, my old flower...' You think you are a hard man, you're well known in the villainy business as a hard man.

J.G.: I'm not hard, I'm not hard, I believe in Ireland.

P.W.: Who do you think did this, John, because whoever it was really stitched you on it?

J.G.: That's right, they stitched me. Very cute, very cute, now. Let's ask you a question and answer honestly, do you think I done it or got it done?

P.W.: I don't know if you got it done or not, John. It is hard to know what is going on when someone on a motorbike pulls up and shoots a woman like that. Everyone I know in the underworld seems upset by this.

J.G.: I'm pissed off about it, too. I'm well pissed off, too.

P.W.: You have to see how it looks. You go away and twelve hours later Veronica is murdered. Did the guards contact you at all since you went away? Will you come home to talk with them?

J.G.: Sure, the last time I was away after the assault, the alleged assault, I was in contact with the cops daily and as soon as they wanted me to come home I did. I don't know, they [the Garda Síochána] must know who was shooting Veronica. Sure, it's not the first time she was, I don't know it's a terrible loss of life for her. There's only one person that we know didn't shoot her and that was herself.

P.W.: You tell me then, Johnny, who do you think would have done something like this, with your extensive knowledge of the Dublin crime scene? You tell me.

J.G.: I don't know. Some cunt, sleveen bastard.

P.W.: Veronica didn't do you any favours by getting killed?

J.G.: "No, she didn't do me any favours, that's for sure. She didn't do me any favours in coming and causing me grief and looking for stories when I had none to give... She got killed, that's the worst thing that could ever happen, I'm sorry for her, I'm sorry for her family, I'm sorry for her child and her husband, I am sorry, believe me, I am sorry. If I wasn't sorry, I would say I don't give a bollocks. I am genuinely sorry. I had the case won.

P.W.: But did you have the case won? It looked that you could get up to three years for the assault.

J.G.: Paul, on my children's lives, right? Lord have mercy on Veronica's life and on her grave, I was going to win the case one hundred per cent. I don't like to talk about the deceased as a liar because she can not defend herself, but I can't defend meself either... I had me case won, one hundred thousand million per cent... trillion per cent!... My record was putting a hole in a factory wall with nobody in it, going in, stealing out of it and if I got away, I got away, if I got caught, I went to jail that was the end of that.

P.W.: What are you doing now? What are you earning a living at now? I hear you're one of the biggest cannabis dealers in the country.

J.G.: Have you? I don't believe you? I have nothing to with drugs.

P.W.: Can you imagine the amount of heat that is going to come down on everyone in your line of work as a result of this murder?

J.G.: Yeah, well, what can I do for them? There's nothing I can do, there's enough on me and I didn't do it. Someone put it down to me, so I don't know. I can't do anything other than face the court or the police or face anybody. If somebody wants me I'll be there, there's no problem... I hope they find the fuck who done the murder and then I hope when they catch him, that you will write and say you blamed John Gilligan in the wrong.

P.W.: What are you working at, what would you describe yourself as now, for the purpose of a story? A retired criminal, a businessman, are you employed anywhere?

J.G.: You can put me down as what you want.

P.W.: But what are you? I am a crime correspondent, that's what I do now, what do *you* do?

J.G.: I'm the main suspect in something I know nothing about, that's what I am.

P.W.: I know that. Describe what you do, then, for a living? You don't work in the equestrian centre, you don't own the equestrian centre, you're not registered as being employed anywhere, so what do you do? Are you a businessman? Are you a drug dealer? I have to describe you as something?

J.G.: A small little fella. I don't think you're upset over Veronica at all 'cause you are laughing and all.

P.W.: I'm not laughing and joking about Veronica Guerin being shot at. It's not a laugh and a joking matter. I'm laughing at the fact that your only answer to me when I'm asking you a straight question is a smart arse remark, when I'm trying to find out your side of the story, when you're accused of one of the most brutal murders in this State... Do you not think I am entitled to an answer, John? You say you are no longer a criminal and you are not a drug dealer. Then what are you, apart from being a small, little fella with a line in smart arse commentary?

J.G.: I breed horses, yeah, I'm a registered breeder. I am, yeah, I am.

P.W.: Oh, so where do you base your activities as a horse breeder?

[Gilligan refused to say where he operated as a horse breeder. Questioning returned to the murder.]

J.G.: I swear to you I had nothing to do with it. If I hated her, I wouldn't do that to her. I would scream and shout at her on the spur of the moment but to go and ask people to do this and do that is just madness.

P.W.: Did you hear that the Independent Group are offering a reward of a hundred thousand pounds for helping to catch Veronica's killers? Would you help the guards if you could?

J.G.: I've never grassed [give information to police] in me life before. That's all I'd say, I hope they catch who done it. Paul, is there something I can do for her family, like, I didn't do anything, but if there is anything I can do because I am genuinely sorry it happened, it's a terrible tragedy... I'm sorry that... I'm sorry she's not around. I don't know, maybe I should be pissed off even saying it, but ring me back if you think I can do anything, even if...

A few hours after that extraordinary conversation with Gilligan, the removal of Veronica's remains took place from a funeral home to the Dublin Airport Church. It was the same church where Veronica attended Mass every Sunday morning with Graham and Cathal. In the church Father Declan Doyle, a close family friend, said of the journalist: "She raised questions of Church, State and institutions, often awkward, difficult, even embarrassing, but ultimately important questions." The parish priest spoke of Veronica's humanity and her ability to love, while her innocent little son, Cathal, confused by all that was happening around him, touched his mummy's coffin and waved as if he could see her. It was as if the angelic youngster had no comprehension of the dreadful wrong that had been done to him and his family. The congregation sang the hymn "Be Not Afraid".

The following morning the President of Ireland, Mary Robinson, and Church and State leaders mingled with several hundred friends, colleagues, police officers and ordinary citizens in a deeply sad and poignant funeral ceremony. A lot of people cried that day. Before the funeral Mass ended, Graham Turley got up to speak about his beloved wife who had been so brutally snatched from him. "The best day I ever had was on 21 September, 1985, the year myself and Veronica promised to love, cherish and honour each other 'til death do us part. We also promised each other that we would have fun. And we really did, believe you me, we had a lot of fun. Then we were rewarded seven years ago with Cathal. After that we were one small group together that no-one could get between." Graham's voice was calm and gentle.

Then, for a moment, his voice faltered, as he said: "I am also saying goodbye today to my best pal." As he walked back to his seat the congregation stood and applauded a man whose courage was deeply moving in the face of such overwhelming despair. During the Mass, gifts which encapsulated Veronica's life were offered on the altar: the cherished picture with Manchester United star Eric Cantona, her national and international sports medals, her wedding picture, a football, Manchester United gloves and the FA Cup semi-final programme. Veronica's sister Claire read from Veronica's own Bible, reciting the words: "Over wisdom, evil can never triumph."

Little Cathal followed his mother's coffin, clutching a spray of lilies with a red rose at its heart. Graham lifted the child to kiss his mummy's coffin. Cathal wrapped his arms around President Robinson's neck, hugging her like an auntie. She fought back tears as Graham, clutching his boy's hand, told her: "He was very good."

"You did her proud," the President reassured the brave victim. At Dardistown Cemetery, under the flight path of noisy jets, Veronica Guerin was laid to rest on Saturday, June 29. Cathal prayed the "Hail Mary", while his father crouched beside him at the graveside. When the prayers had finished the little boy blew a kiss into his mummy's grave. "Goodbye Mummy," he said. For most of us there that day the scene was heart wrenching.

The following day, Sunday, Graham and Cathal visited the gates of the Dáil to see the mountain of flowers and messages of support which had been placed there by the thousands of angry citizens, whose tolerance for John Gilligan and his ilk had evaporated. He and his gang had awoken a monster which would eventually devour them. They had awakened an entire nation.

The following day at 1 p.m. the country came to a standstill. In factories and farms, offices and on the streets everywhere, people stood and observed a minute's silence for Veronica. But by that time in the High Court, John Traynor had succeeded, like his fellow gang members, in silencing Veronica a second time. Graham Turley went to the court in the company of *Sunday Independent* editor Aengus Fanning. Traynor, who was in hiding somewhere in the countryside, decided to let his lawyers continue in their quest to stop the *Sunday Independent* running a story about his drug trafficking operation.

Veronica was portrayed as unstable, irrational and threatening in Traynor's affidavit, against which she could not defend herself. Traynor claimed that Veronica had admitted that her story about him was false. As one observer recalled, it was like watching a boxing match in which only one boxer can throw the punches. Veronica was depicted as an aggressive liar. First she was murdered and then the mob moved in to take her reputation. The court granted the injunction prohibiting the *Sunday Independent* from publishing any story stating Traynor was involved in the sale or supply of drugs. It was all in accordance with the letter of the law.

A week later it was John Gilligan's turn to benefit from the murder of Veronica Guerin. On Tuesday, July 9, exactly two weeks since the murder, a large group of reporters dwarfed the normal attendance at Kilcock District Court. Veronica's former colleagues were reeling from the shock of her murder. The whole country was still numbed. Garda sniffer dogs were brought in to check the courtroom for a bomb, something which had never been seen at the local court before. But suddenly Ireland seemed to be a country where everyone was fair game for the organised criminal terrorists.

Neither Gilligan nor his lawyer were anywhere to be seen. There was no need for them to attend. In the stuffy health centre waiting-room which had taken on the monthly role of courtroom, Judge John Brophy took his seat at the bench. A number of cases had to be processed before the *D.P.P. v. John Joseph Gilligan* came up for mention. Judge Brophy looked down at a local youth who had pleaded guilty to a malicious damage charge. He asked him how he would like three months in prison. "Not very much, your Honour," the youth replied.

"There is no room in there for you anyway," mused the judge and fined the young troublemaker £1,100.

The court clerk then announced Gilligan's case. The packed courtroom fell silent. Superintendent Brendan Quinn, who was handling the case for the State, rose to his feet. "Is Mr Hanahoe in court?" the Judge asked about Gilligan's solicitor. There was no reply. Supt Quinn told the court his instructions were to have the case struck out because the State's only witness, Veronica Guerin, was dead. The Judge wrote the words "struck out" on the copies of the court summons in front of him with a quick flick of his pen. He took off his watch, placed it in front of him on the desk and asked the court to stand with him to observe a minute's silence in memory "of the lady who was the principal witness in this case".

The Judge explained the legal process in case anyone was in any doubt about the law. "The reason it can not go ahead is because there is no effective evidence that can be offered in a court of law because of her untimely death within the last two weeks," he said.

When the minute's silence had ended, the Judge described the murdered reporter as a "crusader in her own right". He urged the media to continue to expose the godfathers. "Remember the hymn at Dublin Airport church, "Be Not Afraid". If you are afraid, then

the barons and the major gangland people in this country will take
away your rights and freedoms which this country has fought for
over many decades. Ms Guerin lost her life as a result of what she
did. I hope that other people in the media will follow on in her
tracks."

As the Judge was speaking, in Dublin the Government
announced the appointment of a new Garda Commissioner, Pat
Byrne. Noel Conroy, the former head of the Serious Crime Squad,
who was by now an assistant commissioner, was promoted to the
rank of Deputy Commissioner in charge of operations to replace
the vacancy left by Byrne. Between them they would lead the
counter-offensive against organised crime. Nora Owen also
announced a package to alleviate the immediate difficulties and log
jams in the criminal justice system. The measures included the
recruitment of extra gardaí, a new prison building programme, the
appointment of extra judges, and extra administrative staff for the
Department of Justice and the courts.

Most significantly, there was also a commitment to establish
an (as yet unnamed) "special unit" which would be headed by the
police but would comprise officers from the Revenue and Social
Welfare. One of Pat Byrne's first tasks as Commissioner was to
advise the Taoiseach, John Bruton, and Nora Owen about the new
unit. The Government had planned to put it in the control of civil
servants, but Byrne argued that it should be led by the police, whom
the criminals would not like to take on. "If you don't do this, then
in a year you will come back and say that it was a mistake not to put
the gardaí in charge. Organised crime knows we won't be bullied,"
Byrne urged Bruton. The Government agreed with their top police
officer.

Legislation on the disposal of criminal assets was also in the
process of being drafted, based on a Private Member's Bill put
forward by the then opposition Justice spokesman, John
O'Donoghue. The legislation would reduce the standards of proof
required to seize a criminal's assets. Nora Owen pointed out that
the proposed legislation would have to be adjusted to ensure that it
was constitutional and stood up to legal scrutiny. These new laws
created the entity that would become known as the Criminal Assets
Bureau.

In less than two weeks after Veronica Guerin's murder, more sound legislation was enacted or mooted against organised crime than at any other time in the history of the State. The fight had begun.

Thirteen

The Investigation

The investigation of the murder of Veronica Guerin was never going to be simple. The unprecedented public outcry at such a high-profile act of terrorism put intense pressure on the political establishment. The public demanded answers and swift action against those responsible for the atrocity. The wall of flowers at the gates of the Dáil, the newspaper editorials and the countless calls to chat shows from an angry public summed it up. A well-organised criminal gang had declared war on society. It had been the ultimate wake-up call that crime was getting out of control. Rarely in Ireland's history had there been such a palpable sense of public anger, fear and frustration.

Ireland was in a state of crisis and the people were looking for leadership and reassurance. The political establishment had to do something about the situation. They looked to the Garda Síochána for answers and resolution. The individual who would lead the biggest criminal investigation in the State's history had to be carefully chosen. In career terms it was something of a poisoned chalice. That officer had to be experienced, capable and focused under the intense pressure which would come from all sides – criminal, political, media and public. That man was Chief Superintendent Tony Hickey.

Hickey was standing in a supermarket queue while on holiday in Portugal when he overheard two Irish people talking about the murder. Hickey never got excited in a crisis. From the time the Kerryman first became a cop in 1965 he was known as someone who stood back and considered all the options before reacting. He went back to his apartment and called his office at the Central Detective Unit in Harcourt Square. He was briefed on the current situation. The police, like everyone else that day, were still reeling from shock at the enormity of what had happened.

Lucan Garda station had been chosen as the base for the investigation in the first hours after the incident. The nearest station to the scene of the crime, Clondalkin, was too small to accommodate the number of officers required. To the then Deputy Commissioner Pat Byrne and Assistant Commissioner Noel Conroy, Hickey was the natural choice to head up the enquiry. Byrne rang Hickey and told him he was in charge. Hickey spent the last three days of his holiday plotting his strategy and making calls to Dublin. "This is definitely a step too far. The criminals have crossed the Rubicon and this murder simply has to be solved," Hickey told me in the early stages of the investigation.

In the first days after the murder there was chaos in the incident room in Lucan. Officers from specialist squads and district units all over the city were being called in. Everyone had a theory and wanted to play a part in the investigation. An army of angry officers turned up to volunteer for duty. One member of the investigation team recalled of the time: "There was sheer bedlam. We were trying to get a structure and a focus on the situation. There were so many gardaí coming in to work, the place was literally jammed. The scene of the crime had to be forensically analysed and statements taken from eyewitnesses to build a picture of what happened. Everyone was stunned at the murder coming so soon after the murder of Jerry McCabe. There was a sense that this just couldn't go on."

Detective Inspector Jerry O'Connell and the local district officer, Superintendent Len Ahern, took charge of organising the incident room and co-ordinating the investigation. Detectives from Hickey's Central Detective Unit (CDU) also arrived. Like Hickey, O'Connell knew of the mammoth task ahead. No one could afford to screw up. As soon as Hickey arrived back from Portugal on the following Saturday, he dropped his bags at home and drove the short distance to Lucan station. He began sifting through the various statements and reports and was briefed by his officers on the scene. He began to organise the single biggest assault on organised crime in gangland's history.

Hickey, a graduate of the FBI Academy in Quantico, Virginia, had been trained to use the Scotland Yard system of organising a major crime enquiry. When used properly, the system worked very effectively. An investigation needed control, direction and focus.

Everything at the scene was documented thoroughly and comprehensive statements taken from witnesses. That was followed up by house-to-house enquiries. Every call and tip from the public was documented and followed through. A detailed suspect list was collated and everyone on it accounted for to the satisfaction of the investigators. Regular conferences were held and everyone kept up-to-date with the flow of information and developments.

On Monday morning Hickey and O'Connell began putting together the group of officers who would become known as the Lucan Investigation Team. They were hand-picked people he and his senior officers knew and trusted. Detective Inspector Toddy O'Loughlin, another unflappable investigator who had been attached to the Investigation Branch at Garda Headquarters, was brought in. So, too, was a quiet-spoken sergeant called John O'Driscoll, a trusted confidant of Hickey's who had spent most of his career in charge of a secretive surveillance squad attached to CDU. O'Driscoll was the quintessential "spook".

In turn, the senior officers in the team selected cops they reckoned were up to the task ahead. Officers from detective and uniformed branch were chosen from units across the city and Garda headquarters. They included experienced investigators and younger cops who were prepared to work hard. There would be no room for slackers. At first the enquiry team was broken into two smaller teams. One of these, headed by O'Connell, would collate all available information about the crime and run the nerve centre of the investigation. They would gather the forensic evidence and all other relevant evidence. O'Driscoll was given the sensitive and time-consuming task of analysing every call made by every known suspect in and around the gang. Surveillance had to be co-ordinated between Lucan and Crime and Security Branch (or C 3) in the Phoenix Park, who provided phone taps, and the National Surveillance Unit (NSU).

The other team, under Todd O'Loughlin, would compile and investigate a list of suspects. Information was gathered from collators in every district in the city, Crime and Security Branch, CDU and Special Branch. Within days the list included over two hundred names, largely those of known criminals and members of the IRA and the INLA. All the gangs in the city were targeted. Every criminal Veronica had ever written about or threatened to write about was analysed. The known movements, associates and family connections of each suspect were carefully scrutinised. It was a trawl of massive proportions. Hickey ordered that each suspect be individually approached and asked to account for his movements on June 26, 1996.

Sitting at the top table of the incident room, Hickey told his men that he wanted the investigation to be methodical and proceed on a broad front. It would be slow, systematic and strictly by the book. The poker-faced chief would not allow the enquiry to be compromised by pressure from either the media or the politicians. He was acutely aware that he and his team were in the full glare of public attention, but there would be no rush to assuage the public with a result. Hickey had seen such investigations end in failure in the past. Everyone expected them to produce results. The pace of the investigation would be dictated by the pace of progress being made.

Everyone in the country knew the prime suspects within twenty-four hours. John Traynor and John Gilligan had become household names overnight. Gilligan had already admitted that he was the man in the frame in interviews with the *Sunday World* and the *Sunday Tribune*. In an interview with *Sunday Tribune* crime correspondent Liz Allen, Gilligan actually admitted that he had threatened to murder Veronica and kidnap and rape her son Cathal. Despite this, Hickey did not want the usual suspects rounded up. To successfully smash the gang responsible he would need hard evidence that stood up to rigorous examination in court. Pulling Gilligan in for questioning now would be a waste of time. If he and his gang were involved, then they would be prepared for a "pull". They were all hardened criminals. Hickey believed in carefully shadowing and unnerving his target, making him look over his shoulder, not knowing what was coming next. He wanted the gang's weakest links identified and isolated.

In the previous two years there had been twelve gangland murders in Dublin alone and none of them had been solved. Hickey had been involved in most of those investigations. The police had identified the hit men and their motives, but the problem was putting together a case that would survive in the courts. In each case there had been people who secretly gave information but refused to stand up in court. In the absence of an outright confession from the killer, there was nothing to sustain a charge. Several files on gangland murders had been sent to the Director of Public Prosecutions recommending that individuals be charged. In each case the State's criminal law officer decided not to prefer charges because there simply wasn't enough evidence.

Organised crime was protected by an impenetrable wall of silence. Its foundations were fear and violence. The more cases that went unsolved, the higher and harder the wall became. Hickey knew that breaking down that wall required a wholly new and revolutionary approach. Members of the actual murder gang held the key to success. This presented the biggest headache. There was no mechanism in place, such as a witness protection programme, to encourage individuals to come clean in safety. Like everything else in the Irish criminal justice system, the people on the ground would have to improvise. Hickey resolved to cross that obstacle when he had to. The killers of Veronica Guerin had launched the Lucan Investigation Team into the most dangerous of uncharted waters.

On top of this, there was also the distinct possibility that Gilligan's mob was not responsible. In the past, a rush for vengeance in the face of overwhelming public outrage had resulted in infamous miscarriages of justice, such as the cases of the Birmingham Six and the Guildford Four. The killing could easily have been a devious plot by a rival organisation designed to set Gilligan up. After all, Gilligan and Traynor had two very public motives for the horrific crime. They couldn't be so stupid and arrogant as to organise a murder and think that there would not be any repercussions – or could they?

A team member recalled Hickey's strategy. "He would say, 'Ok, Gilligan is our main suspect because he had the motive and was capable of the crime.' But he said this had to be a thorough and professional investigation. We had to work from the outside and move inwards, like the ripples on a pond. We had to peel away each layer to get to the next and all the time pick up information and evidence. If Gilligan's gang was responsible, then they would only emerge from a process of elimination and not speculation. We were told to look for a chink in the gang's armour, the weak link that could bring the whole house of cards down on the mob.

"In the early days a lot of us felt that we would be just going through the motions. Certainly at the time Gilligan's gang believed that that was what would happen. But Hickey was a great leader of men. So, too, were O'Loughlin and O'Connell. They never panicked or got excited. Hickey brought out the best in everyone because he had such energy and conviction. One day, after we spoke to an associate of John Traynor's, one guy at a conference told the chief that the criminal, who was also an informant, said we were going the wrong way about the enquiry, that we should be looking at such and such. Hickey never loses the head, but you could see he was angry. 'It would be a bad day when a fucking thug is going to tell us what we should be doing. *We* are in charge of this investigation,' he said. That was a turning point for everyone. We all thought, 'Yeah, Hickey's right.' From then on everyone on the team was determined that we would solve this one."

The intelligence that had been gathered on Gilligan and his gang by Kevin Carty's Operation Pineapple team proved invaluable when shared with the Lucan Investigation Team. Detective Inspector Tim Mulvey from the National Drug Unit had collated the names of members of the gang who were known, such as Meehan, Mitchell and Ward. Lists of telephone numbers, addresses and bank accounts had also been identified which would give the investigation a kick-start. But nothing was yet known about Bowden or Warren, or how the gang operated. No-one suspected the kind of money that was actually involved.

Within a week of the murder, Hickey had a team of around a hundred officers working on the case. The actual investigation team consisted of a core of thirty detectives. Another large team was dispatched to conduct detailed enquiries in Naas in the hope of obtaining some clue as to whether Veronica was being followed on the day of her murder. Hickey knew that the reporter would most likely have been stalked before the crime. It was too well planned an attack to have been opportunistic. Attention to detail paid off. At least one eyewitness recalled seeing Russell Warren, and a caretaker discovered that a roof tile had been dislodged on the court building. Three months later these seemingly innocuous observations provided corroboration when Russell Warren began to talk. Gilligan, he claimed, had told him another person was watching from a rooftop. The witness could place him in the vicinity of the courthouse when Warren said he was there.

At the same time, O'Loughlin's team went to work on the underworld. Unlike most gangland investigations, the criminals approached by the team were prepared to co-operate. Any villain with half a brain had by now realised that one of their number had taken a step too far. They were witnessing universal outrage and the authorities rush to tighten laws. Whoever pulled the trigger had screwed them, too. It had not escaped them, either, that Veronica was a woman, a mother and a well-known public face. Suddenly the hard men of the underworld did not want to be linked in any way with the crime or its perpetrators.

One investigation team member described the underworld trawl: "We would approach a known criminal and ask him to account for his movements on June 26. No matter how low he was in the criminal scale, he got a visit from the team. We showed that we meant business. In other cases you would expect to be told to fuck off, but the vast majority of them told us where they were and how we could check out their alibis. We talked to the criminals. We'd ask: 'What do you think about the murder? Do you know that this is going to fuck everything up for the lot of you?' The criminal fraternity were genuinely upset by the whole thing and didn't want to be seen to be suspects. We started getting a lot of information which kept going back to Gilligan and his outfit. The gangsters wanted us to know that they had nothing to do with it and that's why they talked. We also got information about other serious crimes which was passed onto other units.

"We made huge connections with the underworld, which had never been done before because there hadn't, I suppose, been a good enough reason or the resources there to conduct such a campaign. When we called to see suspects we demanded that they talk to us. We weren't prepared to leave without some information. After about three weeks or so the list was getting smaller. The intelligence was pointing all the time at Gilligan. Former members of the old Factory Gang began talking because they no longer wanted to be associated with him. We were hearing that Meehan and Ward had been on the bike. Every day we were making progress."

One criminal associate of John Traynor's, a cocaine dealer who operated under the guise of a building contractor, refused to co-operate with the detectives. They weren't prepared to walk away, however. The drug dealer's house was searched and documents removed for further examination. The officers couldn't prove any crime against the man but they did discover from the documentation that he had not paid his taxes. As the Criminal Assets Bureau had not yet been set up, the matter was passed to the Revenue Commissioners, who eventually issued the "builder" with a tax demand for fifty thousand pounds. "That wiped the smile off his face," a team member remarked later.

Two names on the list of suspects who were also less than co-operative were Brian Meehan and Peter Mitchell. On July 21 Sergeant Fergus Treanor and Garda Andy O'Brien called to see Brian Meehan at his apartment. When they asked about his movements on the day of the murder, Meehan said he couldn't remember. Then he paused and said: "I was with me father Kevin at his workplace." When O'Brien asked if anyone else had been there that day to verify his story, Meehan replied, "No", and walked away, shutting the door behind him.

Three days later the same officers visited Peter Mitchell. They met him near his home in Summerhill. O'Brien asked him where he was on June 26. "Probably doing what I normally do, driving around the place gettin' stopped by the fuckin' guards," Fatso replied in an aggressive tone. Then he said he had probably been on Moore Street talking to his mother Eileen, a street trader, when they heard the news of the murder around 2 p.m. Mitchell walked away. O'Brien tried to ask him another question, but Mitchell told him to "Fuck off". He climbed into his sports car and drove off at speed.

The same officers called to see Brian Meehan's father, Kevin, at his home on Stanaway Road in Crumlin on July 29. When the officers asked him about his whereabouts on the day of the murder, Meehan replied that he had been working at the roofing company part-owned by his brother, Thomas. When the officers asked Kevin if his son had called to see him at the yard on June 26, Meehan replied: "I don't know. I can't say. I would have to check. I am either at the yard or doing deliveries. I don't know if I can help you. What's it all about?"

The two officers explained that Brian had told them he had

been at the yard. They asked if Kevin could check that was the case. Kevin Meehan became aggressive. "I said I don't know and I'll check and get back to you. I don't have to check anything, I don't see what this has got to do with me," he said. The officers arranged to call back in two days. When they met Meehan again, he had a much clearer memory. "Yeah, Brian was with me alright. We made a cash sale for felt and the customer paid with sterling. We were offering it to anybody who might have been going on holidays. Brian called into me at 12.45 p.m. Well, I should say that it was definitely between 12.30 and 1 p.m.," Meehan recalled. When asked who else was present, Kevin named Peter Mitchell. He refused to answer any more questions and told the officers to leave. The gangsters couldn't even get their alibis straight. They had guaranteed a permanent spot for themselves on the list of suspects.

When approached, Paul Ward claimed that on the day in question he had been at home looking after his heroin addicted niece, helping her through cold turkey withdrawals. His girlfriend, Vanessa Meehan, could corroborate his story. When Dutchie Holland was asked to account for his movements, he said he had been with a friend, an elderly man, in Finglas. The same man, coincidentally, had provided Dutchie's alibi after the murder of Paddy Shanahan in 1996.

About three days after the murder, a man out walking along the banks of the River Liffey at the Strawberry Beds saw what looked like a motorbike in the water. It wasn't far from Lucan Garda station. The man had heard the appeals for information after the Guerin murder and reported what he had seen to the police. A uniformed officer made a half-hearted effort, but didn't find the bike. It wasn't reported to the investigation team. A week later the same man noticed the bike again and decided to pull it out himself. Ironically, he was spotted "acting suspiciously" and was reported to the gardaí. This time members of the investigation team went to the river and found the man and the bike.

Paul Ward had dumped it at that spot two days after the murder. With the help of another criminal, he had cut the bike up and brought it to the river in a van. The motorbike was taken to the Garda Technical Bureau and rebuilt. At that stage it wasn't known if it was the right motorbike, but Hickey was preoccupied with the find.

Why, he thought, would someone go to such lengths to cut up a bike and then dump it? Obviously, the bike held a clue. It was a promising development.

While the investigation was picking up pace, Gilligan's operation continued to flourish. Although other villains in the same boat would have gone to ground until the dust settled, Gilligan, Meehan and the rest of the Firm were actually increasing the size of their shipments. Every other drug dealer was keeping his head down, but Gilligan's men showed no fear and enthusiastically filled the void. In fact, the supply of hash would have dried up in the country in the first few months after the murder had it not been for Gilligan. During the first two months of the investigation, July and August, they received over two thousand kilos of hash and collectively made a profit of £2.6 million.

The ongoing investigation and furore changed nothing for the swaggering gangsters. The drugs were picked up as usual from the Ambassador Hotel and brought to the Greenmount distribution centre, from where Shay Ward and Charlie Bowden did their deliveries. The supplies were getting larger and were at times driving around Dublin with anything up to one hundred kilos in the back of the van. All it would have taken would have been an eagle-eyed cop at a road traffic checkpoint to rumble the largest drug trafficking operation in the State.

Russell Warren, who had been deeply disturbed by the murder and had become a bag of nerves, continued to work as the Firm's "financial controller". He became more important to the organisation because other former bagmen, like the Bookie and Meredith, wanted nothing more to do with Gilligan. In the weeks following the murder Warren recruited his parents, his sister and her husband to begin counting the huge sums of money rolling in. His parents' house became the equivalent of a gangland bank, where huge piles of cash were sorted, counted and packed. Russell wasn't very generous to his folks and paid them only fifty pounds each time they counted the dirty money. In July and August alone the jittery bagman's family counted over two million pounds, which Warren then transported and exchanged for Gilligan. As the operation continued to spiral, Warren found himself caught up in the middle. He was too weak and afraid to try and extricate himself.

One of the gang's main concerns now was the pace of the Lucan team's investigation. Through the gangland grapevine and the media they knew that their crime was being pursued with unprecedented vigour. Arrogantly, they still believed they couldn't be caught. They expected the enquiry to fizzle out after a few months. In the meantime, they would conduct their own investigations into the police and try to plant false leads where they could. Two days after the murder, a young uniformed cop named Rory Corcoran arrested Brian Meehan when he caught him driving despite having been disqualified for forty years. When he brought Meehan back to the Bridewell station to process him, Meehan offered to help the cop recover guns and get information on whoever it was had killed Veronica Guerin. The enthusiastic policeman was all ears, but he was clever enough to inform his Detective Inspector of the offer. Meehan arranged a number of meetings with Corcoran, which were attended by the senior detective. It quickly turned out that Meehan was looking for more information than he was actually giving. The cop was told to keep Meehan on side and feed him a few false lines about what the police knew.

In the first months of the investigation Gilligan's cronies leaked information to the media about police corruption. It was a clever and devious ploy designed to add to the public's lack of confidence in the police and create an atmosphere of mistrust within the Lucan team. Gilligan's men decided to cash in on their "investment", Garda John O'Neill. "We've paid O'Neill enough money, so it's time that he started earning his keep," an underworld source overheard Paul Ward saying to Brian Meehan in early August. Ward had just had O'Neill pull a warrant for Meehan's girlfriend, Fiona Walsh, relating to casual trading offences. Meehan told Ward he wanted to meet the Buffalo in person for a "chat". The crooked nightclub manager who had set up the initial meeting with Ward called O'Neill.

A few days later, Meehan and the nightclub manager arranged to meet the decorated officer at Beechfield Road in Crumlin. They were sitting in the manager's BMW car when O'Neill arrived around 6.30 p.m. with his wife and children. They began watching a children's five-aside soccer match, while O'Neill sat into the back seat of their car. Meehan had no fears about coming to the point. He knew the cop was already in way over his head and was therefore trustworthy. Meehan told O'Neill that he was putting him on the "payroll" at five hundred pounds per week. For that sum he was to "look out" for Peter Mitchell, Ward and himself. Meehan wanted him to report back anything he heard being said about the gang or any intelligence documents going through his station about them. He also wanted to know if surveillance was being placed on them. O'Neill was to continue "looking after" outstanding warrants and court summonses and, when required, to process passport applications. He was going to be a busy man. O'Neill didn't care how much he was betraying everything he stood for. In the end it was all about the money.

The Garda top brass had already begun checking up on the involvement of officers with Gilligan and other underworld gangs. There was concern that officers were on the mob's payroll; if it was so, then it had to be identified and neutralised. An investigation which had already been going on into a rogue detective based in Rathfarnham called John Ryan was stepped up. Ryan had been involved with John Traynor and Sean Fitzgerald in the dodgy used car business. The two fraudsters actually complained that Ryan was ripping them off in a number of their crooked deals. He was subsequently convicted for a crime relating to car theft and jailed.

Another officer attached to Special Branch was found to have visited Gilligan at his home in Jessbrook six days before the murder. The officer's identity, John O'Shea, came to light after he made a number of anonymous phone calls to the Lucan incident room which were subsequently traced. Using the name Joe, O'Shea claimed that he had information about Gilligan but needed guarantees about his safety and that of a friend who, he said, had been in his company when Gilligan asked for information which would discredit the reporter. The officer was investigated during an internal inquiry and switched to other duties.

In the atmosphere of paranoia now sweeping the gardaí in Dublin, the officer who had been handling Traynor also became a suspect. He was grilled by a senior officer after an incorrect story about the "relationship" between the cop and the crook appeared in a newspaper. The detective was stunned by the officer's insinuations and moved from the Central Detective Unit. He had never been involved in any criminal offence and it has since been acknowledged that the officer was above reproach and should never have been treated with suspicion. While this was going on, John O'Neill was still working for the Gilligan gang without being noticed by anyone.

On July 25 the Dáil passed the Proceeds of Crime Act 1996 as part of the government's new anti-crime package, which also included the Disclosure of Information for Taxes and Other Purposes Act. The Criminal Assets Bureau officially came into existence on July 31, although it would have no statutory powers until the Criminal Assets Bureau Act was made law on October 15. Chief Superintendent Fachtna Murphy, who had spent most of his career investigating fraud, was appointed as the chief bureau officer. Financial and taxation fraud was a highly specialised area and few garda officers had Murphy's expertise. The proposed powers and structure was an exciting and innovative departure and much more sophisticated than similar units in Europe. Nevertheless, its success would depend on how it was organised and run. Like Hickey, Murphy knew that this could not be seen to fail.

The State Solicitor for County Cork, Barry Galvin, was brought in as the CAB's chief legal officer. For several years Galvin had been a source of embarrassment to the gardaí and the government over his public claims that Ireland was being used by international crime syndicates to launder drug money. He had gone on national television to expose the fact that several major international traffickers had bought luxury homes in the south west of the country, from where they co-ordinated their drugs empires. Galvin demanded that new powers be introduced to target these criminals and seize their assets, but the response from the police and the Department of Justice was predictable. Galvin was derided as an over-ambitious solicitor who fancied himself as some kind of Elliot Ness. They believed that the drugs empires he was describing simply didn't exist and. like the murdered journalist, Galvin was exaggerating the problem. The Gilligan gang proved the anonymous bureaucrats to be wrong. Times were changing.

The new Garda commissioner, Pat Byrne, in consultation with Murphy, chose Detective Superintendent Felix McKenna as the Bureau's second-in-command. The officer who had achieved Gilligan his longest prison stretch was about to become a thorn in the little man's side once again. There was chaos during the first days of the new bureau. For a start, McKenna and Murphy did not have office space and began operating from three separate rooms in different parts of the Dublin Metropolitan HQ at Harcourt Square. Murphy and McKenna hand-picked the garda team who would form the nucleus of the new bureau: two detective inspectors, four sergeants and ten gardaí. However, there was the difficulty of gelling the four separate agencies – Garda Síochána, Social Welfare, Revenue and Customs – together in one task force, a thing that had never before been done anywhere in Europe. McKenna was given the task of devising a plan setting out a modus operandi for the CAB. At first there was considerable friction between the new partners. Customs and the Garda Síochána, for example, had had a long history of bitter rivalry which successive governments had failed to resolve.

McKenna chaired an expert committee comprising senior representatives of the Revenue, Customs and Social Welfare with a view to drawing up a document outlining how the agencies would work together. Several operational and security problems were identified by the group and Fachtna Murphy relayed these to the Department of Justice for drafting into the Criminal Assets Bureau Act. Security and information technology experts were brought in from the U.S. and Britain to advise on security structures. The civil servants who were attached to the new bureau were nervous about the joining the CAB because of the possible dangers from organised crime. In the new Act it was forbidden to photograph or identify any members of the CAB, apart from Murphy and Galvin. Cork's "Elliot Ness" was given armed garda protection and became the first civilian to be allowed carry a firearm.

As soon as news broke about the Proceeds of Crime Act, Gilligan's gang scurried to clear their bank accounts and hide their money. In the space of a week from July 24 to July 31, Geraldine Gilligan withdrew over two hundred thousand pounds from several bank accounts she had held in her name. In August, Brian Meehan began clearing out his cash with the help of his father, Kevin, and his uncle, Thomas. Both men had helped Brian Meehan hide his wealth by lodging large sums of money in bank accounts using their own names. Several other crime figures rushed to clear out their ill-gotten gains. For them, it was the most severe repercussion of the Guerin murder. One gangster, who was particularly agitated by the CAB, declared to an associate: "Gilligan or one of those fuckers with him will have be whacked for this. They've fucked everything up."

In August, Meehan and his father opened two sterling deposit accounts in the Creditanstalt Bank in Vienna, Austria, and lodged a total of £619,491 during a number of visits over several weeks. All the money had been withdrawn from accounts in building societies and banks across Dublin. The father and son signed non-resident statements and produced their passports for identification purposes. They gave the bank specimen signatures and requested that no correspondence be sent to their homes in Ireland. The Meehans both signed "code word agreements" which allowed them to make withdrawals and receive information about the accounts on simply mentioning the code words. Brian Meehan gave the bank the code word "Meener" and his father selected the word "Green".

On the very day the CAB came into existence, Kevin Carty's Operation Pineapple team raided Jessbrook and took away all financial documentation for analysis. These was passed on to Murphy and McKenna, who were working closely with the Money Laundering Unit of the Fraud Bureau. With the money gone there was no point in freezing any bank accounts and, if there was money in the accounts, at that stage the CAB did not have the power to freeze them. The first major investigation conducted by the CAB involving all of agencies was assessing Geraldine and John Gilligan for tax based on the seized documentation and banking records. It was calculated that between them they owed over £2.5 million in unpaid income tax for the year 1994–1995. When the assessment was drawn up at the beginning of September, none of the tax inspectors assigned to the bureau would sign the document. In the absence of an inspector's signature, the assessment could not be served. When the CAB Act was finally drafted, these tax assessments would be merely signed "Criminal Assets Bureau". To get around the problem, Barry Galvin officially became an inspector of taxes. The documents were signed and sent to Jessbrook. When the demands arrived, Geraldine contacted little John, who lost his head with rage. He called a friend in a state of fury. "Who in fuck do these pricks think they are... Are they fucking mad? It's daylight robbery, that's what it is!" he ranted to his pal. Gilligan later tried to get some of his associates to shoot one of the Revenue people with a view to scaring them off, but the plan never got off the ground.

Back in Lucan, forensic reports revealed that the bullets used in the murder were unusual in that they were reloaded bullets. Reloading bullets is the illegal practice of recycling old, used bullets done mainly by deer hunters because the ammunition required is so expensive. Operations Mauser 1 and, later, Mauser 2 were launched in Lucan in a bid to locate the individual who made the rounds. Gun enthusiasts and hunters throughout the country were arrested and questioned in swoops by dozens of officers attached to the Lucan Investigation Team. The vast majority of the people lifted were respectable professionals. One man actually worked for a foreign embassy. The hunt for the reloaded bullets was a huge success in that it resulted in the seizure of over eighty illegal firearms, including assault rifles, pump-action shotguns and automatic pistols. Twelve people were arrested and charged with firearms offences. A weapon used in the murder of a biker in County Wicklow was also traced by the Lucan team.

The motorbike find had also brought about a breakthrough. The Lucan squad had compiled a list of all stolen motorbikes in the greater Dublin area. When the bike was pieced together, the gardaí were able to trace it to Ian Keith, who had reported his bike as stolen shortly before the Guerin murder. The in-depth analysis of the phone traffic between the known gang members had thrown up the names of several other associates of the gang. Det. Sgt John O'Driscoll, using a specially designed computer programme, had done an extraordinary job in cross-referencing numbers to identify the gang members and build up a picture of their activities. Particularly interesting was the volume of traffic between at least four phones on the day of the murder. "It was clear from just looking at the calls being made between the four phones that something was going down on June 26. It was more evidence that Gilligan and his gang were the right people," a member of the team recalled.

Each phone owner was profiled and checked against the huge bank of intelligence information the Lucan team now had compiled from all branches of the system. Russell Warren and Paul Cradden were among those identified. A phone belonging to a Paul Conroy was also featuring prominently on the lists, but by late August he still had not been identified. Conroy was the false name being used by Charlie Bowden. Through Cradden's connection with Warren and the theft of Ian Keith's bike, the Lucan team now had a potential link connecting the bike with Cradden and Cradden in turn with Warren.

Hickey was quietly happy that things were going in the right direction. Warren was approached by the team and asked to account for his movements on the day of the murder. Like the other gang members, Warren lied. The detectives took the opportunity to weigh him up. They reported back to Hickey, O'Loughlin and O'Connell that the bagman was definitely the weak link. Warren's details were passed to the National Surveillance Unit and he was put under watch. Things were looking good.

On the Monday night following the murder I was a guest on Chris Barry's late-night radio chat show on FM 104 in Dublin. The programme, which later moved to 98 FM, had a lively format that encouraged people to call in and get things off their chests. That night we were discussing Veronica's murder. After about half an hour of calls and debates with listeners, I was informed that a guy claiming to be the Coach was on the line and wanted to talk to me. As soon as I heard the slurred speech I recognised that John Traynor was drunk and emotional. Live on the air he exhorted me to agree to meet with him and discuss the murder. "I thought the world of that girl and you know that's true, Paul. I want you to ring me after that show and meet me. You know that I am telling the truth."

I reminded Traynor of the warning he had given me over the past year about Gilligan and what he said he would do to Veronica. Traynor denied that he ever made the comments. I then put it to him, still on the air, that he had staged the accident in Mondello as part of his alibi, an accusation that he also denied. He claimed that he had won his case against the *Sunday Independent* and, had he not crashed, said he probably would have been passing the murder scene around the time the hit took place. It was obvious that the Coach was scared of something.

The next day we had a long conversation on the phone about the murder. Traynor was distraught and refused to meet me after seeing the picture of himself talking to Veronica which had been surreptitiously taken by the *Sunday Independent*. A few days later Traynor left the country and went into hiding in France.

On July 12 Traynor phoned again, claiming that the INLA were about to issue a statement which would clear his name. On the subject of a face-to-face interview, Traynor was trying to ascertain whether I believed he was involved in the murder. On the following weekend the *Sunday World* exposed the relationship between Gilligan and the INLA, especially his friendship with Fergal Toal and Dessie O'Hare in Portlaoise. The INLA issued a statement from Belfast, which Garda headquarters took as a serious threat, condemning me for the story. An INLA figure then tried to intimidate me over the story, leading the gardaí to search my car for a suspected booby-trap device.

The day same day the story appeared Traynor called me. He asked if would I be prepared to leave the country to meet him. He was also concerned about the story in the paper and said the INLA had "nothing to do with Veronica's murder". He was also aware that by that stage the Lucan team had visited individual members of the INLA asking them to account for their movements. On the afternoon of Tuesday, July 16, he phoned and said he would meet me the following day in Lisbon, Portugal. The next afternoon I met Traynor in a cafe in Lisbon international airport. Wearing slacks with a shirt and tie, he looked hassled and uncomfortable in the sweltering heat. His face was grey and he looked genuinely worried. He constantly chain-smoked and talked on his mobile phone. At the time I had no idea that one of the regular callers was John Gilligan, inquiring about how things were going with "that reporter".

Over the next two days I interviewed Traynor in two locations, in Lisbon and in a downmarket seaside resort called Costa Da Caparica, twenty miles from the Portugese capital. During those meetings Traynor denied any knowledge or involvement in the murder and implied that it had been the work of two men he named as having been involved in the murder of Gilligan's old friend John Bolger in 1994. Significantly, the two men Traynor referred to had fallen out with the INLA gang in Dublin. They were fair game for Traynor's accusations. He kept trying to divert my attention away from the INLA and suggested that I was in some danger from them. "I'll do you a favour in relation to that," he reassured me. Later on he told me he had just received a phone call "from some of my people saying that they are planning to approach you and talk to you. I told them not to lay a finger on that man because he is helping me while he is out here," Traynor claimed. If he was trying to scare me, it certainly wasn't working. Throughout our meetings, which lasted several hours, Traynor seemed worried and scared of someone. He didn't say who but it later became obvious that it was Gilligan. Whenever I tried to bring the conversation around to Gilligan, Traynor simply refused to discuss him. He claimed that there was "no way Gilligan would do anything like that".

He refused to speak about Gilligan, but began discussing his association with Veronica and the day of her murder. "Despite the fact that we had fallen out, I still had a deep regard for Veronica and have been genuinely, deeply saddened by her murder. I considered her a good friend. She had a warm, bubbly personality and I got on with her from the moment we met until she revealed to me that she was going to write a story about me. I liked her from the minute we met. Veronica was full of life. She was very intelligent and had a nice manner. She always had a twinkle in her eye and I suppose I was mesmerised and fascinated with her. I admired her for her courage and eagerness to get a story, especially being a woman. I considered her a good friend and we regularly met for coffee.

"Since I came out of prison in 1990, I had tried to put my criminal past behind me and had begun socialising with decent people. If a story like the one Veronica was writing appeared about me, it would make them think I was some kind of animal. The week before Veronica was murdered my legal team told me that they were almost one hundred per cent sure that I had won my case and that no story would be appearing about me. On the day of the murder I was the happiest man in the world that morning, as I headed off with my two boys to Mondello. If I had been planning to kill Veronica, Naas would have been the last place in the world I would have gone to.

"People say the accident was staged, but I was lucky to get out of that car alive. I was in shock and covered in glass and I had hurt my shoulder. Anyone who saw the accident will say that I could easily have been killed. When I came out of the x-ray room in Naas hospital, one of my sons who had my phone said that someone had been shot. My daughter had passed the scene where Veronica was shot about five minutes after it had happened.

"Within the space of five minutes I had several calls telling me that someone had been killed. When I was told that it was a woman in a red Calibra, I knew it was Veronica. I was very upset. I said to the nurse who was looking after me: 'I knew that person who was shot... She was a good friend of mine.' I got a lift to the garage I owned in Naas and got a car and drove my sons home. I went around by Saggart because I just could not face driving by the murder scene, I couldn't stomach it. Veronica and I had fallen out but I still had a lot of respect and feelings for her. I was feeling very, very sad. In the following days the press started hounding me and then the injunction hearing came up and I was in every paper in the country. I was astounded that people began to look at me as if I did it. I don't believe Veronica would have wished this kind of damage on me in a thousand years.

"My home was besieged by photographers and my family started to get threatening phone calls. I left because my nerves couldn't stand it any more."

I returned to Dublin on the Friday morning. That weekend the *Sunday World* ran a front-page story and four pages of Traynor's interview inside. He had even posed for pictures. It was just another aspect to the story of Gilligan's gang, which was beginning to unfold at an incredible pace, but then the most bizarre development in the whole sordid story occurred.

Sometime before lunch on the following Wednesday, July 24, I received a call on my mobile phone from someone with a Dublin accent purporting to be a friend of John Gilligan's. "John Gilligan is concerned that you are being threatened and blackmailed by Traynor not to write about him [Gilligan]. Mr Gilligan would like to talk with you, if that is alright, on the phone," the voice informed me. I was astonished and confused about the call. As far as I had been concerned, Traynor's interview had gone without a hitch. There had certainly been no overt threats of any kind and he had stayed away from talking about the little man.

At about 12.15 p.m. my phone rang again. This time John Gilligan was on the line. It was one of the most bizarre conversations I ever had with a member of the criminal underworld. "Traynor is a very dangerous man. When you left Lisbon, he [Traynor] rang me and said he had threatened you not to write any more stories about me. He is blackmailing you with compromising pictures which he showed you before you left Portugal. The pictures are of you with a woman and I wouldn't like to be in your shoes dealing with that man," Gilligan's voice sounded calm and deliberate. I had no idea what pictures he might be talking about.

The little godfather went on to deny any involvement with the murder of Veronica. "I hate to say it, but I hate that fucking woman now for all that she has done to me and my family. But if I were you I would be very careful because Traynor might put those pictures in the paper," Gilligan's voice had become menacing and threatening. It was an obvious attempt to try and stop me writing about him. From his tone it was clear that he believed Traynor was blackmailing me.

I told Gilligan that neither he, Traynor, nor any other thug would blackmail me. If he had anything compromising about me in his possession, I told him to keep it and do what he liked with it. "If you do come across any pictures of me, send me some for my family album, you sleazy little bastard," I replied angrily. Gilligan appeared to be taken aback that someone would dare talk to him like that. "Now, I don't want you to be upset with me. I just don't want to be involved between you and Traynor, do you understand me? Now, this conversation never took place, is that alright?" Gilligan added before I ended the conversation.

Immediately afterwards I called Traynor's mobile phone. When he answered I demanded an explanation about what was going on. Traynor sounded scared. It was then that whole outrageous plot was revealed. "Before you came to meet me in Portugal, Gilligan told me to set you up and get pictures of you. He told me: 'Set that man up with a few slappers and then we'll have him on side and shut him up'," explained the con man. "While you were with me Gilligan kept ringing, asking had I done it. When you left I told him that I had set you up and had pictures in my possession. I am scared of Gilligan and he is so volatile at the moment that I was afraid at what he would do to me if I refused. The easiest way out was just to say that I had done it. When he [Gilligan] phoned you, he thought he had you in his hip pocket," Traynor added.

I told Traynor that I thought that I would write a story about what had just happened. The following Friday morning Traynor phoned again. This time his call lasted nearly an hour, during which he apologised about the attempted "blackmail". He sounded worried and nervous. He claimed that Gilligan was intensely angry with him, that he hadn't set me up. "He told me that he was sending people to get me... You don't understand, you don't say no to Gilligan and hope to get away with it. He is a very bad man. I have a family in Dublin and his has a big network of people," Traynor told me.

At that stage I asked Traynor to come clean about the murder of Veronica. I said that if he, Traynor, was going to be killed by Gilligan's people, then it would be better if someone knew what really had happened. In a moment of truth, Traynor admitted for the first and only time that Gilligan had ordered the murder. From my extensive dealings with the gangster, I believed what he was saying. Traynor had indeed set Veronica up by giving the gang the information about her murder. He claimed that he had no knowledge of how Gilligan had planned the murder or who he hired to do it. He begged me not to write the story in the *Sunday World* or to tell the gardaí.

I didn't run the blackmail story because of the fears Traynor had for his family's safety. They were, after all, innocent victims of the whole sorry episode. But I did contact the Lucan Investigation Team and make a full statement.

Fourteen

Gang Busters

Gangland had never seen an offensive like it before. Several weeks into the investigation and there was no let up in the pressure coming from Lucan. By the end of August the investigation had intensified to become the largest search and arrest operation ever mounted by the gardaí. After weeks of a painstaking process of elimination, Hickey, O'Loughlin and O'Connell were satisfied that the Gilligan gang were their primary suspects. All other avenues of enquiry had been either exhausted or led directly back to them. The investigation was now focused on one primary objective, namely to smash Gilligan's mob. The long hours of plodding investigative work were paying off. but there were still large pieces of the underworld puzzle missing.

Gilligan, Traynor, Meehan, Mitchell, Paul and Shay Ward, Denis Meredith, Paul Cradden, the Bookie and Warren were all now in the frame. Dutchie Holland's name was also featuring prominently throughout the various phone records. Hickey had a major interest in Holland, whom he had jailed twice in the past. Holland's name had also featured on the list of suspected hit men. Bowden had not yet been linked to "Paul Conroy", although he had been mentioned by detectives from the North Central Divisional Drug Squad as an associate of Meehan and Mitchell's. Within weeks Bowden would become a central player in the unfolding drama.

Early in the investigation, individuals considered to be on the periphery of Gilligan's organisation were arrested and questioned. Then, the Lucan team adopted a different approach from that used in past investigations. As the team honed in closer to the gang, the friends, relatives and associates of each individual suspect became arrest targets. Each suspect had someone in whom he confided and Hickey's men were determined to find out what those confidants had been told. The smallest morsel of information could give the investigators a new break. Everyone in each target's contact group was arrested at the same time in large, co-ordinated swoops. The strategy was to play hard ball as the team tore down the protective layers the gang members had erected around themselves. When the police hit, they hit hard for maximum effect.

Horrified civilians found themselves being ordered out of bed and arrested in the early hours of the morning by armed detectives. Some of them had never before received so much as a parking ticket and now they were in the surreal world of an interview room, looking into the grim faces of experienced interrogators. They found themselves answering blunt questions about a loved one or friend in relation to a crime that horrified them, as it did the rest of the nation. An arrest in connection with the Veronica Guerin enquiry was a source of great shame. Almost everyone was willing to co-operate in order to distance themselves from the culprits. In the course of the Lucan investigation, over 330 people were arrested, 1,500 people were interviewed without arrest and 3,500 were statements taken.

The gangland crackdown was organised with such meticulous precision that it has been described since as a template for other complex serious crime investigations. Targets were selected during secretive conferences involving the core team members in the incident room. The conferences were chaired by Jerry O'Connell and Todd O'Loughlin. Every member of the team was consulted for his opinion on a suggested course of action. One team member gave a behind-the-scenes description of how the investigation was conducted:

"Everyone was working together and no-one tried to win points over anyone else. When you were given a job, you did it and did it right. There was no room for mistakes. There was great team spirit. The focus was on how best to achieve the task at hand. The basic garda's opinion on the team was as valid as Tony Hickey's. That was the way he ran the investigation. Once a target was picked, intelligence on the whole group was collated before we made a move. Each target group would have been analysed for what they might be able to offer or should know. Team leaders organised arrest and search parties. Various stations were selected where prisoners were to be taken and interrogation teams picked. Extra manpower would be summoned from across the city as well as specialist armed backup from the Emergency Response Unit (ERU). The National Surveillance Unit would have been in position for days beforehand and could pinpoint the locations of those who were to be pulled in.

"Before a raid, everyone involved was required to meet in the incident room for a briefing on the identities and locations of the various targets. It was decided that reinforcements should be treated on a need-to-know basis, simply to avoid loose talk. Searches were slow and meticulous. We were told to search for evidence and clues that could be used for potential leads and during questioning. If there was something illegal there to sustain a charge, it would be considered a bonus. Practically everyone who was arrested was run for the full length of their [statutory maximum] 48-hour detention period. We used the full scope of our powers. The majority of 'prisoners' gave us some information. The tactic was very successful and had the added effect that when people were released from custody the word spread like wild fire that we meant business."

The investigation team worked all day, every day, for most of the first six months. Adrenaline and sheer determination kept everyone going. Officers considered themselves fortunate to get one day off each week to rest and spend time with their families. The morale of the team was boosted when Commissioner Pat Byrne announced the promotion of Tony Hickey to the rank of Assistant Commissioner. Breaking with normal practice, Byrne decided that Hickey would remain head of the Lucan investigation. By September they were gearing up to make a direct attack on the Gilligan gang.

Det. Sgt John O'Driscoll, operating from a room full of phone records, had produced a detailed analysis of the gang's calls on and around the day of the murder. The Gilligan gang had used the phones like walkie-talkies. The times and length of each call showed a structure. The records could show roughly where a suspect was at the time of the call. The phone traffic effectively helped to identify the gang members who had been involved in the murder. It was the first time that mobile phone records had played such a pivotal role in an investigation.

Flowcharts mapping out what was known about the gang and its structure were placed on the wall at the top of the incident room. The room was also overlooked by a picture of Veronica Guerin, which Tony Hickey had pinned up during the first week of the investigation. No matter where one stood in the large room, they met Veronica's smiling face. "It was as if she wouldn't allow us to forget what all this was about. It was what she had died for, exposing evil bastards like Gilligan and his outfit," a team member recalled almost five years later. A montage of pictures of the gang members was also put up on the wall. Representatives of the various police forces who had been asked for assistance in the investigation were brought to Lucan and given a full briefing about the murder and the gang. "When the various police officers got the briefing they also saw the picture. It was a poignant reminder about what this was all about and they were very sympathetic," the team member added.

The Lucan strategy was working. After a few months Brian Meehan phoned a friend and discovered that yet another group of people had been lifted. He was incredulous. "The cops aren't still fucking chasing after us? I thought that would be over ages ago." Meehan, like the rest of the mob, had believed in all sincerity that the investigation would fade away and be dropped within a month. Instead, the pressure was a source of annoyance. In August Garda intelligence learned of a secret meeting in Holland between Meehan, Gilligan and George "the Penguin" Mitchell.

Mitchell had been one of the godfathers whose business had been disrupted by the gang's actions and as a result had moved to establish permanent residency in Holland. He wanted the problem of the ongoing investigation sorted out, so that things could get back to normal. He advised Gilligan and Meehan to shoot a garda. "Anywhere in the country, set one [garda officer] up and riddle him, using machine guns. There'll be so much hassle with that investigation that they'll put all their good men onto the cop murder. If it's done right, then they'll think it's the Provos. Anyway, they have murdered cops before. The Guerin thing will be forgotten in no time," Mitchell was reported as having said at the meeting.

When the intelligence filtered through to Crime and Security Branch, Tony Hickey was warned about the latest development. Members of the investigation team were advised to be extra vigilant and wear their firearms at all time. Two detectives armed with Uzi machine guns were placed on around-the-clock duty at Lucan to protect the always-open incident room. Extra patrols were put in place in and around Lucan village to watch for suspicious activity in the vicinity of the station house. Bomb and fireproof safes were specially imported and part of the station was refurbished to accommodate them. The threats had to be taken seriously. From the flood of hard intelligence coming through, Hickey realised that he and his team were up against a pernicious, evil empire. The criminals were dangerous men who, when they were cornered, would do anything to wriggle free.

By September the investigators were beginning to get a handle on the huge amounts of money the gang had at its disposal. Cash which could buy hit men. The gang had extensive contacts in Europe. Hired killers from Eastern Europe were as plentiful as prostitutes and drug barons in downtown Amsterdam. The close link between Gilligan and the INLA had also been uncovered. The renegade, drug-dealing paramilitaries were already suspected of providing the hit man. Intelligence suggested that the once political organisation had been used as a veritable private army by Gilligan.

In an extraordinary act of bravado, several members of the INLA in Dublin posed for pictures, sitting at a table wearing balaclavas and holding firearms. They declared that their "army" was going to take on the drugs gangs across west Dublin to purge the working class estates. The incredible stunt, organised by a violent thug from County Armagh called Declan Patrick Duffy, was designed to maximise on the public's sense of apprehension after the Guerin murder. In reality, they were reaffirming John Gilligan's supremacy in the drugs business because they were his allies and scaring off the opposition. Behind the balaclavas they were nothing more than drug-dealing thugs themselves. Hickey and his men came down hard on Gilligan's henchmen. The entire leadership of the INLA and their associates were arrested in another major swoop. Some of the terrorists underwent dramatic conversions during their detention in stations across west Dublin. They offered their tormentors valuable information about Gilligan and his associates.

At this stage the Provos began to show an interest in Gilligan and his gang. Claims that the Provos had been planning to have Gilligan assassinated before Veronica's murder were not true, nor were claims that they had kidnapped the little man twice before. The truth was that the Provos had been happy to allow Gilligan

John Traynor on the run in Portugal, 1996.
Sunday World

Dutchie Holland being brought to court in 1997 by Det. Garda Sean O'Brien (right) and Sgt Fergus Treanor to face drug trafficking charges.
Liam O'Connor, Sunday World

Brian Meehan being taken off an Air Corps transport plane by Lucan Investigation Team members Det. Sgt John O'Driscoll, Sgt Fergus Treanor and Det. Sgt Noel Browne in September 1998.
Padraic O'Reilly / Liam O'Connor, Sunday World

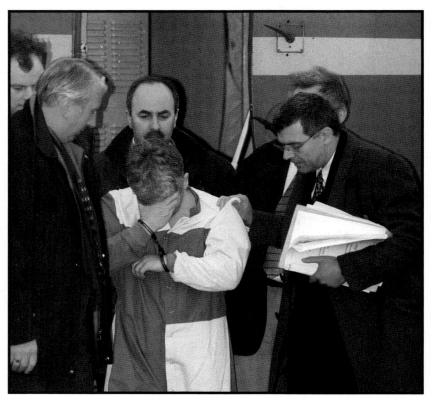

John Gilligan, still wearing his distinctive British prison uniform, being taken from a military transport plane by the Lucan Investigation Team, Det. Insp. Todd O'Loughlin (right), Det. Bernard Masterson (middle) and Det. Garda Bernie Hanly.

Padraic O'Reilly, Sunday World

Gotcha!

Peter Mitchell caught hiding on the Costa Del Sol during Brian Meehan's trial, 1999.
Padraic O'Reilly, Sunday World

Peter Mitchell with his girlfriend Sonya Walsh on the balcony of his luxurious hideout in Spain, 1999.
Padraic O'Reilly / Liam O'Connor, Sunday World

Mitchell's split-level Spanish mansion, complete with private pool.
Padraic O'Reilly / Liam O'Connor, Sunday World

Brian Meehan's parents, Kevin and Frances, in Amsterdam to visit their son in prison, February 1998.
Padraic O'Reilly / Liam O'Connor, Sunday World

Vanesssa Meehan with her father, Kevin, leaving the hospital after he was shot, 1999.
Padraic O'Reilly, Sunday World

Geraldine Gilligan and the author pictured at Jessbrook in November 1996 when the Criminal Assets Bureau moved in to seize the Equestrian Centre and the Gilligans' home.
Liam O'Connor, Sunday World

State Supergrass Charlie Bowden being led away amid tight security after he was sentenced on drugs charges.
Sunday World

John Traynor shortly before Veronica Guerin's murder.
Sunday Independent

John Gilligan used this picture to convince various customs and police units that he was a legitimate "business investor".
Sunday World

The complete haul of drugs, guns and ammunition seized by the Lucan Investigation Team in the months after Veronica Guerin's murder.

Graham Turly on his way to court on the day that John Gilligan was acquitted of the murder of Turly's wife, Veronica Guerin.
Padraic O'Reilly, Sunday World

The first Head of the Criminal Assets Bureau, Det. Chief Superintendent Factna Murphy, and the Bureau's Chief Legal Officer, Barry Gavin.

Former Serious Crime Squad officer Felix McKenna, who was appointed second in command of the then newly formed Criminal Assets Bureau. He became the Bureau chief in 1999.

Asst Comm. Tony Hickey, who lead the Lucan Investigation Team.

Inspector Padraig Kennedy.

Garda Commissioner Pat Byrne at a news conference following Gilligan's acquittal for murder.

Lucan Investigation Team Detectives Bob O'Reilly and Tom Fallon.

operate. He had often helped them out in the past. Gilligan, like Coyle, had never been touched by the Provos before, even though they had been in competing negotiations with the UVF for the sale of the Beit paintings.

After the murder of Martin Cahill, Gilligan and Traynor were among the only criminals who were not summoned by the Provos to one of their infamous interrogation sessions. They had not been touched in the Provo trawl of gangland, which was nothing more than a fundraising exercise. Through Paddy Farrell and Brendan "Speedy" Fegan, Gilligan was also supplying the loyalist terror groups in the North with ecstasy, hashish and cocaine. The hard men of the IRA showed no interest in these dealings, but in a cynical gesture after Guerin's murder, they put the word out that Gilligan was to be shot in revenge. It created beneficial publicity, with Provos being seen as defenders of the people. In reality, they were trying to manipulate the situation.

In the summer of 1996 Tommy Coyle and another close friend of Gilligan's, who had also been a member of the Factory Gang from Cabra, were approached with a proposition. A senior figure in the Dublin Brigade of the IRA told the pair that the organisation wanted Gilligan to "organise" a big drug deal with two named members of the notorious Portadown-based UVF. One of the named UVF men had also been involved in the Beit paintings deal and was now co-ordinating the gang's drugs business. The Provos wanted Gilligan to lure the two men to the south, where they would ambush them. It would be a spectacular publicity coup. Two members of a loyalist murder gang shot dead as they picked up a load of drugs in the Republic. In return, the top Provo informed Coyle and Gilligan's other associate, they would leave the little man alone. "The movement will leave Gilligan's problems to the police. Otherwise Darren Gilligan will be in trouble," the Provo explained. Gilligan was given the message during his brief stay in Dublin in September. Nothing ever came of the plot. One of the UVF men was subsequently murdered in an internal loyalist feud.

As the pressure continued to build in Ireland, things were not running so smoothly for the gang in Holland. Before Veronica Guerin's murder, the Dutch side of Operation Pineapple was called the "Paddy

Team". In early July, further requests were made for assistance by the Departments of Justice and Foreign Affairs. The Dutch then organised Operation Setter, named after the Irish red setter dog, targeting Martin Baltus and Simon Rahman. Baltus had already begun to talk to the Dutch police after the seizure of Gilligan's counterfeit dollars. Rahman had told police that the notes belonged to Baltus. Baltus felt betrayed by his former partner in crime and also suspected that his arrest in March 1995 with the Agram machine gun had been set up by the drug trafficker. Operation Setter began trawling through Rahman's myriad companies to track down his criminal empire.

With Baltus in prison on the counterfeit money rap and Johnny Wildhagen officially "disappeared", Rahman was forced out into the open. From his base in Belgium, Gilligan was ordering larger shipments of hash. Rahman never refused a deal as long as there was hard cash coming. In order to fill Gilligan's orders, Rahman was forced to begin buying up stock from the other major traffickers based in Amsterdam. Without his henchmen, Rahman had no-one to pick up and pack the drugs for shipping to Ireland.

On August 1 an undercover surveillance team watched Rahman as he drove to meet one of his associates at a McDonald's restaurant in Zoetermeer. Rahman was in a hurry to fill one of Gilligan's orders. He took his associate's car and drove to his secret warehouse at Wiltonstraat. He didn't trust his associate with knowledge of the location. The police couldn't believe their eyes when they actually saw Rahman carrying bags of hashish to the car. As he drove off, they moved in. Rahman was arrested with over two hundred kilos and counterfeit currency.

Rahman had finally been caught actually with his hands on the drugs. Fifteen thousand kilos were recovered in the warehouse. In a search of his house, two receipts from the GWK bureau de change at Centraal Station were found. Both were for over a hundred thousand pounds each and in the name of John Gilligan. During interview Rahman admitted that he knew Gilligan but claimed that he never did business with him. Rahman was subsequently convicted, sentenced to two years in prison and fined the equivalent of twenty thousand pounds. The international crime figure was dignified in defeat but he would never do business with John Gilligan again. After Rahman's arrest the Operation Setter team began investigating the supply route to Ireland.

In the meantime, Gilligan's mistress Carol Rooney had left Europe and fled to Australia to stay with a relative. On August 12 Rooney boarded Qantas flight number QF 002 from Heathrow to Sydney, via Bangkok. The twenty-year-old bookie's assistant would never see her nasty lover again. A year later she would tell the Lucan Team that she had been terrified of Gilligan since the murder.

On September 14 Gilligan slipped back into Ireland through Rosslare, on the ferry from Roscoff. He travelled around Dublin in taxis and stayed in different houses, and did not scruple to stop over at Jessbrook. He met Meehan, Mitchell and Ward to find out exactly what was happening with the police investigation. They reassured him that their man on the inside, John O'Neill, would let them know if there were any big breaks in the case. Gilligan also attended a small birthday celebration for Geraldine. After the party, she confronted her husband about his mistress and they had a row that resulted in him beating her. The night before he left Ireland, he stayed in Russell Warren's house.

Coinciding with Gilligan's trip home, his old friend John Cunningham escaped from the Shelton Abbey open prison in County Wicklow. Cunningham, from Ballyfermot, was serving the last two years of his sentence for organising the 1986 kidnapping of Jennifer Guinness. He was spotted drinking in a pub near the prison in contravention of the rules and was about to be sent to an enclosed prison as punishment. Unwilling to face it, he ran. He stayed in Russell Warren's house the night before he left the country on a truck that had been organised by one of Gilligan's associates. Once in Holland, Gilligan helped his old friend get set up in the drugs trade.

The Lucan team had been aware of Gilligan's arrival in Ireland but were not anxious to lay their hands on him just yet. They still needed hard evidence. They were working closely with the Dutch, Belgian and British police in keeping tabs on his movements. When the time was right they would make their move.

Shortly after Gilligan left the country, it was decided to place Russell

Warren under full-time surveillance. The investigators reckoned that he was the weak link and the one most likely to provide the key to get inside the gang's operation. They still were not sure of the nature of his dealings with Gilligan, but were particularly suspicious because his alibi for the day of the murder had not checked out. He had claimed that he had been shopping with his wife, Debbie, in Stillorgan at the crucial times and also went drinking in a pub in Rathgar. A check in the shop showed no record of the purchases he claimed he had made and the people he had named for his alibi said he hadn't arrived in the pub until after 3 p.m. He clearly had not given a true account of his movements at the time the murder took place.

Information coming from Amsterdam showed that Warren had been involved in the exchange of huge sums of money. At the same time, the mysterious "Paul Conroy" was finally identified as Charlie Bowden. In Lucan the team had carefully studied whatever intelligence came their way about Bowden, including his army career record. It was believed that, like Warren, he was not a criminal of the calibre of the rest of the mob. Bowden, too, was placed under surveillance and a detailed list of his friends and relatives compiled.

The Lucan team had made the gangsters feel insecure because of their aggressive, unrelenting operation. All the gang members were becoming edgy and nervous because of the level of police activity. There were almost daily arrests or developments in the Guerin investigation. Meehan, Mitchell, and Paul and Shay Wards began keeping their heads down and staying out of sight.

On September 23 Meehan was given a week's holiday, courtesy of the State. He was jailed for indecent behaviour, specifically for masturbating in front of gardaí in the Bridewell Station. Meehan's solicitor, Michael Hanahoe, said that his client had been at a funeral on the day of that incident the previous April and had been drinking. "I accept his behaviour was something he could not be proud of, but the difficulty is he knows insults were slung about and he has no recollection of what was said," Mr Hanahoe told the District Court.

Judge Gerard Haughton was not impressed with Meehan's performance. "His conduct was disgraceful and I would have no hesitation in jailing him for six to twelve months if that penalty was open to me," he declared. Meehan didn't mind the chance to unwind for a few days. During the week he was in Mountjoy, however, two more shipments totalling 760 kilos arrived in Cork from Amsterdam and were then transported to Greenmount.

Since Veronica Guerin's murder, Gilligan had instructed Russell Warren to bring the money to him by ferry from England and France. He met Gilligan to hand over the cash in London, Dover and Calais. Paul Cradden, his friend, travelled with him on four occasions. Unknown to Warren, the National Surveillance Unit had also travelled with him and monitored the handover of cash. Hickey wanted to know more about the gang's operation before deciding to move in for an arrest. On Sunday, September 29, a conference was held in Lucan to discuss when it would be appropriate to move against Warren.

Detective Inspector Todd O'Loughlin was working closely with the NSU people on the ground, analysing Warren's movements and possible plans. On the same day, Gilligan phoned Warren in Dublin and screamed abuse at him for not having collecting a bag of cash from Dutchie Holland the previous evening. Warren regularly met Holland to collect cash from his end of the drugs operation. About half an hour later Dutchie called Warren and arranged to meet him outside the Virgin Megastore, near O'Connell Bridge in Dublin. Holland handed over a carrier bag with over seventy thousand pounds in cash. He brought the money back to his parents' house for sorting. The following day he was to make a collection from Meehan and fly with the cash to Schipol airport but, when he phoned Meehan, he was told the money wouldn't be ready until the following day.

On Monday afternoon another conference was held in Lucan to discuss Warren's arrest. A decision was not made as to when to life him. That evening Russell Warren went to the 108 Pub in Rathgar with his wife and a friend, Stephen McGrath. For almost two weeks he had been constantly shadowed by as many as twelve men and women of the NSU. Wherever he went, they went. Shortly before 9 p.m. Todd O'Loughlin phoned Detective Sergeants John O'Driscoll and Fergus Treanor who were waiting with a team of ten officers not far from the pub. O'Loughlin gave the order to move on Warren. The Lucan team strolled through the two main doors of the pub.

Inside the undercover NSU people were scattered throughout. One of them indicated to the two sergeants that Warren was in the toilet. They went in after him.

Warren was just finishing relieving himself at the urinal when the two cops stood either side of him. "You better give that a good shake because it will be a while before you have another piss in here again," O'Driscoll said in a sarcastic tone, as Treanor held up his identity badge and put his hand on the bagman's shoulder. "Russell Patrick Warren, I am arresting you under Section 30 of the Offences Against the State Act 1939 on suspicion that you are in possession of information relating to a scheduled offence, namely the possession of a firearm at the Naas Road and Boot Road on June 26, 1996. You are not obliged to say anything unless you wish to do so, but anything you do say will be taken down in writing and may be given in evidence. Do you understand?"

Warren was speechless and the blood drained from his face; he nodded that he understood. He was searched and his hands cuffed behind his back. As he was being taken out of the toilet, Debbie Warren and McGrath were also placed under arrest. The customers in the bar had no idea what was going on and there was almost a row until the Lucan team produced their identity badges and asked the customers to calm down. The NSU officers, who were dressed like a rag-tag collection of disinterested punters, ignored the commotion. When the prisoners were taken away to Lucan, the undercover people casually left the pub and faded into the background. They had another operation planned in conjunction with the Lucan team. At the same time as the pub swoop, Paul Cradden, Warren's parents Patrick and Yvette, his sister Nicola and her husband Brian Cummins were also being arrested and their homes searched. The officers found Holland's bag of cash during the search. The Bookie, other bookies, and two other associates were also arrested in the swoop.

Warren was held in Lucan garda station for two days during which he was questioned about his involvement with the Gilligan gang. One of the detectives he met was Detective Garda Bernie Hanley, who would play a crucial role in the Guerin case over the following months. Hanley, who was attached to the Investigation Section of Garda Headquarters, was highly respected in the force as one of its most talented interrogators. A colleague described his demeanour during an interview: "Hanley never raises his voice. He quietly works on the subject analysing him for signs of little weaknesses and chinks in the armour. Eventually he establishes a relationship with the prisoner who starts to trust him and talks. He has turned the hardest men in the business."

On this occasion Warren was too terrified to admit that he knew anything about the murder, although he gave details of his activities as Gilligan's bagman. He also admitted knowing and collecting money from Brian Meehan. He denied any knowledge of the motorbike or the murder and refused to explain the telephone traffic between him and the other Gilligan gang members on the day of the murder. On October 1, Warren made his first statement to Hanley: "When I first started collecting money for Gilligan there used to be £20,000 or £30,000 in it. This figure would be the lowest amount; it would go as high as £160,00 some times but most of the time it would be around £70,000. At first I was told this money was from betting and the sales of smuggled cigarettes and tobacco. As time went by, I got more involved. I realised that this was money from the sale of drugs. I was only involved in looking after the money for counting and delivering it to him [Gilligan]. Meehan is very closely connected with Gilligan. I think he looks after his drug business for him. I am sorry for getting my family [involved] in all of this."

At the same time, Warren's family members gave statements describing his connections to Gilligan and how they had been recruited by Russell to count money. Patrick Warren, his father, said: "I am disgusted that he [Russell] has got me and my wife into this position. He will never get us into it again."

When asked if he thought his son was involved in Veronica Guerin's murder, Patrick Warren told Detective Sgt Padraig Kennedy: "I don't think Russell would have the guts to pull the trigger because behind it all he is a coward at heart."

The next day the only thing on Brian Meehan's mind was ensuring that the drug money kept moving. He was becoming agitated and excited. Meehan called Charlie Bowden and told him to go to Paul Ward's house. He said Warren was in custody, so "everyone will have to lend a hand". When Bowden arrived,

Meehan, Mitchell, Paul Ward, "Speedy" Fegan and an associate of his from Newry were already busily counting and wrapping the large bundles of used notes. Meehan told the other hoods that they'd have to hurry because Dutchie Holland was due to collect the cash for delivery to Gilligan in England. The thoughtless police had no idea how much they had already inconvenienced the gang.

Meehan instructed the gangsters to sort the cash with the notes facing up, in batches of a thousand pounds, wrapped with elastic bands at the ends. Each batch was then wrapped in batches of five with more elastic bands. Sterling was sorted separately. This, Meehan explained, was to make it easier when exchanging the money in Amsterdam. The cash would look like it had come from a bank. When they had finished counting, there was over a quarter of a million pounds. Later the gang members went to a local pub, where they handed the cash over to Dutchie in two hold-all bags.

The gang's fatal flaw was their sheer arrogance and greed. They were increasing their business and cash flow while at the same time knowing that the police was circling around them and making every effort to get through to them. They expected to be arrested for questioning any day. They were also running the risk of being caught with drugs while under police surveillance. Somehow, in their cocaine-induced confidence, they believed they were still untouchable. Gilligan's gang was spiralling out of control.

Gilligan was extremely worried when he heard Warren had been "lifted" by the police. The gormless bagman he had bullied about the place was weak and liable to spill the beans. Gilligan was staying in a hotel at Russell Square in London waiting for the delivery of his cash. Holland arrived on the ferry and took a train to London to deliver the cash. The two henchmen discussed what kind of action they would have to take if Warren did decide to talk. Dutchie advised his little boss to order Warren over to England, interrogate him and "put the fear of God in him". If he had made a statement to the police, it would mean nothing if he refused to get into the witness box, Holland explained. There was also no witness protection programme in Ireland. Warren should be left under no illusion of the dangers inherent in becoming a tout (informant).

Back in Lucan, time was running out in Warren's detention. The investigation team met to discuss progress. They had made a breakthrough in that someone close to Gilligan had given them an insight into the gang's operation, but they felt that Warren knew a lot more. Hanley had made a connection with Warren and laid the foundations of trust. In the meantime, there was enough evidence in the statements to sustain charges against Warren and his family under the new Proceeds of Crime legislation for handling money they clearly knew to be the proceeds of drug trafficking.

The connection between Warren, Cradden and the motorbike used in the murder was still a source of concern. Neither Cradden nor Warren had given any indication that they knew anything about the bike, but the Lucan team now suspected that Warren had been one of the gang's look-outs during the murder. The structure of the plot had been deciphered in John O'Driscoll's phone analysis. It was decided to release Warren and his family and send a file recommending charges to the Director of Public Prosecutions. In the meantime, Hanley would make informal approaches to Warren and, when the time was right, the gardaí would lift him again. The murder investigation was about to step up dramatically.

On Wednesday evening Warren left Lucan station in a taxi. As soon as he switched on his mobile phone, Gilligan rang. "Can you talk?" he inquired urgently of his bagman. Warren said he couldn't, but he would be at home within twenty minutes and Gilligan could call him back then. Gilligan rang another three times before Warren got home. The little man was impatient and angry. He abused his bagman for not getting home sooner. As soon as Warren arrived at his house, the phone rang yet again. Gilligan began demanding to know what happened while Warren was in custody and what he said. Unlike the cops, Gilligan adopted a different approach when interrogating.

"I'm now tellin' you, you're dead and your family is dead and everyone around you will be dead. I want the truth, tell me exactly what was said and what your family said," Gilligan hissed into the phone. Warren told him it was all about the money that the detectives had found in his parents' house. Gilligan berated Warren for not collecting the money earlier. Warren said he hadn't had time.

"When I tell you to do something, you do it," Gilligan retorted and then demanded to know again what had been said in Lucan. "Get on a plane first thing in the morning and meet me here in

London," Gilligan ordered.

"I can't. Everyone here is upset after the arrests," Warren pleaded.

"Come over here, or I'll go over to ye and I'll kill ye all," the little man snarled and hung up.

The following morning at 8 a.m. Gilligan was on the phone to his bagman again. "Why aren't you over here? If you're not fucking over here I'm going over to you and I'll kill you and I'll kill you if you tell me lies," threatened Gilligan in a furious rage. Warren could only respond that he had no money to travel. Gilligan told him to call Meehan and he would give him the money.

Later that day there was further evidence that the police were stepping up their offensive. Officers attached to the Money Laundering Unit of the Fraud Bureau and the Criminal Assets Bureau visited the offices of Gilligan's solicitor, Michael Hanahoe. The officers came with a search warrant and were given every assistance by Hanahoe and his staff, who at all times conducted themselves with the utmost professional propriety. The gardaí took possession of files and other papers relating to Gilligan's affairs. Due to a leak to the press, the incident was widely publicised the following morning. Photographs were taken of officers taking the documents from the building. The solicitors subsequently sued the authorities in relation to the leak and were awarded significant damages.

That evening Warren met Brian Meehan, who handed him a thousand pounds in cash so that he could go to London. Meehan was much calmer than Gilligan. He asked Warren about what had been said while he and his family were in custody. He wanted to know how much the cops knew about the bike. The bagman reassured Meehan that no-one had said anything. By now Russell Warren was teetering on the edge of a nervous breakdown. He was sandwiched between the police and Gilligan on the other. One group could probably put him and his family in jail; the other could have him and his family wiped out. It was an appalling situation. After the murder Warren had been a nervous wreck anyway. He hadn't been able to sleep at night or eat much. On June 26 he had condemned himself to misery. He wasn't cut out for running with gangland's most dangerous killers.

Warren flew to London on Friday afternoon. Before leaving he told his wife, the Bookie and Stephen McGrath that he was meeting with Gilligan. He wanted them to know his plans, in case Gilligan did something to him. He didn't expect to live. When he arrived in Heathrow, Warren was instructed by Gilligan to take a train to Russell Square in central London. When he arrived at Russell Square, a man Warren had never met before walked up to him and asked if he was "Russell". The man led Warren to the hotel and to meet Gilligan in his room. Warren was shaking with fear and sat down.

Gilligan paced up and down the room as he began his inquisition. He was in the kind of mood which had terrified Veronica Guerin a year earlier. He began by threatening his bagman. "You and your family are dead, and Debbie, no matter how long it takes, I'll get you all. I want the truth. Now put the words 'I'm going to be killed' in the back of your mind. You have to answer questions for me and don't tell me lies." This was John Gilligan's equivalent of the garda official caution. He spent the next few hours interrogating his petrified bagman.

Gilligan said that he intended reclaiming the cash that the Lucan team had seized. He wanted to know exactly how it had been wrapped and packed, so that he could identify it when it came to claiming it. Warren told Gilligan that he had been only asked about the money and to account for his movements on the day of the murder. He convinced the little man that everything was fine. Apparently satisfied with his bagman's answer, it was back to business.

"I want you to bring money to Calais this evening for me," Gilligan demanded. Warren said he couldn't travel because he didn't have a passport with him. Gilligan verbally abused him over this. Warren explained that the police had taken it from him. Gilligan paced up and down the room as he ranted about the Calais trip. Gilligan pointed to a silver case in a press. "There is £300,000 in there and who is going to bring it for me now? I am the fucking boss around here and you're working for me. You should be doin' this, not me. I'll just have to do it meself!"

Later, in a statement to the Lucan team, Warren said that he had plucked up the courage to ask Gilligan about the Guerin murder.

"I said to him something like, if you knew it was going to cause all this trouble, would you still have gone through with shooting Veronica Guerin. He said: 'Are you joking? I even tried to ring Brian [Meehan] to call it off, but I couldn't get through to him.'... During the same conversation in the hotel room, John Gilligan said, sure, it wouldn't have made a bit of difference, because she was dying of cancer anyway."

Carol Rooney would later tell the Lucan team that Gilligan had also made the bizarre claim about Veronica "dying of cancer anyway" in the days after her murder when they were in Amsterdam. That evening Warren returned to Ireland. The next time he and Gilligan met was in the Special Criminal Court.

At the time Warren was getting on what he thought would be his last flight to London, Brian Meehan was also due to appear in the District Court on a summons arising out of his arrest by Garda Rory Corcoran. By this stage the *Sunday World* was aware that Meehan was one of the prime suspects in the case. For several weeks the newspaper had been building up background information about the gang. I was unsure about what Meehan looked like and sat in the back row of District Court number five watching out for him. Outside, two *Sunday World* crime photographers, Padraig O'Reilly and Liam O'Connor, were sitting outside in cars waiting for Meehan and Mitchell to turn up. In the end I hadn't much trouble identifying Meehan. When he walked into court, he spotted me.

Meehan walked over and stood in front of my seat, staring menacingly into my face. I smiled and winked at the evil thug who had murdered my colleague. "Fuck you," I thought at the sheer arrogance of the thug, who was clearly trying to intimidate me. I was determined that we would expose this bastard to the world. I left the court and signalled to my colleagues. Meehan and Mitchell left the court covering their faces but the photographers caught them in their lenses. The two thugs ran away. During the previous weeks we had also focused on the connections between the gang and the INLA. A week later the *Sunday World* ran a story about Meehan in which the newspaper nicknamed him "The Tosser" because of his indecency charge. At the time we couldn't name him legally. Overnight, the name stuck.

Later that afternoon Meehan and Mitchell met Juliet Bacon.

Meehan told her that he was expecting to see the gang exposed in the *Sunday World*. At that very moment the Lucan Investigation Team was preparing for an all-out swoop on the Gilligan gang. Special Branch, the Emergency Response Unit and scores of other reinforcements were being mobilised for the move. Over the next week the team would be responsible for the largest arrest and search operation in history. The gang's days were numbered.

The Lucan plan was to hit Charlie Bowden first, followed by a swoop on Paul Ward's group, then the Meehans, Mitchells and finally Traynor and Gilligan. But their hands were forced when they learned that Bowden was planning to fly to London on Saturday morning, October 5, with a mistress for the weekend. The police feared that Bowden might also be planning to go into hiding. At 5 a.m. on Saturday a large team gathered in Lucan for the first swoop. Bowden's plans for a dirty weekend were to be rudely interrupted.

At 6 a.m. Det. Sgt Fergus Treanor knocked on Charlie Bowden's front door at the Paddocks. Bowden answered the door and six detectives piled in. He was spread-eagled against the wall of his hallway and handcuffed. Det. Garda John Roche formally arrested the ex-soldier. When he was asked if he had he anything to say, Bowden calmly replied: "I don't know what you are talking about." He was taken away in a squad car to Lucan station. Julie Bacon was also arrested and taken in a separate car to Lucan. In a search the officers found cocaine and a large amount of cash. An hour later Michael Bowden called to his brother's house to bring him to the airport. He, too, was arrested. In a search of Michael Bowden's home, he gave the police a bag containing five thousand pounds that he had been holding for his brother. Michael Bowden was then brought to Cabra for questioning. At the same time, two other friends of Bowden's, Julian Clohessy and Paul Smullen, were also lifted.

In the beginning Bowden claimed he knew nothing of Veronica Guerin's murder. He protested that he was a hard-working hairdresser struggling to make a living. For most of the day Bowden refused to budge. One of his first interrogators, Det. Sgt Des McTiernan, was frustrated by Bowden's silence and decided to give him some food for thought. He slammed down photographs of Veronica's body in her car in front of his prisoner.

At 9 p.m. Bernie Hanley and another able interrogator, Det.

Inspector John O'Mahony, walked into the interview room. O'Mahony had been a member of the Drug and Serious Crime Squad. They were calm and assertive. They somehow put Bowden on edge. He would later recall that he had psyched himself up for an arrest. "When I saw these two guys coming in suited and booted, I knew that I was in trouble, I was fucked. They seemed to know everything about me," Bowden recalled.

O'Mahony and Hanley asked Bowden about his association with Meehan, Ward and Mitchell. Bowden said he didn't know them.

O'Mahony: I am putting it to you, Charlie, that you know Brian Meehan, Paul Ward, Shay Ward and Peter Mitchell, and you were in contact with some of them by telephone on the day that Veronica Guerin was murdered.

Bowden: OK, OK, I know them. I know them through Peter Mitchell. Look, I want to tell you about the money you found. I know nothing about the murder. I would have nothing to do with anything like that, it would scare me shitless. I have been working with Meehan, the Wards, Mitchell – and that's where the money is from. If I was talking to them on the day of the murder, it was only about business.

Hanley: What business would that be, Charlie?

Bowden: Selling drugs, that's my involvement with them.

It was at this moment that the Veronica Guerin murder investigation made its biggest breakthrough. The two clever interrogators had found the chink in Bowden's armour. He was prepared to talk about the drugs but was terrified of implicating himself in the murder. It would only be a matter of time before they had the whole story. At first Bowden told a concoction of truth and lies. As the hours wore on, the lies were being weeded out. O'Mahony and Hanley had found their opening and began breaking down the wall of silence that had protected John Gilligan's evil empire.

The officers were surprised at Bowden's reply when they asked him how much money he made from selling drugs for Mitchell and Meehan. "I don't know, a lot. Lately I couldn't handle the amounts. It was getting on top of me. I will show you where I have it hidden offside [off site]." At 10 p.m. Bowden was brought in a squad car to show the investigators his shop on Moore Street. He also pointed out a friend's apartment on Mespil Road in south Dublin where the cash was hidden. An hour later Det. Inspector O'Loughlin and a search team raided the apartment and recovered almost a hundred thousand pounds in cash sterling and punts hidden in a hold-all bag.

While sitting in the back seat of the police car, sandwiched between O'Mahony and Hanley, Bowden began to drop the facade. He said he hadn't told the full truth about how he got to know Mitchell and he described his drug-dealing activities. The officers tried to hide their astonishment when he blurted out how the gang had built the empire. He told how Gilligan was the boss and of giving money to him. He talked about Russell Warren. Every sentence he came out with provided another lead, another piece of the picture. They couldn't write their notes of the conversation quick enough.

When they returned to the station Bowden was placed in his cell for the night. It was only a matter of time before Bowden would tell the whole story, the officers informed the rest of the team. The news coincided with another dramatic lead that resulted from the other interviews. One of the prisoners described how Bowden brought him to the Greenmount lockup. The gang's quartermaster had broken his own strict rule of never bringing anyone other than gang members to the warehouse. A search warrant was obtained and surveillance teams sent to watch the place overnight.

On the following Sunday afternoon, a team was sent to search Greenmount. The officers took turns with a sledgehammer to break down the door. When they walked inside, they couldn't believe their eyes. They found forty-seven kilos of hash, false driver's licences, a substance for mixing cocaine, weighing scales and the cardboard boxes used to ship the drugs from Holland. The boxes still had the false shipping labels placed on them by Martin Baltus and Simon Rahman. The most significant discovery was Bowden's weekly delivery sheet. On it were the names of the gang's customers and the quantities they had ordered. Everyone on that list was later arrested. The officers decided to pull back and call in forensic experts. The scene was preserved. Later, keys found in Bowden's house were proved to matched the locks on the doors of Greenmount.

Todd O'Loughlin was phoned from Greenmount with the good news.

At 1.50 p.m., armed with the information about Greenmount, Hanley and O'Mahony rejoined Bowden in the interview room. The pair had struck up a good relationship with Bowden and he had begun put his trust in them. Their strategy was to make Bowden feel comfortable and not push him too hard. They knew a lot more than Charlie thought they did. They asked Charlie about the murder of Veronica Guerin again.

"I am not involved in the murder. I am not a heavy. I just do the drugs for Meehan and Mitchell for the money," Bowden replied.

They asked him where he got the drugs. Bowden said they were delivered by Meehan or Mitchell. O'Mahony looked at Charlie. "Do you know where the drugs are stored, Charlie?"

"No, I don't."

Hanley asked, "Do you know where they come from?"

"No, I don't ask questions. I just deliver the hash to the list of customers given to me by Meehan and Mitchell."

Hanley decided to tell the prisoner that they had found Greenmount. He leaned forward on the table and looked into the prisoner's eyes. "Charlie, the gardaí have located a warehouse at Greenmount Industrial Estate and they are searching it. They've discovered a large quantity of cannabis and other suspected drugs."

At that moment, Bowden realised that there was no longer any point in diluting the truth.

"Have ye found it? I should have told ye last night. Fuck it. I was going to tell ye when we were driving back from Mespil Road. Now you have found it, I will tell you everything I know. I am sorry for not telling ye about it already," Bowden gasped.

O'Mahony was gentle. "All we want is the full truth. We want you to tell us all you know about the drugs operation and give us whatever information you have regarding the murder of Veronica Guerin."

Bowden replied, "I will tell you everything. I am scared, if Gilligan hears that I have ratted, I am dead."

In the hours that followed, Bowden gave the two detectives every detail of his involvement in the drugs operation and how the system worked. He started dropping bombshells which took them totally by surprise, candidly telling them about the guns being brought in with the drugs and the location of the gang's hidden arsenal. The detectives were surprised at the size of the weapons cache.

To their amazement, Bowden also began describing the gang's attack on Martin Foley. The police had no idea who had been responsible for the second attack. "They [Meehan and Ward] made a bollocks of it [the attempted Foley hit] and he got away. Meehan couldn't handle the gun." He related how Foley's hit was planned, the weapons used and what happened afterwards. Then came the final piece of the puzzle.

Bowden: In January of this year another sub-machinegun and a .357 Magnum with twelve rounds came in.

Hanley: Where is the .357 Magnum now?

Bowden: I know that is the gun you are looking for, for Veronica Guerin's murder.

Hanley: How do you know what type of gun we are looking for?

Bowden: I got it wrapped up and put it in the graveyard, too.

The ex-soldier then described Dutchie Holland as the man he believed was the actual hit man.

O'Mahony: How can you be sure that the .357 is the one used to murder Veronica Guerin?

Bowden: Because I cleaned it and got it ready before the murder. There were refill bullets in it. Brass with silver heads, the tops were turned in, rather than coming to a point.

Charlie Bowden's terrifying story of drugs, guns, money, greed and murder took almost three hours to tell. It blew the lid on a secret underworld that none of the authorities had dreamed existed. His statements made for astonishing reading, but as Bowden was been exposing gangland's secrets, there were other startling developments elsewhere.

Fifteen

Closing In

International co-operation was vital if the murder investigation was to succeed. Det. Garda Pat Bane, one of the officers co-ordinating the investigation from its nerve centre in the incident room, was in regular contact with Roger Wilson of H.M. Customs and Excise in Manchester. Wilson had been aware of the developments since the Guerin murder and of Gilligan's involvement. Wilson had good reason to remember the little man. He had been placed under constant armed guard when Gilligan threatened to have him murdered for seizing his drug money at Holyhead in December 1994. The British authorities feared that Gilligan had recruited Tommy Coyle to organise some of his Provo or INLA friends to hit the vigilant officer.

Police and Customs officers in Holland, Belgium, France and Britain were now monitoring the movements of Gilligan and his cronies. Each time any of them passed through an airport travelling between London and the Continent, he was flagged. A report on each flight eventually arrived on the mountain of paper work building up in Lucan. On the morning Bowden was arrested, Gilligan took the 8.30 a.m. KLM flight from Heathrow to Schipol, clutching a case of money. Without Warren he had no bagman. With the increasing heat coming down from the police in Dublin, he could not find a quick replacement to move the cash directly to Holland. He became his own bagman. That night he returned to London.

The next morning Gilligan met with Michael Cunningham, John Cunningham's brother. As a favour to Gilligan, Michael brought a parcel of cash to him. This was particularly dangerous for Cunningham at the time because he was wanted for questioning for a 1985 armed robbery in West Yorkshire during which a police officer was killed. As a result of intelligence from Ireland, he had also been flagged as a suspected drug trafficker for Customs' attention. At 9.55 a.m. the two men booked seats on the 1 p.m. flight KL 120 to Amsterdam. The Club Class tickets were one way. Over the next two hours there was frantic telephone activity between Customs and Lucan garda station. The incident room was already buzzing with activity. Hickey, O'Loughlin and O'Connell anxiously waited for news from Heathrow.

Fachtna Murphy and Felix McKenna had also been alerted to what was happening. There was a possibility that Gilligan could be carrying drug money. If he was, then the British would require assistance putting together a case against him. Customs and armed police officers drifted into the departures lounge to watch the two underworld pals who had started their criminal careers together as kids on the streets of Ballyfermot. They had probably often dreamed of being big-time bad guys. That dream was about to become a nightmare.

Ten minutes before the flight was due to depart, Gilligan walked up to the boarding gate with his passport and ticket. He was carrying a large, silver, metal case in one hand and a briefcase in the other. Back in Dublin, the Lucan squad were limbering up with their sledgehammers to smash down the door on the multi-million pound empire Gilligan had spent the past three years building. Customs had been instructed by Wilson to intercept their target before he got on the flight. The West Yorkshire police had also been informed and they were already making arrangements to receive their prisoner. Roger Wilson was sitting by his phone in Manchester.

Customs officer Andrew Booth stopped Gilligan just before he passed through Gate 16. "Hello, sir, can I see your passport, please?"

Without speaking, Gilligan handed over his passport.

"How long are you going to Amsterdam for?" Booth asked, as though routinely.

"A couple of weeks."

"What is the purpose of your travel? Is it business or pleasure?"

"Business."

"What sort of business is that, then?"

"Racing."

"What sort? Horse racing?"

"Yes, and property."

"Do you own horses?"

"Yeah, I do."

"Whereabouts?"

"In Ireland."

"Is the trip to Amsterdam for racing, then?"

"No, for property. I'm looking at property there."

"Are you buying property there?"

"Yeah."

"Do you have any money with you to buy that property?"

"Yeah, I do. In the case."

"How much do you have?"

"£300,000. It's all legal and above board. Look." Gilligan produced a document headed "statement of affairs" from his briefcase.

"Who does the money belong to?" inquired Booth.

"Me. It's mine. It came from the bank. Here's the receipt." Gilligan was growing impatient as the last passengers for KL 120 rushed past him. At the same time, Cunningham had also been taken aside.

"Look, what's the problem? It's OK to take the money out, isn't it?"

The customs officer explained that large movements of cash were considered suspicious and that such an amount might be detained if it was believed to be linked to drug trafficking. Gilligan found himself standing in a circle of customs officers and policemen carrying Heckler and Koch sub-machine guns. He was asked to sit down while further inquiries were made. In the meantime, his flight had departed. The police arrested Cunningham and took him away to West Yorkshire. Booth returned at 1.20 p.m. and informed the little man that he wasn't under arrest but that Customs wanted to make further inquiries about the money and would appreciate his assistance.

Despite everything that had happened over the past week, Gilligan had decided to brazen it out. Warren had been arrested and questioned, Gilligan's files had been taken from his solicitor's office and the previous day, Bowden, one of the most important men in his organisation had also been lifted. At that stage Gilligan could simply have walked away and said he would return for the money. But he had gotten away with intimidating Customs before. He reckoned that he had everything covered. After all, he was invincible.

In a holding room Gilligan was asked to open the silver case. Inside, the officers found a pillow, some clothing and a large bundle of cash in bubble wrap. "How much is in it?" asked the customs officer.

"£330,000, and there is a receipt in the briefcase," Gilligan replied. In the briefcase the officers found an assortment of photocopies of bookmakers' cheques, a copy of a receipt for the return of the money seized by Roger Wilson in 1994 and what turned out to be a bizarre loan agreement for four million pounds between John and Geraldine Gilligan and a mysterious Lebanese businessman called Joseph Saouma. An electronic gadget for detecting bugging devices was also found in the case.

A Customs officer at Terminal 3 in Heathrow phoned Roger Wilson to update him on developments. "Arrest him now. Don't let him out of your sight. I'm on my way," Wilson told his colleague. As he raced to London, Wilson called Pat Bane in Lucan. There was jubilation in the incident room but everyone had to act fast. Fachtna Murphy and Felix McKenna met with Hickey and his team in the flurry of activity that followed. It was decided to send Felix McKenna and Det. Garda Bernard Masterson from the Lucan team to London to liaise with the British. The Irish evidence would be crucial to prove Gilligan's money was the proceeds of drug trafficking. It was a break that most investigators dream of, a combination of good timing, luck, hard work and John Gilligan's arrogance. Hickey would later comment about the day: "I think you can make your own luck, too." With the little man in custody he would not be in a position to intimidate witnesses back in Dublin at this crucial phase of the investigation. At 2.06 p.m. John Joseph Gilligan was formally arrested by HM Customs on suspicion of laundering the proceeds of drug trafficking.

At 10.30 p.m. Roger Wilson walked into an interview room and sat across a table from the man who had threatened to have him shot. He introduced himself to the little godfather. Gilligan knew he was in trouble. McKenna and Masterson had also arrived from Dublin. When he spotted the two Irish officers walking past the room where he was being held, the penny finally dropped. The authorities were no longer confined within their own borders. That evening he learned a hard lesson in international law.

Over the next two days, Wilson attempted to question the man he had been wanting to get his hands on for two years. Gilligan refused to give any answers. The two Dublin officers met with Customs and the Crown Prosecution Service on Monday. They explained the ongoing investigation in Ireland and related the news about the discovery of the gang's drug distribution centre the day before. They had the drugs. In addition, they had the information offered by Russell Warren which connected Gilligan to the cash and now they had statements from Bowden identifying Gilligan as the boss.

The information about cash transactions and Gilligan's links with Rahman and Baltus had also come from Holland. It was decided that Gilligan should be charged. On Tuesday, October 8, he was brought before Uxbridge Magistrates Court. He was charged with an offence under section 49(1) of the Drugs Trafficking Act 1994, laundering the proceeds of his drugs operation. At the same hearing Wilson was granted an application to hold on to the money. He told the court that Gilligan couldn't offer a legitimate explanation for the source of the cash, that he was associated with two known English drug dealers and that he was linked with the seizure in Greenmount. Gilligan was remanded to Belmarsh maximum security prison in East London where terrorists and other category "A" class prisoners are held.

In Lucan there was no time for celebration. Things were moving at an incredible pace. The incident room was like the nerve-centre of a battle. Phones were hopping, paper work was being processed, and teams were being organised to deal with new information flowing from the interview rooms. Charlie Bowden dictated his statement to O'Mahony and Hanley. It took over three hours to transcribe. At the end of the statement Bowden added: "The only regret I have is that I didn't let someone know what I knew was going to happen. I would like to sincerely apologise to Veronica's husband and son for my part in her murder. I am full of remorse and am glad to have told you the truth." At 11.20 p.m., under cover of darkness, Bowden showed the Lucan Investigation Team where the gang's arsenal was hidden in the Jewish graveyard on Old Court

Road. The find was kept under wraps until the next day. Shortly after midnight on Sunday, Bowden was put back in his cell.

A Lucan team member summarised the events of that day. "After three months suddenly everything began to fall into place. In the incident room there was surprise and disbelief. We had been making good methodical progress and were always confident we would get a good result. Then, within twenty-four hours it all fell together. You hope against hope for a break like this and when it comes, then you are just stunned. By midnight on October 6 we had the guns, we had the drugs, we had the supply route, we had the mechanics of everything that had happened before and during the murder, Gilligan was out of harm's way in custody in England. Technically, the case had been solved."

The Lucan team worked through the night collating the huge bank of information they had gathered. Teams were chosen for surveillance at the Ambassador Hotel. A new consignment of drugs was expected to be delivered that day from Cork. Another team was dispatched to Cork to investigate the involvement of John Dunne and the rest of the gang's supply route. The Criminal Assets Bureau were called in to work with Lucan on the Cork connection, which would provide proof of Gilligan's drug trafficking activities for the English case and also sustain a case for the CAB to seize the various gang members' assets.

The next morning Bowden's detention period was due to expire at 6.30 a.m. It had been decided to re-arrest him under the Misuse of Drugs Act in light of the discovery at Greenmount. Tony Hickey had been in touch with the Director of Public Prosecutions on Sunday and had updated him on the progress made. He wanted Bowden charged with the sale and supply of drugs at Greenmount. A further charge of possession of firearms could be preferred at a later date. Hickey wanted to keep Bowden on side. There was still an enormous amount of work to be done to corroborate what Bowden had told them.

Early the next morning John O'Mahony and Bernie Hanley went to the old Jewish cemetery. Under a tombstone bearing the name Miriam Norcup, they removed a flagstone and found the arsenal. The cache included a Sten machine gun, an Agram machine pistol, five Walther semi-automatic pistols, silencer barrels, spare magazines and 1,057 rounds of ammo. Back in Lucan, Bowden had been released and re-arrested at 6.45 a.m. He identified the property recovered in Greenmount and the cemetery. That afternoon he appeared before a judge at Kilmainham District Court, who remanded him in custody on drugs charges and ordered him taken to Mountjoy Prison.

While the gardaí were watching the Ambassador Hotel, Paul Ward and Brian Meehan decided to pick up the latest shipment themselves. They were both becoming extremely worried about developments. They collected the load of 380 kilos from Cork and brought it back to Dublin, avoiding Greenmount. It would be the last shipment the gang received from Holland. Neither Meehan, Mitchell, nor Ward were under surveillance. John Foy, a former member of the General's gang and a peripheral player in the Gilligan outfit, was located and watched. Bowden had indicated that Foy might know something about the motorbike and where the murder weapon had been disposed of. Foy, who had served time with Gilligan, Ward and Meehan, was a customer of the gang, turning over thirty kilos a week. It was Foy who had helped Paul Ward cut up the motorbike in a lockup off Cromwellsfort Road, a place where Foy also stored stolen cars.

In Lucan the order was sent out to locate the other gang members and put them under surveillance. The team were aware from Bowden and other underworld informants that Shay Ward had been very upset since the murder. Perhaps he could lead them to the murder weapon. Meehan, Mitchell and the Wards had gone into hiding, moving between safe houses and hotels around Dublin. Meehan and Mitchell arranged to meet with Julian Clohessy in Crumlin and interrogated him about what he had said while in custody. Meehan was beginning to panic. Bowden was in prison and he couldn't make contact with him. He put the word out through the underworld network that anyone who agreed to co-operate with the investigation was dead.

On Tuesday night, October 8, Paul Ward took a room in the Green Isle Hotel in Clondalkin. Shortly after midnight the gardaí at Ronanstown were alerted to suspicious activity in the room. At 1.50 a.m. Paul Ward was arrested at gunpoint on suspicion of being involved in an armed robbery. He was alone, asleep in the room, when detectives burst in. Hippo Ward was brought to Ronanstown, where it was discovered that he was not the Ward they were looking for. He was released within the hour. The incident spooked the gang even more. It was time to get out of the country. Paul Ward, Meehan and Mitchell had already decided to get Shay Ward out before the cops got to him. He had a major drug problem and was likely to buckle under interrogation. He had openly told associates that he was not going to take the murder rap. Shay Ward was flustered and anxious that he was going to be lifted after Bowden's arrest.

Around 7 p.m. on Wednesday evening, Paul Ward phoned John O'Neill, who was working in Tallaght station on the night shift. Hippo demanded that the cop meet him within fifteen minutes. He sounded anxious. The two met in the car park of the Belgard Inn. Hippo had two passport forms and pictures of Shay Ward which he wanted O'Neill to stamp and sign in the station so he could obtain a passport in a false name. O'Neill knew that the gangster was trying to get away from his own colleagues.

By now O'Neill's involvement with Ward had been uncovered in Lucan. The telephone analysis showed that on one day alone Ward had called O'Neill an astounding fifty-five times. In the climate of paranoia that gardaí were on the gang's payroll, Hickey ordered that O'Neill be secretly checked out. Collators' reports were examined to see if O'Neill had been filing any information as a result of his contact with Ward. O'Neill's finances were also discreetly checked and it was immediately obvious that the guy had chronic problems. After paying his various loans, he was left with just eight pounds per week. Hickey ordered a covert surveillance team to watch him. He also gave team members strict orders not to discuss the ongoing developments in the case with their own colleagues. If the Gilligan gang knew how near the police were to catching them, they would flee.

The van used by Bowden and Shay Ward to deliver the drugs was located and watched. The NSU spooks planted a device on the vehicle which told them when it was being moved. On Thursday afternoon Meehan called an associate and instructed him to get rid of the van. It was brought to a scrap yard in Dolphin's Barn owned by Alan and Stuart Kessie. The NSU people were following the van. The place was being used as a front for dismantling cars for spare parts. The hoods in the scrap yard had been told that the car was to be taken apart as soon as possible. It had just been parked when the Kessie brothers and their resident car thieves, James and Liam Weldon, went to work. An NSU member made an urgent call to Lucan, where a team was preparing another operation. "If ye don't get here soon, that van won't exist. They're swarming over it like ants." The surveillance unit members had to protect their anonymity and could not physically get involved in the operation.

The Lucan team members raced to the scene. One of the squad cars almost collided with a bus in the frantic bid to stop the "ants" destroying Bowden's "dope mobile". When they arrived, the team surrounded the yard and went in with guns drawn. The dismantlers were ordered to put their hands up and stand back from the car. The four were arrested and taken to Lucan for questioning. The swoop on the yard led to a separate investigation by the Stolen Car Squad. The four men arrested in the yard were subsequently convicted in relation to the stolen car scam and eleven of their victims were compensated.

While the action was going on in Kessie's yard, a total of seventeen other searches were being carried out throughout Dublin, including in the home of Paul Ward. Todd O'Loughlin had given the order to bring him in. The following day he was spotted hiding drugs in a field near Tallaght but he again slipped through the net. That afternoon another five associates of the gang were arrested in co-ordinated swoops. In the meantime, Shay Ward had been smuggled out of the country through Northern Ireland with the help of Brendan "Speedy" Fegan. Speedy also organised false passports for Meehan, Mitchell and Shay Ward. Time was running out for the gang. Meehan and Mitchell decided to leave without the others. The night before they ran, they beat up an off-duty cop outside a nightclub to vent their anger at being forced to leave their home town! They disappeared to England on October 14. Meehan phoned John Dunne to inform him that there would be no more shipments for a number of weeks.

On Sunday, October 13, Paul Ward arranged to meet O'Neill again, this time in the car park of the Cuckoo's Nest pub in Tallaght. O'Neill gave the crooked cop four photographs of Fiona Walshe which he wanted stamped. O'Neill didn't mind that he was sitting beside a man who was now wanted for the Guerin murder because Ward had assured him that he hadn't been involved in it. O'Neill was not much of an interrogator. A short distance away, Det. Sgt Pat Keane of the Lucan team was secretly monitoring his colleague's meeting. There was now no doubt that O'Neill had gone bad.

The same evening a man wanted in connection with the dodgy scrap yard investigation gave himself up. Lucan team members Det. Gardaí Sean O'Brien, Pat Walshe and Mick McElgunn were sent to collect him. On the way back to Lucan the man appeared nervous. He had something to tell them but was afraid. The detectives said that he could talk freely to them. "How can I, when I don't who of you lot are working for Ward and Meehan?" the suspect exclaimed. He went on tell the officers that he had been with the two gangsters when they were arranging passports with John O'Neill to flee the country.

O'Brien reported the conversation to Tod O'Loughlin and Hickey. At that stage only about six members of the team, including Hickey, knew about the O'Neill enquiry. John O'Driscoll had worked the phones and Keane had been tailing him. Later that night O'Brien and McElgunn were called back to Lucan for a meeting. Todd O'Loughlin, Jerry O'Connell and Hickey were in a room on their own. Hickey filled them in on what was known about O'Neill. He was furious. "This is fucking treason. If this happened a hundred years ago, a person would be hung for it. Here we are breaking our backs, the whole force trying to catch these bastards, and one of our own is working for them trying to help them get away. It's nothing but fucking treachery," Hickey fumed. The Buffalo's days as a policeman were numbered. Hickey swore everyone in the room to absolute secrecy.

By the time Meehan and Mitchell vanished, Dutchie Holland had already disappeared. He popped up again in London where he stayed with some relatives. Within a few weeks the South East Regional Crime Squad found him and placed him under surveillance. With Shay Ward also gone, the only gang member left in Dublin was Paul Ward. It was now known that he had disposed of the murder weapon and the bike. All the indications were that Ward was seriously angry at being thrown into the middle of the murder. He was terrified of being linked to the crime. In Lucan it was calculated that Ward might even decide to come across and give evidence for the State but, first, they had to find Hippo before he joined his pals on the run.

At 3.30 p.m. on Wednesday, October 16, Det. Sgt Padraig Kennedy spotted Paul Ward and John Foy in a car near Ward's home in Walkinstown. Kennedy had been patrolling the area looking for the latest arrest target. Kennedy called for backup. Ward had to be arrested now. He and Foy were taken into custody at gunpoint. In Lucan the order was given for a swoop on Ward's circle. Over the next few hours nine members of Ward's family were lifted, including his elderly parents and his girlfriend, Vanessa Meehan. Another twenty-two searches were ordered.

Ward was the second primary gang member to be arrested. Hickey and his men had a glimmer hope that maybe he would come clean. After all, like Bowden, he held a key to the murder gang. He had also played a central role and was a candidate for a murder charge. In addition to the men he already had working the case, Hickey sent for other experienced, hardened interrogators from around the country, including former members of the disbanded murder squad. Ward's detention in Lucan was to become the subject of much controversy. During his interrogation, Vanessa Meehan and Ward's 74-year-old mother, Elizabeth, were brought to see him. They had been taken from Cabra and Ballyfermot stations for the purpose of the visits. Afterwards, Ward began to talk about the crime.

"My part was to let them [Meehan and the hit man] use my house after the shooting. They came with the bike and the gun," Ward was alleged to have told the investigators. Asked where he had hidden the murder weapon, Ward replied: "Nobody will ever be killed by the gun where it is now." Hippo was then asked where the gun came from. "You know well where it came from. It was with the guns and ammunition you got in the graveyard," Ward is said to have replied. In other interviews Ward claimed his only role in the murder was the disposal of the gun and the bike. During his subsequent trial in the Special Criminal Court, these admissions were ruled inadmissible (see chapter 18).

The order to arrest John O'Neill came on Thursday, the day after Ward's arrest. The same day, the nightclub manager who arranged the first meeting between Ward and O'Neill was taken in for questioning. He confirmed the connection between the drug dealer and the cop. Det. Inspectors Todd O'Loughlin and Jerry O'Connell arrived at O'Neill's home with four other officers. Sgt Keane, who had been watching O'Neill, showed him a warrant to search the house. "Is this about my contact with the Wards?" O'Neill asked as he let his soon-to-be former colleagues into his house. During the search the officers found a sawn-off shotgun that O'Neill claimed he had kept after the armed robbery case for which he won his medal for gallantry. O'Neill then agreed to go to the Garda Dublin Metropolitan HQ at Harcourt Square to be interviewed.

O'Neill was brought to a room next door to Tony Hickey's office in Harcourt Square. He wasn't under arrest and was still a member of the gardaí. O'Neill confessed his dealings with Ward and Meehan. In his statement O'Neill also admitted to having approached two other well-known drug dealers for bribe money, Tony Long and Derek "Dee Dee" O'Driscoll, who were both from Ballyfermot. The crooked policeman had approached them in the middle of September after Brian Meehan put him on the gang's "payroll".

At 12.30 a.m. John O'Neill was officially suspended from the Garda Síochána. Immediately after this, he was arrested under section 30 of the Offences Against the State Act and brought to Naas station for questioning about the firearm found in his home and his association with criminal figures. The arrest of O'Neill was a sad victory. It was a source of grave embarrassment to the police force, coming so soon after a murder which had challenged the public's faith in the keepers of law and order. However, it illustrated the determination of the Lucan team to pursue anyone who came to their attention in the hunt for the killers of Veronica Guerin.

The next day O'Neill formally offered his resignation from the police and was accepted. Later on in the day he was brought back to Lucan to confront Paul Ward. O'Neill told the murder suspect that he had told his police colleagues everything about their relationship. He encouraged Ward to "tell the truth". Ward was angered by the visit and shouted at the officers who were interviewing him. "Fuck off! There is no need to do that. He didn't tell me fuck all about the murder. The money is his fucking problem. I am saying nothing else to you."

On Friday Paul Ward was released from his section 30 detention and re-arrested under the Misuse of Drugs Act. Hickey phoned the Director of Public Prosecutions, Eamon Barnes, and outlined their case so far. Barnes directed that Paul Ward be charged with conspiracy to murder Veronica Guerin. He was also charged with possession of drugs with intent to supply. That night Ward was brought before the Dublin District Court, charged and remanded in custody. Earlier, John O'Neill had been brought to the same court and remanded on sixteen charges of accepting bribes. He was released on bail.

It had been a long week for the investigators but it wasn't over. They were making extraordinary progress. Hickey decided that once they were on a roll, they should keep going. On Friday morning, while some of the Ward family and John O'Neill were still in custody, the Lucan team arrested Russell and Debbie Warren for the second time. They were lifted under the Offences Against the State Act for questioning about the gang's arms find. This time Russell Warren was more forthcoming. He described the events leading up to murder, including being sent to Naas to look out for Veronica's car, but this time stopped short at admitting that he had actually witnessed the incident. In his second statement he claimed that after he left Naas he pulled off the dual carriageway and headed back to Tallaght on a back road. It was the following May before Warren finally admitted his full role in the crime. The flow of good quality information had increased dramatically after Gilligan's arrest. Once they were out of harm's way, Gilligan's cronies were not as scared of reprisals as they had been.

By October 25 the Lucan team felt they had enough groundwork done to move on the Cork end of the operation. At 7.30 a.m. a team comprising officers from the Criminal Assets Bureau and the National Drug Unit swooped on John Dunne and the van drivers he used to transport Gilligan's drugs to Dublin. Everyone, including Dunne's wife, were taken to Lucan for questioning. Detective Inspector John O'Mahony, who had successfully obtained the full assistance of Charlie Bowden, had another breakthrough. Within a short while of his arrest John Dunne agreed to tell all he knew. He was up front and to the point. "I was driven by pure greed and nothing more. After the murder I was too scared to get out," he told

O'Mahony during the drive back to Dublin.

Sergeants Pat Keane and Noel Browne arrived at the Seabridge premises where Dunne worked with a search warrant. The staff were utterly horrified when they discovered that their manager had been involved with the murder gang. While Dunne was making statements in Lucan station, Keane and Browne were making a cursory examination of the shipping records to get an estimate of the amounts of hash they gang had imported. As they continued their calculations, one member of the team had to go away and buy a more sophisticated calculator. That evening one of the officers rang Chief Superintendent Fachtna Murphy at his office in CAB and asked if he was sitting down. Then he told him of his rough calculation of the amount Gilligan had shipped through Cork. "They've shipped in tonnes of the stuff, Chief, as far back as April 1994… millions." A member of that team recalled: "We all knew that they had moved a lot of stuff, but no-one had imagined just how large the whole operation was. Those first three weeks of October 1996 were like a rollercoaster ride. Everything had gone well for us. We finally had Gilligan's whole operation."

The John O'Neill investigation became yet another separate inquiry for the Lucan team to pursue. In November they arrested Long and O'Driscoll. While he was being interviewed at Lucan, O'Driscoll admitted to setting up O'Neill when he was introduced to him by Long. He had secretly filmed himself handing over five thousand pounds to O'Neill. "I needed collateral. The banks take your house deeds, I only took a fuckin' picture. He came to me looking for a few bob and I wouldn't like to see one of your men stuck, you know, good citizen and all of that," O'Driscoll told the officers with a snigger.

During his arrest Long told the officers: "I was to put O'Neill on the payroll for warrants and stuff. Dee Dee told me Paul Ward wanted to know the inside story on the Guerin murder and he was going to use O'Neill on the inside. Once he was filmed, he was fucked." Both criminals were subsequently convicted for corruption. O'Driscoll was jailed for a year and Long, who didn't fancy being inside again, paid a forty-five thousand pound fine. In an act of poetic justice, Long's ability to pay the fine attracted the attentions of the Criminal Assets Bureau two years later and they issued him a tax demand for £240,000.

Finally, in early November John Gilligan's family and close personal associates, including his wife and children, were arrested in swoops. Members of Traynor's group were also lifted. On November 6 the CAB began hitting the gang. They seized vehicles belonging to Ward, Meehan and Mitchell and whatever money they had left behind. They also began the process of seizing all the properties owned by Traynor, Meehan, Mitchell and Ward. On November 20 the CAB also hit Jessbrook with a large force of police and Revenue officials. It was the first large-scale operation by the newly formed bureau. To protect their identities, the CAB officers covered their faces with scarves and the registration numbers of their vans were removed. About twenty uniformed officers sealed off the area and the roads.

Det. Supt Felix McKenna supervised the operation, which took most of a day. They seized horses, jeeps, horse trailers, stable and riding equipment, furniture, televisions and video players. Anything of value was taken. All that was left were personal effects and basic household equipment. The raid was in response at the Gilligan's refusal to pay their two million pound tax demand. Talking to reporters at the gates to her home, Geraldine Gilligan said: "I couldn't answer the tax assessment because the police have all my documents of returns and everything else, so I didn't have any documentation to answer with. My demand has gone from £882,000 to £1,292,000. I can prove the source of any income." Less than a year after the gang languished on a beach in St Lucia and joked about crime paying, the big-time, swaggering gangsters had been reduced to the status of fugitives and prisoners.

Sixteen

The Supergrass

Paul Ward was having a tough time in prison. He told his visitors that he thought he was going out of his mind. Ward was frustrated and angry that he had been left to carry the can while his pals had apparently gotten away scot-free. He once complained to another prisoner that he hadn't even pulled the trigger. He had only got rid of the gun and motorbike because he had been told to. Ward felt betrayed. Like Gilligan, he had developed a taste for the good life his drug money bought. Meehan and Mitchell were off enjoying themselves in the sun and he had no idea if Bowden was going to give evidence against him. Ward was about to explode.

Because of his heroin habit and his volatile state of mind, Ward was housed in the prison's Separation Unit, or E Wing. Hippo's home was cell number 3 on level four. Since before Christmas Ward and the other inmates had been frustrated with their living conditions. Ward was a veteran of the infamous Mountjoy Riots of 1990 when Meehan had led the charge to the prison roof and caused millions of pounds worth of damage in the process. On the evening of January 4, 1997 Ward was again in the news headlines when he attempted another protest.

At 6 p.m. the cells on E4 were unlocked to allow the prisoners free movement about the landing, which had a gym, a recreation hall and a shower room. Ward asked one of the officers if he would allow prisoner Stephen Galvin to get out of his cell to go to the toilet. Galvin had been deprived of evening recreation for a disciplinary offence. Within seconds of being released, five prison officers had been taken hostage by Ward, Galvin, Warren Dumbrell, Eamon Seery, Joseph Cooper and Eddie Ferncombe. The general alarm was raised and an emergency operation put in place. Gardaí and trained Department of Justice negotiators were called in. Ward emerged as the prisoner's spokesman. As he threatened to kill one of the officers, Ward told the hostages: "We plan to stage a peaceful protest."

Over the next two days the prison officers were put through an appalling ordeal in which they had razors, knives and syringes held to their necks. One prison officer was placed on a chair and told he was about to be hanged. The hostages were told that they would be forced to drink AIDS and HIV-infected blood. The prisoners walked around squirting blood from their syringes to illustrate the threat. One of the hostages later recalled: "Ward went beserk and I thought he was going to kill me. He became very violent and aggressive. He lifted a bar and brought it down violently towards my head."

Another officer who had been placed on a chair in the middle of the room with a noose around his neck recalled: "Ward was out of control. I was terrified and made my peace with God. By that I mean I was prepared to die. We cowered down on the floor trying to block out what was happening. I wrote a message to my wife, telling her I was ok and loved her. I thought it was a goodbye letter."

As prison negotiators, prison wardens and the police looked on, it appeared that the hostages would be harmed. They were being constantly threatened. At one stage the officer sitting on the chair was put through a mock execution. Ward yelled that if he didn't have access to a solicitor he was going to start breaking arms and legs. He said he would cut one of the officer's fingers off. "It's only a finger and I'll pass it out for the Governor, " Ward warned.

One of the hostages recalled: "Ward threatened us all that he would stab us with needles and break our fingers. The situation got so serious that I offered Ward my hand and told him to break my hand and every bone in my body but not to stab me with the syringe."

The officers in charge of the overall operation called in the Emergency Response Unit with a view to making a forced entry into the recreation room where the hostages were being held. The ERU recommended that the Army Ranger Wing should be called. Explosives were needed to blast the doors open to get inside, which was one of the Rangers' specialist siege-breaking skills. As the ARW were heading to Dublin, the siege grew more intense.

News of the siege and the involvement of one of the Guerin murder suspects reached the media. Ward spoke to the negotiators and demanded that the group of hostage-takers be transferred to another jail. When he saw the first news reports of the siege, Ward became agitated and lost all control of himself. As negotiators tried to calm him from outside the room, he screamed: "I'm going to smash one of their heads in!"

In the early hours of the following morning the siege was again reported on Sky News and once more Ward was named as the ringleader. The Gilligan gang member warned that if his name was used again, he would smash one of the hostage's heads in. Then he demanded that the media be told that he was protesting because "I am innocent of the murder of Veronica Guerin". Later the next morning, Ward again went mad when he read a description of himself in a newspaper.

While the drama was unfolding, the Lucan Investigation Team took a particular interest in the case. Ward was already disillusioned with the rest of the gang and felt hard done by that he was now taking the rap. There was still the possibility that, if the situation was handled correctly, he could become a witness for the State. After Ward's arrest in October he had met Charlie Bowden in Mountjoy. Ward had told his former colleague that he would go over to the State's side but he felt he couldn't handle the isolation that would inevitably follow. He said he was terrified of Brian Meehan and what the gang could do to his family. He had no idea at that stage that Bowden had already agreed to be Ireland's first supergrass. An officer was sent to the prison to offer assistance in the negotiations. But nothing came of the initiative.

In the meantime, the Rangers had worked out a plan to blast off the recreation room door and storm the room within ten seconds. Eventually, however, the siege came to a much less dramatic conclusion when a nun intervened and convinced Ward and his pals to release the hostages. The prison officers were profoundly traumatised and shaken by the ordeal. Ward and the other hostage takers were removed to Portlaoise Prison, where they were placed in solitary confinement for several months. During that period it is understood that Ward received a number of discreet visits from the gardaí as they investigated the prison siege. These contacts were a perfect opportunity to sound out Hippo's reticence to switch sides. A member of the investigation team recalled: "Ward was very shaky throughout this time and we know that he confided to other prisoners that he was going to talk. We knew he could lead us to the murder weapon and we weren't giving up on that."

While Paul Ward was terrorising the hostages in Mountjoy, Brian Meehan and Peter Mitchell were wrecking havoc in Gran Canaria, where they had been spending the Christmas holidays. Over the previous months the pair had moved between Holland, Belgium, France, Austria and the Costa Del Sol. The gardaí had little difficulty tracking their movements in Spain. The pair of arrogant loudmouths hung around popular Irish haunts, making no effort to keep a low profile. In January Fatso's family flew to the Canary Islands for a belated Christmas gathering with the fugitives and spent two weeks with them. Mitchell's mother, Eileen, cooked a traditional Christmas dinner for her favourite son to make up for his enforced absence from home.

While in the Canaries, Meehan and Mitchell approached a number of bar owners offering to invest in the business, but word spread among the Irish business community about their reputations and they failed to make a deal. At one stage they ran into a number of gardaí from Dublin who were also on holiday in Playa Del Ingles. Meehan and Mitchell stood watching their "old friends" and making the shape of guns with their hands. The cops had to seek alternative accommodation.

In the Life Discotheque, near an area of the resort called the Kasbah, the pair encountered the Galway All Ireland Hurling team. Meehan began picking on the GAA men and attacked one of the team's brightest stars, Gregory Kennedy, breaking his ankle and potentially damaging his sports career. After the incident Mitchell turned to other onlookers and declared in his loud voice: "Now do ye see what happens when you fuck with us?" On another occasion the pair gave another man a severe beating outside the same nightclub.

They left the Canaries and headed back to Europe in the first week of February, where they teamed up with John Traynor. The gang members were making every effort to find out exactly what was happening in the Guerin investigation. Since October the investigation had seemed to go quiet, but it was nothing more than a lull in the ongoing battle. The number of large swoops and high profile arrests had slowed down as the inquiry went into a different phase. Although it wasn't attracting the same level of media attention, the incident room was still the scene of intense activity as the team consolidated their progress to date, obtained statements and built their case. So, too, was the Criminal Assets Bureau. There was a mountain of documentary evidence to be compiled.

By early 1997 Bowden and Warren were still not fully on board as witnesses, although they had expressed their determination to give evidence. Hickey and the gardaí in general were trying to overcome each obstacle as it presented itself, improvising as they went along. The police knew that they were taking on an extremely dangerous and resourceful criminal empire. The only way to beat them was to have witnesses give evidence in court. In order to achieve that, the witnesses had to be protected. They would also have to be granted immunity from prosecution.

Hickey put forward proposals for the establishment of a witness protection programme and had informed the Department of Justice that it was the only way in which they could proceed with the prosecution of Gilligan and his gang. There had never before been a situation like this in Ireland. The Lucan investigation had entered its most difficult phase.

Hickey's strategy was to build as much evidence as possible on each gang member to sustain drug trafficking and murder charges. Secretly, the Lucan team aimed to obtain directions from the D.P.P. to charge Gilligan with murder, possession of firearms and drug trafficking. Then they would seek to have the mob boss extradited. The same strategy would apply to Meehan and Holland, if they got the evidence to charge them. Ideally, the team wanted to catch their suspects in Ireland so they would have the opportunity of interrogating them for 48 hours. If they were extradited from another country, the criminal would have to be charged as soon as his feet touched Irish soil and therefore could not be interviewed.

The gang desperately wanted to get back to "normal". Meehan and Gilligan did everything they could to find out what was happening with the case in Ireland. They hadn't calculated on the intensity of the garda response. On January 22 they got their first indication of the State's case against them at a magistrate's hearing in London into whether Gilligan should be sent forward for trial on the money laundering charges. During the week-long hearing, which

Gilligan lost, officers from the CAB and Lucan gave evidence of his financial dealings in Ireland.

CAB officers caused gasps of surprise when they gave evidence of how Gilligan had gambled almost £5.5 million in two-and-a-half years and lost just over six hundred thousand pounds. Details were also given to the court about his Aer Lingus Gold Circle flights between Dublin and Amsterdam. But the blood drained from Gilligan's face with rage when John Dunne was brought to give evidence. Dunne, who was by now under around-the-clock armed protection in Ireland, was the first of the so-called supergrasses to give evidence against Gilligan.

Lucan had sought and obtained the assistance of every law enforcement organisation in Europe in their efforts to keep up tabs on their suspects. At the same time, unknown to the gang, the European dimension of the case had been stepped up. At the beginning of the year Hickey had decided to send an operational team to the Continent to liase with the Dutch and Belgian authorities. Officers from the Fraud Bureau's Money Laundering Unit, Det. Inspector Terry McGinn and Det. Sgt Gerry Giblin, were sent as liaison on behalf of the MLU and CAB. Roger Wilson and H.M. Customs also sent an investigation team. The information being sought would stand up criminal cases in either Ireland or England.

The Lucan team's primary objective was to obtain the evidence and corroboration for the drugs and firearms charges. Det. Inspector Vincent Farrell had already spent time working for Europol and had a good knowledge of the European system. With him were Det. Sergeants Pat Keane and Noel Browne. Over the next year they would spend much of their time working in Europe. The D.P.P. in Dublin sent an official request to the Dutch and Belgian authorities outlining the assistance required by both CAB and Lucan in the form of what is described as an International Rogatory Commission. The list included tracing shipping records from the companies used by Rahman. He also requested assistance in tracing and interviewing a number of named individuals, including the Gorsts, Simon Rahman, Johnny Wildhagen and Martin Baltus. Interviews and statements were sought from the GWK bank and any other casino or financial institution where cash was changed by Gilligan's bagmen.

The three Irish officers made excellent progress in Holland. The two senior officers attached to the "project team Setter", Jacob Vrolijk and Jitse Hans van der Veer of the Haaglanden police, introduced the Lucan investigators to Martin Baltus. In April Baltus agreed to co-operate with the Irish squad. He had been released from a 150-day prison sentence for the counterfeit dollars scam which had caused a serious falling out with Rahman. In fifteen statements Baltus described in detail his involvement in the operation. He revealed how shipments were packed and transported to Ireland. He gave details of the bogus company names he had used and the dates of the shipments.

Baltus described how he had exchanged £2.8 million for Gilligan and Meehan and how he had been present when Rahman, Wildhagen and Gilligan negotiated deals with Havid, the Morroccan hash dealer. Baltus described packing the various firearms which were sent to Cork. He told of his arrest after picking up the Agram machine pistol in March 1995, which had also been meant for shipment to Dublin and which was identical to the one found in the Jewish cemetery. Baltus provided an exciting break in the case. He corroborated Bowden and Dunne's evidence in relation to the drugs and guns shipments. Statements from the GWK bank in Amsterdam confirmed the money he had admitted exchanging. Baltus had cemented together the entire conspiracy of guns, drugs and money.

The detectives were also brought to a Dutch prison to meet with Simon Rahman, the imperious godfather who had supplied Gilligan with millions of pounds worth of hash and guns. He listened with interest to the questions put to him by the Dutch and Irish officers. They wanted to evaluate him as a potential witness in Ireland against the gang. When Gilligan had been arrested in London, Rahman had lost at least three hundred thousand pounds because he had sent a shipment of hash to Ireland having received only a deposit payment. Gilligan had been on the way to pay another instalment of the hash bill. Rahman hinted that he might be prepared to testify if the price was right, but the team didn't pursue Rahman any further. They didn't think him a suitable witness. Despite exhaustive searches, Johnny Wildhagen was never found.

In June the three Irish officers, in the company of senior judicial police officers Gerrit Troch and Guy Gillis, met with Thomas Gorst and his wife Mariette in Antwerp, Belgium. Thomas Gorst was not as forthcoming as Baltus had been. He admitted participating in the exchange of only one hundred thousand pounds for Gilligan. He had been sentenced to six months imprisonment for that offence in January. He also admitted knowing Denis Meredith, whom he said he had met seven years earlier.

Mariette Gorst said that she knew Gilligan and that she had rented a house for him and Carol Rooney shortly before the murder of Veronica Guerin. She told the men from Lucan: "As far as John Gilligan is concerned, it now appears that I grossly misjudged his character. I only realised that I was dealing with a criminal when I saw an American newspaper and read an article about the arrest of John and four others. He was described as an important drugs trafficker, arms dealer and ex-member of the IRA. You may be rest assured that I am quite prepared to assist in the investigations and to provide all useful information which may provide evidence against Gilligan in Ireland. I am prepared to testify in court in Ireland if necessary." Thomas Gorst also agreed to testify in Ireland but, within a few weeks of giving that agreement, both he and his wife left Belgium and are now believed to be in hiding in Mexico. Before he disappeared, Gorst was holding over eight hundred thousand pounds of Gilligan's drug money. When he vanished, so did the money.

The investigation team still had their star witness on their side. In October Baltus was secretly slipped into Ireland with Senior Detective Vrolijk and whisked to Lucan station amid tight security. While there, he identified the boxes and guns which he had organised and packed for Gilligan. He also made a number of detailed statements to Keane, Farrell and Browne. Baltus told the Lucan detectives: "I have had many thoughts on this and I have given a number of interviews to the police of The Hague concerning these and other matters. I am here in Ireland freely and I acknowledge that I have been involved in bad things and I wish to put all this behind me in my life. I am prepared to travel to court here in Ireland and give the truth."

Six weeks after his arrest, Bowden was released on sixty thousand pounds bail. Meehan had paid a quarter of the bill and the rest was raised among Bowden's family and friends. As soon as he was released in mid-November 1996, Meehan was on the phone to Bowden. He was agitated and sounded dangerous. He demanded to know what Paul Smullen and Julian Clohessy had told the police. Meehan was particularly worried about Clohessy because he had bragged to him about the murder. Now Meehan's big mouth was catching up with him.

Meehan ordered Bowden to write a report of everything he had said and everything his friends had said while in custody. The reports were picked up and sent to Meehan. Then he ordered Bowden to get Smullen and Clohessy to go to a criminal lawyer and swear affidavits to the effect that they had been forced to implicate him (Meehan) in the murder. He wanted the pair to claim that the police had threatened to charge them with murder if they didn't agree to implicate Meehan.

"If anyone who has made a statement against me doesn't sign an affidavit, I will have them taken care of. There's no way I'll let Clohessy get into the witness box," Meehan warned his former partner in crime. "The guards won't be able to protect any witnesses because there is no witness protection programme in Ireland," Meehan declared confidently.

The gangster didn't necessarily mind people cracking under questioning, as long as they didn't get into the witness box. It was something he learned from his master, Gilligan. In his earlier career the little man had gotten off several serious charges by intimidating witnesses. In February 1997, when Paul Ward's charge was upgraded to a charge of murder, Meehan phoned Bowden to tell him it was now likely that he (Bowden) would be charged with conspiracy to murder. The gang's former quartermaster said that there was no way he wanted to be charged in relation to the murder.

The Tosser suggested that he would fix Charlie and Juliet up with false passports and money and set them up with a new life in Australia. It was gangland's equivalent of a witness protection programme. Bowden sent passport photographs to Meehan through an intermediary. By now he was in fear of being charged in relation to the murder. Bowden had never been in prison before and the six weeks he had been in custody were the hardest in his life. He had had trouble contacting O'Mahony and Hanley. Bowden had asked them several times about whether the State was going to grant him immunity in exchange for his testimony against his former colleagues in crime. The two officers couldn't answer him because Tony Hickey was still anxiously awaiting the mandarins in the Department of Justice to come up with a response to his proposal.

In a fit of panic Bowden decided to make a run for it. On February 8 he jumped bail and went to England with Julie Bacon. There they stayed in a guesthouse using false names. In Lucan there was consternation when the ex-soldier disappeared. Hickey and his men were angry at the apparent procrastination at the Department of Justice in coming up with a proposal to ensure their witnesses gave evidence in court. Over a week later, however, a surveillance team from the South East Regional Crime Squad spotted the couple having a meeting with Dutchie Holland. For a number of months the SERCS had dedicated an undercover team to watch Dutchie's every move for the Irish authorities.

The gang's enforcer had made contact with Bowden on Meehan's behalf and asked to meet. Dutchie would never know that it was he who helped the gardaí get their star witness back in custody. The undercover men watched as Bowden and Julie Bacon met with Holland at the Angel Tube Station in Islington early in March.

Dutchie told Bowden that he intended getting a media campaign together to win himself the right to have any interviews with the Lucan team videotaped. Holland had been anxious to return to Ireland after a front-page story appeared in the *Sunday World* that featured his picture and a story revealing that he was the suspected hit man. Dutchie asked Bowden what he had told the police about his (Holland's) involvement in the murder plot. Bowden said he hadn't mentioned Dutchie's name in relation to the murder but had given a statement naming him in relation to the drugs operation.

Holland was friendly and remarked that Bowden wasn't to worry. "Everybody makes a statement but there are ways of dealing with people who do. They either don't get up in the witness box or, like you, they are given the option of running away. Or they could get popped," Holland said with an amicable smile. Dutchie denied any involvement with the murder and reminded Bowden that there was no witness protection programme in Ireland. Holland blamed John Foy for putting his name into the murder equation.

The meeting terrified Bowden and Julie Bacon. Despite his abilities and physical strength, the ex-soldier felt scared and isolated. Luckily for him the secret police team had used electronic equipment to eavesdrop on the conversation. They reported back to the Lucan team, who requested that Bowden be arrested as he wanted for skipping his bail. The former soldier was still considering his options when he got the feeling that he was being followed. One morning he was feeling particularly paranoid and stood at a bus stop for ten minutes, watching to see if someone was following him. Suddenly, both ends of the road were blocked by police cars. Officers wearing bullet-proof vests and armed with HK rifles trained their weapons on him and told him to lie on the ground. He was arrested under the Prevention of Terrorism Act.

Initially, Bowden gave the police a false name but they knew everything about him. He was presented with an extradition order from Ireland which he could opt to contest. He decided to return voluntarily. He spoke to O'Mahony on the phone. "I want to come home. I want to co-operate," he told his garda handler. On March 10 Bowden and Julie Bacon were escorted under armed guard to London City Airport. John O'Mahony and Bernie Hanley were waiting for them and they all flew back to Dublin together. The Lucan investigation was back on track.

The CAB had sought an order freezing Dutchie Holland's luxurious country residence near Brittas Bay in County Wicklow, as the first step in seizing it for resale. Holland was very upset when he heard the news and decided to have the house bought by an alleged boyfriend of his wife. He was also busy trying to reclaim a figure in the region of almost one million pounds which was owed to Gilligan by other drug dealers and money launderers but never paid because he was now a resident of Belmarsh Prison. Holland was to receive a percentage of the money he collected from the debtors as commission.

In February, sixteen officers from CAB and Lucan swooped on Holland's country house, arresting his wife, Angela, and a close family friend. His wife's arrest exacerbated his sense of anxiety and he contacted a friend, who in turn set up a meeting with Dublin-based freelance reporter Ray Managh. Managh was a well-respected journalist who had been covering the courts for several years.

Holland wanted to give a newspaper and radio interview declaring his innocence.

Pat Kenny, one of the country's most popular radio and television hosts, and his researchers were extremely interested in the prospect when Managh tipped them off. On March 5 Pat Kenny recorded an interview in the Jury's Kensington Hotel in which Dutchie denied that he had any involvement in the murder of Veronica Guerin and, indeed, that he was a hit man at all.

Holland also declared: "I will be in Dublin in hours if the police give my legal representatives a written assurance the interview will be videotaped. I want to look Graham Turley in the eye and tell him: 'I did not kill your wife.' I want to tell her son: 'I did not kill your mother.'" Holland also denied murdering Paddy Shanahan, but talked openly about other crimes in which he had been involved and about how he got the nickname "the Wig".

Holland claimed that he had been forced to leave Ireland because of the *Sunday World* article. "Where did the newspaper get my passport picture from?" he asked in the interview, strenuously protesting his innocence. He wanted to know where the journalist's information had come from. Dutchie was being economical with the truth. What he hadn't revealed was that he had been in hiding in England at least three months before the offending article appeared.

Holland avowed that, despite his former criminal record, he had never been charged with violence or assault and he had never laid a hand on a woman. Although he had carried a gun in robberies, he had never used it. "When I heard she had been killed, I didn't think much about it. I didn't follow it up. I didn't know the girl. All I knew was that she wrote articles. I'm not running the girl down. I heard she was dead. I didn't hear the details. It was later I found out it was in Clondalkin and that. I'm not saying it's right. I don't know anything. I just heard this girl got killed and I knew the name. I don't know details. I just got a news flash," he said in another interview with Ray Managh, which was published in the next morning's daily newspapers.

Following the Pat Kenny interview, there was considerable controversy in the national station, RTÉ, when the Director General prevented the interview being aired. He told a furious Pat Kenny that he had made the decision on the advice of the Garda

Commissioner, who was afraid of prejudicing any future investigation involving Holland. The broadcasting chief also argued that transmitting the interview could create legal problems.

Four days after the interview was taped, however, Dutchie's eventual fate was sealed when Charlie Bowden was flown home.

The undercover squad watching Holland reported to Lucan that he had been observed visiting a London store which specialised in providing high-tech bugging and surveillance equipment. Jim Orange, Holland's solicitor, contacted Det. Inspector Todd O'Loughlin to inform him that his client would be turning up voluntarily for an interview on April 4. On that date Mr Orange again contacted the Lucan detective and told him Holland would instead be turning up on April 7. Again, he did not appear. The SERCS undercover squad in London, however, had more accurate information about when the Lucan team could hope to see Dutchie. On April 8 they called Lucan and told them that he was on his way to catch a late-night sailing on the ferry from Holyhead to Dun Laoghaire.

In Lucan a large team was mobilised to intercept Gilligan's enforcer. To be on the safe side, officers watched the North Wall ferry port in Dublin and Rosslare in County Wexford and posed as car checkers as cars rolled off the 5.45 a.m. Stena Sea Link ferry. The first line of officers didn't spot Holland, who was wearing a baseball cap and sitting in the passenger seat of a car driven by a young woman with a child. A few hundred yards further on, a checkpoint had been set up. Det. Garda Marian Cusack spotted Dutchie and pounced. She arrested him under the Offences Against the State Act. He was searched and, before being brought to an interview room at Lucan station, his clothes, shoes and socks were removed and he was given an overall suit to wear. At 8 a.m. Det. Sgt Fergus Treanor and Det. Garda Sean O'Brien began interviewing Dutchie.

The station house sergeant tried to contact Holland's solicitor, Jimmy Orange. At that stage it was discovered that officers from the CAB had arrested Mr Orange for questioning in relation to the sale of Holland's home in Brittas. Later, at Holland's trial, Mr Orange would describe his arrest as a charade designed to prevent him assisting his client at the time of his arrest.

An officer who was examining a Walkman found on Holland suddenly began hearing the voices of his colleagues in the next room, where Dutchie's shoes abd other belongings were being kept. While the interrogation was still going on, officers discovered sophisticated James Bond-style bugging equipment hidden in the soles of his shoes. A technical support team was summoned from Garda HQ, who later discovered receiving and recording equipment in a guest house near the police station. In a follow-up investigation, packaging for the equipment was found in a rented room in a hotel near Tallaght garda station. An accomplice had planned to bug the interviews at Lucan in an attempt to sabotage the whole investigation. From then on the incident room and station house were also regularly swept for bugging equipment, in addition to being protected against physical attack.

When the equipment was found, Holland was asked to account for it. "I am taking responsibility for it and all the rest of the equipment. I've been planning this for a couple of months, lads," said Holland. When asked how much he had paid for the equipment, Dutchie replied sarcastically, "More than you earn in a year. Don't think I am the first one to walk in here with bugs in my shoes."

The Lucan team later sent officers to London to investigate the source of the high-tech devices. They traced the specialist spy shop where Dutchie had ordered the equipment. He had paid in excess of twenty-five thousand pounds. "It was a bit of an unnecessary waste of drug money," an investigation team member quipped.

Holland refused to talk about the murder of Veronica Guerin. "Gentlemen, I am not talking about that," he replied. He was hardly more forthcoming about his involvement in the hash trade.

Sean O'Brien: Paddy, the list which was found in Greenmount has you down for 34 kilos. Is that you, the Wig?

Holland: Yes.

O'Brien: What would you do with 34 kilos, Paddy?

Holland: Look, lads, I had my own customers I am not going to implicate them. I have certain principles.

Later Det. Inspector John O'Mahony visited Holland in the interview room. "You are admitting drug dealing. Is that correct?"

Holland: Yes, only hash. The papers have us dealing in heroin and ecstasy. That's not true.

O'Mahony: Isn't it true that you were selling drugs for John Gilligan?

Holland: I'm not implicating anyone else. I'll speak for myself. I like John Gilligan. He is a nice fella.

Later Det. Sgt Gerry O'Carroll and Det. Inspector Jerry O'Connell went to see Holland. O'Carroll had arrested Holland in relation to the Shanahan murder.

O'Carroll: Well, Gene, it's been a long time. I didn't think that I'd be seeing you again.

Holland: Neither did I, Gerry.

O'Carroll: You know that we are investigating the shooting of Veronica Guerin.

Holland: I'm not talking about that.

O'Carroll: From our investigations we are satisfied that you shot Veronica Guerin on June 26.

Holland: I am not talking about that.

After two days in detention, Hickey decided that there was enough evidence to charge Holland with drug trafficking, based both on his own admissions and the statement of Charlie Bowden. He was released from custody on the morning of April 11, re-arrested and formally charged under the Misuse of Drugs Act. Det. Sgt Padraig Kennedy asked Holland how it felt to be facing a serious drug charge at his time in life.

"It's not over yet," replied Holland. That morning Holland was taken under heavy guard to Kilmainham District Court where he was remanded in custody on drug charges. It had been another bad week for the Gilligan gang.

When Bowden decided to return to Dublin, he signed his own death warrant. The gang needed no further convincing that their quartermaster and distribution manager had turned tout when he didn't fight the extradition process. Meehan made several efforts to contact Julie Bacon. She told the Lucan team that the Tosser wanted to talk to her urgently about Charlie being back in custody. It was decided that if Meehan spoke with Julie, he might say something incriminating. Every piece of evidence or information was crucial to the investigation.

At 4 pm on the same day that Dutchie was charged, Julie Bacon went to the Hole in the Wall pub on Blackhorse Avenue with members of the Lucan team. Det. Garda Colm Church attached a tape-recording device to the public phone in the bar. Julie called an associate of Meehan's in London to tell Meehan the number she was at. A few minutes later Meehan called back. "Charlie is going fucking mad, " she said to Meehan. "He wants to know what the fucking story is with Paddy Holland and how come Holland came home."

Meehan: Paddy Holland came home to clear his name. He's innocent. It has nothing to do with Charlie.

Bacon: He [Charlie] said they nicked him... He got told that someone ratted that he was coming on the boat, or else they said they had surveillance on the boats.

Meehan: Holland has nothing to do with what Charlie got done for."

Bacon then told Meehan that her boyfriend was being kept in a twenty-hour lockup in Arbour Hill, where he was "going fucking mad... He went on hunger strike and everything, he did." She said that Meehan had been put in Arbour Hill prison because he had hit one of the prison officers.

Meehan: But the whole thing, Julie, like, tell me about what [*sic*] whole thing. Like, Holland has nothing got to do with what Charlie got done for.

Bacon: I know, he's just wondering, just worried what the story is, that's all.

Meehan: But it's nothing got to do with the murder and it's nothing. He's clear on the murder, Holland is, because they didn't do him with it, 'cause they've no evidence, right?

Meehan added that Holland was not involved in "the drugs thing" and that he "never touched anything".

Meehan: Now, listen to me and I'll tell you, 'cause I want to get things straight, 'cause things are looking very fucking fishy to me, right, and I'll tell you what, I'm after being good to everybody but I'm taking off my gloves now. If Charlie's going belly-up, if Charlie is going gammy, he better fucking think very strongly about what will happen."
    Bacon: Are you threatening me, Brian?
    Meehan: Threatening, Julie? You'll have no idea what I'm going to fucking do if he goes Turk. Now, I'm telling you. I'm his friend still, I'm helping youse every way I can, but I'm fucking starting to worry and worry and worry, 'cause I'll tell you who goes to Arbour Hill – rapists and fucking rats. I've done everything I fucking can to help him, everything, he has no worries against why Holland is home unless he made a statement against Holland, do you understand?

Bacon again told Meehan that Bowden was "going ballistic" and was wondering what the story was.

Meehan: I'll send someone to fucking kill you this fucking day, do you understand what I'm saying.
    Bacon: What did you say?
    Meehan: You are fucking hearing me. I'll send someone to kill you and everybody around you if he goes Turk. Now tell him I said that, right, and tell him I said I'm fucking considering doing him anyway, so he better not fucking think of going rat, right, that's the message now, right?
    Bacon: You're a fucking knacker, that's all, you're a knacker.
    Meehan: You're the fucking... and Charlie is a rat and if he rats on me, I'll fucking kill you.
    Bacon: I don't fucking blame him if he does, you prick, you.
    Meehan: Yeah, you fucking scumbag.
    Bacon: You're a scumbag. Fuck off.

The conversation ended abruptly and anyone listening was left under no illusion as to just what was going on. Hickey held a conference in Lucan with his senior officers and it was decided to move Julie Bacon out of the house at the Paddocks straight away. That night two thugs from the Cabra area burned the house down on the orders of John Traynor. The gloves had certainly come off.

A special squad of young Special Branch officers were selected to start protecting the witnesses in the Guerin case. The squad later became known as the Witness Protection Unit. Hickey and his team were aware of the amount of money available to the gang and the potential for murder. Several sums of money were offered to murder Bowden over the next two years. By the late summer the bounty on his head had reached a hefty two million pounds. Renegade paramilitaries were recruited to get a sniper to shoot Bowden going to and from court. A disused tower was blocked up near the prison as a result. A rocket attack was also planned on Bowden's security convoy going to court but the plan was dropped because no-one would take the contract.

Then John Traynor tried another, more novel, tactic to get at Bowden. In June he contacted a criminal friend whose brother was doing time in Arbour Hill for a sexual offence. Traynor's contact was to smuggle a poisoned tablet to his brother in prison, who would drop it in Bowden's food. The Coach offered £65,000 for the scam but the contact's brother pulled out of the absurd plot. As a precaution, all the food the witnesses ate was specially prepared to prevent one of them being poisoned. In April 1997 a close associate of Gilligan's was dispatched to Pittsburgh with a case full of money with a view to meeting a mob contact and hiring a professional assassin. It never came to anything. "Speedy" Fegan was then instructed to take photographs of Bowden's three children with a view to scaring him off. This plan, too, had to be abandoned because the ex-soldier's family was now also under heavy guard at their home in Finglas.

On the night of April 27 the Lucan team decided to pay Fegan a visit. The cops burst into a party and caught him snorting cocaine with Vanessa Meehan and another girl. Everyone at the party was arrested. Later, Fegan began giving the gardaí sensitive information about Meehan's movements and plans in return for being let off the hook himself. Loyalty wasn't one of Speedy's strong points.

The gang's lack of success at silencing the State's witnesses was reflected in their efforts to resume their drug business. They began to reorganise, with the help of Speedy Fegan. By the summer, the money was drying up on Meehan, Mitchell and Traynor, and they desperately needed a major injection of funds. On May 7 Meehan strolled into the Creditanstalt Bank in Vienna. He walked up to the bank counter and gave his special code word to access his huge account, "Meener", and furnished his account number. The assistant asked him to wait. Half an hour later the assistant returned with bad news. Meehan becomes suspicious and agitated. The assistant and a manager explained to Meehan that, as a result of a Magistrates Court order, his assets had been frozen.

Meehan broke out in a sweat and began to scan the other customers in the large bank building. There was no point in arguing, he thought. If they had frozen his accounts, then the gardaí might be over waiting to lift him. Meehan ran from the bank. Traynor and Mitchell were waiting for him. They were all stunned but left the city as quickly as they had arrived. They were shocked at how the officers from the Criminal Assets Bureau were well ahead of them. In April the CAB had obtained an international rogatory order and visited the Austrian bank. It proved again that there was suddenly no hiding places left for the remnants of Gilligan's evil mob.

In May the luckless trio organised a four hundred kilo shipment of hash which was to be smuggled to through Northern Ireland to Dublin by Speedy Fegan. He had already moved smaller amounts for the gang. In early June the Northern Ireland newspapers reported that the RUC had seized a huge haul of two hundred kilos of hash. When the gangsters on the Continent read the article, they were furious and blamed Fegan for stealing the other two hundred kilos for himself and tipping off the police about the remainder.

Meehan got on the phone to Fegan and demanded an explanation. Speedy claimed that two of his men had been taking the shipment from Belfast docks when they spotted a British Army checkpoint. To avoid being stopped his two men pulled into a car park, locked the car, put the keys under the wheel arch and left. When the patrol moved off, the pair retrieved the car and drove to the a location to drop the haul. When they looked in the boot of the car, the hash was gone.

Fegan was lying to Meehan. He was well known as a double-crosser and an informant. Meehan threatened to kill him. "Even if I have to go over there [to Northern Ireland] meself, I'll fuckin' kill you." But the loss of Fegan meant the loss of the only strong supply route the gang had into the country. To reorganise the route, Meehan made contact with two drug-dealing brothers from Raheny in north Dublin. He had to put the plan on hold when a pal in Dublin phoned to say he saw Speedy out drinking with the two brothers in a Ranelagh nightclub.

The lack of money was creating tensions in the gang. Meehan turned on Traynor, telling him he was sick of giving him money. Back at home, Meehan's father had to resort to collecting his son's debts. That was interrupted when Meehan and his brother Thomas were both arrested and charged with money laundering by the CAB and the Money Laundering Unit. Things were going decidedly wrong for Meehan, the trusted lieutenant who was desperately trying to hold Gilligan's evil empire together.

In the summer Tony Hickey and his team received confirmation from the D.P.P. that they could proceed and charge John Gilligan and Brian Meehan with the murder of Veronica Guerin. They were also to be charged with sixteen charges of having drugs for sale and supply between July 1, 1994 and October 6, 1996, and with possession of the firearms found in the Jewish cemetery. Hickey and his men went to the Special Criminal Court in June and August 1997 to seek extradition warrants for both men. The two hearings were held in absolute secrecy. Meehan still had to be caught. If he heard any hint that he was to be extradited, he might disappear to South America. For his part, Gilligan might try to pull some type of pre-emptive legal move.

On Monday, September 8, Tony Hickey, Todd O'Loughlin and Jerry O'Connell travelled to London with their extradition warrants for Gilligan. Before they made a move, there had been high level contacts between the D.P.P. and his English equivalent. The Irish would argue that the charges Gilligan faced in Ireland were much more serious than those in England. The British Crown Prosecution Service agreed to stand aside and let the extradition go ahead. Hickey and his men, who had worked virtually non-stop for the past fifteen months for this moment, could scarcely hide their absolute delight.

When he was informed of the extradition warrant and the charges read to him, Gilligan had to be restrained. When he was arraigned before Belmarsh Magistrates Court on the warrants, he refused to recognise the court.

The news of garda plans to extradite the little man rattled Meehan and the rest of the gang in Europe. Who would be next? Meehan was adamant that it wouldn't be him. Garda intelligence had picked up an interesting piece of information about one of Meehan's secret girlfriends, Michelle Dwyer, a beautiful 19-year-old hairdresser. Meehan would meet her on and off in Holland and Spain, behind his girlfriend Fiona Walsh's back. The Tosser reckoned that, apart from a few trusted confidants, the relationship was so secret that he was safe meeting her. On October 8 the Lucan team received information that Dwyer was due to meet Meehan in Amsterdam on Friday afternoon. Hickey sent a request to the Dutch authorities, along with the necessary paperwork, asking them to intercept the Tosser.

Members of Lucan's Dutch team, Pat Keane and Vincent Farrell, were already there following up various aspects of the ongoing case. A specialist undercover police team was mobilised. In Dublin, Dwyer was followed by two officers from the NSU. Meehan had been hard to track around Europe because he was using a number of false passports furnished to him by Speedy Fegan. It was known that Traynor was already in Amsterdam. He had been spotted earlier but lost again. There was no warrant in existence and therefore he had been of no interest at that stage.

The large surveillance squad teamed up with the NSU men, who pointed out Dwyer. She took the commuter train to Centraal Station, but there was still no sign of Meehan. The Irish police officers were beginning to get worried. As she stepped off the train, the target was nowhere in sight. Dwyer got a call on her mobile phone and turned around. The surveillance also took a look. Meehan emerged from the throng of passengers around the entrance to the train station. With him was John Traynor.

The adrenaline began to rise. The three walked through the leaf-strewn streets, chatting and avoiding the oncoming trams. The secret Dutch surveillance squad, about thirty in total, swarmed around the three targets. A woman pushed a pram, an old man walked with a stick, a street cleaner and a young couple kissed as they walk alongside the Dubliners. They were all members of the undercover squad. Pat Keane and Vincent Farrell, who were standing out of sight a safe distance away, confirmed to the commander of the elite Dutch SWAT team that they had the correct targets. After about fifteen minutes Traynor, Meehan and Dwyer reached the magnificent Dam Square. It was a miserable, wet afternoon and the square was unusually quiet. The order was given to move.

Within seconds the police snatch squad were on top of the three. In what was described by one officer as a "blur" because it happened so quickly, Meehan, Traynor and Dwyer were hooded and their hands clasped behind their backs. Traynor began to roar with the fright he got and Meehan soiled his designer pants. Traynor was still roaring as the squad manhandled each of three targets and threw them into the back of vans which had seemed to appear out of nowhere. They were taken to police HQ, where the Irish police officially identified the man they wanted. Traynor was told he was free to go... when he felt his legs could move again! Dwyer was also released. Meehan, who had been given clean pants, was formally charged and informed that he was to be extradited to Ireland to face murder, drugs and firearms charges. He was too stunned to reply. Eight hours later he was still trembling, ashen-faced and staring at the wall of his cell. He looked like a zombie. The Tosser had been caught.

The following day, when he had recovered from his terrifying ordeal, Traynor's instinct for self-preservation kicked in. He phoned Keane and Farrell, who had given him their business cards the previous evening. Traynor met them in a downtown bar. He wanted to know what the prospects were of doing a "deal" with the State in return for his services. The cops, after consultation with Tony Hickey and O'Loughlin, refused the offer.

Traynor suddenly found himself in the gangland equivalent of limbo. His main source of cash, Meehan, was locked up in a maximum security prison. His partners in crime, like Mitchell, were keeping a safe distance from him, and the cops didn't want to know. The clever fraudster would need all his cunning to make a comeback. Ironically, the sudden and violent arrest of Meehan was a blessing in disguise for the Coach. Sources close to the gang later secretly informed garda intelligence that Meehan and Mitchell had been plotting to have Traynor "disappear" in much the same fashion as his Dutch pal Johnny Wildhagen.

After the Meehan arrest, a member of the gang sent a message to John Cunningham in Holland ordering him to organise a hit on Traynor. Cunningham was in the process of establishing himself as the new boss of a multi-million pound drug operation even bigger than Gilligan's. He was shipping cannabis, cocaine and ecstasy to criminals north and south of the border, including members of the General's old gang. Early in 1999 Cunningham travelled to Spain to murder Traynor, according to intelligence sources. But, Cunningham and Traynor had had a long association and the convicted kidnapper couldn't bring himself to whack the Coach. Instead, the pair formed a new alliance. Traynor had survived yet again.

Part Four

Justice

Seventeen

Dutchie's Downfall

As the wheels of justice began turning, the Lucan Investigation Team now had two urgent concerns, namely to organise a long-term witness protection programme and obtain an immunity from prosecution for murder for Warren and Bowden in return for their testimony. They were frustrated at the way the Department of Justice continued to drag its heels. If they did not take action soon and implement the measures suggested by the gardaí, the State's case could fall apart. If that happened, organised crime in Ireland would become stronger than ever.

Hickey stepped up the pressure shortly after Bowden returned from England. In early April he first suggested the introduction of a witness protection programme. It was a radical step, but after thirty years investigating serious crime Hickey knew what he was doing. In their attempts to intimidate potential witnesses in the case, it was the Gilligan gang themselves who put the idea of a WPP firmly in the minds of the police. The criminals had reminded everyone concerned that one did not exist. Hickey decided that should change.

In a memo to Garda Headquarters in April 1997, the assistant commissioner described the situation. "Intelligence indicates that the main players think that the absence of a witness protection programme in this country is to their advantage. There is no doubt that they will resort to murder to prevent witnesses giving damaging evidence in court... I think we should review the situation and if necessary set up a witness protection programme, as all the vital witnesses will be under severe threat if statements are served, and under prolonged threat if and when they give evidence."

In July the Director of Public Prosecutions granted Bowden and Warren immunity from murder. Barry Donoghue, a legal assistant at the D.P.P.'s office who had been liaising directly with

Lucan since the start of the investigation, wrote to Hickey at Lucan station. "The Director has taken the following decision which is unconditional and irrevocable. He will not prosecute Charles Bowden for the murder of Veronica Guerin on the basis of (a) any statement, made orally or in writing by Charles Bowden up to today's date; (b) any further statement made orally or in writing which Charles Bowden may in the future make to a member of the Garda Síochána in the course of their investigation into the possible involvement of other persons in that murder; (c) any evidence which Charles Bowden may give in criminal proceedings against any other person." Lawyers acting for Warren and Bowden were also notified of the immunity deal.

The Department of Justice also gave the go-ahead for the State's witness protection programme. The programme would be primarily the responsibility of the Special Branch and officers were sent to study the system in England, Australia and America. Eventually, the WPP was drafted in law and a specific budget allocated. The families of the three main witnesses were also placed permanently in the programme. Bowden's first wife and three children had a particularly large team of officers with them following the discovery that Speedy Fegan had been trying to photograph them. Wherever the children went, an officer had to be with them. It was an appalling situation to be foisted on a woman and her children, considering that she no longer had anything to do with the selfish gangster. He had brought everyone down with him and changed their lives irrevocably.

Julie Bacon gave an insight into what the programme meant in daily life: "They [gardaí] are like your brothers and sisters after a while. You live with them day and night and share all your problems with them. But they carefully picked good officers who can get on well with people." The State covered every conceivable security risk. The women involved in the WPP even had bulletproof vests specially designed to blend with the contours of their bodies. The basement area of Arbour Hill jail was converted to house the supergrasses.

On September 24 Bowden affirmed his guilty pleas. At that hearing Det. Inspector John O'Mahony told the court that Bowden was kept in isolation in his cell in Arbour Hill prison twenty-three hours a day and was permanently guarded by officers from the new WPP Unit. Bowden's co-operation was given in the full knowledge of the risk to his own life and without any deal being offered to him. "The more threats that are made against him, the more he is determined to give evidence against the members of the gang," said O'Mahony. Judge Cyril Kelly adjourned sentencing Bowden because he said that he needed time to examine similar cases elsewhere in the world. He was the first judge in the Irish criminal justice system with the job of sentencing a supergrass. Later he would be praised by members of Hickey's team for his well-considered judgment.

On October 8 Charlie Bowden was sentenced to six years in prison for the drugs and firearms offences at the Circuit Criminal Court in Dublin. Sniffer dogs swept the building for suspect devices before the Gilligan gang's former manager was swept into court. He was surrounded by armed officers and wearing a bulletproof vest. Bowden's life, Judge Kelly was told, would never be the same again. He would never be able to live a normal life and would have to disappear because of his offer to give evidence against the gang members. "He will attempt to vanish off the face of the earth when he comes out of prison," said Paul O'Higgins, Bowden's counsel.

Judge Kelly sentenced Bowden to six years in prison. As he was taken from the court to begin his sentence, the scene was reminiscent of one of the high profile anti-Mafia trials in Sicily. Members of the ERU kept watch from rooftops while a garda helicopter hovered overhead. Bowden, surrounded by armed officers and a protective, bulletproof shield, was whisked off to Arbour Hill in a convoy of high-powered jeeps.

The following month Russell Warren also affirmed his guilty pleas and was jailed for five years by Judge Kelly. In January Warren and Russell were joined by John Dunne, who was sentenced to three years for his part in Gilligan's operation.

Fears for the safety of the State's witnesses were first expressed when Dutchie Holland applied for bail on July 22 in the Special Criminal Court. Objecting to the release, Det. Sgt Padraig Kennedy from Lucan told the court that Holland, on the morning of his arrest, said that he had no ties with Ireland. In support of this claim, he pointed out that Dutchie had sold his house in Brittas Bay and that he had separated from his wife. His intention was to start a new life in the United States of America. Not being known there, he felt he could blend in better.

Det. Inspector Thomas O'Loughlin gave evidence that Holland was likely to interfere with and harm witnesses. In support of this claim, O'Loughlin cited the meeting between Bowden and Dutchie in London. He also told the court of the phone call between Meehan and Bacon and the subsequent arson attack on Bowden's house. Det. Garda Sean O'Brien said he had received confidential information that strongly suggested that Holland would try to kill witnesses if granted bail.

Holland was cross-examined by senior counsel Peter Charleton, who would lead the prosecution in all of the Gilligan gang trials. Described by his colleagues in the Law Library as "punctilious and exact", the soft-spoken advocate was considered to be one of the country's finest lawyers. Holland explained how he had planted bugs in the heels of his own shoes to record interviews that he had intended to give to the gardaí after giving himself up. He admitted to defrauding the social welfare system and acknowledged that he had not informed the gardaí of his new address in Wicklow because he "did not want any hassle from them". Holland denied issuing threats to Bowden, either at their face-to-face meeting at Islington Tube Station or indirectly through Meehan. Dutchie was remanded in custody.

Patrick Eugene Holland stood trial in the Special Criminal Court on November 18, 1997 after a number of lengthy adjournments in the case. Brendan Grogan, Senior Counsel, led Holland's defence team. Peter Charleton opened the State's case by establishing a link between Holland's prosecution and the Guerin murder. It was, he said, the journalist's death which had prompted a garda operation in a number of particular areas of the city, including the Greenmount Industrial Estate at Harold's Cross and Bowden's home at The Paddocks, near the Phoenix Park.

Charleton went on to say that 47 kg of cannabis had been recovered at the warehouse in Harold's Cross. A search of Holland's house at Brittas Bay had come up with two blank driver's licences which were linked to similar licences found in Harold's Cross. "The entire operation was motivated by greed and motivated by profit at the expense of the people of Ireland and Patrick Holland was part of it."

In his opening Peter Charleton said the premises at Greenmount Industrial Estate had been used as a centre for a major wholesale drug operation in which Holland was a central figure. He said the State would show that Holland had made up to three thousand pounds a week from this enterprise. Holland's name had been found on a list of the gang's customers.

Det. Garda Marion Cusack, the arresting officer, was asked to point out the man she knew to be Patrick Holland. She pointed up at Dutchie in the dock, who smiled and gave the detective a little wave. She smiled back. A minute later she wiped the smile off Holland's face when she told the court why she had arrested him. "I had formed the opinion that Patrick Holland was the man who shot dead Veronica Guerin on June 26, 1996. When I saw him coming through the port, I was of the view that he had murdered Veronica Guerin and, as a result, I arrested him." She had placed Holland in handcuffs and brought him to Lucan garda station.

Supt Len Ahern of Ballyfermot said he had issued a search warrant relating to Holland's property at Brittas Bay in February 1997 because he suspected that the gun used to murder Veronica Guerin would be found there. In his evidence, Det. Inspector Todd O'Loughlin recalled how Holland's solicitor, Jim Orange, had telephoned Lucan garda station on April 4 with a message that his client would not be keeping an appointment for that day. Instead, Holland would appear on April 7. The gardaí, he said, believed this was a ruse on Holland's part, intended to give the impression that he would be arriving at Dun Laoghaire or Dublin airport that morning.

O'Loughlin recalled that on the morning of Holland's arrest he had been informed by a colleague in the Criminal Assets Bureau that Orange had also been taken into custody under the Drug Trafficking Act in connection with the sale of Holland's house in Wicklow. A detective from the Criminal Assets Bureau said the property had been bought and sold in February of that year by Holland so that he could disguise his ownership of it. James Orange's solicitor wife, Elizabeth Ferris, was also part of this CAB investigation and, for these reasons, Holland was not allowed access to either his solicitor or Ferris.

O'Loughlin said the gardaí could not accede to Holland's request to have their interviews recorded on videotape as the appropriate facilities were not available at Lucan Garda Station. They were reluctant to transfer him to another station for security reasons. O'Loughlin gave evidence of finding the bugging equipment and later the recording and receiving equipment near Lucan station.

Before the court could continue hearing direct evidence in the trial, Holland's defence counsel made submissions to the court, which was presided over by Mr Justice Frederick Morris, that his arrest had been illegal. In what is referred to as "trial within a trial", on the issue of the legality of Holland's detention James Orange described his own arrest by the Criminal Assets Bureau on the day of Dutchie's arrest as "a circus and a charade".

"I thought it was absolutely extraordinary that my client gets arrested and, within hours, I get arrested. I found it extraordinary that within minutes of his being release, I got released," Orange declared.

He had first met Holland in London in December 1996 when his client wanted advice about divorcing his wife, Angela. About the rumours circulating in the media that he was suspected of the murder of Veronica Guerin, Holland had expressed concern that if he was ever charged, he would not receive a fair trial, such was the prejudicial nature of the publicity. He had advised Holland that if he returned to Ireland, he could take legal action against the newspapers concerned.

Holland gave an interview to the Pat Kenny Show to express in advance his fears about the manner in which the gardaí might investigate his role in the crime. In particular, he was concerned that any interviews would not be recorded. He claimed the gardaí might make up quotes and attribute them to Holland. Orange said that he had advised Holland to return as soon as possible to Ireland and to enter the country through Belfast to avoid reporters. Orange had offered to collect him when the Belfast train arrived at Connolly station in Dublin and said that he would take him to Lucan garda station personally. "Mr Holland was very much in fear. It was a matter of reassuring him that he would not be deprived of what I thought were his fair rights."

Orange described how gardaí had arrived at his Castleknock home to arrest him. He was in the shower when he found out that he was being arrested for questioning about the sale of Paddy and Angela Holland's house. "At a very early stage I told them to stop the charade, that the whole purpose was to stop me being able to assist Mr Holland at the time of his arrest," the solicitor recalled.

Det. Garda Sean O'Brien dismissed an allegation put by Holland's defence that he and Det. Sgt Fergus Treanor had knelt on the floor and said a Hail Mary during an interview with Holland at Lucan garda station on April 9. O'Brien said he didn't know about the death of Holland's mother and sister and he also denied that the gardaí had mockingly suggested that their prisoner pray for the deceased members of his family. He also dismissed as untrue the claim that the gardaí had told Holland that they had all the evidence they required to secure a conviction.

Brendan Grogan, in summing up his argument at the end of the "trial within a trial," claimed that the detention of Holland and the denial of access to Orange made for a clear breach of his constitutional rights. It was, he said, a deliberate act to prevent Holland from consulting with his solicitor. "The resolve to arrest Mr Orange was done for the purpose of preventing access between Mr Orange and Mr Holland," said Grogan. "This amounted to a clear breach of Mr Holland's constitutional rights. It cannot be a mere coincidence that the events happened in the sequence in which they did."

Grogan also drew attention to the fact that his client's request to have his interviews with gardaí videotaped were not complied with. The counsel did accept, however, that there had been nothing illegal or improper with the subsequent arrest of Holland under the provisions of the Misuse of Drugs Act.

Peter Charleton responded by telling the court that there had been no conspiracy by the gardaí to infringe Holland's constitutional rights when they arrested Orange. While there was a constitutionally protected right to have access to a lawyer, this provision did not give a prisoner the right to have a lawyer of one's choice. No evidence had been given which suggested Holland had been prejudiced because he had a different lawyer to Orange or Ferris.

The three judges ruled that Holland's arrest had been legal and on November 25 the trial resumed.

There had been much anticipation of the appearance of the State's first supergrass. Security was tight for the appearance of Charlie Bowden. Everyone entering the court had to pass through metal detectors and be searched. Members of the ERU stood watch from the rooftops, cradling HK rifles with sniper sights. Bowden was ushered into the witness box for his debut as a supergrass by six bodyguards who stood within feet of him. Looking smart in a suit and wearing a goatee, Bowden appeared relaxed and confident. Dutchie folded his arms and fixed his gaze on his former partner in crime.

Bowden told the court how he got involved in criminal activity with Peter Mitchell and became a central player in the Gilligan gang. Bowden explained the meaning of the entry "the Wig" on his customer list which was found in Greenmount. When he was asked to identify the man he knew to be the "Wig", Bowden looked up for a second at Holland and pointed his finger. "That's him there," he said. Holland frowned.

In answers to questions put by Holland's defence, Bowden admitted that he had lied to gardaí during his initial interviews in October 1996. He talked about the attempted murder of Martin "the Viper" Foley and how he had loaded the weapon used to murder Veronica Guerin. Bowden also told of being with Mitchell, Meehan and the Ward brothers when the murder was being discussed. That was the extent of his involvement in the Guerin murder, he added.

He told Brendan Grogan that he knew he would never be charged with complicity to murder Guerin, despite his admissions about his role in the preparation of the gun. "I knew that they had planned to shoot her," Bowden stated. "When I cleaned the gun, I knew that that was the gun they were going to use to shoot her."

He said that he had agreed to come clean about his role in the murder during an interview with Det. Garda Bernie Hanley and Det. Inspector John O'Mahony. He had no idea how much money he had made from the distribution of drugs, except for the hundred thousand pounds which had been confiscated by gardaí. The seizure of his money caused the closure of his hairdressing salon, he said.

In his own evidence Holland claimed that he had never received large amounts of cannabis from Bowden. He claimed that he had always intended co-operating with the gardaí but had reservations about the their refusal to videotape interviews he might give them. It was for this reason that he placed electronic transmitters in his shoes. He also complained about the manner in which the gardaí had carried out their interviews with him at Lucan Station. In particular, he claimed that two detectives had gone down on their knees and said the Hail Mary in a mocking fashion in front of him and that files on the Guerin murder case were produced in a threatening manner.

Holland claimed to have met Bowden on just three occasions: twice in the West County Hotel in Chapelizod and once in London. At the meetings in Dublin, the topic of discussion was Bowden's hairdressing business which Holland offered to assist by distributing advertising flyers to "country women" outside Bus Aras. He said that Bowden had not been particularly friendly towards him.

But Holland's strongest denials related to the contents of an interview with the Lucan team. "All the gardaí did was talk and say prayers," he recalled amid chuckles from the public gallery and press bench. "I know it's hard to believe. I know that I am not going to be believed but I am telling what happened. Members of the Criminal Assets Bureau never mentioned drugs to me. That is a damned lie. If I had a taped interview, this would not happen. I made a mistake and shouldn't have come home."

Det. Garda Bernie Hanley gave a different version of events: "During interviews in Lucan Holland said: 'I am a practical man. I know when I'm caught. Believe it or not, I was going to give myself up.'" Hanley added that Holland said he was driven to selling drugs because his printing business was not going well. He claimed that the accused had said jokingly to him: "I was only interested in building my dream home in County Wicklow. They will not get that now, as I have sold it."

In his closing submission, Senior Counsel Eamon Leahy, who would appear in all the Gilligan gang cases alongside Peter Charleton, said that the prosecution case rested on two "separate and distinct pillars of evidence". He was referring to the evidence of Charlie Bowden and to the testimony of various gardaí about admissions made by Holland while in custody. Leahy expressed reservations about the quality of accomplices' evidence but on this occasion he was happy that it had been reliably corroborated. He said: "It is capable – individually and collectively – of amounting to evidence that would ground a conviction."

Brendan Grogan, on the other hand, drew attention to Bowden's "ulterior motives" and complained that the accused's legal team had been given notice as late as October of Bowden's willingness to give evidence. "The times involved are capable of supporting the contention that Mr Bowden was holding out and hedging his bets," he said. He added that it had been proven that his client was right to be concerned that evidence would be fabricated by the gardaí. This was evident in the testimony of various garda officers who differed on key matters of fact, he claimed.

After two weeks of evidence Mr Justice Richard Johnson delivered a verdict on Thursday, November 27. The judge said the court was "satisfied beyond a reasonable doubt" that the prosecution had proved that the accused had been in possession of large amounts of cannabis and that those quantities were meant to be sold on or to be otherwise supplied. "We are conscious that it is dangerous to convict on the uncorroborated evidence of an accomplice. But the evidence of the accomplice has in this case been corroborated by the admissions of the accused," the Judge said. "The court does not accept the evidence of the accused relating to the interviews and does not find that it might be reasonably true."

The judge said he accepted the evidence of Det. Sgt Fergus Treanor, who had maintained that Holland acknowledged that he was in fact the person known as "The Wig" and whose nickname had been found on customer lists at the premises in Harold's Cross. Mr Justice Johnson said he also believed that Holland, when asked about the thirty-five kgs of cannabis, had replied: "Look lads, I have my own customers and I am not going to implicate them."

Holland showed little emotion as Mr Justice Johnson said that the court found him guilty as charged and adjourned sentencing to the following morning. As he was being led away, Holland clutched a shopping bag which contained his files. The following morning in the packed courtroom Det. Sgt Padraig Kennedy gave a résumé of Holland's past life in crime. Holland, said Kennedy, came from a decent family on St Laurence's Road, Chapelizod, in west Dublin and had gotten involved in crime at a relatively late age.

Peter Charleton reminded the court that a prison term of fourteen years had been provided for by the Misuse of Drugs Act but that this term had been increased to life. Holland's counsel pleaded for leniency based on his elderly age and the fact that the conviction related to a single incident.

Mr Justice Johnson, however, said Holland had been convicted of an "extremely serious offence". Apart from the age of the accused man and the positive manner in which the trial had been conducted by both the prosecution and the defence, he said there were no mitigating factors. He said: "This is an extremely serious offence which is compounded by the fact that it took place within thirteen months of the accused being granted temporary release from jail on other drugs offence. Accordingly, the court is satisfied that the minimum sentence which the court considers appropriate for this offence is twenty years imprisonment to date from the date of the accused's arrest on April 9, 1997."

As Dutchie was being led down the stairs to a waiting prison van, I was standing beside the dock and said: "Goodbye." He looked at me and made a strange comment. "It was just a job." His bald head disappeared. Patrick Eugene Holland's sentence was subsequently reduced on appeal to twelve years. He is unlikely to be charged with the murder of Veronica Guerin. He is due for release sometime in 2005.

A chill ran through the confidence of the rest of the Gilligan gang. Clearly the State would show no mercy on conviction.

Eighteen

The Trial of Paul Ward

The Air Corps twin-engined CASA troop carrier had been sitting on the edge of the runway at Eindhoven military air base for almost two hours. Detective Inspector Todd O'Loughlin and other members of the Lucan Investigation Team didn't mind the extra wait. They'd carefully planned their strategy over two years earlier when Veronica Guerin was murdered. It had been almost a year since their hard work had paid off with the dramatic arrest of Brian Meehan. Now, on September 3, 1998, after exhausting every legal avenue, he was being extradited back to Ireland. O'Loughlin and his men were bringing the Tosser home to face justice.

At 1.15 p.m. the convoy of large armour-plated police station wagons raced across the tarmac to the waiting military aircraft. When the cars stopped, several special anti-terrorist police jumped out wearing balaclavas and cradling sub-machine guns. They pulled Meehan from the back of one of the vehicles. He was hooded, with his hands cuffed behind his back. O'Loughlin swapped paperwork relevant to the extradition process with one of his Dutch colleagues. He thanked the official and, taking Meehan by the arm, led him up the ramp into the aircraft to his seat. No-one spoke.

As the aircraft taxied and nosed upwards, a team member removed the Tosser's hood. He squinted his eyes and looked around. He was disoriented. Detective Sergeants, Noel Browne, John O'Driscoll and Fergus Treanor sat beside him. They smiled at the once-cocky hoodlum. He was no longer untouchable.

The flight took almost three hours. Just before it began to make its descent into the Air Corps base at Baldonnel, Meehan demanded to go to the toilet. O'Loughlin told him he would have to hang on a little longer; they'd soon be on the ground. But Meehan was in a bad way. "If you don't let me use the toilet, I'll do it here," Meehan shouted over the noise of the engines. He began to unzip his trousers.

Meehan was allowed to go to the toilet, watched all the time by the men who had smashed his evil little world. They didn't want to risk giving Meehan the opportunity of doing something stupid at this stage. A fleet of Garda vans, jeeps and motorbikes were parked on the apron waiting for the aircraft. Members of the Emergency Response Unit with rifles and machine guns were on standby. The garda helicopter was warming up to escort the Tosser's convoy to the Special Criminal Court.

When the plane taxied to a stop, Meehan was escorted down the steps from the Casa light aircraft. As soon as his feet touched the tarmac, Todd O'Loughlin placed his hand on Meehan's shoulder and formally arrested him for the murder of Veronica Guerin. Meehan was brought to a waiting police van where O'Loughlin read out the full eighteen charges relating to murder, drugs and guns. It took him forty-five minutes. Shortly after 5 p.m. Brian Meehan was brought before the Special Criminal Court and half an hour later he was on his back to Portlaoise Prison under a heavily armed escort.

Paul "Hippo" Ward's trial had been due to begin in January 1998 but was adjourned when Ward's legal team sought access to forty statements which had been made to the gardaí by twenty people, including informants. The State refused to disclose the statements because they contained information of a highly confidential and sensitive nature that could put people's lives at risk. The statements were from people close to various gang members who gave valuable information during the Lucan swoops but who were terrified of getting up in the witness box and facing the gang members. In support of the State's case, Assistant Commissioner Tony Hickey said that the gang would "resort to anything" to stop people giving evidence. "We know from intelligence that the people concerned [the Gilligan gang] have the resources, the money and the firearms and will resort to anything to maintain this wall of silence which they believe is necessary to protect themselves," he said. The Special Criminal Court, however, ordered that Ward's defence team be given limited access to the files.

The Director of Public Prosecutions appealed the decision to the High Court. Their counsel, Peter Charleton, said the High Court ruling granting access to statements would affect not only the administration of justice, but how gardaí went about their investigations. He said that the D.P.P. had decided to drop the case against Ward rather than disclose the sensitive information. On March 18 the High Court upheld the D.P.P.'s application and ordered that the trial go ahead without Ward having access to the statements.

The Ward trial began on October 6, 1998. It would be the first trial of its kind in Irish criminal justice history, one in which a supergrass was used. It would be the first serious test of the controversial system. Paddy McEntee SC and Barry Whyte SC, the two most formidable and experienced defence lawyers in the country, appeared for Ward. Peter Charleton SC, Eamon Leahy SC and Tom O'Connell BL appeared for the prosecution, as they would in the Meehan and Gilligan trials.

Peter Charleton gave the court a rundown of the events leading up to and following the murder of Veronica on the fateful day in June 1996. Paul Ward, he said, had been "complicit" in the crime. While he was not one of the two men on board the motorbike on June 26, 1996, he had taken part in discussions and had given comfort to the killers by helping in their escape and disposing of the vehicle and the gun. Charleton went on to give a preview of the evidence on which his allegations would be grounded, including the testimony of Charlie Bowden and verbal admissions made by Ward while in custody in Lucan.

In the first stage of the 31-day trial, the court heard eyewitness and forensic evidence. Nurses Michelle Wall and Brenda Grogan told how they had been on the Naas dual carriageway at the time of the murder. They described finding Veronica Guerin slumped over the passenger seat of her red Opel Calibra car, bleeding heavily. Grogan checked for pulse but found none. Veronica was already dead. Truck driver Michael Dunne saw the motorbike pillion passenger pull alongside the car and smash the driver's window with an implement he had taken out of his jacket. Both men on the motorbike had helmets and wore black leather jackets. "I saw Veronica just slumped across the seats, her whole chest was blood and gunshot wounds," he recalled. Veronica's husband, Graham Turley, and brother, Jimmy Guerin, listened to the heartbreaking evidence from the public gallery.

Det. Sgt Patrick Ennis of the Ballistics Section at the Garda Technical Bureau described the scene on the Naas Road shortly after the shooting. He saw Veronica in the car, her upper body, arms and hands heavily bloodstained, as were the seats. Her lower left arm was entangled with the power lead of the car's mobile phone, which was switched on. An examination of the phone showed that the last number had been redialed.

Ennis removed a number of bullets from the floor of the car. One round had passed through the passenger seat and the passenger door, causing a dent in the outside of the vehicle. He said the reporter had been hit by six bullets fired from the same .357 inch Magnum revolver. He described the bullets as semi-wadcutters of a type often used in gun sports which "create a neat, rounded hole". The bullets were fired through the driver's window at an angle of 40 to 45 degrees and 75 degrees from the rear and were either .38 inch or .357 inch Magnum calibre bullets, both of which could have been fired from a .357 inch Magnum revolver. A microscopic examination of the bullets suggested that they had been reloaded bullets rather than factory loaded.

The State Pathologist, Dr John Harbison, gave clinical evidence that belied the horror of the devastation the gun attack had caused to the reporter. He said the cause of death was "shock and haemorrhage" resulting from "an injury to the right sub-clavial artery and laceration of both lungs". The first two shots – fired from behind – were probably responsible for the fatal wounds, he said, and it appeared as though she had grappled for her car phone and leaned over towards the passenger seat after the first shot. In all, there were eight wounds on the body, including entry and exit wounds. A series of minor lacerations were also found which were consistent with being injured by glass fragments when the window was smashed. He said that one bullet had entered the lower part of her mastoid muscle and her sub-clavial artery was severely lacerated and torn. This seemed to be the most significant injury and the main cause of blood haemorrhage.

The second bullet, which had been fired from below, had fractured her left collarbone. A litre of blood was found in her left chest cavity. Her right lung was lacerated after a bullet had passed through its lower lobe. The same bullet, he reckoned, had previously

penetrated her liver. As the first bullet had struck the glass, it would
have been deformed and, consequently, it would have caused a larger
wound than might otherwise have been the case. Two of the latter
bullets had entered her back and the base of the spine. Another had
passed through the fleshy part of her upper right arm, continued
into her breast, crossing her chest, and followed a "slightly
downward trajectory". Whether she was propelled to the left by the
bullets was not possible to ascertain. She might have moved to the
passenger side of the car to avoid the fire.

Padraig Kennedy, who had been promoted to the rank of
Inspector, gave evidence of arresting Ward under section 30 of the
Offences Against the State Act at Windmill Park in Crumlin on
October 16, 1996 on suspicion that he had information relating to
the possession of firearms on the Naas Road on June 26. At that
point Barry White challenged the validity and legality of his client's
arrest. Ward had been arrested on October 8 at the Green Isle Hotel
on the same offence, White claimed.

Inspector Kennedy replied that the earlier arrest related to an
attempted armed robbery on October 2 and not the murder of
Veronica Guerin. The decision to arrest Ward for the murder had
been taken on October 9 when Charles Bowden implicated Ward in
a statement. Ward was taken to an interview room at Lucan station
but no interview took place because Ward's nose began to bleed
after he stuffed tissue paper up both nostrils. Kennedy denied that
he tried to seize the tissue paper involved because he understood
that Ward was a drug addict at that time. The Inspector said it was
his belief that Ward had met Dutchie Holland and Brian Meehan
on the day of the shooting and that Ward he had helped to dispose
of the gun and the motorbike.

On Monday, October 13, a "trial within a trial" began over the
legality of Ward's arrest and detention in Lucan garda station on
October 16, 1996. His lawyers maintained that their client had, in
effect, been arrested twice in connection with the same offence and
that custody regulations had not been complied with during his
detention. They also contended that Ward had been deprived of
prescribed medication.

Det. Gda Bernard Sheerin of Ronanstown said he was called at
1.50 a.m. on October 8, 1996, to the Green Isle Hotel in Clondalkin

by the manager who was suspicious of two people who had booked into the hotel. Sheerin, who was armed that morning, had the manager open the suspect's bedroom door with the master key. He was accompanied by two uniformed gardaí. He saw Paul Ward asleep in the bed.

"I had confidential information in my possession that the accused was involved in a robbery at the SDS premises on the Naas Road in which firearms were used on October 2, 1996," Sheerin said. The detective maintained that he had drawn his revolver only on entering the room. Once he was satisfied that Ward posed no threat to his safety or that of his colleagues, he reholstered his gun. Sheerin strongly denied a suggestion from counsel Paddy McEntee that Ward had his face slapped in order to wake him up. Sheerin also dismissed the claim that Ward's room had been turned upside down in the search for incriminating evidence.

Sgt Mick Mulhern, who was in charge of Lucan station when Ward was taken in for the murder, said he had arranged a solicitor at Ward's request. When Ward requested a doctor, one was also summoned to the station. Mulhern denied that Ward had been strip-searched and said that £412 had been found in Ward's pockets. His mobile phone was confiscated.

Garda Catherine Moore said that she brought Ward a prescribed dose of physeptone, the heroin substitute, on the orders of Dr Lionel Williams. She was unaware of the effects of not taking the drug but at 9.10 p.m. on October 16 she saw Ward drinking the prescribed dose from a tin container. Dr Lionel Williams said he saw Ward again two days later and gave him a further 40 mg of physeptone, although it was his professional opinion that the prisoner did not need it. On that occasion, Ward pointed to a red mark on the left side of his neck and complained that he had been assaulted by the gardaí while in custody. Dr Williams noticed a mark but reckoned that Ward appeared physically well and fit for interview.

Dr Williams told McEntee that Ward had asked that his mother not be informed about his drug habit. He complained to him on October 18 that he had not been given the physeptone prescribed on October 16 until a day later and only then after he had protested to his solicitor.

Det. Sgt Oliver Keating said that Ward "looked alert" during

the interview at Lucan on October 18. Garda Derek Quinn gave
evidence that Ward had been visited by his mother, Elizabeth, at
2.27 p.m. that day. She stayed for sixteen minutes before Dr Williams
arrived. This was important, said McEntee, suggesting that the
custody record had been doctored; he claimed that Dr Williams had
visited the prisoner before Mrs Ward. Garda Quinn alleged that at
3.30 p.m. on October 18 he released Ward and showed him out the
front door. He stated that he was "surprised" when Det. Sgt Jerry
Healy arrived back in the station five minutes later with Ward again
in custody, after arresting him under the Misuse of Drugs Act. Garda
Quinn denied seeing his colleagues follow Ward as he left the station
with his jacket pulled over his head.

   In reply to questions from the defence, Det. Sgt Healy said he
interviewed Ward on three occasions over the two days of his
detention from October 16. He appeared fine and to have no
difficulty understanding questions. However, something seemed to
be wrong with him after he had been visited by his mother on October
18. He was unaware of Ward's drug problem on October 16 or that
Dr Williams had left physeptone for him. Healy denied that he had
held on to Ward's jacket as he was walking out the station door
after being released. Healy was accompanied by two or three gardaí
outside the gates. He said it was never the intention of the gardaí to
meaningfully release Ward.

   Det. Garda Gerard Dillon denied that Ward had been offered
his "ticket to freedom" in return for leading gardaí to the gun used
in the Guerin murder. Barry White claimed that his client had been
told he would be jailed for twenty years if he didn't help. Ward had
been asked to "tell the truth" in an interview and Dillon denied
drawing a picture of a car with a figure of a man on which Ward's
name was written. Dillon said he may have been doodling on a
sheet of paper, but he hadn't written Ward's name beside the words
"twenty years".

   Sgt Con Condon denied allegations that he had held Ward in
an arm lock and that he had "smacked" him in the face in an effort
to "soften him up". The red mark on Ward's neck had nothing to do
with the manner in which he was dealt by the gardaí, he added. Sgt
Condon said that he had known Ward for eight to ten years and had
only found out about his drug habit during the Guerin murder
investigation.

Paul Ward took the witness stand and claimed that he had been assaulted during questioning at Lucan garda station and that he was not given the heroin substitute left for him by Dr Williams. "I was after being assaulted and I was deprived of my medication," he told the trial.

In answers to questions from his counsel, Barry White, the gangster recalled how he had been driven to the Green Isle Hotel on October 7 by two brothers. One of these two brothers had been suspected of involvement with a drugs courier operation and this was causing Paul Ward concern. He remembered being awoken by a detective who had slapped him on the face before arresting him on suspicion of firearms offences. A short time after being put in a cell in Ronanstown, he was released and given back his possessions. The SIM card had been removed from his mobile phone. He said the gardaí agreed to his request to ring for a taxi to take him home but claimed that he was later told that a taxi would not arrive "because they must not like the Wards".

Ward then told of his arrest nine days later in Crumlin for the Guerin murder. On arrival at Lucan garda station, Ward claimed he asked for a solicitor and a doctor. He denied a suggestion made by gardaí that he had placed tissues up his nostrils to deliberately cause a nose bleed. He acknowledged that he had a runny nose, which was part of the withdrawal symptoms associated with heroin addiction. On the first day of his detention, October 16, he met Dr Lionel Williams who was asked to supply physeptone. He got the impression that a prescription of the heroin substitute would be supplied to him by the gardaí, but no physeptone was given to him until the afternoon of October 18.

While he was being released from custody that afternoon, Ward alleged that his bomber jacket was held tightly by a detective who then arrested him on a drugs offence and brought him back to the station. Under cross-examination by Peter Charleton, Ward spoke of his heroin addiction and how he scored drugs mainly in the south inner-city. When asked whether he reckoned he had been in sufficient health to be questioned in custody, he replied: "I am saying I wasn't well. Whether I was fit or unfit, I don't know. I can't answer. I was going through withdrawals and wasn't well. I refused to speak to the police because the police were the ones that assaulted me."

Ward's mother, Elizabeth, told Patrick McEntee that she was seventy-four years old and that her health was poor. On October 16 she, too, was arrested and taken to Cabra garda station. Her husband, Michael, who was seventy-nine years old, was also arrested and taken to Cabra. Mrs Ward said: "They kept on saying I knew more than I was telling them. They were asking me questions I couldn't answer. I was nervous, shaking, frightened. I remember the garda with a scar, a big man and he was beating the table. The gardaí told me that all my family had been arrested."

When asked by Mr Justice Barr about the relevance of Mrs Ward's evidence, McEntee said that it highlighted that the accused's mother had been subjected to "quite unnecessary pressure." He reckoned that both Vanessa Meehan and Mrs Ward had been improperly used by the gardaí to visit the accused with a view to putting him under pressure and obtaining confessions. Such a tactic amounted to a breach of Ward's constitutional rights.

"There are verbals [verbal admissions] which the prosecution contend followed the enforced visit of Ms Meehan to Mr Ward," said McEntee. "All of this is of utter importance because it begs the question that if they had the verbals already, what were they up to? If they were done to overbear Mr Ward's will in an attempt to make him talk, when he otherwise would have stayed quiet, then that is a breach of his constitutional right to silence." Peter Charleton said that his colleagues must have had the benefit of hearing the mind of Paul Ward when he gave evidence. At no stage did he express displeasure at being visited by his girlfriend or by his mother.

The following day the Special Criminal Court dismissed the defence application that Ward's trial was illegal. Mr Justice Barr said the court did not believe Ward's account of what happened in the Green Isle Hotel or that he had been deprived of his physeptone. Mr Justice Barr also threw out Hippo's claims that he had been beaten or had not been in a fit state to be interviewed due to his drug problem. The trial continued.

Det. Gda Gerard Dillon said that Ward had made an admission shortly after a visit from his girlfriend on October 17, 1996. Ward allegedly told the gardaí that he got rid of the "gear" (the motorbike and the gun). It had been planned that Brian Meehan and Dutchie Holland would go back to Ward's place immediately after the murder. Ward declined to answer when asked if it was John Gilligan who had ordered the hit. He made no reply when asked about the identities of the men on the motorbike.

Det. Gda Bernie Hanley said the accused denied that he had offered to take the rap for the Guerin murder; Ward claimed his role was confined to the disposal of the motorbike and gun used in the crime. "I was only asked to look after the bike and the gun," Ward told Hanley. "After the shooting, it was left in my house. I had to get rid of the fucking thing. My part was to let the two men involved use my house after the shooting. They came with the bike and the gun."

When Hanley asked Ward to give a full statement about the murder, the prisoner replied: "Are you mad? I am fucked up enough. Charge me with taking the gun and the bike for them. But I won't take the murder rap." Hanley added that Ward had said that he would plead guilty to the possession of drugs and to his role in the concealment of guns at the Jewish cemetery, offences for which he believed he would be sentenced to no more than ten years in jail.

Det. Sgt Jerry Healy told how Ward had complained about being repeatedly questioned "about the poxy murder", an event about which he claimed to know nothing. Ward had answered "Yeah, that's it," when he was asked had he got rid of the gun used in the shooting. "I am only a fucking junkie," Ward had said. "I needed the money. I was promised a few bob. When this was being planned, I was asked to let the two men, Patrick Holland and Brian Meehan, into my house and to get rid of that fucking gun when they left. I am not saying any more. That's it. Anyway, I am not that big a fucking eejit." Ward then asked the detectives not to hassle Vanessa Meehan. She had not been involved, said Ward, and "her head is done in over this."

Healy related that Ward was annoyed after the visit from his mother and said: "Some of youse fuckers told me Ma I was on gear [heroin]. What was that for?" When he was asked where the gun had come from, Ward said: "You know well where it came from. Don't be acting the bollix. It was with the guns and ammunition youse got in the graveyard. That's it. I'm finished. I am saying no more. I'm not going to make a statement. Get wise, you know I won't do that."

Healy, in cross-examination by Ward's defence team, rejected the suggestion that the admissions were "classic planted verbals".

Inspector Padraig Kennedy said that he had interviewed Vanessa Meehan in Ballyfermot garda station on the evening of October 17, 1996. She repeatedly replied "I don't know" to questions. When she asked to see her "husband", Kennedy brought her to Lucan. Barry White saw the incident less as facilitating two lovers than as more of an effort to get her "to perform a certain task".

Det. Garda Mary Murphy denied that the visit to Ward by his mother had been part of a "grand plan" to cajole Ward into making a statement. Murphy had been in the unmarked garda car with Det. Gda Paul Gilton on the afternoon of October 18, 1996, when Elizabeth Ward was driven from Cabra to Lucan. Gilton denied that they drove at high speed so as to intimidate the elderly woman. At no stage on the journey did Mrs Ward make a complaint.

On November 3 Charlie Bowden took the witness stand for the second time as the State's star witness. Again he outlined in detail his role in the gang and the events surrounding the murder.

He recalled one of the gang's meetings during which Veronica was discussed. "Meehan said that John Gilligan was upset about the assault charges, that he was going to have something done about her," said Bowden. "Meehan said that if Gilligan was sent down [to prison] for the assault [on Guerin], he was the only one that knew people to contact to get the cannabis and the whole operation would fall apart. Gilligan was apparently pissed off with Veronica Guerin for this case [the assault]. Ward was pissed off that the gun had been left in his house and that he had to get rid of it. So he jumped on a bus," added Bowden. "He said he was scared shitless."

The defence focused on the amounts of money Bowden had made with the drug gang. McEntee did a calculation based on what Bowden said he was earning, which came to around three hundred thousand pounds in just over eighteen months. Bowden disagreed that the money involved was as much as that. The real figure was "somewhere between £150,000 to £200,000". The shortfall was accounted for by his cocaine habit, which would set him back about four hundred pounds per week. "I also spent it," he said. "I lived well. I bought designer clothes and went on foreign holidays. I would go out. I would live well. I would buy stuff for the kids."

He said he felt the pressure come on him in the weeks after the Guerin murder. He sensed that the gardaí were circling members of the gang and he felt it was only a matter of time before they would come looking for him. In the meantime, he became concerned about how he would safely dispose of his cash. "It was blatantly obvious to me that the gardaí were on to me and, having this money in the house, I had to get rid of it," said Bowden. "This was a constant refrain throughout the whole time when we were earning this type of money. We spoke about offshore accounts and how we would go about doing it. We were thinking about getting the money into a bank account in the Isle of Man."

When questioned about the plans for a weekend trip to London which had been rudely interrupted by the Lucan team, Bowden admitted that it was to be a "weekend of infidelity".

"Juliet did not know I was going to London with this girl and 'infidelity' is the word I would use, that's exactly what it was." He denied that he had planned to leave the country permanently.

Bowden denied that he had done a deal to get immunity from prosecution in return for testifying against the gang. He agreed that he had been granted immunity and agreed to testify only after the gardaí had assured him that his wife and children would be protected. "There was [*sic*] absolutely no negotiations between myself and anyone else in relation to giving evidence – none," said Bowden. He acknowledged, however, that he had pestered the gardaí about whether he would be charged with the murder and had received no reply. He also admitted that he had been placed in a grievous position because he had owned up to prior knowledge of the murder weapon and had implicated his wife and family.

"They [the gang] did implicate me. I was part of that murder. I was fully aware of the role I had played in that murder, absolutely aware." His original intention was to lie to the gardaí but when he saw the photographs of Guerin lying dead in her car, he changed his mind. "It was unreal," he said. "I could detach myself from it and my role in it. When I saw those photos of the girl lying in the car shot, I went to pieces. I just couldn't handle it. My wife and my children were going to suffer from my giving this evidence, for me talking to the police. By the same token, I wanted to tell the police exactly what my role was."

Mr Justice Barr asked Bowden why he wanted to tell the gardaí about his role in the murder. Bowden looked up at the judge and replied: "Guilt. The reality and the horror of it. All the time in the cell, my brain superimposed Julie's and the children's faces on the photos. I was caught between the fear of telling them and my own desire to clear my conscience. It sounds trite. I just couldn't hold back what I knew. I had to tell them." Referring to a meeting with Assistant Commissioner Tony Hickey, he added: "I explained to him that I wanted to tell all I knew but asked if they would guarantee protection for my wife and children. That's all I asked him for. He said if I made a full statement, he would examine it, check it and that he would protect my family. He would do his best to protect my family."

Bowden recalled the events of the afternoon and evening of the murder and his meetings with Meehan and Mitchell. He denied an allegation from the defence counsel that Meehan had given him the murder weapon to dispose of. He also denied that he knew Guerin was going to be killed. "It sounds very naïve that I didn't know she was going to be killed, but that is the truth. I didn't think they would be stupid enough to kill a journalist. It's one thing to kill a criminal, but to kill a female journalist to get out of jail for six months – it didn't make sense then and it doesn't make any sense now. There was a high probability in my mind that they were going to shoot her or shoot at her. I was devastated when I heard. I was just sick because I had played a major part in the shooting of that woman. I told Juliet some weeks before that Gilligan was going to get something done about Veronica Guerin and that politicals would have something to do with it to convince her that Gilligan had republican connections.

"Mr McEntee is trying to suggest that I met Brian Meehan to take the gun off him. Meehan is at the scene of the crime. He comes from the scene of the crime and then he strolls down Moore Street with a recently fired weapon which has just killed a woman where he is regularly stopped and searched by the gardaí looking for contraband cigarettes. He stops and waits in the middle of Moore Street with the murder weapon. That is what he is suggesting."

Bowden said he had suffered from a mental disease when he loaded the gun. "Yes, definitely. Sick in the head describes exactly what I was at that time. When I heard on the radio that a woman had been shot, I did my damnedest to ignore my part in the murder."

He contradicted a claim made by journalist and next-door neighbour Senan Molony that he had a party in his house that night to celebrate Guerin's murder. "There may have been a couple of friends back to have a few drinks, but it wasn't a party. It was a regular occurrence for us to go back to have a few drinks."

Later Molony said that Bowden had bought the house next door to his in October 1995. He recalled that he had been covering the story about Veronica's murder that day and when he came home from work that evening, he noticed trays of beer being carried into his neighbour's house. He was "very distraught and upset" by his colleague's murder. Subsequently, it dawned on him that Veronica's death had been the source of mirth in Bowden's house that night. "They were in some way celebrating what had happened," he said. "It seemed to me that they were not cast down by it."

Molony described life beside his neighbours from hell. "Bowden was a different type of neighbour," he said. "He was constantly active and moving around at night. He often had people back to his house five or six times a week. There was incessant, blaring 'techno' music from Bowden's house. It was very monotonous, insistent, repetitive music, which was also very loud. I found it was enough to knock down the walls of my house – like the Walls of Jericho." On one particular occasion Molony went to Bowden's door in his pyjamas, thinking the action might have "a visual impact", but he was disappointed. The music was not turned down by Bowden, who said starkly that he did not care about anyone else. On another occasion Molony said Bowden, who claimed to be an army officer, asked him into the Phoenix Park for a fight. Luckily, he declined.

In his own evidence Paul Ward described Bowden as "more of an associate than a friend". Ward admitted that he had been involved in crime but denied that he had any part in Guerin's murder. "I am accusing Charlie Bowden of telling lies and implicating me in something that I had nothing to do with whatsoever. Mr Bowden is the one I blame. He is the man who told those guards this and he convinced them," stormed Hippo.

"That man should be in the dock. I was asked to do the same thing that that man did and I refused because I knew nothing about

Ms Guerin's murder. I am a victim of being accused of this. Mr Bowden is the main man, the main person who has me here. I know the guards have to do their job. I am not making myself out to be a saint – far from it. I don't blame the guards. I blame Mr Bowden for the lies he said about me and he is after convincing the guards. He is putting poison in the guards' minds, saying that I was involved in that woman's murder. I wasn't."

Amazingly, Bowden's evidence was voluntarily corroborated by Ward, who admitted that he had made three hundred thousand pounds from selling drugs. He spent most of it. Ward said that the members of the gang would pay Gilligan two thousand pounds per kilo of hash. Any margin above this was kept for themselves. Ward calculated that he had collected three million pounds on behalf of Gilligan from the sale of cannabis but said he had no idea how his boss had spent his money. Ward would collect his money in the car parks of two pubs in Walkinstown and carry the cash in plastic shopping bags to his house. He had a hiding place for the cash which was later uncovered by gardaí during their second search of his home.

Ward even talked candidly about the trip to St Lucia in March of 1996. He described lounging about the hotel pool. "The woman's [Guerin's] name was brought up and they [Mitchell and Meehan] were laughing at Gilligan. He was convinced he would get off the charge. It was funny that they were slagging Gilligan and winding him up. They were slagging him about what happened. He was laughing back and saying he didn't think he would go to jail [for the assault]."

Said Ward of the actual murder: "I felt it was terrible. It never entered my head why that lady was killed. I think it would be crazy for anyone to kill a woman to save themselves from going down for six months." He understood that the reporter had been shot because she had threatened the continuation of a "multi-million drugs empire". That said, he had little knowledge of the journalist.

"The woman never stood out in my mind," said Ward. "Paul Williams – now I'd know what he is about. The man is never out of the papers."

Vanessa Meehan described living comfortably on Ward's dirty money. She believed her boyfriend was "rich" but that his wealth had come from the sale of cigarettes and loose tobacco. When they once bought an expensive bathroom Jacuzzi, Ward said that he was paying for it with money received from the sale of hash. She told the court how there was never any shortage of money around the house. She would buy nice clothes in expensive shops, such as Brown Thomas. He had bought her a Mitsubishi Lancer car worth ten thousand pounds and, in 1996, they went on three foreign trips: Santa Ponsa, St Lucia and Lanzarote. She suspected that he was taking heroin after she noticed that he had lost weight, that his pupils were reducing in size and that he was "goofing out". Despite her efforts, he had never shaken off the habit.

She complained of ill-treatment at the hand of the gardaí, who told her to get Paul to say where the gun used to kill Veronica had been kept. "They were very aggressive towards me and they were screaming at me saying that I was lying. They were threatening me. I was very confused and very frightened. They said: 'If you ask him that, we'll let you go home and we'll let Paul go home.' I was more concerned about myself. I just wanted to get out of the police station."

"They were screaming at Paul to go into the [interview] room and Paul wouldn't go into the room. I was crying and I called out to Paul to come in. I was very upset. I was asking him to tell them where the gun was, so that I could go home. He said he had nothing to do with it."

Vanessa told Eamon Leahy that she recalled reading newspaper reports about Guerin's action against Gilligan. Her boyfriend had told her that Guerin had trespassed on Gilligan's property. She said she was "shocked" by the murder but that she hadn't connected it with her boyfriend. "Sure, I'd be mad to do that!" she recalled Ward telling her.

In his closing speech for the prosecution, Eamon Leahy claimed that the case against Ward rested on "four pillars". Three of these comprised alleged verbal admissions made by Ward to the gardaí on October 17 and October 18, 1996. The fourth pillar was the evidence of Bowden. Any three of these pillars would be enough to convict Ward of Guerin's murder. Leahy said that Bowden's evidence was corroborated by Ward's own admissions. The evidence about the telephone calls made to and from Ward's phone lines was "capable of tending to support the case made by the prosecution".

The weekly meetings of the drugs gang, about which Ward had himself given evidence, were also important pieces of testimony.

Patrick McEntee did not agree. He said the court should consider the case in Northern Ireland involving supergrass Harry Kirkpatrick, of whom the North's Court of Criminal Appeal had grown sceptical. Indeed, the use of supergrasses was ended after the trial at which Kirkpatrick had given evidence. "The real danger in this case is that the witness can appear to be very confident," said McEntee, "giving all the appearance of being truthful. He knows the facts better than anyone else because he was a participant in them but he has a lot of self-interest to serve. He is a person who lies when it suits him, who is a ruthless person who was engaging in very serious criminal activity, who has been brought to book and who has thought out the process of serving his own interests and not the interests of justice."

The "insoluble" problem with Bowden was that it was impossible to tell when he was telling the truth. "This case has serious and difficult implications. It is an extremely difficult and emotive case. There is no doubt in the world that Ms Guerin was murdered in the most foul, ruthless, unspeakable manner, mowed down in the prime of her life for doing her duty. No person could or would want to be unmoved by that." He then asked the judges to ensure that their "natural human sympathy" did not invade their deliberations.

The garda investigation only got into "top gear" when Bowden began to spill the beans in October of 1996. "There is not one pick of evidence of any description, shape or make, apart from the contested statements and the evidence of the informer, Bowden, which puts Patrick Holland and Brian Meehan into this frame at all. This is a very, very stripped down case and depends entirely on a contested series of alleged verbals and the word of an informer and absolutely nothing else."

McEntee's closing submissions continued into the next day. He told Judges Barr, Smyth and Ballagh that they would have to be judges of fact and of law. He cautioned against becoming "case hardened" and asked them to approach the issues from the standpoint of a sensible man from "another walk of life". Would the sensible man be satisfied with the alleged admissions by Ward? Would he be satisfied with the evidence of Bowden?

"Bowden's evidence should not and cannot be relied on in any case, never mind a case like this, and he is not by any standards, even the least demanding standards, an honest man. He is a man who tells lies when it suits him to tell lies and he seems to tell these lies simply because he wants to," McEntee went on. "The crux of the problem is that he can't tell the truth. He is all the time telling lies for a great variety of reasons, he is telling lies to save his bacon, telling lies to save his face. His modus operandi is to lie when it suits him and when it becomes apparent that the lies cannot be sustained, he makes concessions."

After thirty-one days of evidence, the Special Criminal Court gave its verdict on Friday, November 27. It was to prove a landmark judgment. It took Mr Justice Barr almost an hour to read the judgment to the packed courtroom. After outlining the crime, Mr Justice Barr said the evidence against Ward consisted of admissions allegedly made by him while in garda custody in October 1996. Referring to the statement he made in the aftermath of the visit from his girlfriend about "getting rid of the gear", the judge said: "The coincidence that the accused's capitulation after more than fourteen hours of silence during interrogations had occurred immediately after the visit by Ms Meehan is a remarkable volte face which gives rise to unease and raises a series of pertinent questions." No tenable explanation had been given as to why Ward and Vanessa Meehan had to meet, said the presiding judge.

A red mark on Ward's neck was consistent with his contention that he had maintained silence and admitted to nothing during this period of his detention. The meeting with his mother was "another very disquieting episode" and "most disturbing. The visit from Mrs Ward was a deliberate ploy devised and orchestrated by the police in a final effort to prevail on the accused to disclose what he had done with the gun.

"As to the visit from Ms Vanessa Meehan to the accused, the court accepts her evidence that she was successfully subjected to grievous psychological pressure by Det. Garda Hanley and perhaps other officers also to assist the police in breaking down the accused who up until then had maintained consistent silence over many interrogation sessions.

"Both meetings amounted to an conscious and deliberate

disregard of the accused's basic constitutional right to fair procedures and treatment while in custody.

"Another alarming feature relating to events during the period of the accused's detention at Lucan garda station is the extraordinary fact that a number of significant documents are now alleged to be unaccountably missing. In all the circumstances, the court is satisfied that in the interests of justice and fairness, all admissions allegedly made by the accused during the period of his detention at Lucan garda station are ruled inadmissible.

"The court is not making a finding that the verbal admissions were in fact planted by the police as alleged but the evidence suggests such a possibility and the accused must be given the benefit of the doubt which exists."

Mr. Justice Barr said Bowden was by his own admission an accomplice and the court felt he was "a self-serving liar". However, the court found that his account of Ward's involvement was accurate and credible. Bowden had no vested interest in trying to shift responsibility for his own actions on to Ward.

"Having reviewed the relevant evidence in this trial with meticulous care – and in particular that of Charles Bowden and the accused – the court is satisfied beyond reasonable doubt that the accused, Paul Ward, was an accessory before the fact to the murder of Veronica Guerin on June 26, 1996 and therefore is guilty of the offence charged in the indictment."

The Ward judgment was a crushing reprimand to the Lucan investigation team, but they considered it a victory nonetheless. Paul Ward, drug dealer and killer, was on his way to prison with a life sentence. It was Bowden's evidence alone which had brought about the guilty verdict. Tony Hickey later met with his team and told them that they had got what they set out to achieve, a conviction which a lot of people had predicted they wouldn't get. He told them to put the case behind them and get ready for the next trial. There was still a lot of work to be done. Their star witness had gone through a ferocious grilling by Patrick McEntee. The court did not wear Bowden's declarations of remorse. There was no advantage to him telling lies about the murder.

As a result of the comments made during the trial, relations between Ward and Brian Meehan deteriorated. Ward was isolated from the other criminals on E1 in Portlaoise for his own protection. On July 30, 1999 Ward was back in court on charges relating to the Mountjoy prison siege. He pleaded guilty to the false imprisonment charge and was sentenced to twelve years. As he was being brought back to his isolation cell, his former pal, Brian Meehan was awaiting his fate in the Special Criminal Court.

Nineteen

The Trial of Brian Meehan

Brendan "Speedy" Fegan was bound to run out of luck sometime. The fact that it was at the end of an IRA gun wasn't surprising. The young, flash and brash drug trafficker had annoyed too many people. He had become one of the biggest drug dealers in Northern Ireland. He played with both loyalist and republican paramilitaries. He had ripped off Meehan and Paddy Farrell, the gangster who brought him into the business. He had even tried to blow up the offices of the *Sunday World* in Belfast because the newspaper had exposed him and his links with Gilligan.

"It's the Provies," were his last words on Sunday, May 9, as the masked gunmen came looking for him in a packed Newry pub. He died instantly from bullet wounds to the head and body. Another of the Tosser's enemies had been eliminated.

On July 5, 1999 there was more "good news" for Meehan. Russell Warren's parents, sister and brother-in-law were ordered to begin serving jail sentences for counting drug money for the supergrass. The four had been sentenced in February and granted bail while they appealed the severity of their sentences. Patrick and Yvette Warren, both aged sixty-nine, were given eighteen months each after they pleaded guilty to handling the cash between May and the time of their arrests in September 1996. Nicola Cummins, Warren's twenty-six-year-old sister, was jailed for one year and her husband, Brian Cummins, got eight months. None of them had ever been in trouble with the law before. It was a severe blow to Russell Warren and the Lucan Investigation Team, who had hoped that they would receive suspended sentences.

Judge Kevin Lynch, presiding in the Court of Criminal Appeal, said the court had sympathy with all four applicants. They had been drawn into an "appalling situation" by the "wrongdoing of a very close relative, Russell Warren".

The smile was wiped off the Tosser's face on May 21, when gardaí attached to the Criminal Assets Bureau arrested him father, Kevin, and his uncle, Thomas Meehan. The two brothers were brought before the Special Criminal Court and charged with a string of money laundering offences. Kevin Meehan was accused with handling a hundred and sixty-five thousand pounds of his son's drug money, while Thomas Meehan was charged with handling over a hundred and ninety-three thousand. Both men were remanded in custody.

On Wednesday, June 2, Kevin Meehan was back in the Special Criminal Court. Brian Meehan's trial began that day, after he had lost an application to be tried separately for the drugs and firearms offences. Meehan's defence team was headed by the highly respected Northern Ireland Queen's Counsel, John McCrudden, Michael Sammon SC and Michael O'Higgins BL. Peter Charleton SC, Eamon Leahy SC and Tom O'Connell BL made up the State's prosecution team. Mr Justice Frederick Morris presided.

The case for the prosecution was opened by Peter Charleton. He said that the court would hear that Meehan had been the driver of the motorbike on June 26, 1996. It would also be told of Meehan's part in conversations concerning the planning of the murder of Veronica Guerin.

Meehan, the court would hear, drove the motorbike away from the murder scene on the Naas Road and arrived shortly afterward at Paul Ward's bungalow on Walkinstown Road. Later, they went to Aungier Street via Harold's Cross, a journey which took about twenty-five minutes. Charlie Bowden, he said, would give evidence that Meehan had been a member of his gang along with Gilligan, Ward and Holland. Several conversations with Meehan would be recalled by Bowden, including one in which the accused enquired about the .357 Magnum revolver stored at the Jewish cemetery. On another occasion, Meehan had offered to shot Guerin but was told that a more experienced hit man, Patrick Holland, had been chosen instead.

Mr Charleton said that Russell Warren would tell how he had repaired the motorbike test-driven by Meehan before the murder. The bike was collected by Meehan, who instructed the bagman to go to Naas to look out for the red Opel Calibra driven by the doomed journalist. The trial would also hear the testimony of Bowden's pal, Julian Clohessy, who would tell of a conversation at the POD nighclub on Harcourt Street in which Meehan was alleged to have said of the murder: "I was involved. I was there."

Direct evidence in the trial started on Thursday, June 3, 1999, when various eyewitnesses and forensic experts gave the same testimony as was given in the Ward trial over eight months earlier. Det. Garda Fergus Treanor described approaching Meehan to could account for his movements on the day of the murder. Meehan first said "No," then paused and said he was probably with his father in the yard at Pimlico. A short while later, he ignored garda requests to continue the conversation and walked into his flat at Clifton Court.

Det. Garda Michael McElgunn told the court that he and Det. Garda Michael Moran retraced the journey from the murder scene to Paul Ward's house on Walkinstown Road on three occasions. The time taken varied from four minutes and twenty seconds to seven minutes and thirty-four seconds. A tape recording of the telephone conversation between Brian Meehan and Julie Bacon on April 11, 1997, was played for the court. Bacon later identified the voice as that of Meehan, who she pointed out in the dock. There were smiles in the court as the petite hairdresser's recorded shouts echoed through the courtroom calling Meehan a "fucking knacker".

Det. Inspector John O'Mahony of the National Bureau of Criminal Investigation said that Bowden had told him that Meehan claimed to have been the driver of the motorbike on the day of the murder. Meehan was said to have described the killing as "a good job" and "a good hit". Meehan had told Bowden of his involvement when the two men met for a drink in on the night of the murder. Meehan did not appear relaxed and did not elaborate on the details.

In his first statement, Bowden acknowledged that he had met Meehan and Holland on Moore Street on the day of the murder, but had not spoken to either man. But in his second statement, made in March 1997, he told gardaí that he had actually spoken to Meehan on Moore Street on that occasion.

O'Mahony told John McCrudden that he had attended the wedding of Bowden and Bacon at Arbour Hill prison on July 24, 1998 because he had been invited and because he believed it would have been impolite to refuse. He was accompanied by a number of

gardaí from the Lucan investigation team, including Det. Garda
Bernie Hanley and Det. Sgt John O'Driscoll. O'Mahony
acknowledged he had a measure of respect for Bowden because he
had "put his life on the line". Bowden had been threatened and his
house burned down by members of the Gilligan gang the night after
Meehan's recorded phone call with Bacon.

Julian Clohessy, the former sales assistant in a men's wear shop,
was also in the witness protection programme. He had been flown
back to Ireland from Australia for the trial. He told the court that he
had met Meehan on a number of occasions in 1995 and 1996, both
in his men's wear shop and in the POD nightclub. A conversation
about Guerin's last words took place on July 11, 1996, when Meehan
told Clohessy of his involvement in the murder. Meehan told
Clohessy that Veronica's last words were: "Please don't shoot me
in the face!", to which Meehan replied: "Fuck you, you bitch!"

Around the time of the murder Clohessy was in Cyprus with
his girlfriend. On the day of the murder, local television relayed the
news which "shocked" him because he had been "a big fan" of
Guerin. When he returned to Ireland on June 29, he had little money
and was pleased when one of the gang members, Peter Mitchell,
paid for a weekend trip to Manchester with Meehan to see Steve
Collins fight Nigel Benn. Peter Mitchell was with Meehan and a
group of others at The Brasserie Bar, off Grafton Street, on July 11.
Afterwards, they went to the POD nightclub where the Tosser made
his sick boast.

"At that point," said Clohessy, "Meehan looked at me in a way
that I could not forget. He said he was there, he said he was involved.
He led me to believe that he was there at Veronica Guerin's murder
and he was involved in Veronica Guerin's murder. I remember what
he said to me."

Clohessy said that the day after his release from questioning in
Lucan about the murder, he was summoned to a meeting in a bar in
Crumlin by Meehan, his father Kevin and "Fatso" Mitchell. At one
stage Meehan, Mitchell and Clohessy went outside the pub to talk
about what had happened while in custody. "I was very confused
and very angry that I was arrested," said Clohessy. Meehan and
Mitchell brought Clohessy to a local park but ran off when they
spotted a garda squad car passing. Later that month Clohessy was

working in his men's wear shop when a man came in carrying a mobile phone and told him that someone wanted to speak to him. Clohessy was handed the phone. It was Meehan on the other end. He ordered Clohessy to walk to the door of the shop. Clohessy was too busy at the time and the conversation ended.

Under cross-examination by John McCrudden, Clohessy admitted using drugs, including cocaine and ecstasy, but only on a "social" basis. Bowden had given him free cannabis and cocaine. He had stayed at Bowden's house at The Paddocks on several occasions and described the former soldier as a friend. He also said that Meehan had shared a room with him on the trip to Manchester and that Meehan had bought him a jumper. He claimed that they did not discuss the murder during the trip.

Clohessy denied a suggestion from McCrudden that the conversation in the POD was "a complete fabrication, possibly underpinned by drugs and alcohol." He acknowledged that on the night in question he had taken alcohol and drugs. Clohessy said that he told his friend, Paul Smullen, of the conversation with Meehan on the evening in the POD but couldn't recall clearly whether he had mentioned the information about Guerin's last words.

On June 17, 1999, Juliet Bacon began giving evidence in the trial. She told prosecuting counsel Tom O'Connell that she had first met Bowden in August 1994 and for the first period of their relationship they had shared a flat in Ballymun. In October 1995 they bought a house at The Paddocks for seventy-seven thousand pounds. She had worked at Clips, Bowden's hairdressing salon in Moore Street. Early in 1996 Bowden had begun to hang out with Meehan and Ward. Around this time, sums of between five and thirty thousand pounds would be counted in their home. She suspected that its source was "shady" but wasn't sure.

Deliveries of drugs would arrive at the house two or three times per week. Bowden would then bring the money to Meehan's flat at Clifton Court. Sometimes the money would be taken to the East Link Toll Bridge where Bowden would give it to another man. Bowden gave Bacon money when ever she asked. She never enquired where the cash came from and he never told her.

"I was quite shocked," said Bacon referring to the day she heard of the murder. She recalled seeing Meehan and Mitchell tap on the window of Clips at around 1.45 p.m. on June 26 and of being at the Hole in the Wall pub later that evening with other people, including Meehan. She remembered how Meehan had a "ruckus" with a member of the public in the men's toilet. In the period of time between the murder and her arrest, she and Bowden, now her husband, continued to count money in their home and bring it to Meehan.

Meehan had been worried about his photograph appearing in the *Sunday World* in October 1996. On the night he was charged, the Tosser had phoned and asked Bacon to access the teletext on television to read what charges had been laid against Bowden. When she told him that Oldcourt Road was referred to in the charges, Meehan said: "That must be the graveyard." Once Ward was charged with the murder of Veronica Guerin, she said that Bowden began to get frightened. He broke his bail restrictions and travelled to London.

Meehan later asked her why Bowden had not fought the State's extradition application. Under cross-examination by the defence she denied ever being in the Greenmount warehouse. She said she had no idea that Bowden was involved with John Gilligan, who used to be referred to as "the Little Man". Bacon said that, as a result of what Bowden had told her, she believed the Little Man was perturbed by Veronica Guerin's work and that he planned to have her threatened. She understood that the Provisional IRA might be asked to perform a role in scaring off the journalist.

She dismissed the description of herself and Bowden as a "sort of latter day Bonnie and Clyde" but admitted that she had counted, and enjoyed, the money which flowed from her husband's criminal activity. She acknowledged that both herself and Bowden used cocaine, but denied that he had sold it to others.

The following day Bacon told the court that she had initially lied to the police in order to protect Bowden. "I never wanted to believe that he had anything to do with it… I think it was pretty horrific, his involvement." She told John McCrudden that she had met her husband in jail the previous week but the topic of her evidence did not arise in their hour-long conversation.

"I have no reason to lie," she declared. "My husband has already admitted he was a drug dealer. I am telling the truth here." Referring to the Guerin murder, she said: "I have no means of blanking it out.

I live with it. I have had to undergo counselling since this happened. I live with two detectives. I am on constant 24-hour protection. I can't forget it."

She denied she was "a barefaced and shamefaced liar" when she said she believed that Guerin was to be threatened rather than shot dead. "I went through an array of emotions when I heard about the murder," she said. "Fear, surprise, shock, apprehension and probably guilt. My first emotion was to find out exactly what my husband's involvement was in it – especially after the conversation we had." When Bacon was asked why she hadn't told the gardaí about the threat to Guerin's life, she replied: "I could have warned her. I don't know if I could have prevented it."

Bacon agreed with McCrudden that her life had been "turned upside down" by the trauma of the murder. Her husband had fully intended coming clean about his involvement in the murder prior to his return to Ireland in March 1997. Nevertheless, she said in court the following day that she and Bowden had planned to flee to Australia after the murder and had passport photos taken to facilitate their move. Meehan had given the couple fifteen thousand pounds in cash, two-thirds of which was to go towards her husband's bail and the rest to herself. The bail contribution represented just one-sixth of the total bail amount; the remainder was put up by Bowden and Bacon's families and a friend. She denied that the fifteen thousand pounds had come from a stash of cash in their house in The Paddocks.

She also denied there had been a party in their home on the night of the murder. On that point she questioned her husband's memory in relation to the number of people who may have gone back to their house after drinks in the Hole in the Wall pub.

The next witness to give evidence was John Dunne. The shipping manager, told how he had started working for John Gilligan early in 1994. He gave details of how the gang's import/export system had worked for over two years. He pointed to Brian Meehan in the dock as the man who had been identified to him by Gilligan as "Joe". Meehan had regularly picked up shipments from Dunne in Cork. Dunne said he initially believed the consignments from Holland were tobacco, but his suspicions were raised in 1996 when he read newspaper reports of Gilligan's involvement in drugs.

When asked by Tony Sammon SC about visits Dunne received in jail from senior gardaí, including Assistant Commissioner Tony Hickey, he denied that he had done a deal with the gardaí in exchange for his evidence. He conceded, however, that he had struck up friendships with some of the members of the Lucan Investigation Team. They had not moved to seize his profits from drugs importation, which had amounted to around twenty-five thousand pounds. He had spent all the money, as he was sacked from his job shortly after being charged with drugs offences.

Charlie Bowden then began his third ordeal in the witness box. He explained how he got involved with Meehan and the gang, how he had managed the gang's drug operation and looked after their arsenal of weapons. He outlined the conversations he had witnessed at various meetings during which Veronica Guerin was discussed and plans were laid to shoot her.

He claimed to have met Meehan and Peter Mitchell on the afternoon following the murder. He claimed Meehan told about the murder. "Meehan said to me: 'It was a good job this morning. I thought he [the hit man] was only going to fire one or two shots at her, but he emptied it into her. Fair play to him. We legged it up the Belgard Road on the bike.'"

"Gilligan had decided to shoot her or to have something done about her," Bowden claimed. "Meehan had offered to do it himself but because he [the hit man] owed Gilligan a favour, he [Gilligan] had chosen him to carry out this." Bowden denied suggestions from McCrudden that he had done a deal with the gardaí in relation to his evidence.

John McCrudden asked Bowden if he had any contact with the media. Bowden said he hadn't. He also denied that he had tried to capitalise on the publicity. The defence then produced a copy of a short, hand-written letter which Bowden had sent to this author in March 1999 informing me that he wanted me to visit him in Arbour Prison. When I called to the prison for the visit, I was not permitted to see the supergrass. The defence team had obtained a copy of the correspondence under a discovery order. When the letter was produced, Bowden admitted having lied earlier. He claimed that he wanted to discuss collaborating with me on a book or screenplay. He wanted to be paid for his endeavours.

Bowden said that he had received letters and requests for interview from two other journalists but hadn't responded to them. Since then he had signed a protocol with the Department of Justice which prohibited him from having any contact with the media.

The next day, Bowden was back in the witness box discussing the background to the murder. "As far as I was aware," he said, "and still to this day, the intention I thought they had was that were going to frighten her. They were doing to shoot at her to frighten her off. I knew she was to be shot or shot at. When I loaded that gun, I knew it was to be used against that girl. It was the most powerful handgun in the world."

He acknowledged that he had a "deep involvement" in the murder: "My role in the murder of Veronica Guerin and what happened could hardly be described as heroism." He said the gang were not impressed with Meehan's markmanship after the Foley incident. "Meehan had panicked on a previous occasion when carrying out a shooting and this was the reason why another person was chosen because he would be calm. He [the killer] was a hit man, an assassin, with several hits under his belt."

Returning to the issue of whether there was a deal with the gardaí in relation to his evidence, Bowden said the Department of Justice had given him a written agreement that guaranteed new identities and relocation for himself and his family, though he did not know where or when. Bowden claimed he knew that his life was endangered by the statements he had given to the gardaí. "I knew my life was in danger," he said. "I knew the lives of my wife and children were in danger. I was out on the wing in Mountjoy. I had no protection."

During his lengthy, gruelling cross-examination Bowden told John McCrudden that there were a number of inaccuracies and "lies" in his evidence to the gardaí. These were corrected in later interviews. "The entire pressure I was under in October was that any admission I made was going to put me in some trouble, either with Gilligan or with Meehan and the gang or the police. I made mistakes. I was highly pressurised when I gave statements to the gardaí in March of 1997."

He had not spoken to Meehan on the morning of the murder, as claimed in one of his first statements, but asserted that he had met

Meehan on Moore Street a short while afterwards. He admitted that he spoke to Meehan by telephone later that day when the two men arranged to meet in the Hole in the Wall pub to watch a soccer match. He strenuously denied that he was trying to "stitch Brian Meehan into every allegation".

Bowden described the gang's arsenal of weapons and said it was an aspect of the gang's operation that he was asked to handle. He acknowledged that "there was a fair amount of experience in using guns in that gang". Bowden claimed that guns were used as currency by Gilligan and Traynor.

Bowden finished giving evidence on July 1 and was followed by Russell Warren. Warren said it was often his job to collect money from dealers on behalf of Gilligan and deliver it to airports in Belgium and Holland. The trips to Europe were weekly and the sums involved were cash amounts of up to a quarter of a million pounds. He agreed with Peter Charleton's description of his job as "a bagman, money counter and sometimes chauffeur" for John Gilligan.

Warren gave detailed evidence of his involvement in preparing the motorbike and the various conversations he had with members of the gang in person and by phone. Then he described the chilling moment that Veronica had been gunned down. "He shot once, then he shot twice. He moved to look into the car and he fired three consecutive shots. I froze. I went to get out of the van as if I could help. I just stopped. It was like slow motion. I realised then what I was after doing."

Warren pulled out of the traffic and drove up a slip road to ring Gilligan. Gilligan, he alleged, wanted to know if the shooting victim was dead. Gilligan repeated his threat to Warren that if he opened his mouth to the gardaí, he too would be murdered. It was at that stage that Warren felt nauseous and shocked: "I just felt sick. My legs would not work." He was so affected by what he had seen that he had to stop his van on the Naas dual carriageway to vomit.

Warren told how he continued collecting, counting and delivering cash. He described his meeting with Gilligan in London the day after he was released from custody the first time. He said that he had cleaned his fingerprints off the motorbike the night before it was used. He also used petrol to take off his prints when he had done work on the bike to make it roadworthy. The day after the murder he refused a request from Gilligan to break up the bike and burn it. He rang Meehan, who said he would do the job himself.

Under cross-examination by McCrudden, Warren insisted that the bike had been stolen with a plan in mind but that he hadn't been given details. He claimed not to know who Guerin was and denied that he had been part of a "well-oiled murder machine bearing down on Veronica Guerin".

"The bike was a stolen bike, so no matter where it was found I didn't want my fingerprints on it." He denied that the reason he removed his prints from the bike was that he knew it was going to be used in the Guerin hit. He claimed that the reason he continued to work for Gilligan after the murder was because he was afraid. "The activity became more intense after the murder," he said. "I was afraid not to continue working for the gang. If I had left or had tried to leave, I don't think I'd be sitting here today. You can't say no."

Warren alleged that Gilligan had "everyone in a mess because he had got Veronica Guerin killed." Warren admitted to threatening two other friends with death if they spoke of the stolen motorbike with anyone.

On the next day the court heard evidence from Det. Supt Martin Callanan of the National Bureau of Criminal Investigation. Veronica's last mobile phone call had been made at 12.54 p.m. and lasted just eighteen seconds. There was an eerie moment when Veronica's voice echoed through the court. It was a recording of a message she had been leaving on a garda contact's phone at the moment she was shot. The call ended abruptly with two loud cracks.

Det. Garda Rory Corcoran of the Special Detective Unit then told of arresting Meehan on June 28, two days after he had driven the motorbike involved in the murder. Meehan was apprehended for driving a car without insurance or a licence. During a conversation in the Bridewell garda station, Meehan offered Corcoran some "vital information in relation to serious crime in Dublin". Meehan said he didn't know anything about the Guerin murder and he wrote his phone number on the front of a cigarette box. Corcoran said he could not divulge the nature of his conversation with the Tosser on the grounds that it was "confidential and privileged".

As Corcoran spoke, Meehan shouted from the dock. "That never fucking happened! I didn't fucking write on it." A prison officer stopped Meehan as he tried to take off his shoe to throw it down at the cop. Corcoran told McCrudden that he hadn't invented the conversation with Meehan.

Det. Garda Bernie Hanley reacted angrily to McCrudden's suggestion that he had "nurtured and cultivated" Russell Warren to stitch Meehan into the murder. He said that between October and Christmas of 1996 he had weekly meetings with Charles Bowden in a car in the Phoenix Park. The meetings lasted ten to fifteen minutes, during which Bowden provided information on the gang's activities.

Ruairi Gogan, a principal officer in the Department of Justice, said Bowden, Warren and Dunne were now being held in extremely restrictive conditions in Arbour Hill prison. Only inmates undergoing punishment were held in more "onerous" conditions. He told John McCrudden that if either Bowden or Warren "cracked up" in the witness box, he would have no hesitation recommending to his Minister that they be allowed out on short, temporary release.

Gogan said that he had reinstated words in an internal memo which had been deleted by a more senior departmental colleague who feared that the document might be discovered by the defence legal team. The memo concerned the possibility of Warren and Bowden getting temporary releases and the reinstated words were "and would be dependent on their performance in court". Gogan said there was no reason why the Department of Justice had to be concerned about the disclosure of these words. The official who had earlier deleted the words, Michael O'Neill, denied that the prisoners were ever given the impression that their likelihood of temporary release was dependent on their performance in court. "At no stage during that meeting or after that meeting was it suggested that these prisoners would be rewarded with temporary release depending on the evidence they would give," said O'Neill, who was the Assistant Secretary-General in the Department.

Later, Meehan's lawyers applied to have the trial stopped because of an abuse of process by the State. In particular, lawyers John McCrudden and Michael O'Higgins argued that it was unprecedented and highly undesirable for three accomplice witnesses, who had mutual interests and concerns, to be incarcerated together. "It is without precedent to have accomplice witnesses put together in a hothouse atmosphere where they have mutual interests. No criminal court can risk relying on the evidence of these people in these circumstances," Michael O'Higgins declared.

Peter Charleton disagreed. "These are witnesses who were threatened, whose families and they themselves are in the Witness Protection Programme and who have to live with their conscience in relation to these crimes. All of this combined with the regime they live under gives rise to strain."

The court ruled against the motion. Mr Justice Frederick Morris said that there was no evidence that the State intended to interfere with the witnesses or with the administration of justice. He added that it seemed perfectly reasonable for them to be incarcerated together. For reasons which were obvious, they could not mix with "mainstream prisoners."

The prosecution's closing speech in the case began on July 20, after twenty-eight days of evidence. Eamon Leahy SC said that Meehan had played a "vital" role in the criminal organisation, working to import and distribute cannabis. Any one of the individual strands would be enough to convict Meehan but when intertwined they consisted of an evidential rope which tied him to the charges.

That night Kevin Meehan was about to go to bed when he heard a knock on the door of his home on Stanaway Road in Crumlin. When he answered the door a man asked him for directions, saying he was lost. In a split second the man produced a gun and fired two shots at the Tosser's father. One hit a wall and the other hit Kevin in the shoulder. He was rushed to hospital but was found not to have been seriously injured. He was released a day later and returned to court as a show of solidarity with his son. No-one has ever been arrested or questioned in relation to the attack. One theory was that Meehan was attacked by the IRA, but there hasn't been a shred of evidence to back it up.

In the meantime, John McCrudden QC started his summing up in Meehan's case. He claimed that the evidence against his client was questionable and that it was tendered by a number of accomplices. "The prosecution's witnesses were a gallery of rogues and convicts whose evidence is laced with implausibility and pockmarked by contradiction and inconsistency," said McCrudden. McCrudden said that if, as he claimed, those witnesses were implausible, then the State's case should fail.

Clohessy, he maintained, was in fact an accomplice despite the assertions of the prosecution. "Clohessy was not a good citizen. He was a drug abusing, cocaine-using associate of Charles Bowden. He was dishonest. He is not independent. He was prejudiced in his attitude to Brian Meehan," said McCrudden.

He claimed that none of the State's witnesses could be believed. "We are dealing with suspect witnesses," he said. "We are dealing with witnesses whose evidence is discredited and degraded. Bowden and Warren had decided to give the cheapest and easiest form of evidence." He reminded the court that it was a tribunal of fact which had to establish the case against Meehan beyond all reasonable doubt. The State's case fell "massively short of that".

"Brian Meehan is no angel," said McCrudden. "I don't come to this court to say he is as good as gold. He is innocent of these crimes but he is a person who has mixed with the wrong people and therefore he is vulnerable. All miscarriages of justice, the Birmingham Six, the Guildford Four, all were people who were vulnerable." McCrudden went on to allege that the real killer of Veronica Guerin was one Charles Bowden, who had sought to distance himself from the murder.

"That which identifies Bowden as the gunman is very circumstantial but the circumstances are compelling. We say that Bowden had something terrible to hide in respect of that day. You have not heard the full truth from Charles Bowden. You have heard a melange of contradiction, inconsistency and implausibility. He tried to reconcile the irreconcilable. It is internally, intrinsically, incredible evidence not capable of belief."

On Thursday, July 29, Mr Justice Frederick Morris delivered the court's verdict in the case of the State versus Brian Meehan. He said the court was satisfied that Meehan was "a high-ranking member of the drugs importation and distribution gang".

"The court accepts Russell Warren's evidence that the accused inspected the motorcycle, directed repairs and renovations to be carried out, later road-tested the motorcycle, returned to collect the motorcycle on the morning of June 26, 1996, directed Russell

Warren to go to Naas and to look out for the red sports car, to report when he saw it, and to follow it in order to report where the car was on the Naas Road.

"The court is satisfied that this evidence leads to only one conclusion, namely that the accused was a fundamental part of the conspiracy or plot to murder Veronica Guerin, that he participated fully in the event."

Mr Justice Morris said Warren's evidence, while it needed to be treated with caution owing to the fact that it was accomplice evidence, was admissible. He added that the court rejected any suggestion that Warren had given evidence at the behest of Det. Garda Bernie Hanley. "The court considers it proper to say that none of the allegations of improper conduct on the part of Det. Garda Hanley were substantiated or indeed supported by evidence. The court is of the view that through the enquiry and trial of this matter, Det. Garda Hanley's conduct has been above reproach."

In a striking contrast, Mr Justice Morris said the court rejected the evidence tendered by Charlie Bowden and his wife in relation to the Guerin murder as unreliable. "In cross-examination Meehan's counsel suggested to Bowden that he was deliberately bolstering the evidence which he was giving so as to be the witness who implicated the accused in the crime and thereby make himself a more 'saleable commodity' if he sold his story to the newspapers or wrote a book." The judge was unimpressed by Bowden's early denial that he had approached this author with a view to writing a book. Bowden's subsequent confession in relation to the contact he had made with Paul Williams showed that he had lied to the court, Morris ruled.

Juliet Bowden's evidence would be treated on the same basis as that of her husband. She had lied to the court on a number of occasions and she was, therefore, also unreliable. While he rejected the evidence of Bowden and that of his wife in relation to the count of murder, the court was prepared to use it to convict Meehan on the drugs and firearms charges. The court regarded the evidence of Julian Clohessy not as evidence from an accomplice but more as an account from someone who had socialised with members of the gang.

Meehan showed no emotion as the verdict was read. In addition to the murder charge, Meehan was given concurrent sentences of twenty and twelve years for drug offences. He received another five and ten years for possessing the firearms for an illegal purpose. Meehan was acquitted on the charge of having the guns and ammunition with intent to endanger life.

Tony Sammon SC said he did not wish to make any mitigating submission because his client wanted to assert his innocence. Three years and one month earlier Meehan had reckoned that he would literally get away with murder. At that moment it had all ended. He was the second member of the gang to take that long one way journey to Portlaoise Prison.

That night the Lucan Investigation Team celebrated. Three members of the gang were now behind bars, two of them serving life for murder. John Gilligan got the news from Dublin. He had been trying every legal avenue available to delay his extradition in the hope that the supergrasses might be released. He knew, deep down, that he would be brought back. He had the fight of his life ahead of him.

Twenty

Gilligan's Last Gamble

John Gilligan had tried every legal mechanism available to prevent being taken back to Ireland to face the charges of murdering Veronica Guerin and running an evil drug empire. But, on Thursday, February 3, 2000, the British legal system finally got rid of the little man who had fought his extradition as strenuously as the Chilean president Augusto Pinochet. Det. Inspector Toddy O'Loughlin and Det. Garda Mick Murray from Lucan had been in London for three days awaiting his final appeal to the High Court there. That morning the High Court threw out his last appeal, describing it as a tactic to delay his return to Ireland.

Back in Lucan, Tony Hickey had decided that as soon as the latest effort to delay the process was over they would not waste a minute more bringing him home. The House of Lords had already ordered that he be sent back to Ireland. An Air Corps plane had already been sent to England to pick up Ireland's most wanted and hated man. On board were key members of the team who had been on the case since the day of Veronica's murder: Pat Bane, Noel Browne, Bernie Hanley and Bernard Masterson. The big, grey troop carrier touched down at RAF Northolt in Surrey, where they were joined by O'Loughlin and Murray.

The Air Force base was close to Highdown Prison, where Gilligan had been transferred from Belmarsh Prison after violent attacks on prison officers. Once again Todd O'Loughlin waited for his prisoner at the steps leading into the aircraft. A convoy of police cars and vans sped up to the plane amid tight security. Gilligan was taken from a van and escorted onto the plane by one of the British officers and officially handed over toe Todd O'Loughlin. The detectives smirked and grinned at the diminutive thug, who looked quite comical in bright green and yellow prison overalls. Later, when he returned to Ireland, the other inmates in Portlaoise nicknamed

Gilligan "La La" after the famous "Tellytubbies" children's programme!

After the plane took off, Gilligan demanded to be allowed go to his baggage and take out his normal clothes. O'Loughlin insisted that Gilligan stay put in his seat, with handcuffs on. When the plane touched down at 4.30 p.m. Gilligan was furious to see at least twenty photographers and cameramen waiting for him on the apron at the Baldonnel Air Corps base. Gilligan stepped off the plane, covering his face with his hand and keeping his head down. On television that night the Irish public caught a glimpse of Public Enemy Number One. The nation that had been stunned and horrified by Veronica's murder were now shocked when they saw the little fellow in the funny suit. It was a mystery how could such an insignificant looking individual could have caused so much grief.

Gilligan was taken in a convoy of garda vans escorted by heavily armed troops to the Special Criminal Court, passing the place where Veronica Guerin was murdered on the way. Gilligan refused to go into the dock at the court until he had changed his clothes, an exercise which was hastily arranged. He stepped up into the elevated dock, flanked by prison officers. He smirked and winked at the large pack of reporters who were seeing the diminutive godfather for the first time. On the last occasion he had stood in the same spot, Gilligan had been sentenced to four years for the theft three thousand pounds worth of hardware goods. The Lucan investigation team members huddled at the side of the courtroom. Gilligan gave them a contemptuous look. They were the ones who had upset the little man's dreams of becoming Europe's top gangland boss.

Det. Inspector Todd O'Loughlin gave evidence of how and why Gilligan was before the court. The presiding judge, Mr Justice Richard Johnson, asked Gilligan if he was legally represented. "No, your Honour," said Gilligan, "I am representing myself." Gilligan stood tapping his fingers on legal papers and staring up at the ceiling as the list of murder, drugs and gun charges was read out at the arraignment.

The judge asked Gilligan if there was any question he wanted to ask of O'Loughlin. Gilligan responded that he wanted his legal papers back. "He said if I asked the court, he has no problem giving them back." After they were checked by security personnel,

O'Loughlin said the papers would be given to Gilligan. He said Gilligan had "a considerable amount of luggage" with him, which included his legal papers. The blue blazer he had put on over his "Teletubby" prison suit was the only thing he had yet been allowed to take from his sealed luggage.

After a 25-minute hearing, Gilligan was told that he could apply for bail. But Gilligan smirked down at the three judges from the dock. "I think bail would be out of the question, wouldn't it?" But he did ask if he could make submissions about the book of evidence. Mr Justice Johnson said he could do so on another date. Gilligan said he would need up to eight weeks to study the Book of Evidence and the court fixed April 3 for hearing his submissions.

"If you wish to make alibi evidence a part of your defence," said the judge, "you must give notice to the State."

"Without a doubt," Gilligan replied. The court then ordered that Gilligan be remanded in custody to appear again on April 3. "I'll be here!" he said.

On April 3, Gilligan represented himself in the Special Criminal Court. Mr Justice Kevin O'Higgins, presiding, asked Gilligan to move out of the dock and stand in the benches normally used by defence counsel in order to make his submissions. Gilligan moved down to the benches accompanied by his prison guards. During fifty minutes of submissions Gilligan requested that the murder charge and the drugs charges be dealt with separately. "I don't think I can handle it all together," he told the court.

Accusing the prosecution of "moving the goal posts" in relation to the murder charge, he asked for full disclosure of all evidence that the gardaí had against him. In fact, he objected to the court as a whole as it was neither independent, nor impartial, and he submitted human rights documents from the United Nations in support of his claim

He denied any involvement in the assault on Veronica Guerin. The forensic evidence in the possession of the gardaí showed there was no damage to the journalist's blouse or jacket and, on that basis, he claimed that he would not have been convicted in Kilcock District Court.

He cited the prosecution's claim that his motivation for the murder had to do with his fear of six months in jail if convicted on the assault charge that Guerin had brought against him. Referring to the murdered journalist, he added: "Lord have mercy on her." He denied making any threats against people prepared to give evidence against him and said he had not ordered a "price" on their heads.

"From fear of going to prison for six months, I had that lady murdered which is not true," he said later. "The evidence was that I was supposed to have struck Veronica Guerin all around her body, which I didn't," he claimed. "She got more boxes than Tyson could give a man, in her statement. I had no fear of Kilcock. I wasn't going to get convicted." He denied that he was on the run and said he had co-operated with the gardaí in relation to the charges. He also dismissed suggestions that the murder charge was connected with the drugs charges and he contradicted claims that he had threatened potential witnesses.

"I have no problem with any person giving evidence against me," he said. "Them people up in Arbour Hill, they have gone through enough. They have nothing to fear from me. I ordered nothing. The only thing I ordered is a cappuccino. It's all rubbish."

But, after his longwinded attempt at advocacy, the godfather told the three judges he was nervous about representing himself. "I don't do this every day. I am not too sure of myself. I thought I'd be able to handle this case. I certainly can't handle it. I'd like to apply for legal aid. I haven't a penny."

On Monday, May 22, Kevin Meehan was found guilty in the Special Criminal Court on six counts of handling his son's drug money and removing the money from the State to avoid a confiscation order. Delivering the verdict of the court, Mr Justice Barr said: "The court is satisfied beyond all reasonable doubt that the accused man was well aware he was engaged in serious criminal activity laundering money for his son, Brian Meehan."

Thomas Meehan, Kevin Meehan's brother, had pleaded guilty to the charges of handling his nephew's cash. Det. Inspector Terry McGinn of the Money Laundering Unit, who had originally been a member of the Operation Pineapple team, said that Thomas Meehan had found it difficult to extricate himself from the money laundering operation. He had been co-operative with the gardaí from the time of his arrest and had suffered from depression since his arrest. Mr

Justice Barr sentenced Thomas Meehan to three years in prison but suspended the final year.

The court was perhaps not aware that Thomas Meehan had been living in fear that his own nephew, Brian Meehan, would have him shot for co-operating with the police. The Tosser tried to stop his uncle pleading guilty by sending a message from prison that he would be "whacked" if he did so. He accused his uncle of becoming an informant.

Kevin Meehan was escorted to Portlaoise Prison where he shared the same landing as his two sons, Brian and Brad. Brad Meehan had been jailed for a number of armed robberies. Thomas Meehan was sent to another prison for his own protection. The conviction of the two middle-aged brothers was another victory for the Lucan investigation and their colleagues in the CAB who had declared war on John Gilligan and his entire organisation. But their biggest battle was about to begin.

After changing his legal team twice, John Gilligan's trial finally began on December 4, 2000. The legal team was led by Michael O'Higgins. This would be O'Higgins' first major trial since becoming a senior counsel. He would prove himself to be a top-class defence lawyer. Before joining the bar, O'Higgins had been a journalist working for a number of publications including *Magill* magazine and the *Sunday Independent* newspaper. He was the first journalist to get access to the General, Martin Cahill, for a major series of intriguing interviews. O'Higgins was joined by Queen's Counsel Terence McDonald from Northern Ireland and Peter Irvine BL.

Gilligan spent most of the 43-day trial gazing up at the skylight in the ceiling of the courtroom. Whenever the State's protected witnesses were mentioned in the opening address to the court, Gilligan's gaze dropped from the skylight into the body of the court and a dismissive smile broke across his small, round face.

Gilligan stood in the dock as each individual charge was read to him. To each count he was asked: "How do you plead? Guilty or not guilty?"

"Not guilty."

When the last count was read out to Gilligan, he replied with a contemptuous grin: "And my final answer is not guilty."

Michael O'Higgins said that his client was "probably the most vilified person ever to come before a court of trial" and in support of this claim he cited the *Evening Herald* newspaper, which went out to County Kildare, photographed his home and published various details about his life and business immediately after the murder. Gilligan had given a newspaper interview in which he had admitted that he was the person suspected of masterminding the Guerin murder. Thereafter, every story written referred to him as "the self-confessed suspect in the Veronica Guerin case."

O'Higgins then said that Gilligan was not lawfully before the court and that he should be discharged because the court had no jurisdiction to try him. He also asked the court to conduct an inquiry into the events surrounding Gilligan's extradition from Britain in February 2000, over three years after his arrest at Heathrow Airport in London. O'Higgins also submitted that the court should prohibit evidence to be heard from protected witnesses Charles Bowden, Russell Warren and John Dunne. He claimed that Bowden and Warren had been given immunity from prosecution by the D.P.P. for the murder of Guerin and that a deal had been done which was dependent on their performance in court.

This was denied by Charleton who said that the court had no power to carry out an inquiry into the extradition of Gilligan or to grant a habeas corpus order. If Gilligan was released in accordance with O'Higgins' wishes, the prisoner would be promptly rearrested on foot of an instruction from the D.P.P. The court rejected O'Higgins' application that the court conduct an inquiry into the circumstances surrounding Gilligan's extradition from Britain and into the arrangements surrounding the three supergrass witnesses, Charlie Bowden, John Dunne and Russell Warren.

Charleton said that Gilligan had inspired the murder because he wanted to protect his drugs empire and to ensure that he stayed out of jail at a time when he was making a great deal of money. Gilligan, he said, was the "controlling mind" behind the criminal gang which he "cloaked in secrecy and terror". The murder was organised on his instruction, through agents who were members of his gang. It would be the prosecution's contention that Gilligan and his gang had imported thousands of kilos of cannabis and a small amount of cocaine, as well as some firearms and ammunition.

"The motivation for the murder of Veronica Guerin was the protection of that empire and the protection of the lie that he was not involved in these offences," said Charleton. From the earliest days in July 1994, Gilligan was an "integral part" of the importation of cannabis resin. The importation of cannabis was initially eighty kgs per week but the amounts rose to "gigantic amounts" subsequently.

Charleton dealt with Gilligan's contacts in Holland. Chief among them was Martin Baltus who, he said, would give evidence for the prosecution that Gilligan had met him on several occasions in January 1995 with a view to laundering the accused's ill-gotten gains in holiday homes. Baltus had attended negotiations for a major drug deal with Simon Rahman and John Gilligan. Baltus would be telling the court that he had made out false invoices for the shipments which were routed through Cork and labelled as machine parts. He saw guns being loaded into boxes containing drugs and he had also seen blank Irish driving licences and fake passports. To illustrate the progression of Gilligan's business, it was stated that the first cannabis shipment in August 26, 1995 had comprised seventy-five kgs, while the last one on October 7, 1996 contained three hundred and eighty kgs.

On September 15, 1995, Veronica Guerin visited Gilligan's home in Enfield. The next day she made a complaint to the gardaí that she had been assaulted. This, said Charleton, was the incident which provoked Gilligan and was ultimately responsible for her murder. On June 13, 1996, Gilligan purchased a ticket to Amsterdam and left Dublin on June 25, the day before the murder. Charleton said that Gilligan "deliberately left the jurisdiction having put in place the elements whereby Veronica Guerin was to be murdered and from abroad he directed that murder".

Peter Charleton detailed Gilligan's dealings with Russell Warren in relation to the motorbike used in the murder and Gilligan's comments to detectives outside Kilcock Court the day before the murder. He also referred to evidence of telephone records between the accused man and the members of his gang on the day of the murder. When the Lucan team arrested Russell Warren it "was the beginning of the end of the criminal gang based in Greenmount and controlled by John Gilligan".

Senior Counsel Felix McEnroy then told the court about hearing Gilligan's threatening phone call to Veronica Guerin on September 15, 1995, which he described as "still imprinted on my mind". The meeting was set up by Michael Kealy, a senior solicitor in McCann FitzGerald, who was representing Guerin in her action against Gilligan for assault. McEnroy said Guerin entered his office around 1 p.m. and that she had the appearance of someone who had been in a fight. "There was bruising or swelling over the left eye," he recalled.

McEnroy said he could hear Gilligan threaten to kill Veronica and to kidnap and rape her son. He heard Gilligan say in a controlled voice: "If you do one thing on me or if you write about me I will kidnap your son and ride him. I will shoot you. Do you understand what I am saying? I will kidnap your fucking son and ride him. I will fucking shoot you. I will kill you."

"Especially the reference to the child," recalled McEnroy. "No one in their right mind could forget it. The imprint is still on my mind."

McEnroy said that when the gardaí first approached him for an interview, he claimed legal professional privilege over his dealings with Guerin. "I knew what had occurred in my office and the significance of what had occurred," he told Terence McDonald QC, for Gilligan. However, he received a letter from Guerin's husband, Graham, asking him to co-operate with the gardaí even if it meant disregarding privilege which normally attaches to communications with one's client. McEnroy, reluctant to disregard legal professional privilege, sought the advice of his colleague, James Nugent SC, then Chairman of the Bar Council. In the exceptional circumstances of the Guerin murder trial, McEnroy was persuaded to make a statement.

"I remember what happened, clear and well," McEnroy said. "I'll never forget it. I have no doubt that I remember hook, line and sinker what happened." He first met Gilligan in 1984 when he was a "devil" or barrister's apprentice. There had been no contact since 1989, when he had last represented Gilligan in court.

"Mr Gilligan does not have much in the way of social conversation. When he speaks, he knows what he wants to say and, more importantly, he wants you to listen, no doubt that. He has what I would call a Dublin city, working-class accent. He is somebody who, when he speaks, knows what he is about. He has good diction and is well capable of expressing himself. He is very direct in the way he expresses himself. He wants you to listen. This man is unusual. He is quiet but when he speaks, he speaks with a level of intensity that immediately grips you. You will know he is talking to you. When I heard that outburst on the phone, I had seen this before and I knew who it was because I had seen that outburst before."

McEnroy said that he had told Guerin to stop the telephone conversation at once and made it clear that she should make a statement to the gardaí. He had then prepared to draft a statement for her. McEnroy denied a suggestion by Terence McDonald that in his own statement McEnroy had used parts of Guerin's statement of complaint to the gardaí about this conversation.

McEnroy recalled spending a full day with Gilligan in 1989 in the Four Courts. He had drafted an important affidavit in a case in which Gilligan was involved.

On December 8, defence counsel Michael O'Higgins asked that the court be cleared of people waiting to give evidence. That included Assistant Commissioner Tony Hickey and a number of people who showed up to give eyewitness evidence. At the request of the prosecution, however, Guerin's husband, Graham Turley, was allowed remain in court. The idea was to prevent witnesses hearing each other's testimony.

The trial adjourned for the Christmas recess on December 13 until January 11. Gilligan was glad of the break, not because the case was getting him down or he liked Christmas. From the safety of his prison cell he was co-ordinating a plot to disrupt his trial. By now Gilligan reckoned that the State witnesses could be discredited. His former mistress, Carol Rooney, who possessed damning evidence had again refused a request from Lucan to return from her overseas hideout to give evidence. Martin Baltus was his biggest fear. Baltus had already shown his willingness to testify after he gave evidence against Simon Rahman in The Hague. He had strong, corroborated evidence to sustain the guns and drugs charges against "De Kliene".

Gilligan sent word through the system to Peter "Fatso" Mitchell and John Traynor to have something done about Baltus. In September Todd O'Loughlin received intelligence through the team's contact with sources close to the gang that serious efforts were being made to prevent Baltus from travelling to the Republic to testify. O'Loughlin contacted Detective Inspector Hans Vrolisk of The Hague police and passed on the information. The Dutch police were patrolling the area near the house where Baltus lived with his wife and son since June when the two police squads had agreed to share intelligence in relation to threats against Baltus. When his police handlers discussed his security, Baltus said that no-one had attempted to intimidate him and he was still determined to appear in the Special Criminal Court in January.

A few days into the new year O'Loughlin and Tony Hickey received heartbreaking news from Holland. Baltus' Dutch police handlers contacted the incident room to say that the key witness had a complete change of heart and was now refusing to travel to Ireland. O'Loughlin immediately flew to Holland in a bid to get Baltus back on side. In The Hague, during a meeting with police, he was told that Baltus didn't want to testify in Ireland out of fear for his family's safety. The Dutch had offered to place him in the equivalent of a witness protection programme but Baltus had refused the offer.

The police in The Hague discovered that Baltus' daughter had been abducted and held against her will over night until Rahman's former manager had a change of heart. Nothing would convince him to travel. O'Loughlin returned to Dublin empty-handed. Someone sympathetic to Gilligan had already scored a major victory against the Lucan team.

When the court resumed after the Christmas break, Det. Inspector John O'Mahony revealed how Charlie Bowden had been initially "evasive" but later went as far as to tell gardaí where they could locate eighty-five thousand pounds of his drugs money. "I believe that because of the whole operation he found himself in, the drugs operation and the murder, it was just too much for him," said O'Mahony. "He had to tell somebody. I am satisfied that Charles Bowden told us everything of relevance to this trial and other trials on the record. I have obviously nothing to hide in relation to this."

"It was a most heinous crime and the people involved in it were ruthless to say the least," O'Mahony told O'Higgins. "It was a professional investigation." In what O'Mahony agreed where off-the-record conversations, Bowden had told the gardaí that he had supplied cocaine to a man called "Arthur." Bowden's initial suspicions were that the drugs importation business had been controlled by Meehan, but he later came to believe that it was Gilligan who was the real authority.

The Detective Inspector was also told by Bowden in 1997 that John Traynor had been involved in the drugs business and was Gilligan's partner. Bowden admitted to having given guns as "sweeteners for the politicals". O'Mahony was not aware of the fact that Traynor had contacted the gardaí on the night of Guerin's murder to protest his innocence. Traynor, having injured himself while racing in Mondello Park, had been in hospital on the day of the murder.

O'Mahony said he was aware of the speculation that Traynor had supplied Gilligan and Meehan with information on the movements of Veronica Guerin on June 26, 1996. He was not able to recall whether Traynor had been involved in legal proceedings against the *Sunday Independent* around that time because Guerin was about to name him as a drugs dealer. It was, he conceded, a "powerful motive" to silence the crime journalist.

The following day O'Mahony told the court that Bowden had given money to Gilligan outside the Gresham Hotel in Dublin. O'Higgins claimed that the only direct evidence given by Bowden in his statements to the gardaí was that he got a call from Gilligan in relation to a drugs consignment containing five semi-automatic pistols. "He was very fearful of what he had told us getting back to the criminal gang," said O'Mahony. "He was absolutely terrified of what he had told us getting out into the public domain and back to his criminal associates.

"Bowden had so much money he didn't know what to do with it. My assessment of him was that he certainly became addicted to a lifestyle that he could only support by drug dealing. He did this of his own free will and knowledge. He knew what he was getting into. The money was easy come, easy go with Bowden at that time."

Bowden, he added, had been "drip-feeding" the truth to gardaí in October 1996. At a meeting in London City Airport in October

1996, where he had been detained by British police, Bowden had agreed to return to Ireland voluntarily. He was duly taken to Lucan and remanded in custody in Mountjoy. O'Mahony insisted that Bowden had agreed "unconditionally" to give evidence without any offer of immunity from prosecution for the Guerin murder. However, the D.P.P. had decided to grant Bowden immunity.

John Dunne gave a frank explanation for his role in the Gilligan gang's operation. "It was pure greed," he told the court. He said he had made approximately forty thousand pounds from his illegal activities. When asked by Michael O'Higgins about his arrangement with the Department of Justice, he claimed to have fought hard for an early release.

"We have certainly waged war on the Department of Justice because we feel we have matched the criteria required to get early release," said Dunne. The former shipping manager was equally frank when he discussed his future. He said he was looking forward to earning a decent living in a location of his choosing after his release. "I know what I am doing in relation to the Witness Protection Programme, so I am happy," he said. "I've made a decision in relation to what I am going to do and I can cope with these problems. The decision I have made now, I have got my own answers. The Witness Protection Programme has gone along with my decision."

The next day Russell Warren told the court what he saw from where he had been sitting in the traffic on the Naas dual carriageway on June 26, 1996: "I just saw the person the back of the bike put his foot down to stabilise himself. He reached over the roof of the Opel and he fired a shot. The bike was about four cars away. Then he fired another shot. He leaned over then he fired three consecutive shots. He put the gun back inside the waistband of his trousers, then they just drove off. I was stunned and shattered by what I saw."

Since their first meeting in early 1996, Warren met Gilligan more than one hundred times. Warren agreed with Terence McDonald, one of Gilligan's lawyers, that the State had been "blackmailing" him into giving evidence against the accused. McDonald asked: "You thought the State was blackmailing you to make sure you gave evidence against the man in the dock?"

Warren replied: "At the time, yes." He said he had received a "firm proposal" from John Kenny of the Prisons Operations Division

at the Department of Justice regarding a date on which Warren could
be taken into the Witness Protection Programme outside jail. "Every
day is a big deal when you are in prison." He said there was a "wink
and nod" relationship with the Department of Justice regarding his
release. It was the timing of "certain trials" and not his behaviour
as a prisoner which had a bearing on his release.

Although he denied there had been a deal with the Department,
he said his release was "like dangling a carrot" in front of him. He
admitted that he had a criminal record and that he had told lies
under oath during another criminal trial in the 1980s. After stealing
the motorbike in Dun Laoghaire with his "good friend" Paul
Cradden, he spent the night in a hotel in Bray with Cradden's
girlfriend. It was during this evening that he had to ring his sister
with a request that she deliver ten thousand pounds to John Traynor.

Warren broke down in tears under cross-examination by Terence
McDonald QC about the events on the day of the murder. McDonald
told Warren that his account about getting sick after witnessing the
murder was "a complete fabrication, a total lie and out and out
lies". Warren denied this and later again denied that he "can't tell
the truth" and that he was "telling lies" so that Gilligan would be
convicted.

"I drove the woman to her death," he said, after explaining he
had kept in telephone contact with Meehan and Gilligan about
Guerin's movements on the day of the murder. "I only sent the
woman to her death." The court adjourned for five minutes to allow
Warren to recover his composure. "I am very sorry about that," he
said on his return to the witness box.

After the murder, Warren claimed, he drove up a slip road and
phoned Gilligan. He then went home, had a shower and met a friend
for a drink in a Rathgar pub where they watched a soccer match
and placed bets. He remembered someone coming into the pub with
an evening newspaper which carried the news that Guerin had been
gunned down. The item was also leading the main television
bulletins.

While he recalled going to a social welfare office in Naas on
the morning of Guerin's murder, he was unable to point out the
location of the office on a map which was supplied to him in court
by Terence McDonald QC. Warren acknowledged that in earlier

statements he had not been truthful: "I was giving the gardaí dribs and drabs of information, some possibly lies and some truth." In a statement he had made to gardaí on October 19, 1996, he admitted lying about whether Gilligan had told him to go to Naas on the day of the murder. At the time, he didn't want the gardaí to know that he had followed Guerin's car from Naas.

"I was trying to cover myself because I just didn't want them to know that I was on the Naas Road. I know that Gilligan told me to go to Naas. It was the morning or the evening over the phone. He said: 'Do what Brian Meehan wants you to do, go to Naas.' It was the evening before or the morning before the murder. Brian said: 'John wants you to go to Naas. I was speaking to John and John said: 'Go to Naas, do what Brian wants you to do. Those were my instructions," he claimed.

Immediately after hearing these words from Warren, McDonald read from transcripts of the Meehan trial in which Warren said: "I cannot recall that John Gilligan told me to go to Naas but Brian Meehan was after saying that John wanted me to do this." McDonald reminded Warren that he should recall this because he was a critical witness in the prosecution's case against Gilligan. Warren had given "an instinctive and foxy" reply to the question regarding his whereabouts when he was allegedly contacted by Gilligan.

Warren reckoned he was in his house when he got the call from Gilligan. He also remembered that Meehan was running late on the day of the murder but that he had met him at a lockup close to where he lived. "I don't recall his exact words but I know it's how it ended up in Naas," said Warren who was given the number of Guerin's car by Meehan but didn't take it down. He agreed with McDonald that he had been mistaken in the evidence he had given in the Meehan trial about the length of the journey to Naas.

Warren said he had been paid a lump sum of seven thousand pounds by Det. Garda Bernie Hanley in April 1997. This was in addition to a sum of £1,920 paid by the same garda the previous December. The money, claimed Warren, was part of his legitimate earnings from his industrial cleaning business and not the proceeds of crime as suggested by McDonald. Warren also denied that he was a garda informer. He admitted having a row with his wife Debbie when she came to visit him in prison. He said he didn't hit her, as had been claimed earlier, because she refused to go away with him after he had finished his five-year jail term.

Warren denied that alleged conversations he had with Gilligan about the Guerin murder were "a figment of his fertile imagination" and "a nonsense and a lie". He said McDonald was wrong to suggest that Gilligan was "never anywhere near the bike or Terenure" the week before the murder when an inspection of the vehicle had taken place. McDonald had earlier claimed that his client was "innocent" of Guerin's murder and that he had no knowledge of the events on the Naas dual carriageway on June 26, 1996.

Warren said that in March 1997 he had got quite close to two detectives. Around that time he remembered being afraid at the prospect of having to meet the accused's brother, Thomas Gilligan. "I didn't want to go on my own because I was afraid something would happen," said Warren, who had received a letter from John Gilligan a short time previously. In the letter, sent from his prison cell in England, Gilligan asked Warren to contact his wife, Geraldine, and his brother, Thomas.

"I hope you are doing OK and I'm sorry for the shit you and your wife and family went through but I could do nothing as I did nothing wrong but I have a big, big fight on my hands," wrote Gilligan to Warren. "I will say good night and God bless. Please take care and I wish you all the best."

In another letter Gilligan comforted Warren, saying that there was no need to have his family worried about "people trying to get at them". Warren said that Gilligan had told him that "me, Brian and Paul [Ward] aren't even thinking like that". In another letter Gilligan wrote that there was no need for Warren and his family to leave Dublin. All Gilligan wanted was for Warren to "tell the truth" in court. "It should not be lies," Gilligan said in a letter. He ended the note by saying: "Letting you know I only need the truth to come out in court. If that be the case, the witnesses I have in court, I will not need to call them. It's not too much to ask. My life is in your hands when you tell lies."

In another letter, he told Warren: "Please tell your friends to stop taking notice of all the shit in the newspapers. Believe me, I wish I could help your families." It was signed: "Your friend, John Gilligan." Gilligan wrote in a subsequent letter: "You don't need to

leave your country over me, say what you like in court. Run away.
You have a home and family now and your new child may well
want to come back to where he was born. You have my word on it.
No one is after you. The papers are mad. Anything to sell them.
God bless and take care and I wish you all the luck in the world.
Your friend, John G."

Charles Bowden gave evidence of the conversations he had in
a car in the Phoenix Park with Det. Garda Bernie Hanley. When
Gilligan's counsel, Michael O'Higgins, suggested that this "sounds
like James Bond," Bowden agreed.

"It was subterfuge," he replied. "I was still in contact with Brian
Meehan and I was relating to Det. Garda Hanley the contents of my
conversation. I was telling Mr Meehan what he wanted to hear and
I was telling the gardaí what was being said." Bowden said that he
had been given a thousand four hundred pounds by Hanley after he
had claimed that some of the money taken from him actually
belonged to his brother.

Bowden named the five men involved in the distribution of the
drugs shipments: himself, Brian Meehan, Paul Ward, Shay Ward
and Peter Mitchell. "If there was £30,000 left over, or £27,000 or
£10,000, that would be distributed between the five of us and the
rest of the money sent to Gilligan," he said.

"I would open the boxes – they started out as wooden crates –
and whatever was in the boxes I would take out. Mostly it was
cannabis. On a couple of occasions it was cocaine or weapons. I
would drive down to the Ambassador Hotel with my driver. My
van wasn't big enough and we would take the courier's can to
wherever the lockup was we were using at that time and I'd go
back to Dublin to the lockup and break up the boxes. I distributed
them out in that fashion that evening."

Bowden remembered meeting John Gilligan and later his
brother, Thomas Gilligan, "sometime after the murder of Veronica
Guerin" and Bowden "sat at the table with him and Brian Meehan."

"I went into the kitchen. John Gilligan was sitting at the table.
We sat down. There was money being counted. The gist of the
conversation I can't remember but I'd imagine it would be something
to do with deliveries of cannabis." The conversation also dealt with
money and lasted "ten minutes, max". When the two men would

speak by phone, Gilligan would simply say: "This is John, what's the count?" He would never have to introduce himself as "John Gilligan".

Bowden claimed that, through the gardaí, the Guerin family had sent him a message supporting his application for temporary release "because of my decision to give evidence". He admitted that the prospect of being charged with the Guerin murder had been of concern to him.

"It definitely was a factor, a major factor," he said. "I was very apprehensive about being charged. It was definitely a subject I was concerned with. I would agree that the vast majority of meetings I had with Det. Hanley and Det. Insp. O'Mahony had to do with whether I would be charged. Every time I asked the question, I was told it wasn't their decision. I hoped to reap the benefits of having co-operated with the gardaí in any charges that would be brought against me."

He agreed with O'Higgins that he regarded Hanley as a "confidant" with whom he was on first name terms. He said that Hanley had given his wife, Juliet, money but he couldn't say how much.

Bowden described his decision to jump bail and flee to England. He also recalled his arrest and decision to return home to give his evidence. "At that stage, I was left with only one option," he said. "To go home and co-operate with the police." He recalled telling the gardaí that he had feared that charges would be brought against him. Nobody was taking his calls and he felt that it would be best to flee the country.

His alibi had "fallen" because his wife had given the gardaí a different account of his movements on June 26, 1996. He acknowledged that, initially, he had said that Meehan had confessed to the murder in the Hole in the Wall pub on the night of the shooting. Later, he changed the location of the alleged confession to his hairdresser's shop on Moore Street on the afternoon of the murder.

He agreed that he had added "the ghoulish line" in his statement in March that the Wig had emptied the whole gun into her and "fair play to him". It took Bowden a while to understand why he was in prison. "I know why I am in prison. I know the reason I am sitting here is because a girl died, that's why I'm here." Six weeks after he was sentenced, he applied to be released early. Getting out of jail was a "preoccupation" and he said it was a "culture shock" to find himself in Mountjoy Prison. The prospect of life in jail was "absolutely horrifying".

Asked by Michael O'Higgins about the arrangements which had been put in place for after his release date in September 6, 2001, Bowden said: "A lot of things have to be taken on trust. The fine detail has yet to be worked out." He said he didn't know what the total cost of the package of measures would be but he assumed his living expenses, including the cost of a house, a car and any training or education would be covered.

"If I act the maggot or don't live up to the guarantees that I have given about my future, then the State do have sanctions against me." He had no problem with the manner in which the gardaí had handled their side of the Witness Protection Programme but he did have concerns about the approach taken by the Department of Justice. While the Department had not forced him to give evidence, it had told him that it would not be dealing with his application for early release until after he gave evidence. "They have," he said, "set aside the merits of my case in qualifying for early release while these trials are going on. It is my belief that if the trial had happened at any time in the past four and a half years, my case would have been dealt with on its merits. I always had difficulty with the conditions I was being held under."

Bowden felt that the State had put him under pressure in the sense that it had not given him any information. He denied that he had received favourable treatment, although he agreed with O'Higgins that he had received a "light sentence" for his criminal activity. "The State would have to be open and honest in its dealings with me and outline in a coherent fashion what its management of my sentence would be." He had filed an application under Article 40 of the Constitution citing "oppressive conditions of confinement", the lack of a review date for his sentence and the reluctance of the Department of Justice to clarify its position. Since then some progress had been made in relation to his future treatment.

Dublin criminal Martin Foley had successfully sued him, he said, and a judgment of a hundred and twenty thousand pounds had been registered against him. Asked if he would pay the money due, he said: "I am not prepared to comment on that. It's ongoing." At one stage, he said he was so concerned about the treatment of his case that he asked the prison authorities to allow this author to visit him. He wanted me to document his plight but the request was turned down by the prison authorities.

Asked if he thought he would be released if the Gilligan trial had been concluded earlier, he said: "I can't say I believe I would be out by now but I do believe that the management of my sentence would have been handled differently if this trial had happened." He said he was not interested in seeing whether certain other persons who are outside the jurisdiction are brought back to Ireland to face charges in relation to the Guerin murder. "There is no real prospect of them being tried and convicted," he said. "It is not important to me whether these people are convicted or not."

The solicitor who represented Gilligan in the assault case taken by Veronica Guerin, Michael Hanahoe, said his client was "extremely confident" that he could win his case. "I had advised him in relation to it and we were happy with our position on it," said Hanahoe. "It was a contested case." On the day before the murder, Hanahoe represented Gilligan at Kilcock District Court in relation to the assault case. Afterwards, they went to Gilligan's equestrian centre at Jessbrook to inspect the site of the alleged assault. From there, Hanahoe drove Gilligan to Dublin Airport.

This author gave evidence on February 8 about telephone calls between myself and Gilligan. In one of the calls, two days after Veronica's murder, I interviewed Gilligan. In the other call he had tried to blackmail me. When asked by the court what had been discussed in the second phone call, I replied that it had been one of the most bizarre conversations I ever had with anybody. Gilligan's defence objected to me saying anything further about the call.

I also explained how I had received a letter from Charles Bowden asking me to visit him in Arbour Hill prison. When I arrived for the visit, I wasn't allowed in. That was the end of it. There was no particular subject mentioned in the letter, so I didn't know what he wanted to talk about. I was then asked by McDonald if there was any reference to a film script and I answered that the first time I had heard about a film script was during the Meehan trial.

Det. Garda Bernie Hanley confirmed that sums of a thousand

and then £1,920 had been given back to the protected witness but had nothing to do with making statements. The money was sourced from the industrial cleaning business that Warren had run previously. "There was no question of payment for information," insisted Hanley, who added that Warren had been "in extreme fear" for his own safety after he agreed to give evidence for the State.

He said that Warren was "a more jittery type of fellow" than Bowden and he acknowledged that it had been "at the back of my mind" that Warren might skip the country at the early stages of the investigation. "Warren and Bowden were facing serious charges," said Hanley. "If they were willing to give information about other members of the gang, I was willing to take it."

Det. Garda Robert O'Reilly, the exhibits officer in the case, said there was "organised chaos" in the Guerin murder trial in late 1996 and early 1997. He denied the suggestion made by O'Higgins that he had "executive control" over the money that he handed back to Bowden and Warren around that time. Assistant Commissioner Tony Hickey said he was surprised to learn that money seized from Bowden, Warren and Dunne could not be passed to the Criminal Assets Bureau because of new legislation. The money was instead in the possession of the gardaí.

Hickey said he had made files on Gilligan available to English barristers who were preparing a case against him in England. Plans to prosecute Gilligan were dropped just two or three days before the trial was due to begin in September 1998. He said that, regardless of what happened, Bowden and Warren were prepared to give evidence in the Gilligan case. Their co-operation had nothing to do with whether they were to be charged in relation to the Guerin murder. He had no particular sympathy for these witnesses in light of the crimes they had perpetrated but he was aware of their paranoia regarding their security while in custody.

Michael O'Higgins sought details of the Witness Protection Programme from the garda officer in charge. The garda officer responsible for the programme said that to give details of the sums paid would jeopardise the security of those involved because, inevitably, a profile of the persons' new identities would be built up. While the programme was the first of its kind, it echoed earlier precedents where witnesses were protected and relocated. "The devil is in the detail," said the officer, whose own identity was to be kept confidential by order of the court. "The problem for me is in relation to the detail and in the significance of the detail when it is joined up. The phrase I use with those on the programme is that I am responsible for your future; the governor is responsible for your present."

The court ordered that references to the witnesses relocation and other security issues not be revealed. But Mr Justice O'Donovan ruled that documents relating to complaints made by the witnesses in custody could be disclosed to the Gilligan defence team.

The prosecution's case closed on February 23 after which Michael O'Higgins submitted that there had been "improper conduct" between the gardaí and the British authorities in relation to the continued detention of Gilligan during the investigation of the Guerin murder in 1997. O'Higgins said Gilligan should have been released by the British in September 1997 when it was decided not to proceed with the prosecution of his client. For that reason, the man accused of Guerin's murder in this trial was not properly before the court.

Terence McDonald QC added that the evidence of Warren could not be relied upon by the prosecution because the witness should be treated "potentially as an accomplice in the murder of Veronica Guerin". Just as Warren had admitted to perjury in a previous trial, the court should believe that he had committed the same offence in this trial. He had, said McDonald, lied "on fundamental matters".

A mutual dependence had developed between Warren and the garda which made his evidence unreliable. His account of his movements on the Naas Road on the day of the murder had been contradicted "at every turn" by eyewitnesses. Warren was "a person of bad character" who without any compunction had incriminated his entire family and subjected them to the risk of imprisonment to "satisfy his own selfish needs".

McDonald was followed by O'Higgins, who submitted that their client had no case to answer in relation to the drugs and firearms counts because the only evidence against him was supplied by Bowden, "an accomplice, a police informer and a man of bad character".

Bowden had the day before the murder "sat polishing bullets" in the knowledge that the gun would be placed in the hands of a "trained hit man". Bowden had committed perjury many times, he had committed perjury in this trial and his evidence was therefore "inherently unreliable".

"Mr Bowden doesn't land a single clean punch on Mr Gilligan," concluded O'Higgins.

For the prosecution, Peter Charleton said there was evidence before the court which was capable of being taken as corroboration. In this regard, the phone records, the threats made against Guerin and the motive for the murder were important.

On February 28, the thirty-seventh day of the trial, O'Higgins applied to have the trial stopped because there was no case to answer in relation to the murder and other drugs and firearms charges. It would be unsafe to continue, he argued, because the evidence tendered by Bowden and Warren was "inherently unreliable". Mr Justice O'Donovan, however, insisted that to accede to the application would be to adjudicate on matters of fact and on the credibility of the witnesses. He was satisfied that a reasonable jury, properly charged and warned of the dangers, could bring a verdict against the accused on one or all of the counts against him.

The Verdict

John Gilligan had become something of a barrack-room lawyer during the past almost five years of fighting the system. Even before that he had convinced himself that he had a good legal brain. When the court retired to consider its verdict on Friday, March 9, Gilligan walked back to his cell boasting: "It's all over. I'll be out of this kip next week." In fact, he was so confident that he would be cleared that he organised a party for his chums on E1, ordering in steaks the night before the judgment was due to be delivered. On the morning of Friday, March 15, as he was being led to his garda and army convoy for the trip to Dublin, he turned and told a prison officer: "I won't be back. I'll never be back in this kip again."

A large group of newspaper, television and radio journalists queued outside the Special Criminal Court from early that morning. After four years and nine months, John Gilligan's case was to be finally disposed of. In a judgment which took almost two hours to read, the court made it clear that the uncorroborated evidence of an accomplice witness will not be sufficient to secure a criminal conviction in this State.

Gilligan smirked and gazed up at the skylight in the court building as the judgment was read out. In summary, the court was satisfied that Gilligan was guilty of the eleven drugs offences of which he was charged. This determination was made on the evidence of protected witness John Dunne, whom the court regarded as credible. It was also based on parts of the testimony of Charlie Bowden and Russell Warren, two individuals of whom the court was deeply suspicious.

On the murder count, the quality of evidence tendered merely gave rise to suspicion. The main grounds for the prosecution were in the testimony of Russell Warren, which the court called inconsistent and uncorroborated. Similarly, on the four firearms and ammunitions counts, the only evidence was from Charles Bowden and it was not corroborated independently.

In the early part of the court's judgment, Mr Justice Diarmuid O'Donovan said that there was no rule of law which prevented a court from convicting a person on the uncorroborated evidence of an accomplice. But, he added: "the court recognises and acknowledges that, insofar as it is uncorroborated, the testimony of persons who would be deemed to be accomplices of the accused must be subjected to absolute scrutiny before it is deemed to be worthy of acceptance."

The judge then went on to explain the standard of proof that would be required to assess whether John Gilligan had killed Veronica Guerin. He said that if it could be shown that Gilligan was in control or command of the murderers, he would be judged to be every bit as guilty as the man who had pulled the trigger.

Even though they were granted immunity from prosecution in relation to the Guerin murder, the court held the view that the three men weren't necessarily unreliable. Referring specifically to Bowden and Warren, the judge said: "No matter what evidence these two men gave at whatever trials they chose to give evidence on behalf of the prosecution, including this trial, they can never be prosecuted for the murder of Veronica Guerin and, therefore, is there sense or logic in their giving perjured evidence? The court thinks not."

If a witness was not creditworthy, said the judge, his or her evidence must be rejected and the question of corroboration does not arise. The court accepted the validity of the witness protection programme but went on to criticise aspects of the arrangements which were put in place, particularly for Bowden and Warren. The fact that Det. Garda Bernie Hanley had not kept records of his meetings with Bowden and Warren was of concern. Moreover, the decision to return money to these two men was also wrong. Indeed, the judge said he was satisfied that there was no reasonable ground upon which the gardaí could have believed that either man had a legitimate claim on the money involved.

"In the view of the Court, there were certain aspects of the evidence of each one of the them [Bowden and Warren] which was creditworthy and capable of belief and while the Court was not prepared to act upon any piece of evidence given by either of those two men which stood by itself; notwithstanding that the Court may have believed that piece of evidence to be true, in the event that the Court was satisfied that there was significant corroboration for it, the Court was prepared to act on it."

The court was satisfied with the evidence given by Bowden and Warren in relation to the drugs importation because it was corroborated independently. It was particularly comfortable with the testimony of John Dunne, who was described as "a credible witness". His account of the importation of hundreds of consignments of was supported by senior executives in shipping and importation companies in Cork.

"It is the view of the Court that under cross-examination, he [Bowden] was exposed as a self-serving liar in a variety of different ways; so much so that the Court was compelled to conclude that, in the interests of justice, it would be unsafe to rely on any evidence which Charles Bowden gave unless it was supported by circumstantial evidence."

Bowden's evidence in relation to the collection of cartons of cannabis from the Ambassador Hotel in Naas and the transportation of same to lockup premises in Inchicore was plausible. His claim that John Gilligan was the controlling force was consistent with the testimony of Dunne and it also tallied with independent evidence gathered by the gardaí, including a home video of a wedding in St Lucia in March 1996.

"It seems to the Court that a reasonable inference to be drawn from such evidence as has been available to the Court with regard to the distribution of the proceeds of the sale of cannabis resin which Mr Gilligan was responsible for importing into this State is that he was the largest beneficiary," said Mr Justice O'Donovan. "That would suggest that he was the supreme authority among the members of the gang but in the view of the Court, the evidence falls short of establishing that Mr Gilligan played an active role in the day-to-day activities of the gang."

The court dismissed the evidence of Russell Warren out of hand. "Mr Warren was a self-confessed perjurer, a proven self-serving liar (under cross-examination, he specifically conceded that telling lies did not worry him as he said 'if you can get away with lies, you would.') and a person who, apparently, did not care who he hurt, if by doing so there was some benefit to himself."

Although the court was sceptical of Warren and of his evidence, it was prepared to use parts of his account which could be corroborated. In particular, the letters he received from Gilligan while in jail supported other evidence of the existence of a gang and of Gilligan's position in it.

The court said there was too much doubt hanging over the prosecution's claim that Gilligan was in possession or control of firearms and ammunition on the dates alleged. Charles Bowden's evidence was being relied on by the prosecution but it could not be corroborated.

Attempts by the prosecution to draw Gilligan into the crime by highlighting his links with the gang were not enough. "The Court is invited to draw the inference that although he was not present at the time, John Gilligan, because he had a history of associating with all of these men at one time or another, must be deemed to be a party to the plan to kill Veronica Guerin. In the view of the Court, that would be guilt by association and that alone, which is not a concept recognised in our criminal jurisprudence."

The court was scathing of the evidence of Russell Warren in relation to his observation of events on June 26, 1996. If his version of events was true, the court said it would have little difficulty in concluding that Gilligan had played "a pivotal role" in the murder of Veronica Guerin, but his story was not credible. Of significance was the fact that he did not tell the gardaí anything about the alleged phone contact with Gilligan on the day of the murder until after he had received money from Det. Garda Hanley. This fatally undermined the prosecution's efforts to link Gilligan to the murder. In addition, there was no evidence from telephone records to support Warren's claim that he had rung Gilligan after he allegedly saw Guerin leave the Court Hotel in Naas.

"As there was no evidence whatsoever to corroborate the events involving Mr Gilligan which Mr Warren said had occurred in the days preceding Mr Guerin's murder and no evidence to corroborate his testimony that he had been in Naas on the morning of that day, the Court could not but have a doubt about all of those matters.

"While this Court has grave suspicions that John Gilligan was complicit in the murder of the late Veronica Guerin, the Court has not been persuaded beyond all reasonable doubt by the evidence which has been adduced by the prosecution that is so and therefore, the Court is required by law to acquit the accused on that charge."

After the judgment was read, the court adjourned for lunch during which everyone tried to absorb the implications of what they had heard. Tony Hickey and his men were obviously shocked by the result. If Baltus and Rooney had testified, it would surely have been a very different outcome. Gilligan at that point had beaten the system. Sitting in the holding cell in the Special Criminal Court, he ate fish and chips for lunch, washed down with a can of Coke. He had phoned his wife at home, who had been busily redecorating Jessbrook for her husband's return, and told her to arrange a car to collect him after the trial. He reckoned that, owing to the fact that he had already been in custody for more than four years, he would be immediately released after being sentenced on the drugs charges.

After 2 p.m. Gilligan was led back up into the dock. He stood with his hands clasped in front of him, gazing once again at the skylight. Mr Justice Diarmuid O'Donovan looked sternly at Gilligan. He said the court had no doubt that Gilligan had "reaped staggering profits" from the drugs racket and was a man of insatiable greed.

"The court is at a loss to find words to express its revulsion for what you have done. You have been responsible for an avalanche of drugs. Never in the history of Irish criminal jurisprudence has one person been presumed to have caused so much wretchedness to so many," the judge said. He said Gilligan may have hidden a fortune and he expressed hope that the Criminal Assets Bureau would find and confiscate it.

The court sentenced Gilligan to a total of twenty-eight years of imprisonment on the drug charges. It was the longest sentence ever handed down in Ireland for drug trafficking. Gilligan was stunned.

Later that afternoon Tony Hickey participated in a press conference at Garda Headquarters in the Phoenix Park, sitting beside his boss, Commissioner Pat Byrne, who described the outcome of the case as "satisfying". Byrne wanted to give some moral support to the investigation team, who were downcast that Gilligan had not been found guilty on any charge relating to the murder of Veronica Guerin.

"We [gardaí] cannot take this on a personal basis. We are professionals and we are tasked to investigate crime, get the evidence and prepare it for the Director of Public Prosecutions. We have dealt a serious blow to organised crime and to a particular group of people in organised crime but we won't rest on our laurels and we know we have a long way to go."

Epilogue

After being acquitted of murder, John Gilligan reckoned he would be freed within a few days. The Special Criminal Court had accepted that his sentence should include time already served while awaiting trial. Within minutes after he had been handed a twenty-eight year sentence, his lawyers revealed that it would be appealed. Unfortunately, it would take at least a year before Gilligan could have his appeal heard. The Little Man could not accept the temerity of the court in handing him such a stiff sentence.

Gilligan didn't like being in Portlaoise prison, even though he had been reunited with many of his old friends on E1. After all, he had sworn that he would never again be a resident in the country's most secure place of detention. On Sunday, March 25, Gilligan and Brian Meehan had a meeting with his lawyers in Portlaoise. As he was being escorted to see his visitor, Gilligan demanded that Assistant Chief Officer Martin Ryan make arrangements to open the wing tuck shop especially for him after his meeting. Gilligan wanted to buy sweets and cans of Coke to take back to his cell. When he was told that this would not be possible, the nasty little godfather began hurling abuse at the ACO. As Brian Meehan struggled to restrain him, Gilligan punched Ryan on the side of his head. The officer was later treated in hospital and put on sick leave.

Following the incident, in accordance with prison rules, the prison officers tried to strip search Gilligan. "I will see that you're fucking killed for this. I will prove that I am not bluffing. I will see that you are got at while going from work. You better bear in mind that I will get your families as well," Gilligan screamed at Ryan and his colleague, Declan O'Reilly.

After this outburst, again on the prison rules, the Deputy Governor of Portlaoise ordered that Gilligan be detained in what is referred to as "the bunker" for a period of two months. Gilligan, with his hands stuffed in his pockets and gazing at the ceiling, was told that he would be confined for twenty-three hours a day for three days. He would lose fourteen days of remission of his sentence and his privileges, including visits, letters, tuck shop, and telephone calls for two months.

Gilligan wasn't prepared to accept the prison rules and applied to the High Court to have the bunker punishment declared unconstitutional. In his judgment, Mr Justice McKechnie said: "In my view it matters not as to the identity of the applicant. It matters not what has been written about him or what has been said about him or what views people might take of him. These matters are entirely irrelevant to me, as is whether he was convicted or acquitted on all, many or most of the charges before the Special Criminal Court. The trial in that court is over and he could be 'Joe Bloggs' instead of John Gilligan. It is entirely immaterial to me. His presence in Portlaoise is of relevance only in that he is a prisoner and in lawful detention pursuant to due process."

Mr Justice McKechnie said that Gilligan was different from a person untouched by the legal process or a person detained prior to trial. He said the little godfather "must accept discipline and accommodate himself to prison life and understand that prison is a recognised form of punishment".

While John Gilligan was arguing with the State, the Lucan investigation team were still piecing together cases against the remaining free members of the gang. John Traynor and Peter Mitchell are still at large and moving between Holland and Spain, from where they are organising drugs shipments to Britain and Ireland. Shay Ward is believed to be in hiding somwhere in England.

Within a few weeks of the Gilligan sentence, the supergrasses Charlie Bowden, Russell Warren and John Dunne were all moved out of the State and relocated as part of the Witness Protection Programme, with new identities and new lives.

The Criminal Assets Bureau began making moves to confiscate all Gilligan's assets, which they told the Special Criminal Court were thought to be worth £14.2 million. On April 23, 2001 the CAB made an application to the court requesting that the High Court appoint a receiver to realise Gilligan's assets, including Jessbrook, his children's houses in Lucan, the family home in Blanchardstown, six vehicles, sixteen bank accounts and more than five million pounds he had staked in bets.

Veronica Guerin's murder changed gangland forever, but her death should not have been necessary to spur change in Irish society. The Garda Síochána has become much more efficient in dealing with organised crime. The Lucan investigation is now regarded as a template for other major inquiries. One of the single most important developments prompted by Veronica's death, the Criminal Assets Bureau, has to date confiscated cash and property worth at least forty million pounds. It has become the most advanced and sophisticated multi-agency weapon against organised crime in Europe. In fact, the CAB now has a unit devoted purely to briefing other law enforcement agencies. It has become a permanent reminder to Gilligan's old friends that crime no longer pays.

As you, the reader, put down this book, new John Gilligans are building their own little evil empires. Organised crime will never go away and the existence of these units and the expertise of a revamped police force will not stop criminal activity. But, it is hoped that never again will a criminal organisation be allowed to consider itself so much above the law that it can take on the State. Then, perhaps, Veronica Guerin will not have died in vain.

We should never forget what this story is about.

Paul Williams
May, 2001